The Medical Teacher

EDITED BY

Ken Cox

MB, MS, MA, FRCS, FRACS, FACS

Professor of Surgery;
Head, School of Medical Education;
Director, WHO Western Pacific Regional Teacher Training
Centre for Health Personnel,
University of New South Wales, Australia

Christine E. Ewan

MB, BS, MA, PhD

Associate Professor of Health Sciences,
The University of Wollongong, Australia

SECOND EDITION

CHURCHILL LIVINGSTONE
EDINBURGH LONDON MELBOURNE AND NEW YORK 1988

CHURCHILL LIVINGSTONE
Medical Division of Longman Group UK Limited

Distributed in the United States of America by Churchill
Livingstone Inc., 19 West 44th Street, New York, N. Y.
10036, and by associated companies, branches and
representatives throughout the world.

First edition 1982
Second edition 1988

ISBN 0-443-03421-4

British Library Cataloguing in Publication Data
The Medical teacher. — 2nd ed.
   1. Medicine — Study and teaching
   I. Cox, Kenneth R.   II. Ewan, Christine E.
   610'.7'11   RS34

Library of Congress Cataloging in Publication Data
The Medical teacher.
   Includes index.
   1. Medicine — Study and teaching. I. Cox, Kenneth R.
II. Ewan, Christine E. [DNLM: 1. Education, Medical.
2. Teaching — methods. W 18 M4896]
R834.M435 1987   610'.7   87-15815

Produced by Longman Group (FE) Ltd
Printed in Hong Kong

Preface

This second edition continues the intention of providing a useful set of 'hands-on' ideas which teachers may use within their personal responsibilities within their faculties. New chapters on the basic themes extend and elaborate the original ideas.

What has been added in this issue is much more attention to the context of that teaching, and the medical teacher's role in a rapidly changing scene. Previously the system was taken as a given, and the focus was on the teacher–student relationship in grappling with subject matter. Now we raise questions about the teacher and educational planning in the faculty, about the directions of the medical school and the relevance of subject matter, and about the teacher in relation to the patient and the community.

Change always involves choices about what is important, what 'must' be covered, what is desirable. These are choices based on values. Values are not usually explicitly exposed in faculty meetings, but are widely used implicitly in debate, particularly about resources (such as money, staff or student time, the distribution of which is always 'political'). We have attempted to surface these values when we recognize them.

These values must be tempered, however, by whatever relevant quantitative data can be gathered about their significance at reasonable cost. How extensive is the problem you want to teach about, how many people are affected, how long will the need last, who deals with that issue now, exactly what are the deficiencies in current understanding, what are the consequences of doing something and of doing nothing?

No clinical or scientific decision would be made without gathering the data relevant to the decision, but data-free educational decisions are glibly made daily.

Medical schools face many dilemmas in charting their course over the next decade. Given the long lag time between any educational decision taken today, and the time of graduation of any student affected by that change in teaching, the choices made today will affect doctors practising a decade from now.

Medical schools may respond as patients often do, by denying that a problem exists, or if so its not their problem, or by waiting passively for the future when they will be told what to do, or they can play their parts in creating their own future. Medical teachers, individually and collectively, are part of this decision making process.

Consequently, we have added chapters on the social, professional and educational contexts within which these decisions are being made.

This edition also has a stronger 'ideological' stance on student learning and on student autonomy as the only reasonable focus of teacher activity. Consequently, we have greater emphasis on self directed learning, on learning by experience, on self assessment, on adult learning and the student as adult, and on the personal growth of the student in preparation for accepting heavy emotion-laden responsibilities.

Lastly, we have allowed a little more theory to creep into what has been essentially a 'how to' book, mainly because 'nothing is so practical as a good theory' in providing a framework from which readers can take their own leaps into innovation.

1988

K.R.C
C.E.E.

Contributors

John I. Balla MB BS, FRACP FRCPE, MA
Professor of Postgraduate Medical
Education, University of Hong Kong,
Hong Kong

Raja C. Bandaranayake MB BS, PhD, MSEd
Senior Lecturer, School of Medical
Education, WHO Western Pacific Regional
Teacher Training Centre for Health Personnel,
University of New South Wales, Australia

David J. Boud BSc, PhD, CPhys, MInstP
Senior Lecturer, Tertiary Education Research
Centre, University of New South Wales,
Australia

Henry Brodaty MB BS, MD, FRACP,
FRANZCP
Senior Lecturer, School of Psychiatry,
University of New South Wales; Director,
Psychiatry Unit, Prince Henry Hospital,
Little Bay, Australia

John P. Chalmers BSc, MB, BS, PhD,
FRACP
Professor of Medicine; Chairman of Computer
Assisted Instruction Subcommittee of School of
Medicine, The Flinders University of South
Australia, Bedford Park, Australia

Rufus M. Clarke MA, MD, FRACS
Professor of Anatomy, Faculty of Medicine,
The University of Newcastle, Australia

Kenneth R. Cox MB MS, MA, FRCS, FRACS,
FACS
Professor of Surgery; Director, WHO Western
Pacific Regional Teacher Training Centre
for Health Personnel, Head, School of Medical

Education, University of New South Wales,
Australia.

Adrian V. Daniel RBI
Director for Education Technology, Faculty
of Medicine, University of Newcastle NSW;
Director, The Medical Communication Unit,
Newcastle,
New South Wales, Australia

Christine E. Ewan MB BS, MA, PhD
Associate Professor of Health Sciences,
The University of Wollongong, Australia

Grahame I. Feletti PhD
Director of Curriculum Development
New Pathway Project
Harvard Medical School, Boston, Ma. USA.

Neville Hatton BA, MEd
Senior Lecturer in Education, School
of Teaching and Curriculum Studies,
The University of Sydney, Australia

Elizabeth Hegarty-Hazel BA, BSc (Hons), MSc,
PhD
Senior Lecturer, School of Microbiology
University of New South Wales, Australia

Joy Higgs BSc, Grad Dip Phty, MHPEd
Senior Lecturer, Cumberland College of Health
Sciences, Lidcombe, New South Wales, Australia

Gerald B. Holzman MD
Professor of Obstetrics and Gynaecology,
Department of Obstetrics, Gynaecology and
Reproductive Biology, Medical College of
Georgia, Augusta, Georgia, USA

Susan S. Irvine MB ChB, MPH, SM
Lecturer, School of Medical Education,
University of New South Wales, Australia

Norman I. Kagan PhD
Professor and Chair, Department of
Educational Psychology, University of
Houston, United States of America

Adrian Lee PhD
Associate Professor of Medical Microbiology,
School of Microbiology, University of New
South Wales, Australia

Jack Marshall MB BCh, FRACGP
Director of Educational Research and
Resource Development, Royal Australian
College of General Practitioners, Family
Medicine Programme, Australia

David I. Newble Bsc (Hons), MD, Dip Ed,
FRACP
Reader in Medicine, Department of Medicine,
University of Adelaide, Australia

Michael J. Oakey ADIPP, AIMBI
Medical Illustration Unit, University of
New South Wales, Australia

John P. Powell BA, MA, PhD
Director, Tertiary Education Research
Centre, University of New South Wales,
Australia

David E. Richmond MD, MHPEd, FRACP,
FRCP
Professor of Geriatric Medicine, University
of Auckland, School of Medicine, New Zealand

Gloria Robbins BSc, Dip Comp Studies
Computer Development Officer, Computer
Department, Education Development Unit,
Bruce
TAFE College, ACT, Australia

Ruth White RN, BA, MEd, EdD,
Senior Lecturer, WHO Regional Teacher
Training Centre, School of Medical Education,
University of New South Wales, Australia

Contents

Context and expectations

Introduction

The doctor's role is evolving continuously in a process of negotiation between the medical profession and the society it serves. At different points in the history of the profession the relative power of the profession and of society has varied. In the recent past, scientific and technological advances, the consequent growth of the tertiary care teaching hospital, and specialist expertise have tended to place much of the power to define a doctor's role in the hands of the profession which was best able to understand the scientific aspects of that role. The following chapters examine some recent changes in the way in which health care and the doctor's role are viewed. The net effect of these changes is that the balance of power in the negotiation of doctors' roles is changing to give a more equal share to society and the profession.

This negotiation of roles has implications for medical education. Medical schools exist within a society whose defined needs for medical care must be met by the graduates of those schools. Attention to the internal imperatives of biomedical science is no longer sufficient for the definition of the medical curriculum. A variety of other imperatives must also be considered. The first chapter in this Section examines the imperatives arising from the practice of medicine and medical education, the second chapter summarizes the expectations of the medical profession which various sectors of the community hold. The third chapter turns its attention to the 'raw material', the students who are selected to study medicine and become doctors. Some critics of the current roles which doctors fulfil have sought to change the nature of doctors by changing the selection of medical students. Chapter 3 examines the contribution which selection makes to the process of medical education.

Professional & educational context of medical education

Medical teachers work in a context in which the old verities about medicine and medical practice can no longer be taken for granted. The awareness of change, and the need to prepare students to work in new roles, are evident in the plethora of meetings and papers directed to 'Medicine in the 21st Century'.

How can a teacher plan teaching for tasks which have not yet been defined? What can we do about the future?

WHO DEFINES THE MEDICAL TASK?

We have four options. We can wait, and respond as roles and tasks emerge. We can speculate about the future, and plan for all contingencies. We can extrapolate from current trends, using the past and the present to predict the future. We can set about creating our own future.

Medical schools and the medical profession face many dilemmas in choosing among such pathways, but may be organizationally incapable of debating the issues thoroughly or of reaching consensus. The medical teacher is inextricably bound into these issues. The choices to be made reflect assumptions about the roles of medicine and the tasks within medical practice which colour every teaching decision.

What are some of the determinants of the medical task? How are they likely to change practice and, consequently, teaching of students and graduates?

1. Patterns of disease and illness

Preventable mortality turns on factors of life style (50%), environment (20%), and human biology (20%) more than on defects in health care provided (10%) according to the US Surgeon General (1975).

Will practice and teaching shift towards persuasion to cease smoking and alcohol and drug intake, to promote exercise and weight reduction, to accident prevention, in short, to include a major focus on prevention and early detection of disease, health education and health promotion? Currently, these are not areas of serious study in medical schools, skills are little developed within teachers, curricular time devoted to them is negligible, and they do not figure in the examinations.

An increasingly elderly population will suffer chronic and irreversible disability for which prevention and cure are no longer relevant.

Will the medical profession and the medical student accept a role of maintaining function in such deteriorating situations, when active intervention is so much more exciting and intellectually stimulating? Can doctors team effectively with all those others involved in the care of the patient?

2. Professional practice

The growth of knowledge and technology ensures progressive specialization of practice. Hospital organization follows the same pattern of differentiation of care basing responsibilities on organs or procedures which, from the patient's point of view, 'disintegrates' care. Even the career structures of the general physician and general surgeon are disappearing as teaching hospitals abolish their 'general' clinics.

The organ focus emphasizes the hospital as the technical 'body shop', and the specialist as 'body mechanic'. If integrated management is not included in the tasks assigned by the hospital, then the patient is unlikely to receive integrated (holistic) care.

An effect of specialization in both basic and clinical sciences is progressive ignorance of every area outside one's own specialty, what they can do, at what risk, for what varieties of patients. Such ignorance is most pronounced about what other health professionals do, and can do, unless the clinician functions wlthin a multi-professional team.

If hospital-based teaching is inevitably provided by separate specialists, on what criteria can each decide what to teach? Should an ophthalmologist teach an overview of the field as exemplified in clinic patients, or skills in uslng the diagnostic tools of the specialty, or the common conditions likely to be met in a general practice, or recognition of the important emergencies, or the growing edge of the field, or when to refer patients to an ophthalmologist?

How can a group of different specialists decide what is 'important' to be taught for the future when each has such limited awareness of the others? If each has a focused view of medicine, how can they teach an overview? Will the curriculum become solely the sum of its separate parts? Will that matter?

3. Society

Extensive community surveys (Heath et al 1985) have expressed strong desires for effective communication, for integrated or 'holistic' care (while doctors are usually employed to provide differentiated care), for team work among all those providing care, for health education and promotion, and for the doctor's involvement in the community.

Is medicine ready, willing and able to respond to such expectations? How and where should they be learned? How could they be examined?

If medicine is a service profession, who decides what services will be provided, the doctor or the professional association or the patient or the family or the funding system? What are the implications for schools of 'medicine as service' as well as 'medicine as science'? Medicine functions with coherent theories of disease, but has only weak concepts about illness, and none about health or commmnity.

4. Government

Resources for health care (money, staff, space, equipment, training) are finite. Governments and other third party financers (insurance companies, health funds, employers) need to contain expenditure, and to ensure value for money. Is medical care effective? Has the health dollar purchased a health benefit? Pragmatic values of utility and effectiveness, political values of social equity, and economic values of efficiency, are being added to the social values of humanity and caring.

VALUE IMPINGING ON MEDICAL PRACTICE

The practice of medicine has a well-established commitment to altruistic service. Medicine has been less an occupation than a way of life. The practice of medicine has been an intensely private interaction.

Today medical decisions are the stuff of public debate, media exaggeration, and legal disputation, as well as the focus of resource limitation by government. Clinical practice is being required to respond to an increasing number of strongly expressed expectations. Each expectation reflects underlying values of what is important:

1. *effectiveness* of therapeutic intervention, seen as cure of disease, resolution of illness or reduc-

tion of the burden of illness, control of symptoms, avoidance of side-effects

2. *utility* to patient, absence of disability, physical independence

3. *humanity*, caring, acceptance

4. *autonomy* of patient, fully informed consent, assistance to selfhelp and emotional independence, death with dignity, euthanasia

5. *responsibility* for continuity of care, certification of illness, social support

6. *equity* of access to health care, equity of costsharing, availability of quality care, minimal cost to the patient, availability of the doctor at the time of illness

7. *efficiency* of use of time and resources, parsimony in use of low cost investigations, drugs and services, awareness of opportunity cost in other possible use of resources.

Unfortunately, not all expectations can be met. To some extent, the values are always in conflict in a particular case. Is the medical school responsible for ensuring thorough and rigorous debate on how this widening spectrum of social expectations can be reconciled with professional values on how practice should be conducted?

Teachers can, for example, assign a different value to be the responsibility of each student in the group in dealing with a specific patient. Students can then argue for their value, and find for themselves where trade-offs are necessary and how conflicts among values can be negotiated rather than manipulated.

Teachers can usefully bring out the paradox that concern for humanitarian care (which has emerged as a result of the inter-personal detachment that can accompany specialization and hospital-based investigation and treatment) comes at a time that other values are now thrusting themselves into the clinical equation and competing with humanity which had been the principal value when few diagnostic and therapeutic tools were available.

Medicine is receiving mixed messages, to be a warm human yet to incorporate all these other values such as hard-nosed efficiency, to be all to the patient yet to share all with other health workers, to know high tech yet practise low tech, to cure all yet care for all, to be socially aware yet not to medicalize social illness.

Medical students need opportunities to work through their feelings about society's ambivalence to medicine. On graduation, their responsibilities as interns will impose severe strains on their feelings. Without resolution of some of their confusion about values, and clarity about their own position, their responses can be automatic, or depersonalized and somewhat dismissive of patients as fellow humans.

As graduates they will face increasing value strains. Competition for resources already exists (eg. across hospitals with the 'rationalization' of facilities), across maladies (with 'interesting' cases being admitted before varicose veins), and may extend to competition across age groups or generations (eg. with intensive care for 80 year olds competing with vaccination for 8 year olds).

The health care system is currently disjointed without connections between preventive and curative medicine, public and private practice, medicine and other health professions, medical practice and medical schools, undergraduate, vocational and continuing education. Will study of health care organization become part of the medical course? Few medical teachers have the breadth of knowledge and practical experience to guide students into a thorough understanding of medical organization and management.

WILL DOCTORS UNDERTAKE (PRIMARY) HEALTH CARE?

Governments frequently support the management strategy called primary health care (often mistakenly understood as general practice or as primitive rural medicine). Primary health care is especially concerned to see equity of distribution of health services and a shift of responsibility to the community.

If preventable mortality relates to matters of life style and environment, what is the role of the medical profession, and consequently of the medical school? Will the profession limit its services to illness care, or expand its coverage to health care at primary, secondary and tertiary levels? If so, how can medical schools prepare graduates for a broader set of tasks? The breadth of abilities required of the graduate far exceeds current expectations of medical student training.

The range of responsibilities within (primary) health care entails:

1. medical care skills

to manage episodic and chronic illness

2. communication skills

to establish how patient, family, community, colleagues see the problem

3. epidemiological skills

to comprehend the chain of events and the ecology of disease and vectors

4. sociological skills

to understand beliefs, values, habits, culture and expectations in what may be largely a social task

5. decision making skills

to judge how far to explore a situation, what factors are critical, and when to take action

6. team skills

to cooperate with other health workers and other sectors responsible for factors which impinge on health

7. educational skills

to inform clearly, to guide, and to persuade to change behaviour

8. leadership and organizational skills

to mobilize, manage and supervise a joint attack on health problems

9. research and evaluation skills

to tackle complex health problems with rigour, and to assess empirical studies when experimental methods are not permissible.

Is medicine ready, willing and able to encompass such a set of additional roles and responsibilities? What would be the implications for the medical school?

HOW ARE MEDICINE AND MEDICAL TEACHERS TO RESPOND?

The medical profession and medical school have dfficulty responding coherently because they are not homogeneous. The study and practice of medicine present many faces as a result of its complexity and diversity. Different participants in the decision making hold different images, seeing medicine as one or more of:

1. science, researching diseases and inventing cures
2. applied science solving illnesses in patients
3. specialist/hospital investigation with high tech intervention
4. service profession providing consultant advice
5. community-based care and social support
6. multi-disciplinary team care
7. prevention of disease, promotion of health
8. counselling, psychological support, healing

All these images are more or less true. Not all can be fully comprehended within an undergraduate curriculum. How are medical teachers to make curricular decisions which optimize the student's grasp of the immensity and variety of medicine, now and in the future?

Two principles or strategies must be understood.

First, a knowledge-driven approach to curriculum design (with each department pushing for extra time to accommodate all the new ideas in its field) faces the Malthusian problem of attempting to fit exponential growth of knowledge into a fixed length course. Slight linear expansion of the course by a year or so cannot accommodate the growth of knowledge.

This growth problem can be to some extent contained by redefining teaching goals around a limited set of priority health problems which the graduate must be capable of handling immediately after graduation. The knowledge to be grasped is that required to comprehend the mechanisms and management of those problems.

Second, the differentiation of roles and responsibilities which flow from the growth of knowledge entails a set of pathway decisions for each possible role and set of abilities, related to 'Who does What', and 'When do they learn to do it?'. Such decisions demand deep consideration, for they turn on fundamental choices about the future roles and abilities of the profession.

Pathway decisions

1. Should the ability be learned by all undergraduates?

2. Should the ability be learned by only some undergraduates, and taken as elective studies?

3. Should the ability be learned after graduation, either in-service or in a formal program?

4. Should the ability be not an exclusively medical responsibility, but be open to study by other health workers?

5. Does the field require substantial research and development until a clearer understanding of theory and practice will indicate whose responsibility it should be?

These are the serious choices for the medical profession and medical schools.

Is medicine to address whole health problems, or solely illness care among those presenting with established disease? What roles will doctors have in managing those problem which medicine chooses to deal with? If the present health care delivery system does not foster medical involvement in the roles medicine chooses, should medicine attempt to reshape the health care system?

To return to the four pathways mentioned at the beginning, medical schools can 'wait and see'. Partly, this is already happening. Medical schools have shown little response to rapid changes in the health care system, in changing public expectations, or in the expanding roles of other health professions. In some countries health departments are bypassing medicine as they develop health care systems based on health workers other than doctors. Many of the academic staff in medical schools do not know or do not care about changes outside their department.

Speculative leaps into the future are not part of the behaviour pattern of medical schools.

Extrapolation from the present has shown many of the developments above. Serious consideration of the factors influencing the disease pattern, the profession, society and government will raise many more predictions, with new technology always a wild card. The medical school needs a forum mechanism to allow these trends to be debated, information collected, and values clarified, if the medical school is to make a rational response.

Or the medical school can create its own future by choosing a view of health care, a range of roles for graduates, and a set of health problems they will be able to tackle. That leap of faith would, hopefully, recognize the complex, multifactorial nature of health problems and of research into them, the many skilled inputs to care which necessitate cooperation and team work, and the central responsibility of the patient in prevention, self-help, and rehabilitation.

Such changes will never be made by schools which produce passive students waiting to be told what they must remember. The school, the staff and the students need to think for themselves, to encourage autonomy and open-ness in thinking creatively about health and health care.

Medicine and medical schools are in serious need of leadership if they are to adapt successfully to a different future.

REFERENCES

Heath C. J. 1985 National Conference on the Role of the Doctor in New Zealand: Implications for Medical Education, Palmerston North, October,

US Surgeon General 1975 Healthy Living US Govt. Printing Office, Washington

The social context of medical education

WHAT DO PATIENTS EXPECT?

WHAT DO OTHER PROFESSIONALS
EXPECT?

WHAT DO THE HEALTH MANAGERS
EXPECT?

CONCLUSION

Medical education performs a service for society in training doctors to meet the need for medical care in society. It is necessary, therefore, for medical educational institutions and teachers to be able to recognize and interpret those needs and design appropriate educational programs.

Most modern medical schools are aware of this responsibility. However, the task is most frequently perceived as one in which needs are assessed largely by surveying the epidemiological characteristics of the population to be served. While this counting of diseases is a highly desirable and necessary component of needs analysis it provides an incomplete picture, particularly in those societies in which basic health care is universally available. In such societies, health care institutions and professionals have already developed complex systems for negotiating their roles and providing a variety of services. In a climate of relative plenty, choices become possible, expectations evolve, and the potential for conflict between expectations and services provided expands. Medical schools must then determine which expectations they should interpret as valid needs to be addressed in medical education. Failure to heed changing expectations is one of the greatest sources of public dissatisfaction with the medical profession and the services it provides.

The following summarizes the multiplicity of expectations evident in modern industrialized societies. Part of the problem for medical teachers is that, in some cases, the expectations held by different sectors of society diverge. The sectors of society which are particularly relevant to the nature of medical practice are the patients or consumers, the managers who administer and fund health services, and the other professionals whose work intersects with the work of the medical profession.

WHAT DO PATIENTS EXPECT?

Patients are those people within a population who consider themselves to be unwell and who choose to consult a doctor for advice or relief. Many people who consider themselves to be unwell do not choose to consult a doctor but use some form of self-management. One study found that 65% of a sample of Australians reported having an illness in the two weeks prior to the survey, but only 18% consulted a doctor (Graycar, 1982). The decision to seek health care is determined by past health and illness experience, health-related behaviour, and personal characteristics such as age, income, status, knowledge and stress level. In industrialized countries the wealthy and better educated are more likely to regard themselves as sick and to seek medical attention (Graycar, 1982). Patients' expectations of doctors are, therefore, influenced by both the patients' background and the prevailing beliefs in the community about those illnesses which are self-limiting and those which require a doctor's intervention.

Patients' expectations of doctors are also influenced by doctors' expectations of patients. Difficulties arise in the doctor–patient interaction when one or both parties disagree on definitions of respective roles, or when behaviour does not conform to expectations on either side. In pluralistic societies the likelihood of mismatched expectations increases. Medical students, therefore, need to understand the variety of expectations they may confront in practice; and they need to recognize their own expectations which develop in the course of professional socialization. For example, to the doctor, admitting a patient to hospital for a minor procedure may be the most efficient way to achieve a satisfactory result. To a patient with a different cultural background and expectations, admission to hospital may signify abandonment by the doctor and imminent death.

A clearcut profile of patients' expectations is difficult to define simply because patients are a diverse group with diverse needs and understandings even within a single social and cultural context. Extrapolating the patient expectations identified in one country or society to other societies is fraught with risks. Local research and definitions of expectations are just as important as local definitions of health care needs based on epidemiological studies.

Difficult though it may be to define the expectations of all patients it is nevertheless possible to assume certain minimum standards which, even if not expected, would be appreciated by most patients. Minimum expectations are that a doctor should be competent, up to date, conscious of environmental and community influences, person-centred, sympathetic, able to attend to some emotional needs, willing to foster long term relationships, be family-centred and visit the home, willing to take time to explain and share information and sensitive enough to know when this is most appropriate whether asked for or not.

In addition, certain areas of concern are common to most societies and should be addressed in medical education. Patient satisfaction is one such area which is important because it has a bearing on patient compliance (Ley 1977, Locker & Dunt 1978). An extensive review of the literature on patient satisfaction with doctors in the U.S.A. concluded that, no matter which criteria are used, patients describe a high level of satisfac-

tion with, and acceptance of, health services (Spiegel & Backhaut 1980). Some studies reveal a primary concern among patients with affective aspects of the doctor's performance (Mac, 1971, Segall & Burnett, 1980). On the other hand, patients attending an urban free clinic in the U.S.A. primarily expected doctors to exhibit technical competence and expected their affective needs to be met by other health workers (Greene et al, 1980). In some health care systems a deficiency of access to other health professionals may mean that affective expectations cannot be displaced from the doctor.

Expectations in relation to information-sharing are also important but also tend to vary. A study of an urban university family practice with a patient population described as cosmopolitan had high expectations of information-sharing and patient education which were met by the doctors in that practice (Chrisman & Baker, 1978). However, many patients, especially those attending free clinics in lower socio-economic areas, apparently do not expect to be asked for their opinion or given details of their treatment regimen (Reader et al, 1957, Kincey et al, 1975, Greene et al, 1980). In general, in free clinics, fewer patients ask questions and fewer doctors feel the need to explain.

Evidently, the characteristics of the context in which health care is delivered also influence the expectations patients bring to the consultation. Economic factors are becoming increasingly important aspects of that context. For example, in some health care systems a doctor's services are purchased like any other commodity. This can create a tendency, in some cases, for patients to expect a tangible outcome from a consultation and for doctors to feel obliged to provide one. These expectations of active intervention and cure have probably been conditioned by the action orientation of doctors and the modern dependence on pharmaceutical and technological developments. Medical students should be conscious of the need to control the health cost spiral and should be taught ways to modify this expectation if they encounter it in their patients.

Perhaps the most important lesson that medical students should learn about patient expectations is that they are formed in interaction with their society and with their doctors. Professional satisfaction and good patient care are most likely to result if students learn to recognize the reciprocity of expectations among patients and doctors. Rather than developing habitual routines for dealing with patients and their problems they could learn how to use that reciprocity to negotiate the most suitable outcome for each patient.

Since most clinical education takes place within teaching hospitals where patient and doctor expectations and negotiations are at a different level from those in the primary care setting most medical students are unprepared for the nature of the expectations and demands they encounter later in their professional work.

WHAT DO OTHER PROFESSIONALS EXPECT?

Doctors interact with other professionals in the course of providing health care. The major groups who interact with doctors directly are the allied health professionals, but another group of professionals is becoming involved increasingly in the analysis of doctors' activities and the health care system. These social and behavioural scientists have raised important issues which should be addressed in medical education. Alongside this social analysis and questioning of long-accepted aspects of medical care has come a heightened awareness among the allied health professionals of the importance of their roles. Changes in the roles of doctors vis-à-vis other professionals have reached different stages in different societies. However, the trend is towards the recognition of mutual interdependence among the health professions.

The new generation of allied health professionals expect to be treated with the respect that their professional training has earned for them. They are less likely to carry out doctors' orders without question than was formerly the case (Bates, 1970), although old interaction patterns persist in some areas among practitioners of older age groups. New curricula in nursing particularly, stress the importance of nurses and other health professionals being able to meet patients' psychosocial needs, solve clinical problems and generate problem-oriented nursing plans and act as patient advocates (Ewan & White, 1984).

The advent of community-based health care, in which the nurse or other specialized staff of community resource facilities is more likely to be in day-to-day contact with the patient and his or her health problems, has done much to strengthen the team concept in which tasks and responsibilities are differentiated and each member, including the doctor, must appreciate and contribute to the tasks of the others. Examples of the increased emphasis on teamwork appear in statements from the professions: Physiotherapy education emphasizes the 'strong, traditional doctor/physiotherapist relationship' and the desirability of a cooperative team approach to physical treatment (Twomey, 1983) while pharmacists expect 'to be treated as a respected and integral part of patient care' (Oscar, 1981): Older (1983), in his criticism of the use of the term 'paramedical', has expressed it simply: 'While working beside a medic may be acceptable to some, working in a subsidiary relation to one . . . is not'.

Medical education must take account of the new relationships which are developing amongst the health professions and must equip future doctors with knowledge of others' roles and with the skills to work effectively as part of a team.

Concurrent with the increased differentiation of tasks within health care, external changes have also had an effect. Economic concerns over health care have placed medicine in the political arena and it has become a popular focus for social comment and investigation by other professionals. The discipline of medical sociology has developed conceptual and analytic mechanisms to explain interactions in health care and to propose alternative approaches to health care. The resulting comment has, in many instances, been critical of traditional medical practices. Members of the medical profession itself have also joined the criticism of the role of medicine in today's society (McKeown, 1976; Bradshaw, 1978; Shapiro, 1978; Taylor 1979). Much of the comment centres on the political power of the profession as a group rather than on the actions of individual doctors.

Representative of the expectations arising from sociological analysis is the conclusion that 'humanized' health care is the desirable goal. Humanized care is described in the following terms: 'Medicine must be more than technically successful; it must have the capacity to provide sustenance, to preserve dignity, and to relieve psychological as well as physical stress' (Mechanic, 1975). Or 'The general practitioner, if he is to be successful, must have a social and preventive orientation as well as a technical one' (Mechanic 1974).

Models of the doctor–patient relationship proposed by various sociologists (Freidson, 1962; Parsons 1967; Szasz & Hollender, 1978) all emphasize various aspects of the potential for information-sharing, reciprocity, equality and patient autonomy.

Not all agree, however, on the limits of the role that doctors should be expected to assume. Stimson (1977), for example, has questioned the desirability of general practitioners becoming involved in social care on the basis that other agencies are better equipped to do so. He argues that, by expanding the general practitioner's role into social therapy, social problems will be re-defined as medical problems.

While these dilemmas appear from time to time in the expressed expectations of the medical profession it is nevertheless obvious that doctors do need to know more about social and cultural relativity, the beliefs and determinants of behaviour of their patients (Kleinman et al, 1978), and the ways in which their own behaviour is influenced by interactions, expectations, personal backgrounds and immediate contexts. The prominence of technical and scientific approaches in traditional medical education ensures that doctors deal with facts, observables and technical definitions. If they are to meet changing expectations, modern doctors must learn to understand alternative definitions of observable reality and alternative interpretations of facts which may lead to 'irrational' or 'illogical' patient behaviour.

Taken together, the main implication of the changing expectations of other professionals is that doctors must learn to accept a changed status which places them alongside their colleagues rather than above them. Skills in evaluating alternative points of view, cooperation and negotiation will need to assume greater importance in medical curricula of the future.

WHAT DO THE MANAGERS EXPECT?

The managers are those administrators and government officials who develop policy and allocate resources to health and health care services. The role of non-medical administrators is becoming more central to health care as economic concerns grow and managerial expertise is required to keep medical institutions within limited budgets. The common concern of the managers is with efficiency and economy.

Doctors occupy a central position in controlling health costs because they control access to many health services. For this reason some governments expect doctors to achieve 'supply restraint' and may threaten to ration available clinical options if restraint is not exercised (Blewett, 1982). Rationing is already in operation in most health care systems and is reflected, for example, in waiting lists for elective surgery and restrictions on prescribing certain drugs.

Governments and managers of health care institutions expect that doctors will recognize that the clinical decisions they take in using available patient care resources are also economic decisions with implications for the society and other patients as well as the individual patient in question (Owen, 1976). In order to meet these expectations doctors must be able to base clinical decisions on updated knowledge of the costs and benefits of alternative actions. Doctors no longer enjoy the freedom to determine the extent of the resources to be used in patient care because governments and third party insurers control the funding of health care. Consequently, managers expect doctors to cooperate in the establishment of profiles of acceptable patterns of practice to enable detection of suboptimal and inefficient services. These expectations are made explicit in the plethora of quality assurance programs which, in spite of their various names (Professional Standards Review Organizations, Peer Review, Quality Assurance Programs) usually measure quantity rather than quality of care. Criteria deal almost exclusively with quantifiable aspects of care such as numbers of investigations ordered, bed occupancy rates, procedures performed and review criteria expressed in statistical profiles, norms of care and written records, and thus reflect the primacy of economic concerns (Spiegel & Backhaut, 1980; Greenlick, 1981).

Increasingly, health administrators' decisions are based on actuarial calculations of cost-benefit and thus impose upon the delivery of health care value judgments other than those of the doctor and the patient. It is possible or even inevitable that doctors will be forced to adopt an actuarial perspective in medical treatment. It has been suggested that medical educators should prepare future graduates to 'accommodate themselves constructively to the requirements of medical practice within socialized markets' (Reinhardt, 1980). Perhaps more importantly medical educators should prepare future graduates to understand the economics of the health care system so that they can, where necessary, counsel or act as advocates for their patients in the resource implications of their illness.

The central issue in the expectations of the managers of modern health services is reflected in the following viewpoint: 'In reality, the move toward cost containment represents a shift from a social view of medicine to an economic view of medicine . . . hospitals and physicians are collectively viewed as an industry producing a product for sale. We used to be a social entity, meeting society's needs, but we are not looked upon that way any more' (Gurtner, 1982).

Medical education must provide learning experiences which reflect the reality of medical practice in an era of increasing technological possibilities but limited economic resources. Students must have the opportunity to consider the ethical and practical aspects of decision-making which incorporates cost-effectiveness as one parameter.

CONCLUSION

In many countries the social context of medicine has changed since the majority of medical teachers were students. The issues facing doctors and society are more complex. Increased biomedical knowledge and technological development offers seemingly limitless potential for medical intervention aimed at cure or life support. Simultaneously has come the recognition that, in industrialized countries at least, much disease has its origins in lifestyle and preventable environmental factors. Governments must allocate finite health resources where they can, potentially, do the most good. Other health professionals and patients themselves have an expanded role to play in meeting the emerging needs for illness prevention and maintenance of healthy populations. In light of these and other changes, expectations of the doctor's role have also changed. To fulfill this new role future doctors will need skills not just in the clinical areas with which they are currently concerned, but also in the ethical, social, political, and economic aspects of medicine.

REFERENCES

Bates B 1970 Doctor and nurse: Changing roles and relations. New England Journal of Medicine 283: 129–134.

Blewett N 1982 Health plan will 'buttress private medicine'. AMA Gazette, July, p. 6.

Bradshaw J S 1978 Doctors on Trial. Wildwood House, London. Chrisman N J & Baker R M 1978 Exploring the doctor-patient relationship: A socio-cultural pilot study in a family practice residency. Journal of Family Practice 7: 713–719.

Ewan C E & White R 1984 Teaching Nursing. A Self-instructional Handbook. Croom Helm London.

Freidson E 1962 Dilemmas in the doctor-patient relationship in Rose A M (ed) Human Behaviour and Social Processes, Routledge & Kegan Paul, London.

Graycar A 1982 Health and social policy in Priorities in Health Care, University of New South Wales Occasional Paper.

Greene J Y, Weinberger M & Mamlin J 1980 Patient attitudes towards health care; Expectations of primary care in a clinic setting. Social Science & Medicine 14A: 133–138.

Greenlick M R 1981 Assessing clinical competence. A societal view. Evaluation and the Health Professions 4: 3–12.

Gurtner W H 1982 The changing relationship between hospitals and surgeons. Bulletin of American College of Surgeons April, pp. 10–11.

Kincey J, Bradshaw P & Ley P 1975 Patient's satisfaction and reported acceptance of advice in general practice. Journal of the Royal College of General Practitioners 25: 558.

Kleinman A, Eisenberg L & Good B 1978 Culture, illness and care. Clinical lessons from anthropological and cross-cultural research. Annals of Internal Medicine 88: 251–258.

Ley P 1977 Patient compliance: A psychologist's viewpoint. Prescriber's Journal 17: 15–20.

Locker D & Dunt D 1978 Theoretical and methodological

issues in sociological studies of consumer satisfaction with medical care. Social Science & Medicine 12: 283–292.

Mace D R 1971 Communication, interviewing and the physician-patient relationship in Coombs R H & Vincent C E (eds) Psychosocial Aspects of Medical Training. C B Thomas Publishing, Springfield Illinois.

McKeown T 1976 The Role of Medicine, Dream, Mirage or Nemesis? The Nuffield Provincial Hospitals Trust.

Mechanic D 1975 Introduction in Howard J & Strauss A (eds) Humanizing Health Care. John Wiley & Sons, New York.

Mechanic D 1974 Correlates of frustration among British general practitioners in Mechanic D Politics, Medicine and Social Science. John Wiley & Sons, New York.

Older J 1983 Point of view — medics and paramedics. ANZAME Bulletin, April, p. 21.

Oscar G 1981 Physician and pharmacist — natural partners. Australian Family Physician 10: 866–970.

Owen D 1976 Clinical freedom and professional freedom. The Lancet, May 8, 1006–1009.

Parsons T 1967 The Social System. Routledge & Kegan Paul, London.

Reader G G, Pratt L & Mudd M C 1957 What patients expect from their doctors. The Modern Hospital 89: 88.

Reinhardt U E 1980 The future of medical enterprise: Perspectives on resource allocation in socialized markets. Journal of Medical Education 55: 311–324.

Segall A & Burnett M 1980 Patient evaluation of physician role performance. Social Science & Medicine 14A: 269–278.

Shapiro M 1978 Getting Doctored. Between the Lines, Chicago.

Spiegel A D & Backhaut B H 1980 Curing and Caring — A review of the factors affecting the quality and acceptability of health care. S P Medical and Scientific Books, New York.

Stimson G V 1977 Social care and the role of the general practitioner. Social Science & Medicine 11: 485–490.

Szasz T S & Hollender M H 1958 The doctor-patient relationship and its historical context. American Journal of Psychiatry 115: 522–528.

Taylor R 1979 Medicine Out of Control. The Anatomy of a Malignant Technology. Sun Books, Melbourne.

Twomey L 1983 What I wish I could tell doctors. Register of Members in Private Practice 1983/1984, Australian Physiotherapy Association, New South Wales.

How should medical students be selected?

Preview

WHAT ARE THE PURPOSES OF
SELECTION?

IS IT POSSIBLE TO PREDICT WHO WILL
BE A GOOD DOCTOR?

WHAT PROBLEMS RESULT FROM
TRADITIONAL SELECTION PROCEDURES?

HOW CAN SELECTION BE IMPROVED?
  Define selection policy
  Recognize that selection and curriculum are
interdependent
  Choose selection methods
    a Academic performance
    b Personality and attitude tests
    c Tests of special aptitudes
    d References
    e Interviews

CONCLUSION

The process of medical student selection has stimulated considerable discussion and research. No
best answers or clear directions can be given,
however, to resolve the problems which arise
when selection is addressed. The following questions and discussion are intended to highlight the
considerations which are relevant to choosing and
using selection criteria and methods.

WHAT ARE THE PURPOSES OF
SELECTION?

The obvious answer to this question is an administrative one. Places in medical school are rela-

tively few while applicants are numerous. Since
medical education is also an expensive process,
selection is used to discriminate among students
on criteria which are believed to predict performance in medical school. More recently it has been
suggested that selection should contribute to the
implementation of social policies, such as affirmative action or equality of opportunity.

Whatever the purpose to which selection is put,
all selection criteria are based on values and beliefs
about medical education and the role of the
doctor. All selection methods are, therefore,
unavoidably biased. The medical teacher's task is
to recognize and understand the values and biases
inherent in selection procedures, and to ensure
that they are the most appropriate values for the
society and context within which the school
functions.

IS IT POSSIBLE TO PREDICT WHO WILL
BE A GOOD DOCTOR?

To answer that question some prior questions
must be considered: What is a good doctor? Is a
good general practitioner recognizable by the same
criteria as a good pathologist or psychiatrist or
medical administrator? What are the characteristics of a young adult which predispose him or
her to become a 'good doctor' five or ten years
later? Can valid and reliable measures of these
desired characteristics be developed? Can those
measures be applied with sufficient confidence to
justify rejection of applicants who are qualified on
other criteria?

Attempts to identify and measure predictive
characteristics such as academic performance,

attitude, problem solving ability, tolerance of ambiguity, interpersonal skills and various aspects of personality have been disappointing (Bennett, 1982, Lipton et al, 1984). Correlations between high school or pre-medical exam performance and clinical performance are invariably insignificant (Bennett & Wakeford, 1982). Interviews and personality and attitude tests are often no more helpful. Correlations between selection interviews and later clinical performance have been reported to be as low as 0.2 (Antonovsky et al 1979). Some small correlational associations have been found between personality variables and clinical performance, but not at a level which justifies rejection of applicants (Gough, 1967, Rezler, 1983).

Despite this reality, however, medical schools continue to select students primarily on the basis of academic performance, with some schools choosing to use additional criteria assessed by interview or some form of psychometric testing. In the absence of better methods the continuation of these practices can be justified on several grounds.

Measures of academic performance are administratively simple, economical, fair and relatively objective. They provide some indication, if not of the student's ability to be a good doctor, at least of the student's ability to work diligently and pass examinations — skills which are required in medical schools. The major shortcoming of examinations is that they offer no insight into the personal characteristics of the student. This deficiency is addressed by some schools which employ additional methods to assess interpersonal skills, maturity, level of motivation, attitudes and thinking styles.

WHAT PROBLEMS RESULT FROM TRADITIONAL SELECTION PROCEDURES?

The major problem which results from traditional selection procedures is said to be the homogeneity of medical student groups. Proof of such homogeneity and its deleterious effects is seldom forthcoming. However, a tendency in that direction can probably be admitted to the extent that medical students are drawn from the upper strata of academic performance, usually with major subjects in the sciences rather than the humanities. Although this has been suggested as a cause of lack of social concern or 'person-orientation' among medical students (Sheldrake et al, 1978, Adams, 1982) such claims have not been proven (Ewan, 1981).

A further aspect of homogeneity which has implications for the nature of health care services is the tendency for medical students to be derived from higher social strata within their society. This tendency varies in extent and importance among different societies and political contexts, and manifests itself in different ways. In some countries students from urban areas are over-represented and students from minority groups under-represented. In Australia students from professional and managerial family backgrounds are significantly over-represented in medical schools (Beighton & Gallagher, 1976, Sheehan et al, 1980a, Ewan 1981). A large proportion of this imbalance is due to differential performance in high schools which may be due to geographic and social variations in the quality of school available and in conditions in the home (Anderson & Vervoorn, 1983). Although no tuition fees are payable in Australian medical schools, it is also possible that students from the lower socio-economic strata either do not aspire to medicine, or are deterred by the extra length and financial burden of self-support during the course.

Alternative selection criteria, however, may be even further biased socially than academic performance. A major criticism of subjective selection methods such as student interviews has been that interviewers tend to prefer interviewees with whom they can interact easily or with whom they can identify. The social bias in such a process is evident. Attempts to avoid this level of subjectivity include employing members of the community on interviewing panels, and predetermining specific criteria by which applicants should be judged. A closer examination of typical criteria, however, raises further concerns. For example, one community-oriented innovative medical school employs tests and interviews to measure characteristics such as creativity, higher order thinking, tolerance of ambiguity, perseverance, self-confidence and compatibility with the school's program

(Sanson-Fisher, 1982). One cohort of students thus selected was even less socially representative than cohorts of students from traditional schools (Sheehan et al, 1980a). A probable explanation lies in the fact that, in the society concerned, the characteristics sought are found less commonly in students from lower socio-economic strata who demonstrate predominantly characteristics such as authoritarianism, intolerance, intellectual passivity, concrete thinking and insecurity (Phillips 1979).

The situation is, therefore, extremely complex and simple solutions will not be found. For example, if alternative selection procedures succeed in producing 'better' doctors by selecting on criteria such as those defined above, will medicine become an even more socially élite profession whose members are out of touch with the needs of the majority of their patients? Further interesting questions arise. Are the characteristics of the 'ideal' doctor also the characteristics of the established middle class? Or has this view of the doctor been defined in its own image by the established middle class in the guise of medical school selection committees? If middle class attitudes are necessary for effective medical practice should only those students who possess those characteristics be selected? Or should students from a broad social range be selected and helped to develop such attitudes as part of their medical education? Every medical school selection committee should ask itself these questions before proceeding to formulate selection policy.

HOW CAN SELECTION BE IMPROVED?

1. Define selection policy

Each medical school within its particular social and political context should define its selection policy in relation to the responsibility it perceives towards its community. Selection criteria may incorporate social as well as professional and academic considerations.

2. Recognize that selection and curriculum are interdependent

The school should examine its curriculum in relation to the type of doctor it decides to produce, and should decide how the curriculum and the type of students selected will interact to produce the desired outcome. An example of this type of planning is the Rural Area Project in Thailand in which students from rural areas are selected and trained predominantly in health facilities in those areas. The curriculum is designed so that instruction can be carried out at a distance from the medical school for a significant proportion of the time. The curriculum differs in several respects from the mainstream curriculum (Sriratanaban & Sangprasert, 1983).

Prerequisites for effective learning within the curriculum must be identified. Some prerequisites (for example, skill in the language of instruction, or basic mathematical ability) may form part of the selection criteria, in that students who do not meet them will not be considered for admission regardless of their other attributes. Such course prerequisites should be chosen with care and should reflect only those criteria which have been demonstrated to affect significantly the student's ability to cope with the curriculum. Otherwise, imposition of prerequisites increases the likelihood that potentially good doctors will be excluded unnecessarily, and increases the tendency towards homogeneity in recruits to the profession.

On the other hand, the school may decide that certain prerequisites can be dealt with by provision of remedial learning experiences. In this case selection methods should be used to identify those students who meet some selection criteria but may require remedial assistance in other areas. Decisions about absolute and relative prerequisites and criteria are determined by the chosen selection policy.

A specific example of the need for curricular adaptation to the characteristics of students occurs when selection policy aims to achieve social equity or representation through some form of quota or positive discrimination in favour of disadvantaged groups. Students from those groups may be admitted with lower academic performance scores than other students, for example. 'Disadvantaged' groups, however, are usually disadvantaged in many ways; and medical students from such groups may require special financial, logistic and academic assistance if they are to succeed in medical schools.

3. Choose selection methods

A variety of selection methods is available. Choice of method may be determined as much by the resources available for selection as by the school's policy. The number of applicants may be so great that the school is forced to implement an initial sorting procedure based solely on academic performance, in order to reduce to manageable proportions the number to be interviewed or tested comprehensively. Nevertheless, attempts should be made to gather information on applicants from as wide a variety of sources as possible. Some characteristics of the more common sources of information are summarized briefly below.

1. Academic performance

Tests may be general tests of performance, such as high school leaving examinations, or specific standardized tests, such as the Medical College Admissions Test. These tests are objective in their scoring, fair in the sense that all candidates face exactly the same known test, and reasonably reliable in the sense of reproducibility. Their ability to predict performance in medical school is, however, insufficiently sensitive to enable them to be used to rank candidates reliably. Cut-off points which admit some students and reject others with a score one point lower are not justified as precise, given the variance of the examination. A better use of scores on academic tests is to categorize students into groups which would be likely to cope well with the medical course and groups which would be unlikely to cope. Used as a first stage filter in this way academic tests help to reduce the numbers of students who will proceed to more labour-intensive phases of the selection process.

2. Personality and attitude tests

The use of such tests in selection of medical students has not yet been proven to be effective in predicting performance as a doctor, and the reliability and predictive validity of tests is difficult to establish. Standardized tests and personality inventories which are available should be used with caution in cultures other than the ones for which they were developed. At this stage in the development of the science of selection, personality and attitude tests are more safely used for research purposes to study the attitudes or personality characteristics of students who wish to study medicine. Several reviews of methods of attitude assessment are available for medical teachers (Rezler, 1976, Weinholtz & Stritter, 1982).

3. Tests of special aptitudes

Tests of special aptitudes are used in some professions, such as dentistry, in which certain aptitudes such as manual dexterity are agreed to be important. Other types of aptitudes, such as creativity or higher order thinking, are more difficult to justify as selection criteria, since reliable links between such aptitudes and performance as a doctor have not yet been proven. Nevertheless, tests are available which measure such characteristics, although the same caution should be applied as with personality and attitude tests. A description of the use of such selection criteria is available (Vinson et al, 1979, Feletti et al, 1985). Tests of moral reasoning have been reported to correlate highly with clinical performance (Sheehan et al, 1980b), and it has been suggested that these could be used as a screen to assess interpersonal skills, allowing the interview to be directed more specifically towards the institution's objectives (Benor et al, 1984).

4. References

Reports from school teachers and principals have been used to contribute to selection of medical students. Reports from supervisors in previous relevant work experience or academic endeavours might also be helpful. The general experience is that such reports are almost uniformly positive and therefore unhelpful in discriminating among students (Vinson et al, 1979). One way of improving the information available from referees is to ask specific questions or to provide a standard framework within which the referee can make his or her comments (Bennett & Wakeford, 1983). For example, the referee may be asked to rate the applicant's ability and willingness to cooperate with others or to cope with a particular given scenario.

5. *Interviews*

In spite of their disappointing performance as predictors of success in medical school, interviews have potential importance as part of the selection process. Their use can be improved by careful prior planning. The purposes of the interview should be decided upon, and all interviewers should be aware of and understand those purposes. Interviews should be used for purposes for which they are best suited. For example, it may be unreasonable to attempt to predict an applicant's academic ability from an interview; but it is quite reasonable to assess his or her ability to converse intelligently and develop rapport with the interviewers. The role of the interview in the selection process should also be clear: Is the interview to be used to rank applicants, or to identify 'at risk' individuals for rejection or remedial assistance?

Interviewers' ability to make judgments about applicants on the basis of an interview is assisted by providing guidelines for eliciting useful information. Interviewers on medical school selection panels are unlikely to find a structured or standardized set of questions satisfactory, since they are accustomed to the clinical approach of following certain 'leads' in the interviewee's responses. A suitable compromise, therefore, is to provide an armamentarium of question types to enable useful information to be gathered. Such an approach is analogous to the 'system review' in medical history taking. The selection committee should identify the type of information to be sought in the interview (for example, motivation to become a doctor, willingness to work in a health team, ability to communicate with patients) and then provide sample questions which probe for this information. The following example in Figure 3.1 is adapted from Bennett & Wakeford (1983).

In addition to providing interviewers with guidance to help them gather relevant information from the interview, the interview protocol should request that interviewers record their judgments on specific criteria and give their reasons for that judgment. For example: 'Do you have doubts

Motivation to become a doctor
Have you ever been ill or in hospital?
What does a doctor do?
What do you think would be the difference between a good doctor and a bad doctor?
What abilities and interests do you have that would make you a good doctor?
Can you describe a situation from your past experience in which you demonstrated those abilities or interests?

Willingness to work in a health team
Can you describe something you have done or achieved completely on your own?
Can you describe something you have done which required working with other people?
Which of these situations did you enjoy more, and why?

Ability to communicate with patients
Pretend I am a patient. Can you explain to me why I should try to lose weight?

Fig. 3.1 Sample questions for selection interview

about this applicant's motivation to become a doctor? If yes, why?' Requiring this kind of thought and commitment from the interviewer discourages snap judgments which may be based on first impressions rather than the interviewee's responses. Where decisions as to acceptance or rejection of the applicant are based on the outcome of the interview, it is essential that interviews be conducted by panels of two or more interviewers who are familiar with the role and who can arrive at decisions by discussion and consensus. A scoring system may simplify this process, but it will not necessarily render the procedure any more reliable unless standardized interviews and rigorous checklists and scoring procedures are used. At best it may make some interviewers feel more comfortable about the process of ranking or comparing candidates one with another.

CONCLUSION

Improvement of selection procedures is a goal worthy of some effort; it is not, however, a panacea for the ills of medical education. Emphasis on selection to improve the quality of medical graduates underestimates the power of medical education and the socialization process.

More seriously, a reliance on selection to ensure the presence of desirable characteristics diminishes the medical school's responsibility to provide experiences which develop or reinforce those characteristics in students and doctors. Selection and curriculum are interdependent.

All selection methods are derived from particular value positions and therefore carry inherent biases. To this extent at least, all methods are in some way imperfect, and trade-offs must be made to achieve the best fit for the individual, the curriculum and the community. Choice of selection methods should be guided by policies derived from the values of the community which the medical school serves, and by a realistic appraisal of the strengths and limitations of the methods themselves. To this end selection procedures should be accorded priority as opportunities for research.

REFERENCES

Adams A 1982 The selection of more socially motivated students would help the cause. World Forum 3: 365–366

Anderson D S, Vervoorn A E 1983 Access to Privilege: Patterns of Participation in Australian Post-secondary Education. ANU Press Canberra

Antonovsky A, Anson O, Bernstein J 1979 Interviewing and the selection of medical students: The experience of five years at Beer Sheba. Programmed Learning and Educational Technology 16: 328–334

Beighton F C L, Gallagher A P, 1976 Socio-economic differences between university and CAE students. The Australian University 14: 162–176

Bennett M 1982 Selection of students for the health professions: A critical review of selection procedures in R D Linke (ed) Selection of students for the Health Professions Australasian and New Zealand Association for Medical Education, August

Bennett M, Wakeford R 1982 Health policy, student selection and curriculum reform. Health Policy and Education 3: 173–181

Bennett M, Wakeford R 1983 Selecting students for training in health care. A practical guide to improving selection procedures. World Health Organization Offset Publication No. 74 WHO, Geneva

Benor D E Notzer N, Sheehan T J, Norman G R 1984 Moral reasoning as a criterion for admission to medical school. Medical Education 18: 423–428

Ewan C E 1981 Report on interviews of incoming students. Faculty of Medicine Papers No. 7, University of New South Wales, February

Feletti G I, Sanson-Fisher W, Vidler V, Admissions Committee of the Faculty of Medicine, University of Newcastle, NSW. 1985 Evaluating an approach to selecting medical students. Medical Education 19: 276–284

Gough H G 1967 Non-intellectual factors in the selection and evaluation of medical students. Journal of Medical Education 42: 642–650

Lipton A, Huxham G J, Hamilton D 1984 Predictors of success in a cohort of medical students. Medical Education 18: 203–210

Phillips S, 1979 Young Australians pp 41 & 84 The Attitudes of Our Children, Harper & Row, Sydney

Rezler A G 1976 Methods of attitude assessment for medical teachers Medical Education 10: 43–51

Rezler A G 1983 Admission to Allied Health, Dentistry, Medicine, Nursing and Pharmacy schools in the U.S. A review of the literature 1960–1980 in C McGuire, R Foley, A Gow, R Richards (eds) Handbook of Health Professions Education. Jossey Bass, San Francisco.

Sanson-Fisher R W 1982 Selection of students for the health professions: Reviewing the experience of the Newcastle medical school, in R D Linke (ed) Selection of Students for the Health Professions, Australasian and New Zealand Association for Medical Education , August

Sheehan M, Colditz G, Western J, Doherty R 1980 Students entering Medicine I: Socio-economic background. Paper presented at Australasian and New Zealand Association for Medical Education Annual Conference

Sheehan T J, Husted S D R, Candee D, Cook C D, Borgen M 1980 Moral judgment as a predictor of clinical performance. Evaluation and the Health Professions 3: 393–404

Sheldrake P R, Linke R D, Mensh 1978 IN Chapter 3 in Medical Education in Australia: Present trends and future prospects in Australian Medical schools. ERDC Report No 16, Australian Government Publishing Service, Canberra

Sriatanaban A, Sangprasert B 1983 The rural area project (RAP) in Thailand: curriculum development. Medical Education 17: 374–377

Vinson T, Cooney G, Turnbull J 1979 Admission to medical school: the Newcastle Experiment. Programmed Learning and Educational Technology 16: 277–287

Weinholtz D, Stritter 1982 How to plan an assessment of students' attitudes. Medical Teacher 4: 95–101

Teaching approaches

Introduction

The following chapters deal with the process of student learning and the teaching methods and venues which are commonly in use in medical schools. Although each method has potential advantages and disadvantages, and specific purposes for which it is best suited, the feature common to them all is the necessity for the teacher to plan their use so that student learning is facilitated. That 'teaching does not equal learning' is by now a well-worn maxim and is discussed further in Chapter 4 — How do students learn?

Good teachers are aware of teaching and learning as a process necessitating two-way communication and an awareness of the conditions which students find helpful to their learning. Theories and models of learning have been developed which seek to explain learning and improve teaching (for example, see Gagne, 1974; Wilson, 1981) and a few general principles which emerge from these models may be helpful to medical teachers.

1. Teachers must decide what it is that students should learn. In other words they should determine clear learning objectives for the session.

2. Teachers must decide what experiences should be provided to assist students to achieve those objectives. At this point familiarity with some principles of learning will be helpful. Specific conditions for different types of learning are discussed in Gagne (1974) and Lovell (1980) and are also discussed in the following chapters.

3. Teachers must decide what resources will be needed to help students learn from the experience. Resources are discussed in more detail in a following section.

4. Teachers must decide how they and the students will know when the students have achieved the objectives. In some cases assessment of learning can be built into the learning experience itself, and ways of doing this are discussed in the chapter dealing with each method. Immediate assessment and feedback on performance are very effective components of teaching and should be used wherever circumstances and resources permit. In other cases assessment may have to be conducted in an examination context. Examinations are discussed in detail in a following section.

The above four steps are a very brief summary of the instructional design process. A more comprehensive treatment can be found in any standard text on instructional design. A useful reference for basic information is Kemp (1971).

Within each teaching session the conditions for learning which teachers should plan to incorporate can be summarized in four main steps. No matter which method you use some attention must be given to each of these conditions if you expect students to learn what you are trying to teach.

1. Motivation

Students must recognize a need or desire to learn what you have to teach them. You must, therefore, demonstrate the relevance of the material to the tasks the student will ultimately perform.

2. Attention

Students must be able to select the key information from the variety of stimuli which present themselves. For example, not everything you say in a lecture will be equally important for the students to know or remember. Some information may be incidental or included simply for illustration. Students, however, are often not aware of the scope of the topic and are uncertain as to which information is the most important. You must help them to recognize this important information, and can do so in a number of ways by using emphasis, handouts and, audio-visual aids. Whichever method you choose, remember that students do not have the same perspective of the topic that you have and they will need guidance in determining which aspects deserve their main concentration.

3. Incorporation

Students may take notes and may learn those notes well enough to allow reproduction of those notes in the examination. Usually, however, learning of that type is short-lived. It has not been incorporated by the student into the stable body of knowledge which forms what students 'really know' — those things they can call on at future times to help them perform tasks and solve problems. Incorporation of knowledge into stable memory storage where it can be used when needed depends on students being able to understand the new knowledge and relate it to what they already know and use. To do this they must have

adequate opportunity to think about, discuss and reflect on the new knowledge and compare it with other things in their experience.

4. Use

To ensure that knowledge remains usable and accessible it must, quite simply, be used. Students must have opportunities, either in that session or subsequent ones, to practise and apply what they are learning. Practice and application not only consolidates new learning but it provides an opportunity for both teacher and learner to assess how well the learner is mastering the skills or concepts involved. In this way feedback and remediation become part of the learning process.

In summary, whichever method you decide to use to achieve the learning objectives which you have defined, always plan the session to ensure that there are activities which will arouse motivation, guide students' attention to the important material and allow time and opportunity for reflection, application and practice. The methods described in the following chapters emphasize these principles and offer many practical suggestions for their incorporation into all common teaching methods.

REFERENCES

Gagne R M 1974 Essentials of learning for instruction. The Dryden Press, Illinois.
Kemp J E 1970 Instructional design. Fearon Publishers inc. Belmont, California.
Lovell R B 1980 Adult learning. Croom Helm, London.
Wilson J D 1981 Student learning in higher education. Croom Helm London.

How do students learn?

INTRODUCTION

Any attempt to answer this question must take account of *why* students engage in learning activities: their intentions, motivations, aspirations and interests. Good teachers have always taken pains to find out what they can about these matters but researchers into learning have, until quite recently, tended to ignore them with the result that many of their findings have not been of much use to the practising teacher.

If we try to look at things from the perspective of the student this enables us to develop a view of learning as an interaction between what students bring with them and their perceptions of the context in which learning takes place. On the one hand are the knowledge, interests, attitudes and aspirations which students bring into the classroom, and on the other the subject-matters, teaching methods, learning tasks, assessment procedures, teachers and departmental environments which they encounter in the university.

It is important to appreciate that students and teachers often have very different views of the context in which learning takes place. These differences frequently result in outcomes which satisfy neither group of participants, a point made by Entwistle (in Marton et al, 1984, p. 2): '. . . as educators we should be much more concerned than we are with the quality of learning. Much of our current teaching and assessment seems to induce a passive, reproductive form of learning which is contrary to the aims of the teachers themselves'.

Further illustrations of this lack of congruence between teachers' and students' perceptions of the context of learning can be found in the reports of some medical educators on their own learning experiences (Powell, 1983, p. 266), reports which would surely have made depressing reading for their teachers:

'I was subjected to a conventional medical curriculum from which I learnt nothing except how to work just sufficiently to scrape through year by year.'

'I latched on to the idea that to learn you got a clear view of what you were expected to know, and learnt it, word for word. Not much thinking. Just learn the sacred text. Unfortunately the apparent success of this mind-stunting technique impressed me and retarded my mind's development for years to come.'

WHAT STUDENTS BRING WITH THEM

When students arrive at university they bring with them a well-formed set of beliefs, attitudes and values; a great deal of information; a large number of concepts and opinions; a rather idealistic view of their chosen profession; an unrealistically high expectation of their future academic achievements; an interest in what they envisage they will be learning; and a determination to succeed in their course of study.

Most medical educators, like their colleagues in other disciplines, often make incorrect assumptions about this 'mental luggage' which students carry into the classroom. This is scarcely surprising as few academics make a serious attempt to discover the nature of the foundations upon which all their teaching must stand (or fall), or to enquire into what stays with their students after graduation. Their overwhelming concern is with what happens between enrolment and the final examinations, and this concern is shaped mainly by the teacher's perspective rather than that of the student.

Space permits mention of only three of the more important items in the students' 'luggage'. First is the approach to study, the general conception of what is involved in learning something. This has been formed by years of experience in school characterized by working under the close supervision of teachers, the mastery of factual information in order to do well in examinations, and the belief that there is one correct solution to a problem or answer to a question. This approach has led the student to success in the past and is thus likely to persist, even though it may no longer be appropriate in the university environment.

Second is the desire and determination to do well academically. This has also led to success and entry into the medical school but, as the earlier quotations indicated, it can lead to study practices which hinder the intellectual development of the student and obstruct the growth of understanding. To succeed within the new environment students are likely to do whatever they perceive to be necessary for success, even though this is often at variance with the aspirations of their teachers.

Third are the concepts which students have already formed in relation to whatever subject-matter they will be engaged in studying. These concepts are often erroneous or poorly grasped, although they are often of a quite fundamental nature. Some examples are the following: normal, average, force and evolution. The set of concepts which students bring with them into the classroom is firmly entrenched as a result of being held for many years. These concepts provide the means by which the student interprets new experiences and attaches meaning to them. They form what Aber-crombie (1969) calls 'schemata', that is, mental structures into which new information and knowledge must be made to fit if it is to be meaningful to the student.

Unfortunately, recent research has indicated that these schemata are extremely resistant to change. Dahlgren, for example, (in Marton et al, 1983) has shown that many students acquire the ability to speak the language of their discipline, and perform well in examinations, yet continue to entertain the naive ideas which they brought with them when beginning a course of study. In order to modify or displace these erroneous concepts it appears necessary to, first, accurately determine their characteristics, and then devise methods of teaching which address them more directly and thus be more likely to succeed in changing them. The evidence of the work of Dahlgren and others indicates that conventional teaching methods have only limited impact upon students' basic misconceptions.

The importance of what students bring with them cannot be over-emphasized. Its significance lies in its power to influence the ways in which they respond to the content of what they are being taught. Teachers often take for granted that students are very much like themselves in that they share a common set of basic ideas and assumptions. This is not true. Students interpret what they hear in lectures and see in laboratories in terms of their own view of reality rather than that of the teacher. As teachers we need to be far more aware of this than we usually are. It is no use blaming undesirable learning outcomes upon the poor preparation, slothfulness or limited intellectual ability of students. It is our responsibility as teachers to discover, at the beginning of each course, the level and extent of the knowledge possessed by students. Even more important is the need to identify the extent to which basic ideas are *misunderstood*. Then we shall be able to design our teaching efforts so that they focus upon the elimination of misconceptions and the development of understanding.

THE CONTEXT OF LEARNING

The medical student encounters an environment characterized by a heavy workload, a variety of subject-matters (many of which are unfamiliar) dense with factual material and new terminology, frequent assessment hurdles, peers who have often acquired an excessively competitive style at school, teachers who themselves carry a heavy workload, a demanding series of learning tasks, and many conflicting demands on their time.

To cope with all this they must adopt learning strategies that will enable them to become qualified. They therefore attend carefully to any signals which seem to indicate what is expected of them. The loudest signals emanate from the assessment system since this is what finally determines academic success and entry into the desired career. It is being recognized increasingly that the most important single force which shapes students' approaches to study and learning is the system of assessment. If we wish to influence how students learn we should, therefore, look very closely at the ways in which we assess their performance.

Staff often say that their teaching is directed at helping students to understand the subject-matter and to develop creativity, problem-solving skills, flexibility, critical thinking, open-mindedness, and the ability to analyse and synthesize complex material. Students, however, often perceive what is required of them in a very different manner which leads them to adopt approaches to learning which favour the reproduction of factual material and the tailoring of assignment work to fit what they think the staff want. The important role of the assessment system in shaping this approach was clearly shown in the findings of Becker et al (1968) and in the work of Snyder (1971) who coined the useful phrase 'the hidden curriculum' to describe the students' view of the most important things they were required to learn.

The work of Marton and his colleagues (Marton et al, 1984) has suggested the usefulness of distinguishing between what they call 'deep' and 'surface' approaches to learning. The first approach is concerned with understanding the content of study material whereas the second is largely aimed at reproducing it. Assessment procedures play an important part in encouraging many students to adopt a 'surface' approach, but many other factors are also involved. These include overcrowded curricula, heavy reliance on lecturing as a teaching method, frequent use of 'cookbook' laboratory experiments, large numbers of assignment tasks, and a workload which leaves little time for reflection and integration. Faced with all this it is small wonder that many students give up trying to understand what they are doing and concentrate upon satisfying what they see to be the requirements of the examiners. As Laurillard (in Marton et al, 1984, p. 143) has pointed out:

'Students take a largely rational approach to learning. They consider what is required of them, they decide on priorities, and they act accordingly. The teacher plays an important part in forming their perceptions of what is required and what is important, and it is this, as much as their style of presenting the subject-matter, which influences what and how their students learn.'

WHAT DO WE WANT STUDENTS TO LEARN?

Medical educators, probably more than any other group concerned with preparation for a profession, have been much influenced by the 'behavioural objectives' movement in curriculum design. This has undoubtedly helped teachers to think more clearly about what they want their students to learn but it has also lead to a concentration upon end-of-course achievements rather than the longer-term effects of learning. It is always a salutary exercise for teachers to ask themselves what they expect students to retain years after almost all the details of the content of a course have been forgotten. The answer to this question can then be used to sieve course content, learning tasks, teaching methods and assessment procedures in order to identify their relevance to the basic aims of teaching.

If we were to do this we would discover that much of what we currently teach would fall through the sieve in much the same way as it passes through the heads of students. This should encourage us to focus much more sharply on the key elements of what we wish students to learn and to modify the curriculum and our methods of teaching to ensure that these things are learnt and learnt in a meaningful manner so as to be more likely to endure into the years of professional practice.

The competencies required for successful medical practice are progressively developed through the daily experience of that practice. The knowledge and skills involved are such that they can never be mastered: learning continues throughout the working life of professionals. It follows from this that the major task which faces medical educators is that of making sure that each graduate is capable of learning from the wealth of experiences that lie ahead. Together with this ability there must also be instilled a desire to continue learning. For this to be achieved the characteristics of undergraduate learning need to match much more closely than is usually the case the ways in which successful practitioners learn from experience. In other words, it should be designed to call into play the same skills and attitudes which enable us to develop our competencies as professional people. All our endeavours as teachers should be shaped by this end so that students are helped to learn in ways appropriate to the requirements of future practice.

The best way to appreciate how this might be achieved is to reflect upon how we go about learning in our own professional practice. Do we, for example, spend many hours each day listening to lectures? Adult learning is firmly based upon experience and its reflective analysis. Frequently it is related to problem identification and resolution (Boud, 1985). Intellectual and practical skills are acquired and developed through constant practice guided by a commitment to achieve higher levels of competency. We should take a fresh look at how we go about our teaching, and the features of the learning experiences we provide for students, in order to ensure that we provide ample opportunities for students to acquire the knowledge, skills and attitudes that will enable them to continue to learn throughout their careers.

FURTHER READING

Abercrombie M L J 1969 The anatomy of judgment. Penguin Books Harmondsworth
Fascinating account of a small group teaching method designed to encourage medical students to question some of their basic assumptions and to sharpen their ability to observe and interpret everyday and clinical phenomena.

Becker H S, Geer B, Hughes E C 1968 Making the grade: the academic side of college life. Wiley, New York
Major study of the effects of the assessment system on students' approaches to learning and the carrying out of academic tasks.

Boud E (ed) 1985 Problem-based learning in education for the professions. HERDSA, Sydney
Valuable collection of accounts by practitioners of ways in which problem-based courses can be developed and introduced into the curriculum. Includes material on medical education.

Entwistle N, Ramsden P 1982 Understanding student learning. Croom Helm, London
Report of a research program into student approaches to learning and the extent to which these reflect teaching and assessment methods. Includes many quotations from interviews with students which provide insights into the ways in which they see themselves as learners and their interpretation of what is expected of them.

Holt J 1967 How children fall. Penguin Books Harmondsworth
Although concerned with how young children go about learning this book contains much of interest to university teachers because its main focus is the ways in which learners respond to what teachers do. Very readable, perceptive and non-technical. Written by a practitioner.

Marton F, Hounsell D, Entwistle H 1984 (eds) The experience of learning. Scottish Academic, Edinburgh
Up to date and authoritative collection of papers reporting recent research aimed at determining the student perspective on learning and how this is influenced by the context in which it occurs. Includes valuable discussions of the implications of the findings for teachers.

Powell J P 1983 The impact of higher education: graduates report on what they learnt. In: Moses I (ed) Research and development in higher education. HERDSA, Sydney, vol 6
Reports a study of how practitioners in the health professions view the significance and value of their undergraduate training in relation to their professional and personal lives.

Snyder B R 1971 The hidden curriculum. Knopf, New York
Examines the relationship between teachers' beliefs about the aims of their teaching and the rather different views that students have of what they think is expected of them. Shows that the 'hidden curriculum' exerts a powerful influence on the ways in which students approach learning.

Wilson J D 1981 Student learning in higher education. Croom Helm, London
Comprehensive survey of research into all aspects of student learning. Valuable summary with many comments on implications for teaching. Extensive blbliography.

How to plan and deliver a lecture

Preview

WHAT IS A LECTURE?

Introductions — gaining attention; arousing motivation; structuring
Development — explaining, especially clarity and emphasis; making links; variations
Conclusions — reviewing and evaluating

WHY A LECTURE?

Purposes — styles of learning

LECTURE — WHAT KINDS?

a. Classical;
b. Problem-centred;
c. Sequential;
d. Comparative;
e. Thesis

HOW BEST TO PLAN A LECTURE?

1. Define key questions
2. Work out links or connections
3. Organize material
4. Adapt to target group

WHAT IS A LECTURE?

Lecturing has been with us for a very long time. The process has been defined as '. . . .giving information, generating understanding, and creating interest.' (Brown, 1978, p. 41). Central to what actually happens during a lecture is the skill of explaining, (Cox and Ewan, 1982; Turney et al, 1983b) as the lecturer attempts to give understanding to his or her students. To come to grips with the complexities of lecturing, it is useful to see any one lecture being made up of an introduction, a development, and a conclusion. Within each section of the lecture, certain skills and strategies of teaching will be applicable. These are considered in turn.

Introductions

During the introduction as the lecture begins, *gaining attention* and *arousing motivation* will be important (Turney et al, 1983b). Obviously, unless students are attending, they will not take in information in order to start understanding the topic. Some lecturers initially gain attention through a position habitually adopted, a regular opening phrase, or a certain gestural signal. The topic may be written up, or the overhead switched on. The teacher is responsible for providing some stimulus which indicates to students that the lecture is commencing.

But it is clear in all learning contexts that unless an external stimulus is quickly followed by arousal of internal motives within students, attention will fade and learning will not take place. Now while the whole area of motivation is broad and poorly understood, lecturers will be more effective in their teaching if they can tap these factors which relate to students' needs, attitudes, incentives, drives, values, understanding, in short, anything which makes them want to learn. Tertiary lecturers should not rely wholly on the assumption that, just because students are there, they will learn, if only to pass the exam. One of our teaching roles is to foster student learning.

One form of intrinsic motivation which energizes learning for all ages is *curiosity*. Forms of conceptual conflict, like surprise, doubt, bafflement, or contradiction, are great motivators, for humans will work to resolve anomalies once they are hooked by that which puzzles them. An unusual item of equipment, an apparently irrelevant diagram, or a brain-teasing anecdote, can enlist the mind's capacity for putting ideas into appropriate boxes. Another type of motivation which may help at the beginning of a lecture is an appeal to *interests*, (political issues, current films, human relationships, controversial value questions, aspects of sport or sub-cultures) which can lead into a topic and establish relevance for students.

Finding ways to arouse motivation is not easy. The always present question for any teacher is one of balance between employing external factors which compel students to learn and enlisting internal motives which make them want to learn. But much educational research shows that intrinsic motivation is a crucial factor in learning.

Another teacher move which is important in introductions is defined in recent research as *structuring*, (Turney et al, 1983b) which broadly entails setting a context for learning. There are three possible ways this can be done early in a lecture.

First, by establishing goals, the lecturer can indicate purposes or objectives, because learning is enhanced when students know where a lecture is headed.

Second, by giving directions, the lecturer can indicate how students might proceed with various activities during the lecture.

Third, by outlining content, the lecturer can indicate in sequence what will be covered in the lecture. Structuring moves serve to make the task in hand clear for both lecturer and students, through the putting into words of where the lecture is going. Check how these moves are achieved in this introduction.

> You will all come across patients who have difficulty breathing through the nose. There are many different pathological processes which cause nasal obstruction.

> Today I want to focus on nasal allergies. Then, in order to help you make an accurate diagnosis, we'll go through a handout on taking a history and conducting a physical examination. Because it is crucial to recognize symptoms accurately, I'll be spending a fair bit of time on slides showing physical examination of nasal cavities. Please listen carefully at that stage. It would be better not to take notes then, as you will get a printed summary of key signs. I intend to leave time for your questions at the end.

Development

Having set the scene through some of the introductory procedures outlined above, the lecturer moves on to development of the topic. The main body of a lecture essentially consists of a series of connected short explanations, sequenced to give information and understanding to students. So the lecturer at this stage will be heavily involved in *explaining*. Several aspects of that process need to be stressed.

Many studies have found correlations between teacher *clarity* and learning outcomes. In lecturing, clarity will be promoted particularly through use of language such as accurate definitions, precise vocabulary, straightforward sentences, fluent speech and the avoidance of vagueness, false starts, incomplete sentences or excessive qualifications.

Another mainly verbal activity, namely *emphasis*, has also proved to be quite significant. The lecturer may emphasize by varying voice pitch or volume, by directly cuing what is important, by restating main ideas in other words, by repetitions of concepts, or by enumerating points in a sequence. These are areas of presentation which any lecturer can improve by careful preparation and practice. Compare these two efforts.

> Now, um, you know we need water to survive. I mean you could live without food for a week. Not water. Anyway, the point is water is not much use to us if it's dirty, full of disease and things. So it has to be treated so people can drink it safely. Which brings me to today's topic — ah, . . . yes, purification. Water purification. Now we might that is I could talk about natural purification, but I guess you all understand it. So let me talk about artificial means. Now, in water from a river there are bits and pieces, dirt, mud and stuff . . . particles you need to get rid of. Some are so light they never sink. So we need to add something to the water to help the mud like stick together . . . get heavier and sink.

> A key issue for much of the world's population is how to obtain a supply of water fit for human consumption. Now water is an effective medium for the spread of such

diseases as typhoid and hepatitis, in fact any sickness spread by water-borne parasites. Today we will focus on artificial means of effective water purification. There are three steps or phases in any effective water purifying system. The first, as in natural water purification, depends on gravity. Large particles of mud in a holding pond will sink to the bottom. But lighter particles require assistance. So in this first phase, coagulation a substance such as alum or $AlSO_4$ is added. This coagulant helps particles adhere, stick together, thus becoming heavier and sinking to the bottom.

As the lecture proceeds, it will be essential to have connections between ideas made explicit. *Making links* entails, for example, concepts which have been treated previously and which are required to understand unfamiliar material. A variation on this theme is to assist understanding by highlighting familiar notions which relate to new content in the lecture. Other instances where specific connections could be formed are between generalizations and the examples which illustrate them, between steps in a process or procedure, among the sections within the lecture itself, or between concepts which are alike or contrasting.

A lecturer should not assume that because the links are perfectly clear to him or her, students can make the implicit jumps or fill in the gaps. Various theories suggest that such explicit moves help students to make sense of new ideas by fitting them into existing cognitive frameworks, in other words, by hanging unfamiliar material on known hooks where it seems to belong.

Further into the lecture, *variations* will be necessary to sustain attention and understanding. A number of studies have shown that attending starts to drop around 15 to 20 minutes into the traditional one hour lecture (Turney et al, 1983 a). A change in stimulus can be provided by the lecturer simply changing position or in some way changing tone of voice, pace or volume.

More directly, the media or materials of instruction can be varied. Switching an overhead projector on or off can change the focus of attention from a diagram to the lecturer's comments and back again as required. Introducing when appropriate a model, real objects, a demonstration, slides, an audio or videotape excerpt, pictures or film restimulates interest and greatly aids understanding.

Even within quite large groups, variety can also be provided by allowing for short periods of inter-action, for example, between lecturer and students by asking or inviting questions, or among students by setting small 'buzz' groups to a task. Note that structuring of such interaction will be very important. Meaningful variations do enhance attending and can promote learning in lecture situations.

Conclusions

Because lectures tend to be discrete units separated by periods of time and other life activities, a conclusion is necessary to help achieve closure for students, a sense that the task in hand has been rounded off satisfactorily (Turney, et al, 1983b). A significant closing strategy for any lecture is reviewing, commonly done by reiterating key points covered in a verbal summarizing. Often this is associated with a progressive or final written summary of the content covered. Certain writers suggest a review aids longterm memory, allowing students to check whether what they remember or have recorded in their notes corresponds with what was covered by the lecturer (Brown, 1978).

Another less frequently used aspect of closure is evaluating, in which the lecturer may attempt to find out in the short term whether immediate aims have been realized. Opportunities for obtaining direct feedback in the lecture context are limited, though as already noted questions could be asked or invited more often than has been the case. Handouts may be organized to encourage student application of concepts, or to direct their enquiries for further information. Follow-up tasks may be designed for associated tutorials or practicals, to allow students to discuss ideas, clarify concepts, or evaluate skills development. Occasionally lecturers may invite feedback where students express opinions about the value or relevance of what they are covering, or even about the way they are being taught. Even if evaluation is difficult in lecturing, any information so gained is invaluable in shaping the approach to successive lectures.

WHY LECTURE?

One simple reason for lecturing is that it has long

been a traditional means of teaching. Another is that current patterns of tertiary education (and funding) ensure that there are few alternative modes available (or affordable). But if we accept that lecturing is here to stay, then there are some safe conclusions supported by research which can be drawn about the purposes which lectures may usefully serve.

Lectures are not effective for demonstrating practical skills or detailed procedures, nor for having students apply ideas, solve problems or clarify values.

But lectures can be used to present and organize information, promote understanding of concepts and ideas, and create interest in a subject (Ewan, 1984). Lecturers should be clear about the purposes which lecturing serves best.

Some findings about student learning may also help lecturers do their job more effectively. It is apparent that for the reception of information both short- and long-term memory are important. The pace and amount of material presented must allow time for rehearsal of key ideas followed by effective memory storage so that later retrieval is possible.

Studies of student note-taking indicate that at best half the material is recorded adequately, while some students get as little as a tenth (Brown, 1983). Also, in examinations of how students go about mastering lecture material, several researchers have independently analyzed two extreme styles of learning, summarized in Table 5.1. below.

Table 5.1 Two extremes of learning

The 'deep' approach	The 'surface' approach
Actively search for understanding	Memorize what will be assessed
Question arguments	Focus on specific facts; do not actively seek connections
Relate ideas to previous knowledge or personal experiences	
Try to see the whole	Learn by rote steps or parts
Risk-taking; confident	Over-cautious; anxious

Effective learners are versatile, able to move between the two approaches according to the demands of the situation. There appear to be links between lecturing styles and the kinds of approaches to learning fostered in particular university departments. Lecturers are left to draw

conclusions concerning their own styles of lecturing.

LECTURES: WHAT KINDS?

To assist lecturers in deciding which lecture patterns may be most suited to their purposes, and as a further guide to planning, Bligh's summaries of five different lecture types are briefly outlined and exemplified from plans and presentations of students in the Master of Health Personnel degree program conducted at the School of Medical Education, University of New South Wales. (Bligh, 1972; Brown & Tomlinson, 1979).

A. Classical

(the most common type)
  * broad sections in a logical order, with branches or related sub-sections developed and exemplified, concluded with a brief summary.
  * suits descriptive topics, often answering 'what' questions.

What is a Conversion Hysteria?
Introduction
hysterical disorders
no organic damage, yet loss of function
basic cause, extreme stress (e.g. wars)
prevents any further harm
simulated? discuss . . . . .

Symptoms
diverse, usually higher functions and sensory motor systems affected (e.g. amnesia paralysis)
can produce pseudodementia
also pain — real? discuss . . . .

Aetiology
many theories including
1. genetic factors — hysterical personality
2. upbringing — dominant traits reinforced
3. psychodynamic explanation, where unconscious conflict or psychic trauma — threat to integrity — switching off of functions — ill, need not continue stressful situation

Fig. 5.1 Example of a 'Classical' lecture plan

B. Problem-centred

(quite common)
  * an issue or case is stated, then alternative solutions are posed and evaluated, with findings summarized.

* suits enquiry and controversial topics, answers mainly 'how' and/or 'why' questions.

> How can those in the 'helping professions' assist patients with depression?
> What kind — reactive or endogenous?
> Assessment
>   current life events — sleep patterns — past history
>   — any records available? — significant others
> If reactive, and counselling possible — ventilation
>   of feelings — cognition and perception of events —
>   setting achievable goals — evaluation — follow up
>   and/or referral
> If endogenous, and team treatment possible — G.P?
>   Specialist? Community clinic?
>   follow up — supportive and educational roles —
>   contact with significant others — evaluation of
>   situation and progress

Fig. 5.2 Example of a 'Problem-centred' lecture plan

C. Sequential

(very common)

   * steps in a process or series of ordered statements, presented, usually in a time sequence, with a built up progressive summary.

   * suits historical accounts, mathematical, scientific or medical procedures, answers 'when' or 'how' questions.

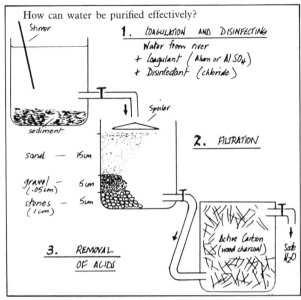

Fig. 5.3 Example of a 'Sequential' lecture plan

D. Comparative

(less common)

   * similarities and/or differences between concepts or procedures are systematically dealt with, usually with a progressive summary.

   * suits evaluative topics, answers mainly 'what' or 'how' questions.

| How can disabled persons cope with their sexuality? | | | | |
Condition	Etiology	Sexuality	Coitus	Orgasm
Cerebrovascular accident	acquired disruption of blood supply to the brain	period of lack of interest	may be difficult, due to spasms or internal rotation	possible, takes time
Cerebral palsy	damage to the brain before or after or during birth	unaffected	may be difficult, due to spasms or contractures	possible
Multiple sclerosis (progressive)	acquired viral or immunological	drive may decrease due to fatigue	may be difficult, due to spasms	difficult due to impaired sensation
Spinal cord injury	acquired damage, disease or trauma	no sensation in genital area or below lesion	may be difficult, due to spasms	not possible other parts of body — erogenous
Poliomyelitis	acquired viral infection	unaffected, complete genital sensation	deformities may interfere	possible
Muscular dystrophy (progressive)	congenital, appears later, cause unknown	unaffected, no lack of sensation	deformities may interfere	possible

Fig. 5.4 Example of a 'Comparative' lecture plan

E. Thesis

(uncommon)

    * a question is posed, then hypothesis provided with evidence or proofs to support the conclusion drawn

    * suits research and theoretical topics, clearly answers 'why' questions.

Why should dietary fibre intake be increased?
Postulate: The average Western diet is deficient in dietary fibre.
This deficiency is causally linked to several illness problems.
e.g. — appendicitis — rural Africans with high fibre diets rarely develop appendicitis.
    — large bowel cancer — studies in Finland show that the incidence of bowel cancer in rural areas is one quarter of that in Copenhagen where meat consumption is greater.
    — breast cancer — evidence links breast cancer with high fat, low plant food diet.
    — gall stones — usually associated with high calorie, high fat, low fibre diet.

Fig. 5.5 Example of a 'Thesis' type lecture plan

HOW BEST TO PLAN A LECTURE?

There are many ideas about planning and preparation for teaching which may be applied to lectures. Here four of the most tried and practical suggestions are presented as a guide. While all the research indicates that actual teaching never goes exactly as planned, the time and effort spent will ensure that the lecturer is ready, clear about directions, sure of content and aware of the target group of learners.

Define key questions

Ask yourself some or all of the following: 'What am I trying to do in this lecture?' 'What are the students to learn from it?' 'Can I pose clearly the questions which need to be answered to understand this topic?'

    If the content can be broken down into a series of 'What', 'How' and/or 'Why' questions, then the lecturer is well on the way to a good presentation, for he or she will be clear about the main focus or purpose (often termed goals or aims or objectives) for the session (Turney et al, 1983b).

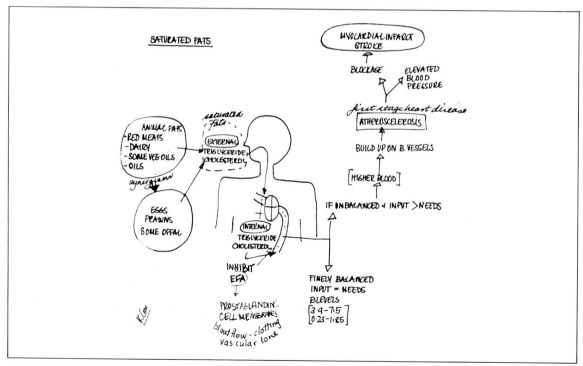

Fig. 5.6 Example of a diagrammatic approach to establishing links between concepts in a lecture

Work out links or connections

With any topic, but especially a new or difficult one, it is helpful to start with a large blank sheet.

Using key questions as a guide, jot down main ideas, generalizations and concepts, together with instances or examples.

Mark the most important ideas (with lines, colour, boxes, arrows. . .).

Delete irrelevant and non-crucial material.

SATURATED FATS

(Lecture 2 in a series on Nutrition for allied health professionals — Final year, 1st Semester, class of 110)

INTRODUCTION
- What links are there between heart disease and diet ?
  - Question without comment to the group.

Group Activities

'Buzz' groups note their answers — keep for later check

DEVELOPMENT
- What are saturated fats ?
  - Outline lecture — quick review including sources — emphasize different types of cholesterol

Students listen — note only new facts

- How do they affect body functions?
  - Build up overhead diagram — current theories — β levels — factors involved, including sex, heredity, body production of cholesterol, exercise and stress

Students add labels, notes to blank diagram handout (given out with basic reading list)

- Why do imbalances contribute to heart disease ?
  - Underline key issues — fine balances — studies on levels — possible sequence of effects

Request careful attention — time to be left for copying down chain of effects

CONCLUSION
- Raise opening question again.
  - Check gaps in understanding — invite questions / alternative — individual consults if no time

Students review initial answers — frame questions about uncertainties

---

Fig. 5.7 Example of a completed lecture plan

Work out where the gaps are, then read to fill them in yourself. Such a diagrammatic approach gets to the essentials. These two points are demonstrated in Figure 5.6 (Brown, 1978).

If it helps, decide what type of lecture best suits the topic.

Lay out the lecture in note form, highlighting key questions, and paying careful attention to the introduction, development and conclusion.

Select sufficient examples to illustrate adequately any laws, concepts, rules, processes or principles.

Especially clarify links or connections between generalizations and relevant examples. This should guide your choice of audiovisual materials, and help decide whether a handout is appropriate (Brown & Tomlinson 1980).

Consider also if the plan will include any opportunities for systematic feedback, student interaction, or immediate evaluation.

Adapt to Target Group.

Check over the plan in the light of your knowledge of the student group whom you will lecture. Some useful questions are as follows: 'Is the conceptual level appropriate?' 'Is the content manageable and adequate?' 'Will certain points require special emphasis?' 'Are the examples within students' experience and capabilities?' (Turney et al, 1983b). These last two points are illustrated in the final plan for the lecture on saturated fats, shown in Figure 5.7.

REFERENCES

Bligh D 1972 What's the Use of Lectures? Penguin Harmondsworth. An older but still useful and sympathetic consideration of the process of lecturing effectively.

Brown B 1978 Lecturing and Explaining. Methuen, London. This text, based on a workshop approach, is full of practical suggestions about how lecturing may be improved.

Brown G, Tomlinson D 1979 How to improve lecturing. Medical Teacher 1: 3: 128–135. An article outlining the five types of lectures considered in this chapter, together with ideas for their improvement.

Brown G, Tomlinson D 1980 How to improve handouts. Medical Teacher 2: 5:215–220 A useful examination of the ways in which handouts may be used according to the purposes the lecturer has in mind.

Brown G 1983 Studies of student learning: implications for medical teaching. Medical Teacher 5: 2 53–56. A look from the receiving end, with particular reference to the work of Marton, Pask, Entwistle and Biggs.

Cox K R, Ewan C E (eds) 1982 The Medical Teacher Churchill Livingstone Edinburgh. A broad view of teaching, with numerous chapters relevant to aspects of lecturing and planning.

Ewan C E 1984 Teaching skills development manual. School of Medical Education, University of NSW. Many aspects of creating conditions for learning are examined in a concise and straightforward manner.

Turney C et al 1983a Sydney Micro Skills Redeveloped Series 1 Sydney University Press. A research based approach to basic teaching skills, the chapter on Variability being specially relevant to lecturing.

Turney C et al 1983b Sydney Micro Skills Redeveloped Series 2 Sydney University Press. The chapter on Explaining considers in some detail both planning and presentation skills, while Introductory Procedures and Closure contains many ideas useful to beginning and ending lectures.

How to help students to learn in small groups*

Preview

Successful small group teaching can, and should be planned. Small group teaching should be selected when it is the most appropriate method for the given situation. Small groups can be effective in helping students gain skills in problem solving, thinking and interaction; and can influence students' attitudes.

WHY USE SMALL GROUP TEACHING?

The goals of small group teaching
Skills in small group teaching

FORMATS IN SMALL GROUP TEACHING

Problem solving
The student presentation
Free or associative group discussion
Role play
Case study
Use of evidence
Games

ENCOURAGING DISCUSSION IN GROUPS

Structured learning programs
Sub-grouping
Use of newsprint

The critical incident
The use of healthy competition
The controversial statement
Brainstorming
Other ideas

THE ROLE OF THE TEACHER

THE ROLE OF THE LEARNER

Perhaps one of the nicest things about group work is that . . . students and teachers have to learn together, because the best way to learn about group work is to get on and do it' (Abercrombie 1974).

This chapter looks at ways in which tutorials can be made more effective. Successful small-group teaching does not simply happen; it can be planned and needs to be. Teachers will spend long hours writing out practical programs and preparing lectures, but often plan tutorials simply by deciding on the topic to be discussed and including it in the timetable. This frequently wastes valuable teaching time. Topics should be selected for tutorials because they are most appropriately taught by small-group discussion. Thus a lecture may be successful in teaching the etiology of urinary tract infection or a printed handout might be as useful. However, small-group discussion would be particularly suitable for teaching students how to interpret laboratory reports on urine specimens, with the reports presented as problems be solved.

* In this chapter, small group teaching sessions are considered to be classes of 60 minutes to 90 minutes duration with 6 to 12 students. The term tutorial is used synonymously with small group teaching.

THE GOALS OF SMALL GROUP TEACHING

The recognized goals and benefits of small group teaching closely parallel some of the principal goals of medical education.

The goals ascribed to small group learning in the literature (Sharan & Sharan, 1976, Rotem & Manzie, 1980, Brown, 1982) include the development of:

* thinking skills
* problem solving skills
* communication skills
* attitudes
* interpersonal skills
* team work skills
* team leadership skills.

These skills are among the key abilities needed by health personnel in today's changing world.

The success of small groups in solving problems is an extension of the principle 'two heads are better than one'; much evidence supports this view (Carpenter, 1956, Evans, 1966, Neufeld & Barrows, 1974).

The solving of a problem can itself be a vehicle for the learning of facts. Each student brings to the tutorial his or her background knowledge based on previous experience which differs from the other students. The combined experience of members of the group will usually provide the necessary information for the solution. As teachers, we tend to forget how much students can work out for themselves.

Small group teaching also facilitates the formation of attitudes. The freedom of group discussion allows individuals to explore their relationships with others, and to understand reasons for their own behaviour which result in problems of communication. Many medical schools now use group work to explore and develop student attitudes to the patient–doctor relationship, and to facilitate teamwork with paramedical and nursing staff members (MacNamara, 1974, Werner & Schneider, 1974, Pigache, 1975).

Finally, medical teachers often include tutorials in their programs as a means of obtaining feedback for themselves and the students. How much students understand about certain topics is often revealed only during discussion. Students do not always appreciate what they do or do not understand — this fact is often overlooked, and is the reason why asking students if they have any questions is so often unrewarding. The 'associative discussion method', described in a later section, is intended to help students discover whether any unconscious assumptions are affecting their ability to learn or understand.

FORMATS FOR SMALL GROUP TEACHING

In small group teaching a variety of formats is essential. A number of useful examples are presented below.

1. Problem solving

Presenting students with problems to solve is a useful approach (Lee, 1976). All too often, however, these problems are presented as a series of questions which form part of the formal assessment in the subject being taught. This is inhibitory to active discussion as the major topic of student interest is what answer would score the most marks, and only the tutor knows that. Problems that could not fairly be used in an assessment in which marks are awarded may be invaluable in providing students with opportunity to assess their understanding and knowledge of a subject. The problem shown in Figure 6.11 illustrates this point; it has been so successful in teaching microbiology to medical students that it may be useful to other teachers.

The probable reasons for the success of this problem are:

1. the answer is not immediately obvious to any students;

2. the answer is found after a process of revision and elimination, which allows students to discover their own weaknesses in this area and learn from other students;

3. the correct answer is not essential, as the session can achieve its purpose even if the answer is not found.

Creation of problems for small-group dscussion is not easy. Another example that stimulates active participation and encourages useful learning is the

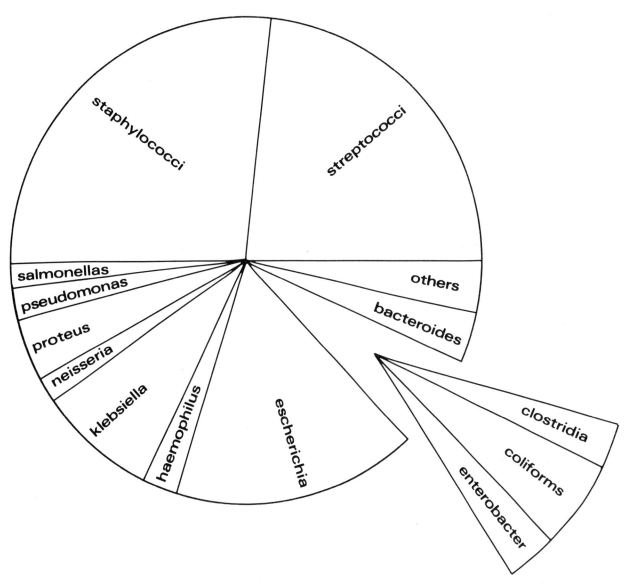

Fig. 6.1 The chart illustrates the relative proportion of bacteria isolated from a certain type of specimen commonly taken from patients — for example, staphylococci are isolated from 25 per cent of these specimens. Examine the figure closely and name the specimen. Give reasons for your answer. (Taken from the Communicable Disease Report of February 14, 1975, published by the Public Health Laboratory Service of England and Wales, and reproduced with the permission of Dr. N D Noah, of the Epidemiological Research Laboratory, who prepared the original diagram.)

following tutorial on influenza: The students are requested to:

Draw a diagram that illustrates the history of influenza in England just before the Asian flu pandemic of 1957 until the Hong Kong pandemic of 1968. There were four epidemics of influenza in Britain during this time. Your diagram should show: (1) the likely severity of each outbreak; (2) the relative concentrations of antibody in the community; (3) incidence of antigenicdrift; (4) a postulated origin of the virus responsible for the 1968 pandemic.

Problem based learning is a very popular focus for current research and educational innovation.

2. The student presentation

Asking a student to make a prepared presentation to the rest of the group can inhibit group discussion. The others in the class know little about the topic, and tend not to consider it their problem. Often the session becomes a mini-lecture presented by someone with limited skills in lecturing. This can be overcome by using techniques to encourage discussion during or after the presentation. For example, the other students could be told that one of them is to be asked to summarize the major points after the presentation; another will be asked to put two questions to the speaker.

The issue of preparation before tutorials is a contentious one. Tutors complain that a major problem with some small-group discussions is that only a few students prepare for the sessions and therefore the discussions fall flat. This is a fact of life; we never will have a tutorial group that is fully prepared (Were we?). There are two ways out of this dilemma. Firstly, students can be allocated slightly different tasks but all related to the central topic. Or secondly, the tutorial can be planned to allow for individual work at the beginning of a session. Students can be asked to work on an individual document for 10–15 minutes before discussion starts. If the major task of the tutorial is related to this individual work, students are more likely to contribute as they have a common experience about which they can comment, question or express opinions.

3. Free or associative group discussion

Abercrombie (1960) pioneered this technique, which incorporates some of the principles of group-analytic psychotherapy. The aim of the original discussions was to help preclinical medical students observe accurately and draw reasonable conclusions from their observations. Students worked on their own for about 20 minutes on a problem that might confront them in their studies, for example, comparison of two X-ray films. This gave the members of the group a common experience to which each of them reacted in different ways. In the discussion that followed, the tutor said little, but encouraged the students to talk freely about their reactions and to elucidate the factors that had influenced them, especially the basic assumptions which they were making, such as the age of the patients.

4. Role Play

The role play technique has been used for many years in management training programs. It is now being increasingly used in the more progressive medical schools (MacNamara, 1974; Pigache, 1975). Students act out short scenes which are relevant to the topic being taught. The teacher first describes the situation and then assigns different roles to the students. For example, the incident might be an interview between a doctor and a mother who is reluctant to have her child immunized. Two students act out the scene; the other students watch. By acting different roles many students gain an appreciation of how people interact. There is a surprising amount of reaction against this technique, probably due to the conservative upbringing of most medical teachers. The method may seem inappropriate to many courses, but is it? Certainly the novelty of the approach would have a positive effect, provided the objectives of the session were clear. One unexpected but interesting paper describes the use of role play in the teaching of chemistry (Trumbore, 1974).

5. Case Study

Medical students are very familiar with dealing with cases in their clinical education. Cases are used as the focus of conferences, presentations, and assignments. An outline of the case study method as it is used at the Harvard Business School follows.

In the Harvard approach the participant/learner is taught primarily by the problem-centered, participant-involved case method.

This method involves several steps:

* students are required to read cases describing a particular problem situation

* the case is analyzed and discussed in the classroom

* students are asked to produce evidence from their reading of the cases to support recommendations and decisions related to solution of the problem.

This process helps to sharpen students' analytical and problem solving skills in dealing with the multiplicity of interacting variables and influences which are part of the 'real world'.

6. Use of evidence

'A useful resource in discussion work is material which can be flexibly used to initiate and feed discussion' (Rudduck 1979). In Britain the Humanities Curriculum Project developed the strategy of using 'evidence' in the teaching of controversial ethical and social issues.

Evidence is any kind of material (eg. photographs, films, printed prose) which has relevance to an issue under discussion. Evidence can be supplied to the discussion group or the group members can seek out this material. The evidence itself does not settle the value issue but is used to delineate the issue. As in life, the evidence is usually ambiguous and this requires interpretation and the use of judgment. In this way students develop their thinking skills and examine their attitudes while at the same time gaining an insight into the situation or issue they are exploring.

There are many interesting aspects to this approach. The teacher has the opportunity of using a method which allows the students to explore issues without the teacher's biases becoming evident. That is, the teacher adopts a position of neutrality during the discussion. There is an absence of behavioural objectives to limit the direction or scope of the discussion. And finally the outcome for each student is his/her own insights into the issues under discussion.

7. Games

How do games fit into the serious business of medical education?

Games, simulation exercises and role plays can provide learning opportunities which other learning activities cannot. They allow learners to become involved, to experience feelings, to examine attitudes, and to experience personal growth. They can also provide a welcome and very stimulating diversion from regular lessons.

Games are potentially very powerful media for facilitating learning. However, they should also be used with care. For instance, problems can arise when participants are not able (or enabled) to de-role after being deeply involved in roles they have played. Indeed the debriefing or discussion of what participants have learned at the end of the game is often more essential to learning than the actual game. Boud and others (1985) explored the

importance of allowing students to stop and reflect on what they have learned from such activities as games, classwork and practical sessions.

Teachers need to consider two other factors when using games:

* Teachers may need to develop new skills to orchestrate the game.
* Games take time to prepare. And new games created by teachers can benefit from a 'dress rehearsal' to iron out the inevitable problems.

For further reading in this area refer to Pfeiffer and Jones (1974) and Scannell & Newstrom (1983).

ENCOURAGING DISCUSSION IN GROUPS

Active participation facilitates learning; and yet tutors often express dissatisfaction with the degree of student involvement in small group sessions.

A frequent question is 'How do you get everybody to take part?' and the unspoken assumption seems to be that something is wrong if any individual remains silent to the end of even one meeting. This seems to be an unnecessary worry, especially when discussions are contrasted with the usual lecture situation where total student silence doesn't seem to bother anybody. Provided there is reasonably good general participation, the tutor can rest content. More will be lost than gained if the silent and shy students are forced into joining in before they feel ready (Cleugh, 1970).

1. Structured learning programs

One of the major messages of this chapter is that small group teaching should be a planned activity. This involves the teacher in planning the design or structure of the learning activity and acting in such a way that an environment is created which encourages learners to participate in the planned activity.

Structure is often condemned by teachers as being synonymous with lack of freedom for students to learn 'what' and 'how' they want to learn. What is needed says Wilson (1980) is an intermediate style between an imposed structure which inhibits participation and 'deprives students of useful opportunities to develop social and analytical skills' and letting students go where they will which 'creates problems of relevance and organization'.

In the small group teaching/learning setting the teacher could, for example, provide an overview of the topic area then ask the students to select a topic within this area for group discussion or investigation. Alternatively, the group could propose both a topic and a mode of study and presentation. The teacher could then review the proposal and endorse it or discuss amendments, endeavouring to ensure relevance and task manageability while at the same time allowing the students to make most of the decisions.

2. Subgrouping

The most powerful way of encouraging active participation is to form subgroups within the small group, and ask pairs, trios, or quartets of students to work on certain problems or perform certain tasks. After a period, the subgroups come together and compare their conclusions. (*See* Lane (1975) for further discussion on subgrouping.)

Students are much more likely to participate when working in threes with the hum of other conversations making their contributions less conspicuous. After this subgroup discussion there is also an increased likelihood of participation in the whole group deliberations. (Refer to Lee, 1976, 1977, 1978a,b).

Tutors should not be afraid to interrupt the discussion to form different groupings two or three times in one tutorial. Learning is improved if a teaching session has a number of breaks in the action (Bligh, 1971).

One difficulty with the use of subgroups is the often boring stage of a session when subgroups are asked to report back their findings to the whole group. A technique that has overcome this problem has been reported previously (Lee, 1977). As soon as each subgroup has agreed on their solution to each of a series of case histories they are asked to record their answers on a central chart drawn up on the blackboard or on a piece of newsprint. The headings on this chart are as follows: Case number; Answer (Diagnosis, etc.); Opinion (agree/disagree) of second subgroup; Opinion of third subgroup (agree/disagree).

The advantages of the use of this table, which has undoubtedly been the major feature in these sessions, are as follows:

1. Each subgroup is forced to commit itself. By having to record a result or an opinion on another subgroup's answer, the students must make a decision. They are unable to hedge or change their minds as often happens if verbal reports are requested.

2. Friendly 'competition' helps the students focus on the task. Members of each subgroup try to get the answer to a problem first so that they on record their conclusions. This friendy competition creates a very good atmosphere in the group.

3. Movement of the subgroups creates a climate of active participation. The fact that students have to go to the front of the room to record their results, and the dialogue between students as they enter their opinions on the table, also contribute to an atmosphere of constructive, active involvement.

4. The completion of the chart indicates that all subgroups have finished the task. By looking at the table the tutor has a clear idea of how the various subgroups are completing the problems, and can go to the aid of any slower group of students.

5. Areas of disagreement are immediately highlighted. This probably is the most useful function of the table. The tutor can clearly see when a problem has been correctly answered and there is no dispute; this problem need not be discussed further. The tutor now has more time to emphasize the disagreements between subgroups and can try to encourage discussion on this difference of opinion and thus resolve the problem.

3. Butcher's paper (newsprint)

By forming subgroups the members of the total group can compare their solutions with problems. It is significant if three groups come up with completely different sets of conclusions; likewise, it is often a powerful experience to find that three small groups of people who are working separately come up with identical opinions. A useful method is to give each of the subgroups a large piece of rough white paper (i.e. butcher's paper/newsprint) with some coloured felt pens and instructions to use very large writing. Students usually produce colourful, easily visible results which can be fixed onto the wall, side by side for rapid comparison.

4. The critical incident

A technique, which uses recall of vivid personal experiences to help the learning of a particular topic, is to ask each student to draw a picture of that experience. They are then asked to explain this incident to fellow students, and, in discussion, the group can make extensive use of paper and coloured pens.

An example would be to ask students to draw a picture of an incident they had seen in the hospital where asepsis had not been properly maintained. After explanation of their pictures in subgroups, a list of principles for correct aseptic technique could be drawn up by the whole group. This may appear to be a childish technique, but it is an excellent way of breaking the ice, and results in very active discussion.

5. 'Us' versus 'them': the use of 'healthy' competition

The introduction of an element of friendly competition into a discussion can result in a fruitful and enjoyable session. The following instruction from a tutorial on chemotherapy is an example of this approach.

Students are given a series of 31 short case histories together with questions on antimicrobial therapy. The following instructions accompany the problems.

Procedure:
1. For half an hour try to answer as many questions as you can.
2. Form a subgroup of three or four students and produce a combined answer sheet. You have thirty minutes to complete as many cases as possible.
3. Exchange your answer sheet with another subgroup and score their answers using the handout provided. Hand in the subgroup score to your tutor.

The handout provided is a detailed analysis of right and wrong answers to the problem.

6. The controversial statement

Even with advanced postgraduate students tutorial sessions need to be planned. Even though there may be active discussion, meetings often fall short of their potential achievements unless they are planned

Nisbet (1966) describes a technique which has been adapted for use in medical microbiology. Students are asked to make a series of controversial statements relating to public health microbiology. Each statement should be 'clear, succinct, important, . . . (and) controversial enough to require careful decision before it is accepted or rejected; . . . (These statements are to) represent the personal belief based on study, experience and reflection of its author.'

In the first session the students present and justify their own statements. At the second session the students have to accept, modify, or reject each statement, and therefore produce a group statement on public health that can be reproduced and distributed to the rest of the class.

As the group is obliged to produce a series of statements which are agreed upon by consensus by the end of the session, lively debate is likely to occur. If readers try to write a few controversial statements in their own disciplines, they will find that they need to use a considerable amount of knowledge and understanding of their own subject.

7. Brainstorming

Brainstorming principally involves the student(s) in writing down as many ideas as they can in quick succession. The idea is to encourage the students to explore a topic by giving free range ø their thoughts. Usually the student is encouraged to think independently at first. This may then be followed by a group brainstorm, i.e. all students are encouraged (spontaneously or in sequence) to contribute their ideas which are recorded on newsprint or on an overhead transparency. During this process all ideas are accepted and no questions or discussion are allowed. These ideas are then used for subsequent discussion. The advantages of this process are:

* all students are encouraged to participate

* the slower-thinking students have time to prepare their ideas before contributing to the group

* students are encouraged to think laterally as well as logically

Brainstorming can be used in a number of ways:

* as a 'warm up' exercise to get discussion started

* as a means of producing a list of ideas which can then be clarified, grouped or prioritized as a lead in to group discussion

* as a 'revitalizer' to get a group 'activated' again

* as a means of producing a wide list of alternatives or problem solutions, rather than simply accepting the 'obvious' or 'most vocal' argument.

8. Other ideas

A number of other ideas for encouraging discussion, especially at the start of group work are given by Frederick (1981). These include:

1. goals and values testing — pairs of students discuss the value of texts and how they fit in with course goals

2. using concrete images — asking students to identify objects or events etc related to the topic for discussion

3. generating questions — students are asked to formulate questions to promote discussion

4. illustrative quotations — students are asked to find and read out quotations (from an allocated text) which illustrate the topic for discussion

5. generating truth statements — students develop 'true' statements about the topic and other students question these

6. forced debate — students are forced to accept one or other side of a debate

7. non-structured scene setting — the teacher sets the scene for discussion (eg. with slides) then the students conduct the discussion

8. asking student how they would like to conduct the discussion.

THE ROLE OF THE TUTOR

To say that the teacher is not the 'dominating member' does not lessen the importance nor lower the status of the teacher. The teacher may be dominant in the student's eyes but refrain from behaving in a dominating manner (Abercrombie, 1974).

Being a good tutor is hard work. Running a successful discussion is more difficult for some people than giving a good lecture. As Bligh (1974) has said, as teachers we are selected for our ability to express ourselves in writing, either in examinations or in publications. Therefore, the teacher is often good at putting thoughts into words, which is helpful for giving lectures. But teaching by discussion requires skills in listening and observing. Usually, the university teacher has no training in these skills and finds listening difficult. It is not easy to keep silent during the long pauses that inevitably develop during a small group session. A tape recording can be very revealing about the amount of discussion time a tutor is using up (Blackie, 1971).

A group does behave in a predictable way. Work in the fascinating field of group dynamics has shown that, whatever the content, all groups develop an operational process, a style of working together that has great impact on the quality of the product. Groups also develop a set of relationships and patterns of interaction among participants that affect the character of the experience. During a session these factors are at work, either facilitating or impeding the achievement of group goals. The usefulness of a knowledge of group dynamics has been shown by Verbrugh et al. (1972) who used small group teaching to teach pathology to medical students. The results were initially disappointing; only 45 per cent of students attended the group discussions. The teaching staff members then attended a course in small group teaching (discussion technique, group dynamics). After this course, attendance at the tutorials increased up to 90 per cent.

We often work, however, in group situations where the basic patterns of group behaviour do not have a chance to operate. Students come together for a one hour period in a timetable that may include 20–30 other teaching sessions during the same week. Trying to achieve group cohesiveness within these constraints is a little naive.

The following extracts from articles on small group teaching describe the major function of the tutor:

> The function of the tutor is to keep the ball rolling (if necessary; it usually is not); to encourage the more silent members of the group

(e.g. if they do say anything, to refer back to it as a useful contribution to the discussion, thus increasing self-confidence); and to intervene with interpretations of students' prejudices when they become evident and no other member does so' (Barnett 1957).

The second extract touches on the difficult issue of how long the tutor allows students to make mistakes:

'. . . where there is an erring majority, it behoves the tutor to keep the discussion open or he may simply give more power to the blind leading the weak. He can usually expect someone in the group to detect unreason and to interpret it. He can step in and do so himself if no one else does' (Allen, 1965).

Note that, in both of these extracts, it is suggested that the tutor enters the discussion only to make a correction after giving other group members a chance to do so.

Perhaps one of the hardest tasks facing the teacher of small groups is knowing when to intervene. How far do you allow the students to lead the discussion where they wish before it becomes 'off the track' and needs to be brought back to the set topic? Should the teacher strictly refrain from giving his/her point of view? When does the teacher's contribution of ideas become 'directing the discussion'?

What teachers need to learn is how to intervene strategically (Richmond, 1984). This depends on such factors as group size, the number of people involved in the incident and the potential impact of the interaction. Richmond presents a model for intervention which readers may wish to explore further.

Richmond (1984) also identifies a number of critical incidents in group work, where teacher input is usually needed:

1. In starting or finishing group discussion
2. To maintain the flow of content
   * when the group is faced with lack of essential information
   * when the group fails to detect erroneous information contributed during discussion
   * when the group gets side-tracked
   * when a task is completed and the leader wishes them to move forward
3. To manage group dynamics
   * to encourage reticent members
   * to manage over-enthusiastic contributors
   * to manage nuisance subgroups
4. To facilitate goal achievement
   * when groups fail to grasp a concept or principle
   * when groups are unable to apply concepts/principles
   * to check group understanding
5. to manage the group environment
   * to help meet time constraints
   * to manage environmental distractions

(For further reading on group dynamics see WHO, 1973; Rotem & Manzie, 1980; Shaw, 1981, Peterson et al, 1984.)

Part of the teacher's preparation for small group work is the preparation of him or herself for the following roles in discussions (Rudduck, 1979):

* the instructor — the teacher contributes some instructional background
* the devil's advocate — the teacher acts as a catalyst, challenging the group
* the neutral chairman — to encourage independent thinking
* the consultant — the teacher withdraws from the group but is available for consultation

THE ROLE OF THE STUDENT

Apathy of the students is often unfairly blamed for an unsatisfactory tutorial. Use of pre-planning and some of the methods described above can overcome this. However, whether learning occurs or not is the responsibility of the students. Students who are reluctant to participate actively in the types of small group discussion which were described here will learn little themselves and will inhibit the learning of others.

Students may find discussion difficult (Brown 1983) because:

* they have not developed skills in communicating their ideas, and the other skills outlined earlier in this paper
* the traditional authority role of the teacher inhibits student input
* teachers tend to become dominant in the classroom.

Research in the area of how students learn

(Ramsden 1985) has emphasized that the quality of the student's learning depends on the student's approach to learning. A 'deep' approach to learning places the emphasis on searching for meaning and exploration of the topic. A 'surface' approach to learning involves such activities as memorizing and learning to reproduce what is learned. The deep approach is generally more effective in most areas of learning. However, the surface approach is very effective for studying certain subjects in which the student is required to absorb and retain a mass of data. The skilled student is one who is capable of adopting whichever approach is required in the given situation.

This emphasizes the importance of the teacher's role in creating and managing the learning context and the student's role in acting as a responsible and critical consumer/participant in the learning experience.

The best way to get students to accept responsibility for their learning in a tutorial program is to talk with them. The reasons for all methods used should be clearly explained; students should be encouraged to speak up if a session is proving to be unsatisfactory. The techniques described here are aimed at promoting active discussion and learning. If this is not happening then the method should be abandoned. Student and tutor should be able to say, 'This isn't a very useful discussion; what can we do to improve it?'. Sitting through a session and then bitterly complaining about a poor tutorial makes the whole exercise a waste of time for staff members and for students. It is essential that students should accept this responsibility. Ideally, if time permits, students should also be given the responsibility of planning some of the discussion themselves.

CONCLUSION

No magic formula exists for small group teaching; however, certain strategies can result in greater satisfaction for both teacher and student. Health personnel educators are encouraged to try out the ideas presented above, to share their experiences and report any particularly successful small group teaching formats.

BIBLIOGRAPHY

For a further exploration in the area of learning to work in groups readers may refer to two useful books by Miles (1981) and Jaques (1984).

A recent publication 'Problem-based learning in education for the professions' (Boud, 1985) will provide readers with a range of ideas and methods to use in their teaching.

REFERENCES

Abercrombie M L J 1974 Aims and techniques of group teaching, 3rd edn. Society for Research into Higher Education, 45

Abercrombie M L J 1960 The anatomy of judgement, Hutchinson, London (paperback edition 1969 Penguin, Harmondsworth)

Allen E A 1965 Group methods of teaching in higher education: the background of some new approaches. Educational Review, 18: 34–44

Barnett S A 1957 An experiment with free discussion groups. Universities Quarterly 12: 170–175

Blackie P 1971 Asking questions. English in Education 5: 77–96

Bligh D A 1971 Techniques in small group discussions. Varieties of group discussion in university teaching. University teaching Methods Unit, University of London Institute of Education, 11

Bligh D A 1974 What's the use of lectures? 3rd edn. Penguin Education, Harmondsworth

Boud et al 1985 Reflection: Turning experience into learning, Kogan Page, London.

Brown G 1982 How to improve small group teaching in medicine, Ch. 12 in Cox K R, Ewan C E (Eds) The Medical Teacher, Churchill Livingstone, Edinburgh

Brown G 1983 Studies of student learning: Implication for medical teaching, Medical Teacher, Vol 5 No 2, p 52–56

Carpenter F 1956 Educational significance of studies on the relation between rigidity and problem solving. Science Education 40: 296–302

Cleugh M F 1970 Educating older people. In: School Sciences, Paperback, Tavistock, London

Evans K M 1956 Group methods. Educational Research 9: 44–50 Harvard Business School — The use of cases in executive programs. Unpublished, undated paper

Frederick P 1981 The dreaded discussion: Ten Ways to Start Improving College and University Teaching 29: 109–114

Jaques D 1984 Learning in groups, Croom Helm, London

Lane M 1975 Clustering. Improving college and university teaching 23: 203–208

Lee A 1976 Problems for small group discussions. Medical Journal of Australia 2: 959–960

Lee A 1977 A single method for encouraging active participation small-group discussion sessions. Journal of Medical Education 52: 432–433

Lee A 1978(a) Small group teaching in microbiology 3. Examples. Medical Journal of Australia 605–607

Lee A 1978(b) Small group teaching in microbiology 4. Comments and revision. Medical Journal of Australia 645–647

MacNamara M 1974 Talking with patients: some problems met by medical students. British Journal of Medical Education 8: 17–23

Neufeld V R Barrows H S 1974 The 'McMaster philosophy', an approach to medical education. Journal of Medical Education 49: 1040–1050

Nisbet S 1966 A method for advanced seminars. Universities Quarterly 20: 349–355

Peterson P L Wilkinson L C Hallinan M (Eds) 1984 The social context of instruction, Academic Press Inc, London

Pfeiffer J W Jones J E 1974 A handbook of structured experiences for human relations training, University associates, California

Pigache P 1975 Training G.P.s on H P World Medicine 10: 67–69

Ramsden P 1985 Student learning research: Retrospect and prospect, Higher Education Research and Development, Vol 4 No 1 p: 51–69

Richmond D E 1984 Improving the effectiveness of small-group learning with strategic intervention, Medical Teacher, Vol 6 No 4, p 138–145

Rotem A Manzie P 1980 How to use small groups in medical education, Medical Teacher, Vol 2 No 2 p 80–87

Rudduck J 1979 Learning to teach through discussion, Centre for Applied Research in Education. Occasional Publications No 8 U E A Norwich

Scannell E E Newstrom J W 1983 More games trainers play — experiential learning exercises, McGraw-Hill Book Co, New York.

Sharan S Sharan Y 1976 Why use small groups? Chapter 1 in Sharan S Sharan Y Small group teaching, Educ. Technol. Pub.

Shaw M E 1981 Group dynamics — the psychology of small group behaviour, McGraw-Hill Book Co, USA

Trumbore C N 1974 A role-playing exercise in general chemistry. Journal of Chemical Education 51: 117–118

Verbrugh H S Vries M J Eastman W N 1972 Group dynamics and audiovisual media in basic pathology course for medical students. Paedagogica Europa 7: 120–126

Werner A Schneider J M 1974 Teaching medical students interactional skills. New England Journal of Medicine 290: 1232–1235.

Wilson A 1980 Structuring seminars: a technique to allow students to participate in the structuring of small group discussions. Studies in Higher Education 5: 81–84

WHO 1973 Introduction to Group Dynamics. WHO Educational Bulletin

Problem-based learning

SUMMARY

WHAT IS PROBLEM-BASED LEARNING?

Problem-based learning in medicine is learning undertaken by a student in response to being confronted by a clinical or bio-medical problem. Its unique features are:

1. A complete reversal of the traditional order of learning: 'Here's a problem; learn from it', supersedes the traditional: 'Learn this, and then you'll be able to solve clinical problems'.

2. A deliberate focus on the process of clinical reasoning.

3. A deliberate focus on the process and effectiveness of student learning.

The sequence of events in problem-based learning runs as follows. Students are presented with a problem (e.g. a middle-aged woman with epigastric pain); they analyse the problem, develop some hypotheses about the cause of the pain, identify what further information they need, and identify the questions that they would like to ask the patient. These questions are put and answered, and the students then refine their hypotheses and reformulate the problem. They may move through further cycles of data identification, information gathering and problem reformulation, gaining information from physical examination, laboratory and radiological investigations.

As they do this, they become aware of areas where their knowledge, understanding and skills are inadequate, and they then formulate their own questions, the answers to which will help to fill their self-identified areas of uncertainty (e.g. what happens in the stomach when a meal arrives? What can you see down a gastroscope? How do you feel a liver?). They then undertake individual study in order to find answers to these questions, and apply their newly-acquired knowledge and understanding to the original problem and to other, related, problems. This activity may reveal new areas of uncertainty, which can in turn be filled by formulating more questions, seeking more information, and subsequently applying it.

Thus, the problem precedes the learning, and the processes of clinical reasoning and self-directed learning are exposed and made available for inspection and reflection. Note the similarity between the cycles of clinical reasoning and self-directed learning: problem analysis, data identification, information seeking, application to the problem, problem reformulation (Barrows & Tamblyn 1980).

WHY USE PROBLEM-BASED LEARNING?

Problem-based learning offers a number of advantages in achieving the aims espoused by most medical schools, and in circumventing some of the problems currently experienced by many of them.

First, the selection of appropriate problems will ensure the acquisition of a core of relevant knowledge and understanding by the students. Second, because students can see the relevance of what they learn, they are well motivated to learn. Third, in addressing the problem, students are obliged to identify what they already know, and how well they know it; their current knowledge thus becomes the point of departure for learning what they do not know (a basic educational premise that is too often ignored!).

Most important, students lay down new knowledge in memory in a format which is accessible for clinical problem-solving, rather than in a format dictated by the intellectual structure of an academic discipline (Bordage & Zacks, 1984), e.g. developmental anatomy. In addition, the learning that they undertake is reinforced by its application both to the initial problem and to similar problems.

Thus, the responsibility for learning is placed on the student, where it should be; in taking on this responsibility, students themselves learn how to learn — an indispensable skill if they are to become competent at managing their own independent learning for the rest of their professional lives.

In addition, they learn about clinical reasoning, not as a theoretical subject, but powerfully tinged with their own emotional experiences as they discover which strategies work and which do not, and as they reflect on the different ways of tackling clinical problems.

Finally, this has implications for the role of the teacher, who becomes an educational consultant rather than a purveyor of information.

HOW CAN PROBLEM-BASED LEARNING BE UNDERTAKEN?

Three issues should be addressed: the stage of medical education in which problem-based learning is initiated, the size of groups of students, and the format of the problems employed.

Stage

Problem-based learning in medicine was pioneered in undergraduate medical schools which also adopted a curriculum featuring vertical integration of basic and clinical sciences, e.g. Newcastle (Australia), McMaster (Canada), Southern Illinois University (USA). However, there is no educational reason why problem-based learning should not be undertaken in a pre-clinical curriculum; a recent book by Howard Barrows addresses this issue (Barrows, 1985), although no persistently successful applications have yet been reported. It is obvious that the horizontal integration of a number of the basic sciences could generate a much more powerful and realistic set of problems and strategies for their exploration, as well as encouraging students to integrate their own knowledge and understanding. Thus an integrated course, for example in neurobiology, is more likely to provide a successful setting for problem-based learning than one which relies exclusively on neuroanatomy. Much current clinical teaching could also be conducted in a problem-based way, if teachers were to place greater emphasis on the processes of clinical reasoning and learning, rather than on the recall of detail.

Problem-based learning is admirably suited to the requirements of postgraduate and vocational education. Much of this stage of education already occurs in a problem-based mode, although few current postgraduate examinations (with the notable exception of the FRACGP (Fabb, 1983)) encourage problem-based learning. Another excellent example is the McMaster experience in helping postgraduates to acquire the skills of critical appraisal of the published literature (Sackett, 1982).

Size of group

Problem-based learning originated in medical schools which also adopted small group learning as an educational strategy. This is not a prerequisite for problem-based learning, but it should be pointed out that the combined experiences of a group of students, even direct from high school, constitute a knowledge-base powerful enough to tackle even clinical problems, let alone pre-clinical ones. Small groups of students, in a clinical undergraduate or postgraduate setting, constitute an ideal vehicle for problem-based learning.

Large groups can also be used for problem-based learning (Joorabchi, 1982), if logistic reasons prohibit the use of smaller groups. As the problem is unfolded by the teacher, students confer with their neighbours to identify the information required and to appraise its interpretation, before identifying their own learning needs, which they satisfy by subsequent private study. The teacher must, of course, be prepared to relinquish some of the sense of control that is a characteristic of the lecture theatre environment. This is just one of the barriers to the introduction of problem-based learning in existing medical schools (Thompson & Williams, 1985).

Format

The range of possible formats for problems is diverse: they may be written, videotaped or audiotaped, on computer, or real or simulated patients. These formats all share the requirement of presenting information in a realistic way, so that they carry conviction with both teachers and students.

Problems presented in writing are inexpensive to produce, but suffer from the disadvantage that much of the information has already been interpreted and encoded for the student. Videotaped or audiotaped materials make excellent triggers for the initial presentation of the problem, but they are less satisfactory for the subsequent unfolding of the problem, because the information presented cannot be accurately geared to the students' questions. This difficulty can be overcome by giving the teacher the responsibility for making appropriate information available on request, e.g. by giving the results of investigations, or by playing the role of the patient.

More sophisticated solutions of this difficulty include Patient Management Problems (for example, those featured in the Check program of the RACGP), computerized Patient Management Problems (still painfully few in number), and the Problem-Based Learning Modules developed by Howard Barrows and his colleagues. These modules comprise a patient simulation in a book format, designed specifically for problem-based learning (Barrows, 1985). Barrows has also pioneered the use of simulated (or programmed) patients, who are people or patients who are trained to present a patient's problem in a convincing and reproducible way (Barrows & Tamblyn, 1980, Barrows, 1985).

HOW DOES ONE CONSTRUCT PROBLEM-BASED LEARNING MATERIALS?

Before actually preparing the materials, it is necessary to make some decisions about what students are expected to be able to do at graduation, and then to decide what constitutes a reasonable level of competence for the stage that the students are at when they undertake the course segment in question. These decisions should naturally include statements about competence in clinical reasoning and self-directed learning, as well as content knowledge and understanding.

Clinical problems should be selected using such criteria as commonness, preventability, the importance of appropriate diagnosis and management to the clinical outcome, and the illustration of crucial concepts. Crucial concepts should also constitute the chief criterion for selection of problems in a non-clinical setting.

The structure of the problem is derived from the natural sequence of problem-solving clinical reasoning. This is illustrated by one of the problems currently in use in the first year of the undergraduate medical program at the University of Newcastle, New South Wales. Figure 1 shows the tutor guide for the first session on the problem. The guide identifies (from left to right): the resources available to the teacher, the clinical reasoning processes that should flow from the clinical information acquired by the students, the questions that should arise, and the learning goals that the students might identify. The last are by no means the only learning goals that the students may identify; they are, however, the ones which

University of Newcastle
N.S.W.
Faculty of Medicine

WORKING PROBLEM 3

BLOCK 1, 1985   TUTOR GUIDE

SESSION 1   FRIDAY 29/3/85 (1½ - 2 HOURS)

TUTOR	CLINICAL REASONING	DISCUSSION	LEARNING GOALS AND RESOURCES
VIDEO 1. Ken Middleton and his mother. Ken is 15 years of age.	CUE RECOGNITION INITIAL PROBLEM FORMULATION	Is there a problem? Who has the problem? Is Ken's behaviour abnormal? What type of behaviour is Ken exhibiting?	1. How can we evaluate behaviour? 2. What common forms of abnormal behaviour are there?

	HYPOTHESIS GENERATION
	
	No problem: normal adolescent behaviour
	
	Physical: inherited
	drugs/chemicals
	disease
	
	Behavioural:
	1. Situational.(Stress)
	   - mother
	   - school
	   - family problems etc.
	
	2. Psychological
	   - interpersonal prob-
	     lems
	   - out of touch with
	     reality (psychosis)
	   - personal distress
	     (neurosis)
	
	PROBLEM REFORMULATION
	
	Discuss ENQUIRY STRATEGY
		What might be the cause of Ken's (perceived) abnormal behaviour?
		
		(i) How to obtain further information (how to deal with Ken's mother)
			3. What factors or experiences may result in abnormal behaviour?

VIDEO 2. Ken Middleton		(ii) Information required - aspects of behaviour which can be assessed and defined - stresses being faced by Ken	4. What is being experienced? (includes 'Mental State Examination') - Appearance - Behaviour - Speech - Feelings - Awareness - Attention - Orientation - Memory - Counter transference - Insight

TUTOR: Ensure hypotheses, essential clinical data, group learning goals are recorded. Distribute prepared Learning Goals; discuss in relation to group goals and ensure allocation of latter.

Group Secretary to meet with Professor Tony Smith, at 5.00 p.m. in the Staff Common Room (613), Medical Sciences Building.

PLEASE NOTE: THERE ARE THREE SESSIONS ONLY FOR THIS WORKING PROBLEM

Fig. 7.1 Example of a tutor guide for a working problem

the problem planners have identified, and for which the planners have provided a starting point for learning in the form of a page or two of overview, and references for further study. The tutor is not obliged to stick rigidly to the guide if the students elect to tackle the problem another way, nor are the students restricted to the learning goals identified by the Faculty.

Students can be helped to reassure themselves that they have indeed reached the expected level of mastery by the provision of materials (e.g. another, similar, problem) with answers, on which they can test their newly acquired knowledge and understanding.

HOW CAN ONE ASSESS PROBLEM-BASED LEARNING?

Unless it is clear to students that the processes of clinical reasoning and self-directed learning and application of knowledge are assessed as well as the outcomes of correct diagnosis and recall of information, the full benefits of problem-based learning will never be realized.

It is therefore necessary to select examination instruments that can and do test the processes of clinical reasoning and student learning. Clinical reasoning may be tested by the use of Modified Essay Questions and short answer questions (see Chapter 21), Patient Management Problems (see Chapter 23) and clinical assessments (see Chapter 24). The Objective Structured Clinical Examination can be used to test clinical reasoning skills, and can be used to tap a wide range of content areas. Simulated patients or programmed patients can also be used. A structured oral examination, based on the sequential supply of information by the examiner, is a powerful tool which has been piloted in Newcastle, New South Wales, but needs further development.

The process of student learning can be examined by using methods such as the Medical Independent Learning Exercise, (Feletti et al, 1984). In this exercise, students identify individual learning needs that arise from a clinical problem that has just been confronted. Having done so, they formulate a series of questions to which answers should be found, and then have a period of time (hours or a few days) to undertake the necessary learning to answer those questions, using whatever resources are normally available. The subsequent oral examination focuses not only upon how the questions were formulated and upon what has been learned, but also on how the learning was undertaken, and how it was applied to the original problem.

HOW SUCCESSFUL IS PROBLEM-BASED LEARNING?

An educational strategy can be evaluated by considering its acceptability, effectiveness and efficiency.

The acceptability of problem-based learning is generally high, both among staff and students. A minority of each find themselves to be incompatible with it, but for most people the excitement, the intellectual challenges, and the freedom to learn, heavily outweigh the stress and anxiety generated by the ambiguity of defining one's own educational goals. The existence of the minority emphasizes the need for pre-admission familiarization and counselling, for both students and staff.

The effectiveness of problem-based learning is reflected in the clinical performance of Newcastle and McMaster graduates, who perform at least as well as their peers on both subjective and objective measures (Woodward & Ferrier, 1982). When considering the quality of intellectual processing, it is becoming clear that students in problem-based medical schools see themselves as adopting approaches to studying which more accurately reflect the intellectual aspirations of universities than do students in conventional schools (Clarke & Newble, 1985). The long-term effectiveness of problem-based learning as a preparation for a lifetime of self-directed learning will, of course, require long-term evaluation.

The efficiency of problem-based learning is harder to document. Any form of teaching that centres on individual students requires more effort, but many faculty members regard the warmth of the human contact with students, and the privilege of watching their intellectual development at close quarters, to be more than adequate reward for the effort invested. In cold financial terms, problem-based schools receive the same level of state funding per student as other schools, and, being newer, are usually less well-endowed with other resources; they are therefore at least as educationally efficient. The student-staff ratio necessary to maintain more contact between students and staff is achieved by going beyond full-time staff faculty members as a source of group mentors or tutors. These part-time staff are valuable role models, who, once freed from the traditionally imposed limitations of the teacher as an information source, are able to stimulate and maintain their own professional effectiveness by the two-way exchange with students. Careful education of this cadre of teachers is, however, necessary.

WHAT ARE THE PROBLEMS WITH PROBLEM-BASED LEARNING?

Some of these have already surfaced, either implicltly or explicitly.

First, problem-based learning requires a high degree of faculty commitment and collaboration, not only because of the need for integration across academic disciplines, but also because of the deliberate emphasis on process as well as on content, both in examination and teaching. Mixed messages arising from the efforts of even a few 'content-pushers' will put the devoted efforts of the majority at risk. Faculty members have to be prepared to relinquish some control of the educational process, and to accept that not all content areas can be covered by the problems. These are potent causes of insecurity for teachers, and the temptation to go back to familiar ways can be very strong, particularly with accrediting bodies and peers looking censoriously over one's shoulder. However, if the problems have been well-chosen, not much important content will have been missed, and students should be well-prepared to deal with such areas when they arise.

Second, the development of the problems and supporting materials is expensive of time, not least on account of the consultation that is necessary to secure a coherent approach, both educationally and clinically. But, once completed, only minor updating will be required for several years.

Third, student anxiety is heightened by the potential vastness of the universe of learning, by the apparently haphazard way in which they explore that universe, and by the lack of self-esteem they feel at the bottom of the professional ladder. One might expect that this anxiety would dimiish as students progress to the senior years and begin to feel confident in their skills and knowledge; but only during the intern year do many graduates begin to realize that problem-based learning has indeed equipped them well for their professional tasks.

SUMMARY

Problem-based learning places the responsibility for learning in the hands of the student, and encourages examination of the processes of clinical reasoning and of self-directed study. The teacher's role changes from that of a supplier of information to being a consultant.

This way of learning seems to offer some advantages at both undergraduate and postgraduate levels. The opportunities for intellectual growth that it offers staff and students can outweigh the admitted difficulties of planning and implementation.

BIBLIOGRAPHY

Barrows HS 1985 How to design a problem-based curriculum for the preclinical years. (Springer Series on Medical Education, No.8). Springer, New York
   Excellent introduction and first two chapters; a good subsequent framework on 'how to', but a little light on detail. Some of these lacunae are filled by Barrows HS, Feltovich PJ The structure of problem-based learning. (Submitted for publication).
Barrows HS, Tamblyn RM 1980 Problem-based learning: an approach to medical education. (Springer series on Medical Education, No 1). Springer, New York
Bordage C, Zacks R 1984 The structure of medical knowledge in the memories of medical students and general practitioners: categories and prototypes. Medical Education 18: 406–416
Clarke RM, Newble DI 1986 The approaches to learning of students in a traditional and in an innovative problem-based medical school. Medical Education 20: 267–273

See also Coles CR 1985 undergraduate medical curricula and the learning they generate. Paper presented to the Association for the Study of Medical Education, Southampton. Medical Education 19: 85

Fabb WE 1983 A review of the Royal Australian College of General Practitioners' Examination for Fellowship 1979–1983. Melbourne, Royal Australian College of General Practitioners

Feletti GI, Saunders NA, Smith AJ, Engel CE 1984 Assessment of independent learning. Medical Teacher 6: 70–73

Joorabchi B 1982 How to construct and use a problem-based programmed lecture. Medical Teacher 4: 6–11

Perhaps too flamboyant a presentation for the British tradition, with no data on effectiveness

Sackett DL 1982 Literature critiques. In teaching clinicians epidemiology: problems and prospects. A Bellagio Conference Report, New York. Rockefeller Foundation. p 93

Thompson DG, Williams RG 1985. Barriers to the acceptance of problem-based learning in medical schools. Studies in Higher Education 10: 199–203

A brief appraisal of the barriers, with some possible solutions

Woodward CA, Ferrier BM 1982 Perspectives of graduates two or five years after graduation from a three-year medical school. Journal of Medical Education 57: 294–302.

Prior learning, challenges and critical thinking in the medical student laboratory

Preview

INTRODUCTION

It would be rare to find a medical school or indeed a university which does not pay its dues to critical thinking (or one of its synonyms) as an educational goal of the highest importance. What is meant by this laudable goal may often be vague but includes a healthy scepticism, the production of new insights, an inclination to develop testable new ideas, and the production of more satisfactory solutions to problems in hand (McPeck, 1981; Arons, 1985).

Critical thinking cannot be done or taught in the abstract, but only through the difficulties of specific subject matter. An isolated course in critical thinking is unlikely to help much. It would be best if critical thinking skills were acquired gradually, in many subjects over several years, with students given sufficient time for the reflection needed.

This chapter describes a way of encouraging critical thinking in the student laboratory — a resource which is frequently misused for the most mundane purposes in medical schools. The value of the laboratory setting lies in its provision of the concrete materials of a discipline and the opportunity for critical thinking in interrelating the theory and methodology of the discipline. Perhaps even more important can be the provision of time for reflection and for discussion with peers and teachers.

The way of encouraging critical thinking advocated here is to provide suitable *sequences* of laboratory exercises. This idea is very well supported in the literature on critical thinking and the related literature on problem solving and scientific enquiry (Karplus et al, 1977, Carmichael et al, 1980, Berner, 1984, Glaser, 1984); it specifically takes into account research which demonstrates the importance of prior learning (Novak, 1980).

In a laboratory setting this means *not* launching students into exercises supposedly encouraging critical thinking before students have the technical and intellectual skills to cope. At the same time it does *not* mean packing early years of a course with facts and recipes, saving the critical thinking for final year. Suitably designed sequences could be used in the laboratories of all science laboratory based subjects from first year on. In keeping with the argument above, it would be best if such sequences and other ways of encouraging critical thinking were to appear in numerous subjects and in non-laboratory settings as well.

The sequence is:

1. Exercises teaching technical skills and knowledge used in practical medical settings.

2. Challenge exercises requiring appreciation of technical skills and knowledge in hypothesis generation and testing, and in interpretation of laboratory results.

3. Critical thinking exercises requiring search for new insights and problem solution, and forms of conscious reflection on thinking and reasoning processes.

Throughout this paper one complete sequence will be illustrated from microbiology (urinary tract infections) (see Figs 8.1–8.6. Additional illustrations will be drawn from other areas of microbiology and from several other laboratory based medical disciplines.

1. PRIOR LEARNING: TECHNICAL SKILLS AND KNOWLEDGE IN PRACTICAL MEDICAL SETTINGS

What is needed in each discipline or problem area is to teach a small number of relevant technical skills, and to teach them well in an interesting manner effectively co-ordinated with related knowledge. Identification of the skills to be taught is an important task for a course designer, and selection should be based on criteria such as likely direct use with future patients and role as prior learning.

When selection is based on more expedient criteria, such as availability of equipment or research interests of the department, then the situation often arises in which students encounter many techniques and operate many pieces of equipment each only once during an entire course of study. Students do not become competent at any of the many techniques and do not find a satisfactory relationship with other parts of their learning. Feelings of incompetence, frustration and generally negative attitudes to medical science are engendered. Such problems were one of the reasons laboratory classes were entirely abandoned in so many U.S. medical schools.

'Although . . . (typical) exercises were often tedious and results dubious, they probably also played a significant role in orientating students towards an understanding of laboratory test characteristics that they no longer possess'. (Benson, 1980).

Obviously a case of throwing baby out with bathwater; and in some of the same U.S. medical school students are now requesting access to laboratories! What is required is to use laboratory resources thoughtfully in ways which are systematic, practical, educationally rewarding and thoroughly cost- and outcome-oriented.

It is a commonplace idea that laboratory technical skills, like other psychomotor skills, involve the senses and the brain as well as the muscles. Good performance requires co-ordination and smooth execution. Accuracy is the most common standard of performance but speed may also be important.

Research on learning (Fitts & Posner, 1967; Gagné, 1970; Gagné & Briggs, 1974; White, 1979) permits some generalizations for course designers and teachers. They should:

1. provide students with a satisfying rationale for learning the techniques (e.g. use with patients or important prerequisite).

2. help students understand the logic or overview of the skills routine and to understand links with related perceptual skills and knowledge.

3. provide opportunities for practice and feedback to improve the accuracy, speed and quality of the comnponent-part skills.

4. take account of the fact that, once mastered, technical skills are well remembered and retained and they continue to improve with practice.

Figures 8.1 & 8.2 show simple exercises taken from a laboratory class in the early stages of the microbiology course at the University of New South Wales. Their purpose is to teach students the skills of collecting suitable mid-stream urine specimens as well as standard techniques for microbiology screening of urine (tests for pH, protein and other biochemical measures of normality, microscopic appearance, culture techniques to determine numbers and types of organisms).

The four criteria above are taken into account:

(a). *Rationale*

Screening of urines is one of the most common clinical procedures and doctors are required to collect and examine mid-stream urines or at least to supervise (depending where in the world they are working). Significant numbers of doctors now in practice are quite inept at this apparently simple collection technique as witness the culture results in microbiology laboratories. These reveal the extent of wastage of time, effort and money on faulty and contaminated specimens. Problems are exacerbated in cases of urines from babies, bedridden and elderly patients. The student exercise allows practice in microscopy and plating tech-

Screening mid-stream urine; laboratory techniques and knowledge
(Adapted from Microbiology Laboratory Manual at the University of New South Wales)

Knowledge
  Lecture and handouts on urinary tract infections
  Text references
  Procedure for collection of mid-stream urine specimens
  Procedure for screening (microscopy, plating and biochemical tests)

Laboratory
1 The 'patient' is you. Signs and symptoms presumably nil. Use this opportunity to learn to collect and screen a mid-stream specimen.

Procedure
  1. Collect the first specimen of your urine passed — together with a mid-stream sample.
  2. Check pH, protein and other biochemical tests using the dip sticks and colour charts provided.
  3. Examine microscopically.
  4. Plate specimen on MacConkey agar using both standardized dip-culture techniques and normal streak plating.
  5. Have your tutor check each of your procedures. Record results. Incubate plates at 37°C for 18–24 hours.

Question
When would screening similar to this be likely to reveal significant numbers of bacteria in mid-stream specimens from apparently healthy adults?

Fig. 8.1 Exercise used to help students differentiate between a specimen well collected and a poor one.

Differentiation of infected and contaminated specimens
(Adapted from Microbiology Laboratory Manual at the University of New South Wales)

Knowledge
  Criteria for recognition of infection on basis of WBC, RBC, epithelial cells, numbers and types of organisms, pH, protein.
  Other materials as for Figure 8.1.

Laboratory
Several specimens are provided from patients with suspected urinary tract infections.

Procedure
  1. Examine microscopically, check biochemical tests, and culture using standard methods (as for Figure 8.1).
  2. Next class examine the incubated plates and confer with your tutor as to likely identity of any bacteria isolated.
  3. Decide whether specimen is normal, contaminated or infected and note further tests required (confirmations, antibiotic sensitivities).
  4. Using the form supplied, complete a laboratory report in a way you consider would be of optimum value to the attending physician.

Question
Suggest reasons for obtaining contaminated specimens. Could these be avoided? How?

Fig. 8.2 Cases for practice in differentiating infected from poorly collected specimens.

niques which are transferable to processing of other specimens. A final rationale is that skill in, and knowledge of, the technique are prerequisites for later exercises involving challenges and critical thinking (see sections 2 and 3 of this paper).

(b). *Overview and links with knowledge*
Students are provided with an overview of the specimen collection technique using both description and a series of diagrams of key steps. Similiar overviews of microscopy and plating techniques have also involved demonstrations of the techniques, movies showing close-ups of key steps, and displays of microscopes and plates competently set up. Links with knowledge are encouraged by time-tabling a lecture on urinary tract infection in the same week as the lab, providing suitable lecture handouts and text references. Laboratory demonstrators specifically draw on this material in discussions with small groups of students at the beginning and end of the lab. Questions in the text of the exercise cue students to important links of theory with method.

(c). *Practice and feedback*
Demonstrators check students' microscopes and watch their plating technique, offering feedback. Later, when incubated plates are returned there is a further opportunity to recognize the effects of poor plating technique. Cases (Figure 8.1) allow students to differentiate between a specimen collected well and a poor one. Other exercises (not shown) permit students to repeat the techniques until a satisfactory standard has been reached and, if required, these can be monitored in the course of practical examination.

(d). (*Cannot be accomplished within single exercises such as shown in Figures 8.1 and 8.2*).
In a somewhat similar manner, MacQueen et al (1976) organized a self-paced student biochemistry

laboratory at the University of Dundee. The early units involved student performance of chromatographic techniques directed towards clinical recognition of abnormal hemoglobins. Demonstrations illustrated both knowledge of hemoglobin structure and knowledge of separation techniques whilst experiments allowed students to practise techniques and to recognize normal and abnormal patterns.

2. CHALLENGE EXERCISES

Berner (1984) described dimensions of medical problem solving which included two common ones which can be well taught in laboratory classes. These arise when (1) both the problem and appropriate solution are known by the problem solver and pattern recognition or use of algorithms is appropriate or (2) the problem remains to be identified but, once clear, the solution is also clear. These two types of problem include those with a diagnostic focus and those in which a hypothesis-testing approach may be appropriate.

Laboratory-based challenges on both types of problem can build on earlier technical exercises and prepare the way for critical thinking in laboratory settings.

Structured case studies (Hegarty & Lee, 1979; Hegarty, 1982) provide one suitable format for challenge exercises. Here students are presented with an overall diagnosis (e.g. urinary tract infection) and a brief case study. A typical example, shown in Figure 8.3, informs students of the types of laboratory investigations performed in microbiological examination of urine and asks for their diagnosis (e.g. whether consistent with a urinary tract infection or not). Appropriately for students at an early stage in the course, they are also asked to compose the section of the laboratory report concerning culture results.

In unstructured case studies (Hegarty & Lee, 1979; Hegarty, 1982), students are *not* presented with an overall diagnosis but are presented with a brief case study and required to evaluate the patient's condition. As Barrows (1983) stressed in his discussion of problem-based learning in practice, patients typically present without their physician's having opportunity for prior specific study

---

Structured Case Study in Microbiology
(Adapted from Laboratory Manual, University of New South Wales)

Case study: urinary tract infection
A woman, aged 26, gave a history of having lower abdominal pain, frequency and burning sensation on micturition. No antibiotic treatment had been given. On examination she had a temperature of 37°C and tenderness over the lower abdomen.
Investigation of the urine revealed:

pH	6	Red Blood cells	$<10 \times 10^6$/litre
Protein	0	White Blood cells	160×10^6/litre
Glucose	0	Epithelial cells	$<10 \times 10^6$/litre
Blood	0	Casts	Present

Material
Gram stain of centrifuged deposit of urine
Standard culture plates

Student tasks
1. Examine the material provided and make a diagnosis in this case.
2. Write out exactly what you consider should be written in the culture section of the laboratory report.
3. Is any more information needed before the laboratory report can be completed?

Fig. 8.3 Example of a structured case study used as a challenge exercise

---

of the case: their conditions have to be evaluated initially on the basis of what the physicians already know (i.e. prior learning of similar cases). Unstructured case studies can provide practice, and a typical example is shown in Figure 8.4, a case of a patient with bacterial endocarditis.

Successful completion of this case involves students in integration and application of a wide range of knowledge and skills in microbiology (as well as clinical studies on physical examinations, differential diagnoses and pathology). Questions 2, 4 and 6 concerning selection and interpretation of laboratory tests are well integrated with questions on treatment, predisposing factors and discussion of the patient's prognosis. In format, the exercise is structured as a simulation of a real life sequence but with a compressed time span. Laboratory materials are provided in concealed kits under the control of a tutor who monitors student requests and gives feedback on relevance.

Clarke (1981) showed how students in the medical school at Newcastle, Australia, are taught to gain experience with laboratory investigations, their interpretation and cost-effective use. These

Unstructured Case Study in Microbiology
(Adapted from Laboratory Manual, University of New
South Wales)

Case study
A 45 year old man was seen by a doctor for a 3-day
history of progressive dyspnea (on exertion especially)
and chest pain. He was previously known to have a
mild diastolic murmur but on auscultation was found
to have also a loud pan-systolic murmur. His legs were
edematous, his temperature 38°C, BP 100/60 and pulse
rate 100.

Material
None supplied initially.
Material available from tutor on submission of
appropriate requests (see below).

Student tasks
Answer the following questions:
  1. What is the differential diagnosis?
  2. What samples would you collect for
microbiological investigations?
  3. When would you commence provisional therapy
and what would you recommend?
  4. Ask your tutor for tests to establish a diagnosis.
  5. Would you modify the treatment in any way? If
so, how?
  6. What additional test is necessary? Ask your tutor
for the results.
  7. What is the source of the infecting organism?
  8. What are the predisposing factors?
  9. What is the prognosis? Give reasons.

Fig. 8.4 Example of an unstructured case study used as a
challenge exercise

challenge exercises build on prior learning of technical skills and knowledge. A flow chart illustrated
steps suitable for use with students in the third
term of the first year in the five year curriculum:

Early steps in the sequence were
  1. Write hypotheses about patient's problem(s)
  2. Inspect list of investigations in Investigation
Resource book
  3. Receive feedback on possible investigations
  4. Rank investigations in order of peformance
  6. Choose first investigation
Final steps in the sequence were
  16. Evaluate usefulness of investigation in
distinguishing between hypotheses in step 1.
  17. Receive feedback on usefulness of investigation
  18. Decide whether to perform any further
investigations
  19. Write brief clinical assessment of patient's
problem(s)
  20. Add up cost of investigations (Extracts from Clarke,
1981)

The Investigation Resource Book available to
these students contained information and questions under headings such as the following:

1. Principle of test
2. Technical factors
  2.1 Availability   2.2 Complexity
  2.3 Reliability   2.4 Patient preparation
  2.5 Notification of result
3. Patient acceptability
  3.1 Risk   3.2 Discomfort
  3.3 Time   3.4 Cost

Other challenge exercises concerning students'
skill in ordering laboratory investigations include
the card game reported by Saunders and Wallis
(1981). Students were required to justify each
investigation ordered and receive scores according
to whether the procedure was unnecessary or even
harmful, competent or (for a bonus) an essential
investigation that is often overlooked.

Ward et al (1976) described the development of
an elective offered at the University of Minnesota
Medical School on Interpretive Aspects of Laboratory Medicine. Teaching methods included
lectures, problem solving sessions, independent
study of case histories and readings i.e. including
study *about* laboratory medicine but no actual
benchwork. Topics covered were interpretive
aspects of single and multiple chemical abnormalities, acid/base balance, fluid and electrolytes,
endocrine function, enzymology and liver function; serology (infectious mononucleosis, rheu-
matoid arthritis, lupus erythematosus and syphilis);
dysproteinemias, body fluids, renal function and
urinary sediment; anemias, leukemias, coagulo-
pathies and platelet function.

Challenge exercises consisted either of giving brief
case histories and asking them to generate clinical
hypotheses and to decide on laboratory tests to
order, or giving them results of laboratory tests
and asking questions ranging widely from recognition of algorithms, through expectations of
results, diagnostic possibilities and additional tests
to advanced decision-making, such as recommendations for surgery.

An evaluation of the effectiveness of this course
at the University of Minnesota was conducted
(Burke and Connelly, 1981). An example of a
typical test was presentation of the clinical
vignette of a patient with hepatitis B surface
antigen (HbsAg) positive chronic active hepatitis,
together with the results of routine blood count
and urinalysis. Students were asked to generate a

series of clinical hypotheses and to engage in cycles of data interpretation, hypothesis evaluation and acquisition of appropriate laboratory data. Students' hypotheses were evaluated according to their specificity, appropriate matching to the vignette, and comparison with experts' correct hypotheses. Students' test selections were evaluated according to appropriateness (range-pathognomonic, helpful, non-contributory, contraindicated) and their interpretations were similarly assessed.

Results of this evaluation suggested that the course of systematic instruction in interpretive aspects of laboratory medicine had helped students to revise their clinical hypotheses toward greater diagnostic accuracy. More experienced students received greater benefit from the course. With some of the vignettes, students failed to recognize the need to revise their hypotheses on the basis of laboratory findings. Both of these outcomes underline again the importance of prior specific knowledge. The problem may be two-fold: lack of knowledge or failure to activate long term memory and to be able to use knowledge in appropriate circumstances (Gonnella, 1970).

3. CRITICAL THINKING EXERCISES

As stated earlier, the term critical thinking can encompass very many intellectual processes (Arons, 1985, specified ten major processes wih many sub-processes). Here the processes will be considered as encompassing two distinct divisions:

(a). Search for new insights and production of more satisfactory solutions to problems in hand (including search for evidence, design of exper-imental investigations, probing for assumptions, drawing inferences, recognizing situations where firm inferences cannot be drawn, hypothetico-deductive reasoning and so on).

(b). Forms of conscious reflection on thinking and reasoning processes.

In their discussions of critical thinking, McPeck (1981) and Arons (1985) cover points (a) in detail and (b) to a much lesser extent. Other writers focusing on knowledge-rich domains such as medicine have stressed the strong interactions between structures of knowledge and thinking

processes. The forms of conscious reflection on thinking and reasoning to which they refer include peer group discussions with reflection on question-answer sessions, or the formulation and criticism of hypotheses (Schmidt, 1983), or students' reflec-tion on their own reasoning followed by exposure to an expert view and reflection on that (Glaser, 1984).

No doubt it is every teacher's hope that the direction of student development would be towards the competent performance displayed by experts (i.e. the organized knowledge structures acquired over-long periods of learning and experi-ence). Research suggests that the knowledge of novices is organized around the facts and objects explicit in a problem presentation, whereas experts use principles and abstractions rather than concrete details (see, for example, the work of Lesgold et al (1981) on the interpretation of X-ray films by novices compared with experts).

Medical teachers can use the laboratory setting for encouraging critical thinking in both dimen-sions (a) and (b). Much of (a) is entirely congruent with the practice of experimental laboratory-based science. Dimension (b) requires time and reflec-tion, peer-group interaction, and stimulus from experts. All are regularly available in laboratory settings, though not unique to them

Conditions for learning have largely been discussed in Sections 1 and 2 above. Teachers should build carefully on prior learning, should attend very carefully to the structure of sessions (e.g. do not allow experts to deliver their views before students have had the opportunity to reflect on their own, ensure students can articulate the difference between an expert's view and their own, provide opportunities for students to criti-cize experts' views). Importantly, teachers should not be too ambitious in hopes for transfer of critical thinking skills from one topic to another. There may be transfer of enthusiasm for critical thinking and transfer between conceptually related topics. Otherwise opportunities for encouraging critical thinking should be provided in all topics, all subjects and at all levels.

In the Microbiology course at the University of New South Wales a two-hour teaching session is presented about two-thirds of the way through the one year course in which

1. Students are presented with a set of reports issued from the microbiology laboratory of one of the large teaching hospitals. In groups of four, the students outline their own interpretations and state, if a medical officer, what actions they would take on receipt of each report (with special emphasis on prescription of antibiotics).

2. The reports were the same ones used in a published study (Ackerman et al, 1979) in which they were circulated to interns, residents and visiting medical officers at the same teaching hospital (experts of different levels of sophistication). Differential analysis of the results were available in the publication.

3. In their groups of four, students have the opportunity to reflect on their own thought processes before negotiating an 'agreed view' for the group.

4. 'Agreed views' are exchanged by two groups of four who are then presented with copies of the journal article and analyses of the expert's views. This allows the students to compare their interpretations with those of the hospital staff and to discuss the pros and cons of laboratory scientist of clinician taking major responsibility for interpretation of a laboratory report. This would typically include the issue of whether laboratory scientists should simply report antibiotic sensitivities or take a step further and make recommendations for therapy.

Critical Thinking: Student vs. Expert Interpretation of Microbiology Laboratory Reports
(Adapted from Laboratory Manual, University of New South Wales)

Laboratory report
Case of a woman aged 62 (from Ackerman et al, 1979, p. 199)
Clinical notes: Laparotomy 1 week ago for bowel obstruction. Progress satisfactory, but now has mild dysuria. Not catheterized.
  Urine microscopy — white blood cells $<10/mm^3$, red blood cells $10-100/mm^3$, epithelial cells $<10/mm$.
  Culture — bacterial count 10^5 ml. Three different organisms present. Mixed growth of Gram-negative rods $\times$ 2 and *Str. faecalis*.

Questions for student discussion
  1. How would you interpret this report?
  2. What action would you take on receipt of this report?

Feedback
  1. Summary of interpretation by 160 clinicians (adapted from Ackerman et al, 1979, p. 200).

Medical group	Interpretation of report				Recommendations	
	No infection	Infection	Inconclusive	Repeat test	Systemic antibiotics indicated	Symptomatic treatment only
V.M.O.s	56*	30	14	45	25	5
S.R.M.O.s	85	8	8	92	15(8)**	15
R.M.O.s	81	19	..	86	19(10)**	10
Interns	60	37	4	67	37	6
All M.O.s	63	29	8	62	27	7

  * All figures in this table are percentages unless otherwise indicated.
  ** If symptoms warrant

  2. Compare your own interpretations and planned actions with those of the experts.
  3. Try to account for differences between the different groups of experts.
  4. Discuss difficulties in interpretation.
  5. Produce a revised report.
  6. Compare the published revision (Ackerman et al, 1979).
  'Mixed growth of two Gram-negative rods and *Str. faecalis*. This result is most likely the result of contamination of the specimen and not a consequence of urinary infection. Antibiotic therapy is probably not necessary. Repeat test if symptoms persist. The presence of red blood cells may be associated with many factors other than infection'.
  7. Try to account for differences.

Fig. 8.5 Analysis of laboratory reports used to promote critical thinking

5. Students are asked to account for differences between the three groups of experts, to locate their own views in relation, and to add a formal critique of their own (or the experts') views.

6. Complementing the critical thinking opportunities (1) — (5) is the dimension of communication between diagnostic laboratory scientists and clinicians. Main reasons for failures of communication were use of jargon, use of changed or unfamiliar names of bacterial species and, importantly, the use of ill-defined reporting conventions. The authors concluded that communication with clinicians would be more effective if microbiologists not only ensured that reports were free from jargon but also used reporting conventions in which they stated what conclusions could be drawn from tests and made recommendations, where appropriate, for antibiotic therapy.

A more advanced and less structured opportunity for critical thinking based in the laboratory is case analysis (Lee & Hegarty, 1981). Here students select the case of one patient with a microbiological problem whom they have seen during the third year of their five year medical course. The case must be one warranting detailed analysis and requiring fairly extensive library research in order to explore its complexities (see Figure 8.6). Students usually choose a patient who presented major difficulties in recognition of their problem/s or one with a variety of microbiological problems precipitated by immunosuppression or underlying pathology.

Some examples will illustrate the level of students' critical thinking in this laboratory based exercise. In 1985, one student submitted a case book on *Streptococcus agalactiae* (Group B Streptococcus) as an extremely unusual case of urinary tract infection, septicemia and endocarditis in the same patient. The student was in a good position to think critically about this problem of a urinary tract infection (and other much more serious sequels) caused by this organism since he had completed several earlier relevant exercises (see Figures 8.1 to 8.5) Brief excerpts from the student's report cannot do justice, but can show that his critical thinking ranged from issues of specimen collection to interpretation of significance of an unusual organism.

Specimen collection: Failure to use standard collection techniques, e.g. 'on interviewing Mrs

---

Critical Thinking: Case Analysis in Microbiology (Adapted from the Laboratory Manual, University of New South Wales)
See text page 15 for details of a student's analysis of a case involving urinary tract infection, endocarditis, and septicaemia. This forms the last part of the sequence depicted in Figures 1,2,3,4 and 5.
A report of some 15 pages was required with headings:
1. *Clinical presentation*. A summary of relevant details.
2. *Specimens*. Evaluation of the selection, collection and transport of materials submitted to the laboratory.
3. *Microbiological diagnosis*. Copies of laboratory reports should be presented if possible; otherwise a summary of results. The interpretation and significance of this information should be discussed.
4. *Initiation of infection*. This section should discuss the factors which may have led to development of the infection; these could range from predisposing factors (for endogenous infections) to epidemiological considerations (for infectious diseases)
5. *Treatment*. Describe the antimicrobial therapy used and discuss it in terms of reasons for selection and the justification of those reasons.
6. *Prognosis*.

Fig. 8.6 Example of a case analysis used to promote critical thinking

---

C. and questioning her specifically on collection technique, she said she had never been swabbed or asked to swab herself before voiding a urine sample. This could account for the repeated requests for specimens to be collected again, since the epithelial cell count was high in many of them and the likelihood of contamination had to be considered'.

Microbiological diagnosis: Problems of assessing Streptococcus agalactiae as a pathogen in UTI because 'Strep.agalactiae is a rare pathogen of UTI, less than 1% as reported by Mhalu. It is part of the normal flora. Hager et al reported up to 12% vaginal cultures showing presence of this organism. The number of epithelial cells was high. Because of these problems, the diagnosis of UTI could not be made confidently, and the lab rightly requested repeat collection of MSU specimens'.

A final high level aspect of critical thinking is insight into new problems (McPeck, 1981). Berner (1984) used the term 'invented' problems in medicine for situations such as discovery of new disease entities and subsequent searches for solutions.

Such situations occur fairly rarely in medicine and of course a medical student would seldom be cast in the role of the discoverer. However, the laboratory is essential to the medical scientists who are responsible for investigation of new disease entities and for searching methods of treatment and prevention. Medical teachers can design sessions so that students can participate vicariously in the laboratory investigations. A final example from Microbiology at the University of New South Wales illustrates this. Each year since 1981, medical students have vicariously investigated the new disease entity of AIDS (Acquired Immune Deficiency Syndrome). In the first year, sessions centred around clinical descriptions (the AIDS syndrome, Kaposi's sarcoma, opportunistic infections) and laboratory investigations. Early laboratory findings were restricted to isolation of the opportunists, e.g. *Pneumocystis*, and search for the underlying causative organism.

Examples of stimulus questions were used (1) Given that this is one syndrome, what would you predict to be a possible mechanism of pathogenesis? (2) What tests could be done to confirm your hypothesis? In later years, details became available of candidate virus agents of the disease, their reactions in cell cultures, nucleic acid characterization, and also of the effects on the body's immune system of T helper and T suppressor cells. Now AIDS is no longer considered a new disease entity: its cause, effects and methods of transmission are known. However, considerable problems remain, and students' critical thinking in the laboratory can engage the difficulties of routine virus isolation, interpretation of serological tests and details of the search for prevention and cure.

REFERENCES

Ackerman V P, Pritchard R C, Groot Obbink D J, Bradbury R, Lee A 1979 Consumer survey on microbiology reports, Lancet, January 27: 199–202.

Arons A B 1985 'Critical thinking' and the baccalaureate curriculum, Liberal Education, 71: 147–157.

Barrows H S 1983 Problem-based, self-directed learning, Journal of the American Medical Association 250: 3077–3080.

Benson E S 1980 Improved use of laboratory tests, Human Pathology 11: 440–448.

Berner E S 1984 Paradigms and problem solving: a literature review. Journal of Medical Education 59: 625–633.

Burke M D, Connelly D P 1981 Systematic instruction in laboratory medicine: effects on the clinical problem solving performance of medical students, Human Pathology 12: 133–144.

Carmichael J W, Hassell J, Hunter J, Jones L, Ryan M A, Vincent H 1980 Project S O A R (Stress on Analytical Reasoning), American Biology Teacher 42: 169–173.

Clarke R M 1981 Undergraduate education in the cost-effective use of laboratory and radiological investigations in clinical decision making, Medical Education 15: 17–25.

Fitts P M, Posner M I 1967 Human performance Belmont California: Wadsworth.

Gagné R M 1970 The Conditions of learning (second edition) New York: Holt, Rinehart and Winston.

Gagné R M, Briggs C J 1974 Principles of Instructional Design. New York: Holt, Rinehart and Winston.

Glaser R 1984 Education and thinking: the role of knowledge. American Psychologist 39: 93–104.

Gonnella J S, Gòrdan M J, Williamson J W, Cotsonas N J 1970 Evaluation of patient care, an approach. Journal of the American Medical Association 214: 2040–2043.

Hegarty E H, Lee A 1979 Effective laboratory teaching in medicine Part 2. Design, Medical Teacher 1, 227–234.

Hegarty E H 1982 Designing laboratory exercises. Ch 26 in The Medical Teacher (Eds Cox K R and Ewan C E) Edinburgh: Churchill and Livingstone.

Karplus R, Lawson A E, Wollman W, Appel M, Bernhoff R, Howe A, Rusch J J, Sullivan F 1977. Science Teaching on the Development of Reasoning; a Workshop Berkeley: The Regents of the University of California.

Lee A, Hegarty E H 1981 Case analysis as a teaching method in the paraclinical sciences, Medical Journal of Australia 1: 250–251.

Lesgold A M, Feltovich P J, Glaser R, Wang Y 1981 The acquisition of perceptual diagnostic skill in radiology (Tech: REp. PDS-l) Pittsburgh, P A: Learning Research and Development Centre, University of Pittsburgh. Cited in Glaser 1984.

Macqueen D, Chignell D A, Dutton G J, Garland P B 1976 Biochemistry for medical students: a flexible student-oriented approach, Medical Education 10: 418–-437.

McPeck J E 1981 Critical thinking and education, Oxford: Martin Robertson.

Novak J D 1980 Learning theory applied to the biology classroom American Biology Teacher 42, 280–285

Saunders N A, Wallis B J 1981 Learning decision-making in clinical medicine: a card game dealing with acute emergencies for undergraduate use. Medical Education 15: 323–327.

Schmidt H G 1983 Problem-based learning: rationale and description. Medical Education 17: 11–16.

Ward C J, Harris I B, Burke M D, Horowitz C 1976 Systemic instruction in interpretive aspects of laboratory medicine Journal of Medical Education 51: 648–656.

White R T 1979 Achievement, mastery, proficiency, competence Studies in Science Education 6: 1–22.

Using the community as a learning environment

Preview

OBJECTIVES FOR COMMUNITY
PLACEMENTS

    Learning behavioural sciences
    Understanding the burden of illness in society
    Learning professional skills
    Learning process skills
        problem solving methods
        research methods
        evaluation methods

STRATEGIES FOR COMMUNITY
PLACEMENTS

    educational strategies
    management strategies
EVALUATION OF COMMUNITY
PLACEMENTS

SUMMARY

A current trend in medical education is to encourage more student learning to take place in the community. Two main reasons account for this — one is medical, the other educational.

Firstly, more of the care of individual patients is taking place outside hospital walls, both in preventive and therapeutic spheres.

Secondly, it is an accepted educational principle that teaching should take place in an environment as similar as possible to that in which the knowledge and skills being learned will be practised.

This chapter is about teaching professional skills in a setting away from the classroom, and away from the teaching hospital. It is not about educating the public or educating patients, that topic is dealt with in Chapter 19.

OBJECTIVES FOR COMMUNITY PLACEMENTS

As many teachers or supervisors are involved in successful community placements the success of those placements depends on defining the goals of the learning experience very clearly as a guide for the supervisors and preceptors.

Areas for which objectives might be set include the following.

Learning behavioural sciences

Students will become better doctors if they acquire an understanding of how people behave when they are healthy and when they are sick, and how culture affects patterns and perceptions of illness. Patients will benefit if doctors are familiar with different value systems, and with the psychological aspects of, for example, growth, aging and death on the life of a family.

All of these aspects can be best appreciated by students when they participate in experiences dissimilar to their own upbringing, and when they can share these experiences with their peers. Common objectives for community placement would be to raise awareness among students of cultural and subcultural differences, and to help them clarify their own values.

Thus community placement can be used to enhance students' learning of cognitive information relevant to behavioural sciences such as psychology, sociology and anthropology.

Understanding the burden of illness in society

Learning objectives for community placement in the preclinical and early clinical years might emphasize that students require an understanding of illness not only in its florid form in a hospital setting, but in earlier stages.

Students can be encouraged to see patients as part of a population, not just as individuals, so that observations of patterns of health and illness become part of the medical students' conceptual framework.

An understanding of the time span of illness might be a related objective. Many factors such as smoking are present for up to 30 years before disease develops. Chronic diseases such as diabetes, epilepsy and asthma and disabilities such as spinal injuries may need to be managed in the home setting for more than 30 years.

Concurrently with understanding the burden of illness in society students learn about the way in which the local health system operates, and how different health professionals contribute to a team approach to care. They also have opportunities to observe the attitudes towards health and illness held by patients, their families, and health professionals.

These goals for community placement and the relative importance of the information and attitudes should be discussed, clarified, and negotiated with the preceptors.

Learning professional skills

Skill development in community placements could include objectives such as the following

* That the student will be able to apply principles of first aid and undertake emergency resuscitation of a patient.

* That the student will be able to teach the elderly patient the correct use of the oxygen cylinder in the home setting.

* That the student will understand the appropriate uses of primary, secondary and tertiary facilities and be able to refer patients appropriately.

* That the student will come to understand

better the role of the doctor in primary health care, and learn to work effectively with other health professionals in community services for rehabilitation of stroke patients.

Learning process skills

Health services are changing as health needs change. Familiarity with processes for gathering, organizing, interpreting and evaluating information will help doctors to make better clinical decisions, and enable them to influence better health policy decisions.

Moreover, the same methods are able to be applied in different contexts, for example in a problem solving process, a research process, or an evaluation process. The following examples illustrate this.

Problem solving methods

Learning a problem solving process which can be applied in later years is possible if individual students (or small groups of students) are given a specific problem, asked to explore it and to recommend a plan of action to improve the situation. This implies that the individual or group would be able to justify the decision; and defend its appropriateness for the community in question. An example of such a problem follows

Example:

Maternal and child health care centre in an expanding township is underutilized although there are serious child health problems in the locality. The location of the clinic can be shown to be a problem. When it was built 20 years ago the young families lived close by, but now they are on the outskirts of the town a few kilometres away. No public transport runs to the clinic and parking is very difficult, so mothers with more than one small child will not make the journey.

There may be several strategies to improve this situation. The students can explore such a problem, and discuss the ramifications of the problem and of various alternative solutions.

Research methods

A community setting can also provide an interesting location for students to learn research methods. They can conduct pilot surveys, design and administer questionnaires, and apply simple statistical analyses to the information gathered.

Example:

> Students could be asked to report on the needs of frail elderly residents for home support, day care centres, and institutional care.

Students could use their existing knowledge to formulate a hypothesis with regard to a relevant question and then seek information to confirm or deny this. If students work in groups each with a specific hypothesis and they are guided by a supervisor the learning experience can be very valuable. Hypotheses for the above example might be

★ that frail elderly people can stay in their own homes if bathrooms are adapted with rails and other aids.

★ that respite institutional care for the elderly who live with their families enables more families to care for their aged.

Evaluation methods

An evaluation project can assist students to learn to identify which information to gather and how to assess that information in order to make better decisions about individual patient management programs or about health services

Example: In one community an accident prevention program stresses road safety, and water safety. It is well planned and well executed and felt to be very beneficial. However, in another community the major safety issues concern occupational accidents and environmental health — the same prevention program will be of less relevance and less value to these people. Skills in analyzing the needs, concerns and goals of individuals or groups are as useful to the practising doctor as they are to the medical teacher.

STRATEGIES FOR COMMUNITY PLACEMENT

Educational strategies

When the purpose of a field training exercise in the community has been defined, the task still remains to determine how the learning experience should be organized. There are many options available, most being somewhere on a continuum between the following two extremes.

★ At one end of the continuum are small group visits to a variety of service centres with students as observers, on the other end, individual in depth attachments over a reasonable period of time with students acting as apprentices actually taking a significant part of the workload.

Some options for community placements are listed below:-

(a). Individual students (or pairs) choose an elective topic and select their own placements, the teaching institution then approves the proposal.

(b). Individual students are assigned to work in a clinical community health centre/social agency from full-time to one half day per week.

(c). Small groups of students visit an organization for an afternoon. The visits are timetabled so that each small group moves over a period of weeks to each organization (i.e. the number of visits and numbers of student groups must be equal).

(d). Students are purposefully assigned to roles different from those in which they will later work.

When considering the most appropriate type of field placement the following questions should be asked:

1. Do I want the students to be aware of this service, and understand its role in health care services e.g. preclinical behavioural science students visiting a health promotion unit?

2. Do I want the students to be aware of this organization to comment critically about the service it provides, and to understand the purposes of diagnosis and treatment (e.g. final year students visiting a handicapped childrens' society)?

3. Do I want the students to be able to work independently in this service, and to make clinical decisions after their exposure to it (e.g. final year medical students undertaking home visits with a family physician)?

4. Which elements of the bio-psycho-social system are most important in this placement — is the objective mastering clinical skills, or is it understanding the complexity of working in a multicultural neighbourhood?

Management strategies

No matter what the learning objective is, and how it is best thought to be achieved certain practical details are very important if community placements are going to be satisfactory. The teacher co-ordinating the placement should ask the following questions:

* Which is the most convenient time for the visit
  — from the preceptors' point of view?
  — from the patients' or consumers' point of view?
  — from the students'/teachers' point of view?
* Which is the most appropriate time for the visits from the point of view of the learning objectives?
* Is there transport available to the placement? Will it be available both before and after the period the students are there? Is this transport efficient, so that the time spent in travelling is not prohibitive?
* Can the subject matter be learnt better by short visits over several weeks/months, or by one or two intensive visits (say one week)?
* Are there any legal issues to be considered (e.g. prescribing drugs, driving vehicles)?
* Are there any ethical issues to be considered (e.g. patient consent, third person present in an interview). Will this visit cause financial repercussions (e.g. GP may see fewer patients if a student is visiting the practice)?
* Who will be the contact person at the teaching institution during the field study period to clarify information and cope with unexpected problems?
* Who will supervise the preceptors and community supervisors and ensure that all teachers both understand the learning objectives and have the capacity to enable them to be achieved?
* Will finding food, and, if necessary, accommodation be problematic for the students?
* Will social activities — to enhance the group process, or provide an opportunity for the medical school to show its appreciation to preceptors — be the responsibility of staff or students?
* Are there cultural or religious differences of which students should be cognizant before undertaking on site activities?

EVALUATION OF COMMUNITY PLACEMENTS

It is essential that the community experiences be evaluated, both from the learning and the teaching point of view. Methods of student assessment can be built into the placement, (*see* Chapters 24–27) but the program as a whole should also be assessed. A structured evaluation needs to be undertaken as with a dispersed group of students and preceptors both positive and negative aspects of the experience may not come to the attention of the medical faculty unless specifically requested.

Educational questions may include:
* Did the students fulfill the learning objectives?
* Did they learn unanticipated knowledge?
* Were they well supervised?

Other broader questions may include:
* Do these placements enhance the medical school relationships with community practitioners, and the public itself?
* Is this method of learning cost effective?
* Are the students contributing to a healthier population?

SUMMARY

Allowing students to undertake learning experiences in the community broadens their perceptions about health and illness, and enables them to learn professional skills for health services which are extending increasingly beyond hospital walls.

It cannot be assumed that learning that takes place in informal community settings requires less planning than learning within an institution. Teaching in the community has as much a management and coordination role as a teaching role, but if an appropriate structure is fostered the experience will be rewarding for all.

How to help students learn from experience

Preview

INTRODUCTION

HOW CAN STUDENTS BE HELPED TO
REFLECT ON EXPERIENCE?

A MODEL OF LEARNING FROM
EXPERIENCE

DEBRIEFING

CONCLUSION

INTRODUCTION

While formal teaching activities play an important
part in medical education, the most significant
forms of learning often occur through learning
from experience. The experience-based learning
can take place as a planned part of the curriculum
through specially planned exercises on, for
example, interviewing skills or clinical examinations, or through less well-defined hospital or
community placements in which students learn
through exposure to genuine problems with real
patients. Much attention has been given to
analyzing and researching teaching methods such
as the lecture or tutorial and how students learn
from these; but much less emphasis has been
placed by both researchers and teachers on how
students can learn from the complex experiences
which they meet outside the lecture room. It is
through developing the capability of students to
learn effectively from their experiences that they
will be able as professionals to be competent
learners throughout their lives.

Learning from experience involves drawing
upon past experiences, examining these and if

necessary reappraising them, and learning from
new, planned experiences through making records
as they occur and reflecting critically on them.
These experiences may be specially contrived in
workshop settings or they may consist of events
such as work on a given ward for a particular
period of time. The term 'reflection on learning'
has been used to describe the general processes of
learning from experience in both case (Boud,
Keogh and Walker 1985a). 'Debriefing' is a more
a specific term usually applied to sessions
conducted in a group after a workshop, simulation
or placement (Pearson and Smith 1985).

What is a workshop?

A workshop is a way of organizing teaching and
learning in which participants are typically
exposed to a variety of activities such as mini-
lectures, structured exercises, small-group
discussion, and simulations. The mix of these and
the emphasis placed on each varies greatly
depending of the purpose of the course and the
role of the workshop in it.

While no single set of activities constitutes a
workshop as such, the term cannot be properly
used unless participants are actively involved over
a significant proportion of the time in ways other
than listening to a presenter and asking questions,
and unless the needs of individual participants are
taken into account.

HOW CAN STUDENTS BE HELPED TO
REFLECT ON EXPERIENCE?

Much lip-service is paid to the need for individuals to reflect and for teachers to debrief their groups. Many teachers acknowledge the importance of these activities, but fail to implement them effectively in their own courses. There is also confusion, even in the literature, about what is involved in reflection and a lack of clarity about what are the key elements. At times debriefing is used as though it were synonymous with a teacher making a summary or conclusion. While it can be useful for one person to review what has occurred, it is important that all participants are encouraged to do this for themselves. There need to be opportunities for differing accounts to be reported and compared, and this may lead some people to alter their interpretation of what took place. The greater students' personal involvement in the activity, for example, performing an examination themselves rather than observing one, the greater the need for their experience to be respected and their views accepted as an account of what happened to them. If this does not coincide with what the person who planned the event would have liked to have happened, then it is for the teacher to reappraise the situation and respond to what actually happened.

Much of the value of activities which focus on learning from experience is in the exchange of experience of different people and the exploration of their various viewpoints. One of the main ways in which people learn in complex areas, such as clinical placements, is by working through their experiences, relating them to their own ideas and to their earlier experiences and those of others, and drawing lessons from them. This is a series of steps which cannot be done for someone else: all that a teacher can do is to provide suitable conditions for it to take place. Teachers can assist reflection through structuring debriefing sessions, but they cannot define the outcomes for others. This is paradoxical in a way, as teachers are normally careful to define the learning outcomes of activities they arrange and to plan a program to meet these ends.

Activities which use experienced-based learning are of many different types, and the ways in which they should be structured to promote reflection will vary according to their objectives and the degree of involvement of the participants. When participants are involved in case-studies, simu-lations, games or role-playing where the objectives are complex and the activities demand more than intellectual involvement, reflection needs to be very carefully planned and substantial periods of time need to be devoted to it.

Experience-based learning opportunities in medical education

Time needs to be devoted to structured reflection in many contexts in a typical course. These include:
Initial skills training in interviews and examin-ation. Behavioural science topics such as group skills and counselling. Community-based assign-ments, for example, mini-projects on reviewing home care arrangements or alcohol and drug services. Practicums and electives in clinical areas such as general practice, accident or emergency work. Mainstream ward work where students act as 'apprentices'.

In all these contexts opportunities for students to record and reflect on their experiences system-atically may be deficient or entirely absent. The kinds of reflection on experience required will differ greatly, and the time spent by teachers on assisting and facilitating these activities will vary depending on the importance of the activity and the stage of the course reached. For example, more time needs to be spent at the early stages of learning from experience to enable students to develop skills of record keeping and reflection.

A wide range of techniques can be used to assist people to reflect on their learning and to maximize the benefits of their experience (Boud, Keogh and Walker 1985b). Most of these fit within a model of reflection on learning which can be applied to specific activities.

A MODEL OF LEARNING FROM EXPERIENCE

To help in understanding the model it may be useful to imagine a session following students' first exposure, in groups, to a hospital ward.

The model of reflection on learning (Boud, Keogh and Walker 1985c) suggests that the first step might be to *return to the experience*, for participants to recall in detail exactly what happened: Whom did you meet? Who said what? How did each person react? What did you feel each time? What occupied your attention? What else was going on? The idea is to recapture, in as much detail as possible, the full experience of the event and the reactions of all those associated with it. This may be done in the mind's eye, but it is helpful to either write it down, recount it to another person or report it to the group. This will pull our further aspects of the experience that may not have been consciously noted, or which at the time may not have seemed to be very significant. Some aspects may remain blurred, or other features may act as the focus of attention and members of the group may become drawn to them. Typically, these will be events that either made an intellectual impact on them, or which gave rise to some positive or negative emotional response.

The second step which is useful in reflection is *attending to feelings*. Some aspects of an event provoke stronger feelings than others. These feelings may be experienced as positive, feeling good, or negative, feeling bad, frustrated, upset or worried. Sometimes these will be quite simple, and participants may have expressed themselves at the time saying that they felt to others. More commonly there will be other occasions when they could recall their feelings but they (quite appropriately) expressed nothing at the time.

These times can often have significance for learning. For example, they may raise questions for a participant such as: Do I always feel at a loss when faced with someone who is inarticulate? Am I usually pleased when a patient answers me eagerly? Do I feel disgusted by certain types of behaviour? Sometimes it may be sufficient for them to acknowledge their feelings, just to savour the good ones and pass over the others; but at other times it will be useful for them to express the unexpressed, to allow themselves to feel angry at the registrar's abruptness, or to feel the anxiety of being confronted by a stranger. At the time, an expression of these feelings may have been unsuited to the circumstances or disruptive. However, it can be necessary for these feelings to arise retrospectively and be addressed if students

are not to remain unsatisfied and anxious about being exposed to similar situations. Again, they can attend to their feelings and express them by themselves or on paper; but for this aspect it is often more useful to have another person to listen and be supportive. Feelings and emotions are an important but too little examined element in learning, especially when dealing with other human beings.

The third step, *re-evaluating the experiences*, logically occurs after the others, but aspects of it take place in parallel with the first two. This is the stage in which new experiences can be related to prior experiences, and new knowledge can be fitted into one's existing way of looking at the world. This step is termed *re*-evaluating the experience because evaluation occurs throughout: we all make judgments about events as they occur, but these immediate, unconsidered assessments may not be an adequate foundation on which we can rest our learning. We need to re-evaluate, to turn again (and again) to our experience to examine what it tells us. It can be useful to think of the separate elements of this step, but many of these can occur in parallel with one another and the particular order may vary.

Components of the re-evaluation stage are:

Association: the connecting of the ideas and feelings which are part of the original experience, and those which have occurred during reflection, with existing knowledge and attitudes. Some of the techniques which can be used for this are: free association, allowing oneself to suspend judgment and note whatever comes to mind; or brainstorming of ideas, a form of group association where ideas are initially collected without evaluation. Some people find it useful, depending on what has taken place, to construct diagrams or lists or to note analogies. For example, after the ward experience a session might be spent on generating ideas about the implications of the experience or producing a list of ideas, say, about how to initiate contacts with patients. This could be done as an individual exercise or profitably in the whole group.

Integration: processing the associations to examine whether they are meaningful and useful. This may involve looking at patterns in associations, grouping them together, drawing simple maps of linkages, relating the ideas generated to others. In the example, this could occur by taking the list of implications and looking for common themes or links between the ideas expressed, by elaborating some and rejecting others.

Validation: subjecting the ideas and feelings which have started to be integrated to what might be called 'reality tests', such as looking for internal consistency between new appreciations and existing knowledge and beliefs, for consistency between these and parallel data from others, or trying out new perceptions in new situations. In the group we may take one of the clusters of ideas and examine how it could be used in a practical situation through further role play, or by checking these ideas out against the individual's experience in the ward.

Appropriation: making new knowledge an integral part of how we act and how we feel. This is an element of the process which someone may or may not experience once they have worked on a particular event thoroughly. This may occur in our example through one or more people having an insight into how they conduct themselves with others which could affect all their subsequent interactions with patients, such as in realizing the off-putting effect that one of their favourite conversational

openings has on others and finding an effective alternative.

In any given situation it may be appropriate to work through these stages systematically using some of the approaches suggested; but on other occasions it might be best to concentrate on one aspect of these in the group and encourage others to take place outside the group, or to plan a separate activity which involves a mixture of group and individual activities. Individuals can facilitate these processes for themselves through keeping diaries and journals, and working systematically on them using devices such as those discussed by Rainer (1980).

DEBRIEFING

A common way of structuring reflection with groups is the debriefing session which usually follows an experiental exercise, simulation, or role play, but which also needs to occur after any period of experience-based learning (Pearson and Smith 1985). Debriefing is the second part of the two part activity of briefing and debriefing which takes place before and after a particular workshop activity or set of activities. Briefing occurs in the early part of a workshop when participants are orientated to the activity that follows. Briefing is often neglected or is inadequate, and this can lead

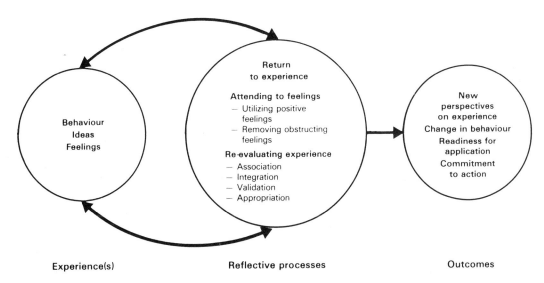

Fig. 10.1 The reflection process in context

to a waste of the potential of the exercise which has been organized. At the briefing stage students may be provided with instructions, goals and the rules which relate to what is acceptable behaviour in a given situation. More important than these, however, is the presentation of the purposes and intentions of the exercise. The purpose of the activity may be to focus on one aspect of a problem rather than another, for example, to focus on the interventions of the doctor in the interviewing exercise rather than being distracted by the narrative of the patient. In briefing it is important to highlight the main emphasis of the activity without prejudging the outcomes.

Pearson and Smith (1985) have broadly followed the model of reflection outlined above and they have translated the three main stages of return to experience, attending to feelings, and re-evaluation into three simple questions which guide debriefing. These are:

* What happened?
* How did the participants feel?
* What does it mean?

Time for reflection

It is essential that adequate time is given to reflection: both scheduled class time and individual study time. The most common mistake of teachers and course planners, and indeed students, is to allow too much time for the experiental activity and too little for debriefing, thus leaving participants dissatisfied and insufficiently equipped to be able to continue their own learning from the experience. The rule of thumb which is commonly applied in workshops is that at least as much time should be given to debriefing and other forms of reflection as is given to the preceding exercise; frequently, this should be multiplied as much as fivefold. This time allocation may appear unrealistic at first sight, but it is impossible to underestimate the importance of adequate processing of experience at the time. Perhaps more people have been put off workshop experiences and practicums through insufficient or inadequate debriefing than in any other way. One useful strategy to encourage learners to devote time to reflection is through the use of learning partnerships.

Learner partnerships

These are essentially informal arrangements between two students in which they share experiences, clarify expectations of the course or placement, receive mutual support, and ask questions they might feel inhibited about revealing to staff.

Partnerships can be fostered by teachers through presentation of the idea and encouragement of initial meetings, but they can continue only through active involvement of individual students.

For details see Robinson, Saberton and Griffin (1985) and Saberton (1985).

CONCLUSION

There are many forms of reflection and many ways of conducting debriefing sessions. In any given situation they are limited only by the imagination of the teacher. What they have in common is that they provide tools which students can use to focus on their experiences and which can help them continue their learning after the formal session has ended.

REFERENCES

Bawden R, MacKinnon C 1980 The portfolio, HERDSA News 2,2, 4–5. An example of a handout to students describing the keeping of a portfolio in a science course.

Boud D J, Keogh R, Walker D 1985a What is reflection on learning?, in Boud D J, Keogh and Walker D (eds) Reflection: Turning Experience into Learning. London: Kogan Page. A description of what is included by the term reflection.

Boud D J, Keogh R, Walker D (eds) 1985b Reflection: Turning Experience into Learning. London: Kogan Page

Ideas and case studies on different reflection strategies. Includes the use of diaries, portfolios, autobiographies, debriefing sessions, and computer aided reflection.

Boud D J, Keogh R, Walker D 1985c Promoting reflection in learning: a model, in Boud D J, Keogh R and Walker D (eds) Reflection: Turning Experience into Learning. London: Kogan Page. A fuller version of the model presented above.

Johnson D W, Johnson F P 1982 Joining Together: Group Theory and Group Skills. Englewood Cliffs New Jersey:

Prentice-Hall. A useful source of communication exercises and group-building strategies.

Pearson M, Smith D 1985 Debriefing in experience-based learning in Boud D J, Keogh R, Walker D (eds) Reflection: Turning Experience into Learning. London: Kogan Page. An account of how to use debriefing in a workshop setting.

Rainer T 1980 The New Diary. London: Angus and Robertson An informal guide to the concept and practice of writing a personal journal.

Robinson J, Saberton S, Griffin V 1985 Learning Partnerships: Interdependent Learning in Adult Education Toronto: Ontario Institute for Studies in Education Department of Adult Education Discussion of the concept of learning partnerships and how they have been used.

Saberton S 1985 Learning Partnerships. HERDSA News 7: 3–5 Concise guidelines for the formation and use of learning partnerships.

Watson H J, Vallee J M, Mulford W R 1981 Structured Experiences and Group Development. Canberra: Curriculum Development Centre A sourcebook of games and simulations for group development.

Teaching professional skills

Introduction

The next chapters embrace areas which have received little attention in medical thinking and teaching, yet all are critical to the gathering, interpretation and use of clinical information.

These areas relate to

1. What we look for clinically, and what we 'see'.

What we notice and what we overlook relate very much to what we expect to find. These can be called the perceptual aspects of clinical observation.

2. How we go about searching for clinical features in the history and physical examination.

Our approaches reflect implicit clinical reasoning strategies or plans. Each plan used in seeking clinical data has its strengths and weaknesses.

3. How we actually weigh up all the possible gains and losses that may result from our clinical decisions.

An extraordinarily diverse number of issues flashes through our minds. Every choice involves some trade-offs in risks and benefits. Every choice is based both on

(a) values (about which are most important among the various possible outcomes) and

(b) probabilities (of how likely is each outcome).

These are the personal and pragmatic factors influencing how we make clinical decisions.

Our neglect of the study and teaching of these everyday phenomena reflects some limitations of our profession. While we readily acknowledge the uncertain nature of clinical features and diagnosis, we have not incorporated probabilities explicitly into our diagnostic calculus at the bedside. While we acknowledge the emotional impact of an illness on a patient, we pretend that decisions by doctors are free from emotions and values.

These limitations reflect what is socially acceptable material for discussion and analysis within a profession which is well versed in the concrete and visible manifestations within biomedical science, but relatively unschooled in cognitive and behavioural psychology as they apply to what doctors do. That is, we are comfortable studying patient behaviour, but we have not seen the study of doctor behaviour as a responsibility of the medical school.

Intangibles, such as values and feelings, can be viewed with suspicion or even derision. Some of these attitudes appear to flow from lack of understanding of the nature of medicine as an applied science within a service profession. While the biological principles underlying the understanding and treatment of disease are developed and tested scientifically, their application in practice by humans (such as doctors) serving the needs of other humans (such as patients, families and communities) always involves choices by each about what is most important and what is of most concern.

Choices and decisions are not right or wrong in any scientific or verifiable sense, but aim to optimize what seems 'best' for that individual case.

Banal as it may sound, study of the application of science to situations requires study of the situations as well as of the science. The situations embrace not only the objective phenomena of diseases and settings but also their subjective significance to the people involved, particularly doctor and patient. What does this illness mean, what do I want to happen, how can I decide what to do? Science does not ordinarily deal with meaning, purpose and choice; but medicine as an applied science always deals with them, whether explicitly or implicitly.

Because of the paucity of previous teaching in these areas, more attention is given in these Chapters to such concepts and their learning. Because the teaching of these concepts and their application is so recent, little experience of a range of teaching methods can be drawn upon.

Nevertheless a number of important principles in teaching these skills do emerge.

First, the teacher needs to provide the *experiences* within which the students can learn these concepts and strategies for themselves. That is, learning seems to take place within the *process* of sensing the data, interpreting the data, choosing what to do next and when to stop, and deciding what to do about what has been worked out.

Second, the number of skills to be learned is large. An obvious consequence is that such learning takes considerable time. Clinical learning should, consequently, begin as early as possible within the medical course.

Third, each of the skills deals with clinical features which may be clear cut and evident, or may be faint and difficult to detect. Students must examine a large number of patients before the skills of detecting delicate clues can be used confidently, and be fine-tuned.

Furthermore, clinical data vary widely in their reliability. Students need considerable time to adjust to the notion that the observations may be ambiguous or illusory.

Fourth, the techniques of physical examination can be learned on normal patients and colleagues, but the perceptual ability to judge the consistency of a lump or the tension of the abdomen or the timing of a murmur must be learned on real signs in real patients. Again, the extremely large number needed of these 'hands-on' experiences speaks strongly for beginning clinical experiences as early as possible.

Fifth, the skills of pattern recognition are built on a 'clinical memory' of images of clinical pictures. That memory must be put together from seeing large numbers of patients until the pictures are recognized intuitively (note that the word 'recognize' means to 'know again'). The number of clinical images to be experienced is so large that, again, exposure to a broad range of these images

must begin as early as possible in as many settings as practicable.

Sixth, clinical pictures are usually incomplete. Students take time to adjust to the same diagnosis being made on the different sets of data found in different patients.

Further, many clinical features (such as fever, pain, vomiting, weakness) appear in a number of illnesses. Students take time to adjust to different diagnoses being made on what may appear to be similar sets of evidence.

Seventh, students find themselves struggling to detect unreliable, non-specific data to fit into an ambiguous, incomplete picture, yet they are expected to reach a logical and defensible diagnosis and management plan which fits the unexpressed expectations of the patient.

Worse, the possible diagnoses do not have agreed sets of necessary and sufficient data which define them. When diagnosis is a matter of opinion, the student must learn opinions. Unfortunately, opinions of teacher/clinicians do not always coincide.

Eighth, the exercise of these clinical skills requires a level of self-confidence, and of feeling comfortable in the clinical setting and with patients. Medical students often take a considerable time to feel at ease in the wards and in examining patients. Not only must that time be provided, but attention to the personal development of the student must not be overlooked.

Society does not ordinarily condone the intrusion into another's 'personal space', asking questions about intimate matters, or examining another person's body. Medical students are expected to move effortlessly and casually into this intimate relationship; medical teachers rarely acknowledge that students may have feelings about such behaviour, let alone assist adaptation to the new roles and relationships. We have, consequently, incorporated chapters on becoming a doctor, on teaching interviewing skills, and on teaching counselling skills.

The intern year similarly represents a dramatic transition to a new range of serious responsibilities under conditions of heavy work load and personal stress. Little attention is paid to whether the intern's consequent (and perhaps self-protective) behaviour is appropriate, or is mal-adaptive from the patient's point of view. Some personal blocks and inhibitions can persist unacknowledged throughout a lifetime of practice.

Ninth, the students need insight into their own values when they find that clinical decision making involves trade-offs among many possible outcomes, and between the doctor's values and the patient's. 'Physician, know thyself' is a prior condition before students (or doctors) can presume to know others. Decision making is so much simpler if the patient is not consulted.

Negotiating trade-offs among values and risks, such as thoroughness in looking after this patient and efficiency in managing finite resources, are time-consuming and difficult. Should the student/doctor 'bother' about such questions?

If you avoid allowing others to have control over 'your' decisions, whose ends are being served? We have added a chapter on how to teach ethical decision making.

Tenth, learning of these skills is much more powerful under conditions of responsibility: 'I learned more in my intern year than I had in the whole of the medical course!' Decision making can be really understood only when one is actually making decisions that matter, for then the full range of issues impinging on the decision must be considered. What guidance does the intern have at this most critical phase of learning? We have included a chapter on preparing students for their continuing education.

All of these points strongly indicate the need for prolonged, supervised, practical experience in real situations. The roles for the teacher are as colleague, coach and evaluator of the student, and manager of the student's learning experiences. Learning obviously must take place within the

student. Ensuring the opportunities for them to do so comprises the teacher's central task. The experiences are, however, somewhat unpredictable, for they depend on what patients are available for examination and discussion. Learning, consequently, runs the risk of being ad hoc and unsystematic, particularly if the teacher uses only routine patient care rounds as the setting for 'organized' clinical teaching.

Chapter 14, then, deals with learning the reasoning which guides the clinical process, and Chapter 15 with collection of the evidence.

Pari passu with these insights into the styles and flaws of clinical thinking has grown a new field of systematic application of probability theory to the steps and assumptions in interpretation of data and in clinical decisions. Where the studies of what the doctor actually does are *descriptive*, this field of decision analysis is *prescriptive* in working out what ought to be done. The decision analytic approach (borrowed from economics and business) lays out the clinical choices (or at least parts of them) in algorithms, such as flow charts or decision trees. Each choice is able to be justified explicitly and pragmatically by calculating how likely is each of the possible outcomes after taking one path or the other. Both descriptive and prescriptive approaches illuminate clinical thinking for students. The principles of clinical decision making are touched on in Chapter 16 which deals with teaching how to decide what to do.

Continuing our concern to represent the context within which medicine is practised, we begin this Section with a societal view of what may be included with expectations about the competent doctor.

What is included in clinical competence?

Preview

COMPONENTS OF CLINICAL
COMPETENCE

Technical competence
Effect on disease
Effect on patient
Efficiency in managing resources
Balanced judgment
Habitual behaviour

What should a doctor be able to do? Who defines these expectations, the profession providing the service or the public being served? Medical practice and medical competence have come under increasing scrutiny as different parties attempt to exert influence over the nature of the medical task. These changing expectations are beginning to cast clinical competence in a different light.

1. The most powerful and recent factor has been the increasing cost of medical care, which has drawn third party financers (Government, insurance companies, employers) into analysis of what they are getting for the money. An economic view of medical care as a service to be purchased is increasingly mixed with the traditional view of medicine as a 'public good'.

Doctors were in a No Lose game[1] in which they were not required to justify their existence or their

---

* Those seeking help are likely to cast the expected helper in a 'magical' role with powers which may not exist. Failure to improve after visiting the 'healer' (or after supplicating to a saint) is not blamed on the healer, but on Fate or one-self or some external influence. The healer cannot lose, whatever the outcome.

effectiveness. Now a health benefit is being bought. Does a health benefit actually result from the medical service? Is it worth the the cost?

2. Such questions require medicine to demonstrate the effectiveness of the services provided. How do you define effectiveness? Whose criteria will be used — doctor's, patient's or financer's?

3. Are medical services efficient? Do the services make optimal use of time, staff, equipment, materials, space, money? If resources are finite, how are decisions made about the most efficient use of those resources? Efficient from whose point of view?

4. Politically, Governments aim for social equity in distribution of services, even professional services. Are acceptable, affordable medical services accessible and available?

5. Socially, expectations are rising about the doctor's responsibility in health education and promotion, in psycho-social counselling, in guiding self-help, and in sharing decision making with the patient. If medicine is a service profession, who decides what services will be provided, the provider or the consumer? Whose criteria will judge whether a satisfactory service has been provided?

6. Legally, what are the limits of medical responsibility? Previously, malpractice litigation was based solely on doctor negligence. As doctors have increasingly taken responsibility for decision making, particularly within complex hospital care, doctors have become more liable for the outcomes of care, not just the processes of care. Does clinical competence include clear allocation of responsibility for all decisions made?

7. How does the doctor handle the possible conflict of values over priorities in clinical manage-

ment, or in use of finite resources? Different views on what 'should' be done are hard enough for a doctor to reconcile, but become increasingly complicated as soon as more than one person has a stake in the decision. Consider who has a stake in questions such as

— intensive resuscitation for the elderly or death with dignity?

— who is admitted to hospital — the patient needing nursing care for advancing cancer or the patient who will be more independent after hip replacement or removal of a cataract?

— a coronary care unit or a dietary lipid reduction program?

— a liver transplant for one child or immunization for 100 000?

All of these issues impinge on daily clinical decisions, either explicitly or implicitly. The medical teacher must decide whether to teach and to examine in all of these areas, if the graduate is to be seen as clinically competent to function in a changing society.

Some criteria for such a societal view of clinical competence can be set out as follows:

COMPONENTS OF CLINICAL COMPETENCE

1. Technical competence in using knowledge and skills of diagnosis and management in patient care
2. Effect on disease
3. Effect on patient
4. Efficiency in managing finite resources
5. Balanced judgment, resolving trade-offs among competing values
6. Habitual behaviour in meeting these expectations

If these are the components of a societal view of clinical competence, what are the facets which must be taught and tested?

Technical competence

These abilities are covered in Chapters 24 and 25, and are not covered further here.

Effect on disease

Medical effectiveness is usually measured prag-

matically as outcomes of disease, which are then frequently interpreted as the results of therapy.

The common criteria for measuring outcomes of disease are:

— survival/death rates counted as frequencies after stated periods (eg. 5 year, 10 year survival rates, peri-operative mortality)

— survival time (eg. as median survival time)

— complication/side-effects/morbidity rates, as frequencies of particular events (such as wound infection, agranulocytosis), but not usually counting the extent, severity, persistence or disabling effects, or the consequent re-admission rate

— recurrence rates (after apparently successful therapy)

— disability (eg. ability to work, ability to live independently)

The medical teacher can engage students in working these matters out around every clinical patient by having them

(i). tabulate the range of possible outcomes, good and bad

(ii). estimate how likely is each outcome in this patient (which frequently demonstrates the paucity of recorded data which could guide clinical decisions)

(iii). estimate how important is each outcome (which requires the student to find out which are the outcomes valued by each patient and by the doctor, as well as attempting to count the impact of each outcome)*

(iv). combine the likelihood with the importance for each outcome.

Since the likelihoods are currently only weakly developed, and the values hardly at all, multiplication of two such numbers to derive the 'expected value' (as in financial decision analysis) may not yet be practicable clinically.

Yet patients and doctors are implicitly making these combinations daily. Death may be the worst possible outcome, but we accept the risk of death

---

* Unfortunately we have no agreed scales on which to measure 'importance'. We can rank outcomes in relation to one another, or on a scale as from 0 to 100, or we can estimate odds to help the patient express personal preferences. The simplest technique is to adjust survival time by a percentage that reflects the lowered quality of life. Such a combination of quality with quantity is expressed as 'quality-adjusted life years' or QALYs as the unit for measuring outcome.

under anesthesia because we estimate the likelihood to be acceptably low in ourselves. The pain of having a tooth removed may be recognized as a short-lived outcome; but avoiding such extremely likely pain by removal under general anesthesia may be valued sufficiently highly to justify taking the (assumed low) risk of dying under anesthesia.

(v). rank what can now be seen as the most serious and reasonably likely issues, good and bad

(vi). modify the clinical decision in the light of what have turned out to be the most serious considerations

(vii). from among these considerations choose a limited set of outcome criteria which the students can use to estimate medical effectiveness in this case.

(viii). help the students extrapolate from this case to develop a set of general rules for estimating effectiveness.

Effect on patient

The effects on the patient can be seen in both the processes and outcomes of care, and fall into a number of categories.

1. Effects related to the doctor:
   (a). effective communication within the encounter
   (b). satisfaction with the process and outcome of the encounter
   (c). understanding of the nature of the illness
   (d). acceptance of the explanation and of the management plan
   (e). belief, faith, mystique resulting in 'healing'
2. Effects related to the illness
   (a). Morbidity, complications (short and long term)
   (b). functional result, disability
3. Effects related to health behaviour
   (a). compliance with regimen
   (b). prevention of recurrence eg. of infant diarrhea
   (c). life style eg. cessation of smoking
4. Effects related to management
   (a). time, interruption to work or family life
   (b). costs of visits, transport, drugs

(c). convenience
(d). side-effects, re-admission rate

Most journal accounts of therapeutic effectiveness disregard or under-estimate the impact on the patient, and on the patient's regular activities. Measuring frequencies of events in which doctors are interested may overlook the extent, severity, persistence and disabling effects of the treatment on the patient's life. These accounts do not usually include the effect on the patient's time (off work, attending clinics and in hospital) or income or family, nor the effects on the resources of the health care system. That is, the trade-offs considered by the patient in assessing whether a treatment is or was worthwhile may be based on very different criteria from those the doctor used.

The burden of illness relieved must be off-set against the burden incurred by therapy. The resource costs of treatment must be subtracted from the gains which result from treatment. The estimate of effectiveness of treatment must be tempered by the expected natural history of the disease, and by the effect of other health interventions (from domestic care to improved housing and diet).

The medical teacher can help the students to work out with each patient what are the most important aspects to them of the illness, the treatment and the implications of both. Failure to elicit how the patient understands the illness can result in under-diagnosis or mis-diagnosis, failure to satisfy the patient, and low compliance with the management plan. These flaws can be diminished by asking the patient three simple questions.

What do you think is the matter?
What do you think caused it?
What do you think should be done about it?

The next task is to ensure that those aspects of care important to the patient are properly attended to, both in discussion of treatment options and in the management plan.

The third is to build that pattern of discussion with the patient into every interaction, since the patient's concerns are the whole focus of the consultation.

The fourth is to have students and patients develop a scoring sheet which could provide a framework for recording the patient's views on what is important within the consultation and within management. The sheet is used for feeding those views back to student and teacher after the consultation to see how well the patient's concerns were met.

The fifth is to help each student modify his or her behaviour in the light of this personal feedback.

Efficient use of resources

This area frequently raises high emotion among clinicians, and even among students. The position often taken very strongly is that it is not the doctor's role to 'skimp' in the responsibility to the patient.

The medical teacher must allow sufficient time for students to work out what are the questions to be dealt with when considering efficiency, what are the elements in the different positions taken by those for or against efficiency, what is the nature of the conflict of view, what are values issues and what are pragmatic issues, and what role does quantitation of clinical practice have in tidying some of the confusion.

These are serious ethical and moral questions for students to work through for themselves. Teachers have no 'true' answers. Nobody has the 'right' answer when the issues are about trade-offs of possible gains and losses. Teachers may participate in discussion as experienced colleagues, and as advisers on what position the profession currently takes, but not as ethical or moral authorities.

The teacher's aim must be that the students are eventually able to resolve such dilemmas for themselves; meantime the clarification must take place with rigour and honesty (see Chapter 17).

Every patient offers the possibility of discussing these issues, even if the patient is merely seeking a doctor's certificate to permit him to stay off work.

The teacher has the opportunity to mount specific questions around the justification for each use of resources. For example,

— Why would you order that test?
— What will you do if the test result is positive/negative?
— How will the test result affect the likelihood of the disease?

— How will the test result affect your management?
— How do you know that is the most useful test to order at this stage? What are the alternatives? How do they differ in the strength of information they provide? How do they differ in risk?

The teacher can divide the group into those taking a cumulative strategy of seeking the data likely to be positive for the provisional diagnosis and its nearest competitor, and those seeking only data which would discriminate between the two diagnoses. Each group then counts the numbers of tests and their costs in money, risks, time, staff and material resources.

Or the class can compete to see who can get the correct and complete diagnosis at the lowest cost. The class can debate which approach is safest, and what is the cost/safety trade-off.

The teacher can then take students through a follow-up of the outcomes discussion above, attempting to establish the most efficient management path that seems to suit the patient's best interests.

A critical concept here is that the focus of the consultation is management, not diagnosis. Information is useful only to the extent that it contributes to management decisions. Management is useful only to the extent that it optimizes outcomes for patients. Consequently, information is useful only if it helps improve patient outcomes. Social information may sometimes be more critical than test information.

Balanced judgment

Like it or not, the doctor must accept substantial responsibility on behalf of the patient. Some doctors automatically assume that responsibility, to the frustration of some patients. Some patients refuse to accept any responsibility, to the frustration of some doctors. All doctors know more about medicine than all patients, but all patients know more about themselves than any doctor does.

Doctors control access to health resources. Patients cannot order their own barium meals or prescribe themselves prednisone. Doctors decide when an illness is 'worth' investigating or not (sometimes expressed as the doctor taking a risk, but it is the patient who takes the health risk).

Doctors often decide (eg. that a hernia should be operated on, or that hypertension need not be treated) or prescribe, rather than offering choices. Choices take time to discuss, open up uncertainty, and may raise questions which are difficult to answer.

Life is full of trade-offs. The medical teacher can find a dozen trade-offs in every patient's management. So the student can be set to find them also. Having revealed every point at which the gains and loses can be seen, the student must struggle with how to make the choices in the patient's best interests. Clarifying the patient's 'best interests' may necessitate considerable consultation with the patient.

Judgment is learned in the process of making judgments. Balance is learned through the techniques of identifying what is important at each point (for which we use the concept of the value or utility associated with an outcome), how likely it is, and how that can be reconciled with other important aspects.

The teacher's task is to keep the student's thinking open and honest, so that the student learns to recognize his or her own values and where they may differ from the patient's. The task faced by the student/doctor is somehow to combine all the positive and negative outcomes and their likelihoods, because that is the professional's responsibility. That medical pragmatism must then be combined with the patient's values, as far as they can be ascertained.

The teacher must be a safe sounding board, helping the student hear his or her own ideas bounce back, perhaps with some Socratic paradoxes thrown in.

Habitual behaviour

Students are adept at 'performing' to meet the expectations of teachers and examiners. The behaviour displayed in Final examnations may not typify the student's behaviour with patients in the ward or the clinic (especially as the 'rules of the game' differ).

How can the medical teacher be confident about how openly and honestly the graduate released on society will behave when unsupervised? What is the medical teacher's task in teaching and testing for habitual behaviour?

To answer that question negatively, the teacher cannot know, if the student has practised only under close supervision. Or if the teacher/student relationship has been dogmatic and authoritarian, in which case the student has had no freedom of choice or of action.

It may sound self-evident, but habitual behaviour is established only by behaving habitually. If no opportunities are provided for trying out behaviour with the opportunity to seek supervision or consultation with the teacher, then those behaviours are not yet established. The process is being left until the student acquires the burden of sudden and heavy responsibilities immediately after graduation, a period for which the term 'practice' is then correctly used.

The teacher's task is to allow progressively increasing responsibility, first for small and limited decisions (such as whether to order this test), then larger decisions (such as whether to put in a urinary catheter), then for complex decisions associated with more uncertainty and more trade-offs (such as whether to arrange admission of a patient to hospital).

In summary, the teacher's task is to allow the student experiences within which to struggle with making judgments under conditions of responsibility, but with ample discussion and reflection on the practical and ethical dilemmas involved, and with guidance on how to elicit what is most important to the patient.

Becoming a doctor

The process of becoming a doctor and a member of the medical profession is a social process. It should be distinguished from the academic process of earning a medical qualification or degree. The latter process certifies that the individual has the required knowledge and skills to practise medicine. The former process, professional socialization, should result in an individual who can use those knowledge and skills responsibly and with sensitivity to the needs of patients, communities and self.

WHAT IS PROFESSIONAL SOCIALIZATION?

Professional socialization is the acquisition or development of values and behaviour patterns which enable the individual to fulfill the role which society expects of members of that profession.

The ideal outcome of the socialization process is a self-image which permits feelings of personal adequacy and satisfaction in the performance of the expected role.

Socialization should not result in the production of stereotypic doctors stamped from the same mould. That is indoctrination. The major difference between indoctrination and socialization is the extent to which the characteristics of individuals are permitted to influence the outcome. Socialization is a specialized social interaction in which students and the people with whom they come in contact develop expectations of themselves and each other in the medical context and respond to each other with those expectations in mind. Eventually, responses develop into patterns of behaviour and ways of perceiving situations which accord with society's expectations of the doctor's role.

The important aspect of this explanation of socialization is that students themselves have an active part in the process. Students are not blank pages waiting to be imprinted with a professional image. Students bring their personalities, dispositions and past experiences to the interaction, and these individual characteristics influence students' interpretations of, and responses to the situation.

HOW DOES SOCIALIZATION OCCUR?

Potential socializing influences are found mainly in students' interactions with patients, institutions, teachers and fellow students.

The process is complex because it involves 'the exposure of young recruits to a great variety of messages delivered by many agents with little necessary coherence or congruence among them' (Shuval & Adler, 1980). Socialization is further complicated by the fact that only some of those messages are consciously or explicitly delivered.

A large proportion of the messages students receive is carried in the 'hidden curriculum', those messages, both verbal and nonverbal, conveyed by doctors, patients, nurses and institutions which run parallel to, and may even conflict with, the formal explicit curriculum.

The student–patient interaction is central to the future capacity of the student to function as a competent medical practitioner. It is critical to the development of self-image and skills in professional judgment. As a result of contact with patients the student learns to balance the roles of student and doctor, and to move from one to the other as appropriate. In one study of socialization (Huntington 1957) students whose patients in primary care attachments treated them as doctors, and who felt that they handled their patients' problems well, showed a greater tendency to develop an image of themselves as doctors rather than students, even in the earlier years of their medical course.

Interactions with teachers are important socializing influences. Interactions with faculty members, exchange of experiences and ideas, and opportunities to observe and evaluate teachers' behaviour no doubt influence the development of medical students' images of the profession and themselves as members of it. However, no direct association can be inferred between faculty influence and student behaviour. Coker et al (1960) report that American students' values don't match those of the faculty members they say they have been influenced by. A major study of Israeli medical students (Shuval & Adler, 1980) found that, at the end of medical school, students and teachers differ on a substantial number of the values and norms observed, and that the pattern depended not only on the qualities of the models themselves or the structure of the situation but on the nature of the norms and values studied. Bonito & Levine (1975) also found that the 'factors that influence the development of medical student attitudes appear to vary from one area of concern to another'.

On the other hand, Harris (1974) found a shared set of professional attitudes among clinical teachers in different British medical schools and also a major degree of modeling of students' attitudes on those of their clinical teachers, (although he also noted that students entering medical school already have attitudes which are more similar to the clinical teachers than do students entering other professions). Feather (1981) has also commented on the tendency for Australian medical students to self-select a profession whose members hold values and attitudes consonant with their own.

Such research into the influence of teachers as role models suggests that variability, even contradiction, is the rule rather than the exception in the models and the messages which medical students experience.

Interaction among students themselves is a major socializing influence which mediates and stabilizes students' responses amidst this variability

Interaction among medical students results in the development of a student culture (Becker & Geer, 1958) which allows students to develop solutions to the problems of learning to be doctors. The student culture provides a perspective from which students can accommodate to the requirements of medical school, while directing their efforts along routes other than those suggested by the faculty if that appears to be the most expedient option. Students actively select options for behaviour by balancing personal goals and needs with faculty and institutional requirements. In this way faculty influence is limited and modified by the student culture. For example, students may decide to maintain a student role and to accord priority to book learning and formal teaching sessions rather than to informal ward attachments and clinical experience. This is likely to occur when faculty timetable formal teaching sessions alongside clinical attachments and emphasize the cognitive aspects of medical experience in the examinations. Immediate concerns over passing examinations assume priority over eventual concerns with gaining clinical experience; and the student culture becomes one which supports postponement of role taking and encourages theoretical learning.

The interactive quality of socialization is evident in this example. Students respond to faculty expectations which seem to be most pressing vis-à-vis their need to pass exams. As a result students accord priority to formal teaching sessions and examinable material. In turn, faculty complain frequently that all that students want to know is how to pass examinations. The process is circular and self-perpetuating.

Students' attitudes and behaviour are flexible and responsive to the immediate needs of their environment. This is the social value of student culture. It provides sufficient support to allow students to bend faculty requirements to their own needs and also to adapt their own responses to experiences they encounter.

WHAT ARE THE IMPLICATIONS FOR THE MEDICAL TEACHER?

Foremost is the implication that the medical teacher must become aware of the subtleties of interaction which influence the socialization process.

Socialization is a two-way process with students possessing the capacity to influence teachers' behaviour as well as to be influenced by it. Teachers may find it necessary, for example, to resist the pressure to provide mini-lectures in ward rounds or to provide answers to problem-solving group sessions. Expectations of this nature held by students are usually the result of past or current educational experiences in which teachers are viewed as 'givers' of learning and students as passive recipients. These habits may be hard to break.

The interactive nature of socialization can be used to help students become more effective and mature doctors by encouraging the development of a colleague relationship between teachers and students. The aim of such colleagual relationships is to share knowledge and experiences and to develop progressively mutual respect and responsibility. Although teachers are unquestionably more clinically experienced, students may have more to contribute in some areas than teachers. Mutuality is therefore possible as well as desirable. For example, because they are only part way along the career path students may have a better understanding of the lay person's beliefs about illnesses. Teachers can seek students' input to clinical decisions at any level which is appropriate to their stage of professional development.

The other major implication is that teachers must re-examine their understanding of their function as role models. In relation to the transformation of students into colleagues, many teachers see their responsibility as being merely to provide a good example for students to follow. However, expecting students to passively absorb and incorporate professional values and behaviour patterns is no more appropriate than expecting them to passively absorb the contents of a medical textbook. Students must be active in experiencing, discussing and evaluating professional behaviour in order to extract personal meaning which can be incorporated into their own professional self-image.

Observing a good role model may help students to understand what is expected of them, but it may not help them to integrate the forces influencing their own behaviour to produce the desired result. Some students manage to do so but many experience some form of strain in accommodating to their professional roles. There is evidence (Ellard, 1974, Schwartz et al, 1978) that doctors and students who experience professional dissatisfaction and who consider suicide or seek psychiatric assistance are often in conflict over the doctor's role vis-a-vis patients and have not developed a satisfactory professional self-image.

The achievement of technical competence does not ensure the ability to perform as a competent professional. Medical teaching often fails to recognize those parts of professional competence which are not encompassed by technical and cognitive mastery of medical tasks (Engel, 1977, Silverman et al, 1983).

Major studies of socialization (Becker et al, 1961, Bloom, 1973, Shuval, 1980) have noted that technical competence rather than psychosocial and personal adjustment to the professional role is the objective of medical education. Medical students '. . . value the chance to do procedures for the symbolic boost given to their self-esteem' (Becker et al, 1961). The symbolic boost derives from the students' observation that responsibility for, and experience with, procedures reflects the dominant values operating in a teaching hospital. Similarly, Bloom (1973) in his study of a US medical school observed that the school chose to concentrate on the technical and concrete 'training' of students rather than fostering their personal growth, self-conception and psychosocial resources. He attributed this to the fact that faculty can agree on criteria of technical competence but not on the attitudinal dimension, creating a 'value-vacuum' which causes students to 'play it safe'. Students tend to 'play safe' because to admit difficulties is tantamount to confessing one can't 'make the grade' (Capaldini & Bickel, 1982). Medical schools encourage denial of problems of adjustment to the professional role and students learn to perpetuate self-protective attitudes in their dealings with patients under the guise of therapeutic distance (Virshup, 1981). Thinking and feeling are separated in the curriculum, and the scientific and technological environment of the medical school inhibits expression of feelings and the examination of those aspects of medical experience which complement technical competence. In such a context 'the teacher must remain unaware of what is happening to the student. The defences freeze into rituals in which teacher and learner alike shut out the human voices of the patient and the doctor in distress' (Marinker, 1974). Teachers can, if they are aware of the need, remedy some of these deficiencies of traditional medical curricula.

WHAT CAN THE TEACHER DO?

Teachers can provide consistent opportunities for taking the doctor's role in a supportive environment with respected senior colleagues who are sensitive to the processes of socialization and who could provide insightful, constructive feedback. Teachers can assist professional development by making the hidden curriculum explicit; by revealing not only the cognitive aspects of clinical reasoning but the intuitive and affective aspects as well (see Chapter 14); by exploring the implications of alternative clinical actions not just from the clinical viewpoint but from the viewpoints of doctor, patient and society (see chapter 17) (Good & Good, 1980; Stein, 1984). Teachers can help students to develop a healthy perspective of professional responsibilities by exploring stressful situations and the variety of responses exhibited by other students and by experienced doctors (see Chapters 13 & 18 and Pfifferling, 1983). Teachers can, by broadening the repertoire of venues for clinical learning, also contribute to the students' experiences of the realities of medical practice in a variety of contexts (see Chapter 9) which do not provide the technical and psycho-social support services found in teaching hospitals.

In summary, medical teachers can recognize that becoming a doctor is a process of personal development which requires time and space for reflection on experience (see Chapter 10). Previous generations of students may have fared better in this respect than recent and forthcoming generations who are subject to increasing pressure of content and specialization in medical curricula. Reflection is a legitimate and necessary aspect of medical education but crowded curricula render it impossible. Curriculum planners and teachers must review the objectives and processes of medical education to ensure that opportunities for reflection and personal development re-emerge.

REFERENCES

Becker H, Geer B 1958 Student culture in medical school. Harvard Education Review 28: 70–80

Becker H S, Geer B, Hughes E C, Strauss A L 1961 Boys in white — student culture in medical school. University of Chicago Press, Chicago

Bloom S W 1973 Power and dissent in the medical school. The Free Press, New York

Bonito A J, Levine D M 1975 Effect of 'attitudinal content' on formation of professional attitudes in medical students. British Journal of Medical Education 9: 22–26

Capaldini L, Bickel J W 1982 Review of 'Coping in medical school' by B Virshup. Journal of Medical Education 57: 734–735

Coker R E, Back K W, Donnelly T G, Miller H 1960 Patterns of influence: medical school faculty members and the values and specialty interests of medical students. Journal of Medical Education 35: 518–527

Ellard J 1974 The disease of being a doctor. Medical Journal of Australian Sept 21 318–322

Engel G L 1977 The need for a new medical model: a challenge for biomedicine. Science 196: 129–136

Feather N T 1981 Values and attitudes of medical students at an Australian university. Journal of Medical Education 56: 818–830

Good B J, Delvecchio Good M J 1980 The meaning of symptoms: a cultural hermeneutic model for clinical practice. In: Eisenberg L, Kleinman A (eds) The relevance of social science for medicine. Reidel, Boston, Mass. pp 165–196

Harris C M 1974 Formation of professional attitudes in

medical students. British Journal of Medical Education 8: 241–245

Huntington M J 1957 The development of a professional self-image. In: Merton R K, Reader G G, Kendall P L (eds) The student physician. Harvard University Press, Cambridge, Mass.

Marinker M 1974 Medical education and human values. Journal of the Royal College of General Practitioners 24: 445–462

Pfifferling J H 1983 Is present medical education obsolete? Journal of Holistic Medicine 5: 74–81

Schwartz A H, Swartzhurg M, Lieb J, Slaby A E 1978 Medical school and the process of disillusionment. Medical Education 12: 182–185

Shuval J T 1980 Entering medicine: The dynamics of transition. Pergamon Press, Oxford

Shuval J T, Adler I 1980 The role of models in professional socialization. Social Science and Medicine 14A: 5–14

Silverman D, Gartrell N, Aronson M, Steer M, Edbril S 1983 In search of the biopsychosocial perspective: an experiment with beginning medical students. American Journal of Psychiatry 140: 1154–1159

Stein H F 1984 The ethnographic mode of teaching clinical behavioural science. In: Chrisman N J, Maretzki T W (eds) Clinically applied anthropology. Reidel, Boston, Mass.

Virshup B 1981 Coping in medical school. Health Sciences Consortium, Chapel Hill, North Carolina

Teaching interviewing skills

INTRODUCTION

Why teach interviewing skills to medical students?

Readers of this chapter are probably aware of the importance of teaching skills in interviewing. We know that virtually all doctors spend most of their time talking with patients but that, until recently, little if any instruction was given on the 'how to talk'.

Medical education is heavily biased toward content: learning facts and assembling patterns of information. The consequent neglect of, the 'how to elicit' rather than the 'what to elicit', has led to major interviewing deficiencies. Maguire & Rutter (1976) reported that over 50% of the medical students used and accepted jargon without probing the patient's understanding of terms like 'run down'; lacked precision such as in obtaining key dates or drug dosages; failed to pick up verbal leads; needlessly repeated topics already covered; failed to clarify inconsistencies or gaps in the history; assumed that there was only a single problem; or were unable to complete interviews in reasonable time. About a third or more of students asked no questions about personal issues and ignored all patient cues; asked questions inappropriately; or showed little or no interest in the patient.

If the widely held clinical aphorism that '90% of diagnosis is history' is true, can poor interviewing skills be improved? Goldberg et al (1980) demonstrated that poorly skilled family medicine trainees could improve after training in interviewing techniques. Skillful interviews result in better information, more accurate diagnosis, improved rapport and greater compliance with treatment.

When to teach interviewing skills?

There is no easy solution to the question of timing. In the early years of the medical course the medical student is most malleable but lacks maturity, has had insufficient clinical contact, and has few if any opportunities to practise skills. In later undergraduate years the student has had a fuller experience of life and of medicine, but bad habits may already be entrenched, and the demands for theoretical knowledge and good examination results loom larger as determinants of future career prospects. Passing exams seems more important than acquiring skills to become a good doctor.

After graduation and residency many doctors are very receptive to learning interview and inter-personal skills but most lack time or opportunity and those who do make a commitment often need it least.

So when should doctors learn how to interview? For qualified doctors, elective courses should be offered by post-graduate education centres or learned colleges.

Undergraduates need either a continuous program of supervised learning, or at least two periods of instruction in their course. The constraints of block teaching in the curriculum and competing school demands usually mean that the latter two-phase model is adopted. Whichever model is used the principles of what is taught are the same. The key to success is continued practice and supervision.

How to motivate students?

Interview theory is not intellectually demanding; and all important practice may be rejected by 'fact-hungry' students. Ironically, those most motivated are those least needy of training. Why do students drop out? Some see the practical side as non-examinable, are too threatened or embar-rassed by the interpersonal process, are too rigid to change, or are too culturally alienated.

The teacher can counter such problems in a number of ways. Small groups with participation by all members *after* observation of model inter-views by the teacher will help lessen embarrass-ment. Humour, fun and warm-up exercises can lessen anxiety. Motivation is improved by making the material more relevant. Relevance can be clinical, using examples or video recordings from different specialties of medicine and general prac-tice, or personal, so that the student learns more about him- or her-self. Students are more likely to model themselves on videotape recordings of interviews by local teachers whom they actually

know, rather than on those made by clinicians from other centres. It is better to make one's own tapes, or do live modelling, rather than using tape-recordings from elsewhere. An obvious way of increasing students' perceptions of relevance is to make interviewing examinable; my experience is that it improves attendance and effort without detracting from the session. The theory of inter-viewing can be tested in written papers; the prac-tice by observation of patient (real or simulated) interviews.

TECHNIQUES IN TEACHING INTERVIEWING SKILLS

Didactic teaching

Didactic presentations benefit from variation in the techniques of presentation. Students can hear a formal short (5–20 minutes) lecture, read hand-outs, watch a videotape of the lecturer talking, or integrate two or three of these methods of pres-entation. Learning can be reinforced by pairs of students summarizing for each other what was taught the previous week.

Videotape

What the, microscope did for bacteriology, the videotape recorder does for the interview. Video-tapes of teacher interviews provide models, and tapes of student interviews allow self appraisal and comments by supervisor and colleagues. Note that students may be particularly vulnerable to criti-cism, and gentle, constructive commentary is required.

The advantages of video-analysis include the facility to pause the tape and ask others what they would say next (not what would they ask *about* but what words they would actually use), and the facility to replay portions of the interview to emphasize certain points. Some students feel better if they can preview the tape alone or even re-do it if dissatisfied.

Videotape recording facilities must be adequate to allow for benefit from the technique. A clear picture of the faces of the interviewer and inter-viewee and distinct sound reproduction are the minimum requirements. While a technician and a number of cameras allow switching from person to person and a more professional tape, these are not essential. One fixed camera with a wide enough lens, good microphones and adequate instructions enable the student to record *and* interview.

Role plays

Medical students are generally shy to role play. Inhibitions are lessened if the teacher role plays as often as possible, or if a couple of extroverted student volunteers 'ham up' a terrible interview early in the course. At first it helps motivation if role plays are made into games, e.g. the interviewer must find out the patient's secret problem by good interviewing technique.

Role plays may be easier if students team up with those *least* familiar to them. Structuring the roles also helps; without a script students seem at a loss to act as patients. Give students protocols to read and then talk to 'patients' and 'doctors' separately to induct them into their roles. Leave students free to embellish the history, though seldom do they do this. It is easier if the patient role can be either sex (e.g. You are Mr(s) Brown, a 54 year old married school teacher worried about the effects of recently diagnosed diabetes. . . .) After the first couple of role plays students are more apt to involve themselves more deeply. It is important to *de-role* — allow the student to discuss any feelings engendered by the role. The 'patient' is instructed to de-role first, then the 'doctor', and finally the observer provides commentary. Students are encouraged to discuss *process*, the interviewing skills being taught, and not to concentrate on finding solutions to the patient's problems.

The size of the group

Smaller groups allow for closer, more intimate supervision. Ideally one supervisor for one (or two) groups of three to four student works best. Alternatives are for the teacher to train students to supervise each other. For example, a class of fifty can be taught the theory, and smaller supervised groups can then disperse preferably into separate rooms.

If no extra staff are available, students can separate into threesomes; interviewer, interviewee and observer. Observers should be instructed in what to observe; the more concrete the observations the easier, e.g. counting the number of open and closed questions, rating the tone of voice. Observers require pen and paper in order to capture the actual words. Students should be warned that the roles will be changed after each role play. Threesomes, once formed should be encouraged to remain together for subsequent weeks. The advantages are group loyalty, higher attendance and less time needed (to reform threesomes) in subsequent sessions.

COUNSELING VERSUS INTERVIEWING

Students should be reminded of the need to discriminate between interviewing and counselling or the establishment of the deepest rapport, merely sufficient rapport to get on with the business of doctoring.

Counseling requires practice and is important as it is at the heart of much of what the general practitioner does daily. Students are being educated to be general practitioners as far as possible, and they need to know the rudiments of supportive psychotherapy. These can be provided within an interviewing course, but can be developed only by repeated practice under supervision. Students can be encouraged to take on cases for supervised therapy during their allocation to community medicine, geriatrics or psychiatry.

GENERAL PRINCIPLES OF THE INTERVIEW

Setting goals and formulating hypotheses

Experienced clinicians decide on the purpose of the interview beforehand. If it is a diagnostic interview they formulate an hypothesis (provisional diagnosis) very soon (within minutes). The major part of the interview is directed at refuting or confirming the hypothesis, constructing alternative hypotheses (differential diagnoses), and eliciting information regarding prognosis or management.

Technique for learning to set goals and formulate hypotheses:

1. Didactic and general discussion — ask students how they decide on goals of an interview.

2. Initial hypothesis generation show several transcripts or videotapes of clinical interviews and each time ask students to write down their diagnostic hypotheses after progressively shorter periods of time: five minutes, then three minutes, then 90 seconds. It is interesting to do one example with the sound turned right down. Student formulations can be discussed in small groups and group findings presented to the larger class.

HOW DO I START AN INTERVIEW?

General remarks

It is helpful to provide some guidelines for students embarking on interviews, especially as they are at a disadvantage in that students must generally impose themselves on patients. Student interviews of patients are unlike most medical consultations; students need patients — patients do *not* need them. Students should wear identification, obtain permission from the doctor or nursing staff prior to seeing the patient, introduce themselves, state the purpose of their interview and, most importantly, ask the patient's permission before proceeding.

Touch

In Australia the Anglo-Saxon tradition of limited physical contact socially inhibits many students from touching patients. Yet touch can establish rapport, reassure and help diagnosis. Shaking hands with patients at the start of the interview (and often at the end) can be helpful. This welcomes the patient, establishes contact and permits assessment, e.g. tremor, perspiration and firmness of handshake.

This raises the whole issue of touching patients. Whom do we find it easy to comfort with a hand on the arm or around the shoulders? Usually the very young and the very old. With whom do we find it difficult? Usually sexually attractive patients. Society sanctions medical personnel touching patients' bodies, all over, even internally. Interestingly, many patients discuss private matters only once they are on the examination couch.

Techniques for learning to start an interview

Students can describe methods of starting interviews which they have observed. The issue of touch provides stimulus for a lively discussion. Students enjoy talking about this issue, describing their experiences and views on medical ethics, and recounting stories of doctors violating patients.

Another technique of introducing students to the importance of touch is having them experience it. This can be threatening but revealing. Ask students to pair off with someone they hardly know and then ask them to hold hands while silent for 60 seconds.

The setting

The setting is crucial to a good interview. Adequate privacy, good lighting, comfortable seats and unhurried time, while obvious, are often ignored. The seating is particularly important. A higher doctor's chair can reinforce the patient's feeling of being 'talked down to'. A desk between patient and doctor may add one barrier too many for the inhibited patient. The angle of chairs to each other has implications, viz.:

1. Confrontational: interviewer and patient directly facing each other.

2. Neutral: both interviewer and interviewee face a common neutral point but are able to face each other quite comfortably without any pressure to do so. It is easy to arrange chairs in this position across the corner of a desk.

3. Alliance: both interviewer and patient facing the (hostile) world 'out there'. This arrangement is useful with paranoid or angry patients.

Other points to consider in the setting are the prevention of interruptions, control of noises from outside the room and having the secretary hold telephone calls. Lighting should not be directed onto the patient in an interrogatory manner (*see* Figure 13.1).

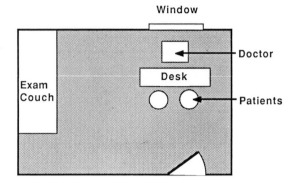

Example 1

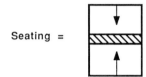

Seating =

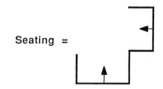

Fig. 13.1 'Is anything worrying you?'

Example 2

Seating =

Techniques for learning about the setting

1. General Discussion
   All students have been patients themselves or have watched consultations. Ask for their observations. Ask students to draw diagrams of the settings of consultation rooms that they have observed, for example see Figure 13.2.
2. Show videotapes of various doctors' consultations noting differences in styles.

Are there any rules?

It is useful to present some rules at the interview (*see* Table 13.1) or have the students generate a list of rules themselves.

Techniques for learning the rules: These can be presented didactically and reinforced by videotapes of naturalistic doctor-patient interviews. A more creative, and often hilarious technique is to

Fig. 13.2 Example diagrams of consulting room settings

Table 13.1 Do's and don'ts of the medical interview

DO
* Be courteous
  — introduce yourself;
  — arrange setting;
  — talk with (collaborate with) your patient
* Consider hypotheses — work out your priorities

* Use the patient's words
* Signal if you want to change the subject or interrupt

* Check to see if the patient has understood you
* Be understanding, show empathy and be helpful
* Use touch where appropriate
* Re-order information into format before presentation
* Be honest
* Assure confidentiality

* Warn a patient a few minutes before finishing
* Ask the patient if there is anything further to add or if there are any questions
* Summarise at end of interview; check that information is understood

DON'T
* Patronize your patient
  — assume patient knows who you are;
  — stand at opposite end of bed;
  — talk down to your patient
* Be rigidly judgmental or follow a form or a list of questions
* Use jargon
* Jump from topic to topic, or interrupt without signalling first
* Ask two or three questions at the same time
* Be too familar or too cold
* Be (physically) seductive (the friend -v- the professional)
* Present information verbatim to a colleague
* Ever lie or make promises you cannot keep
* Make an alliance with the patient that compromises your position on the team
* Terminate abruptly
* Mumble important instructions at the end of the interview as patient is leaving

ask two volunteers to role play an interview while breaking as many rules as they can.

Confidentiality

The guiding principles are that the patient's rights are paramount and that unless unable to do so, the patient should have the option to speak first and in private. This is particularly important when an accompanying parent or spouse may inhibit the patient from discussing certain problems. Sometimes it is necessary to ask the parent to leave, to reassure the adolescent of confidentiality, or to create privacy, e.g. in an examination room.

Occasionally students may be caught in conflicts of interest. One conflict may be between loyalties to the patient and the patient's clinician. A patient may ask the student not to tell the hospital team something which the student realizes has important bearing on management. Students can usually pre-empt this situation by making it plain they are part of a team and anything which is confided in the student can be done only on the understanding that it is available to the whole team.

A second type of conflict may occur between responsibilities to patient and relative. This can often be resolved by further discussion with the patient, although sometimes the right of confidentiality of the patient must over-rule the need for a spouse or parent to know. Finally, there may be a conflict between responsibilities to different

doctors e.g. referring general practitioner and hospital consultant, or between student and doctor. Such conflicts revolve around a request for a certain treatment or investigation or put in a different way, a conflict between doing what is believed to be best for the patient as against satisfying the other doctor.

WHERE AM I GOING? OR WHAT DO I DO NEXT?

After constructing the initial hypothesis the interviewer tries to find better hypotheses.

The best hypothesis is then chosen and the clinician considers prognosis and plans for management, and weighs up complicating factors. Subsequently the clinician will summarize relevant facts for the patient — see Finishing the Interview (p. 100).

Students should actually practise what to do next. The analogy of driving a car illustrates the point. The student has learnt how to start the car (start the interview), has reached the first stop on the route (goals and hypotheses), and is now planning the remainder of the route. Many natural pauses or junctions occur during the course of the interview e.g. after completion of the history of the present illness; and there are often several possible roads down which the interviewer can travel. Indeed there may not be *one* best route;

several will reach the final correct destination (diagnosis and management) and will visit the important spots (e.g. allergy to medication) on route.

Techniques for learning what to do next: Show videotapes of diagnostic interviews used in goal setting and hypothesis formulation. Now as well as generating initial hypotheses students, perhaps in groups of 3–6, should decide on goals for the next part of the interview and what they would say in order to reach these goals. This process can be repeated by interruptions during the interview until enthusiasm for this 'game' wanes. To increase enjoyment, the principles of games should apply — achievement, struggle and (perhaps) competitiveness, and cases should be challenging.

HOW DO I GET THERE?

Techniques in Interviewing — Part 1

Multilevel Interviews

Interviews are conducted at several levels simultaneously. The most obvious is the level of obtaining information for diagnosis and management. The second level is monitoring other (non-verbal) cues. At the third level the interviewer monitors the patient's feelings per se and the patient's feelings to the interviewer. When the interviewer is more experienced, attention should be turned to the fourth level of interviewing, the interviewer's own feelings. Fifthly, the interviewer monitors the *interview process* itself. Mostly interviews are overtly conducted at level one only although the clinician remains aware of the more complicated levels influencing the process of the interview.

An example of the multilevel process occurring in an interview is provided by a 31 year old woman with tenosynovitis who complained angrily about restrictions on her activities while she was wringing a mangled handkerchief in her sweating hands (non-verbal cue for anxiety — level 2). She had not been complying with the treatment regimen (level 3, anger and anxiety about her illness) thereby frustrating the doctor who became annoyed with the patient (level 4, interviewer's feelings of anger and frustration and perhaps

impotence). The interview was tense and turgid (level 5) until the interviewer commented: 'You seem angry about this tenosynovitis (level 3) and we're not making much headway with your treatment (Level 5)'.

Techniques for learning about levels:

(a). Didactic presentation of material by lecture, in person or on videotape, or by giving out written material.

(b). View videotapes of interviews and ask students to comment on different level of communication. It is interesting to use non-clinical interviews, e.g. news interviews, talk ('today') shows, soap operas.

(c). Ask students to interview patients in pairs around the wards so that one can observe and comment on the *process* of the interview (as well as the content).

(d). Videotapes of very brief role-plays of people showing a lot of affect can be used to stimulate students to formulate their responses.

Use of signals

Interviewers should let the other person know before changing topics or interrupting. This minimizes disruption and makes for a smoother interview. For example, 'Would you mind if we moved onto another area?'; or 'Sorry to interrupt but. . .'; or 'I know there's a lot more to say about your home life: perhaps we could return to that later if we have time'. People need signals — signals prevent accidents.

Techniques for learning to use signals: Demonstrate interview with patient or show a videotape of the teacher interviewing a difficult patient such as one who talks in circumstantial manner. The interviewer can interrupt or change topics frequently *after* signalling an intention to do so to the patient. The road driving metaphor can be extended here.

Use of language

Doctors should avoid the use of technical words or jargon; language should be as simple as possible and at the patient's level. There are some specific points about the discussion of psychological issues. It is best to use the patient's own words even if the patient uses an expletive to describe a feeling. Interviewers should be particularly acute to the patient's use of swear words as they usually signal issues of deeper emotional importance. Thus if the patient complains of 'feeling uptight' or feeling 'pissed off', then paraphrases by the doctor such as 'feeling anxious' or 'feeling angry' lose impact. Doctor and patient build a common vocabulary which is then shared in future sessions.

Techniques for learning about language: (1) Didactic and discussion; (2) Video clips of role-played interviews to demonstrate points.

INTERVIEWING TECHNIQUES — SPECIFICS

An effective way to teach the specifics of interviewing techniques is the course in micro-counseling skills developed by Ivey and Authier (1978). This breaks up interviewing into single skills which can be taught individually and then amalgamated. Ivey and Authier recommend the use of several workshops each focusing on one of the following skills:

1. Attending behaviours

(*a*). *Eye contact:* provides diagnostic information, helps establish rapport and demonstrates the interviewer's involvement. Breaks in eye contact, by either interviewer or patient, may indicate embarrassment or difficulty with a particular topic.

(*b*). *Body posture:* non-verbal communication is a two way process and the patient is very aware of the doctor's body posture which should indicate attentiveness, usually by a slight forward lean. The interviewer should remain relaxed and not look unnatural, nor should the interviewer stare at the patient.

(*c*). *Verbal following:* the interviewer can convey to the patient his or her interest, by use of the patient's own words as much as possible, repetition of the last few words of what has been said, and avoidance of interruptions or changes in topic.

2. Use of questions

(*a*). *Open questions* or exploratory interventions are those that begin with 'How . . .?', 'What . . .?', or 'Tell me about . . . .'. They encourage the patient to be open and do not make any presuppositions about the response.

(*b*). *Closed questions* can be answered by a 'yes' or 'no', structure answers, impose the interviewer's framework on the response, and make demands on the interviewer to supply further questions.

3. Minimal encourages
are small indicators of interest to the patient. These can be in the form of brief utterances: 'Oh?', 'So?', 'Then?', 'Hmm', 'Uh-huh'; repetition of the last few words of what has just been said; simple statements such as 'Tell me more'; or, silence which is not too prolonged so that it becomes uncomfortable.

4. Paraphrases
are useful in clarifying points, especially dilemmas, and checking the accuracy of what has been heard. Paraphrases put into other words the essence of what the patient has said: 'Basically you are saying that . . . .' or 'It sounds like you cannot decide between . . . .'.

5. Summarizations
highlight themes from one or several sessions. They help the patient put thoughts and feelings in order and move the patient from exploration to action, and they enable the doctor to correct distortions in his or her perceptions. Summarizations are useful at the end of discussion of a topic or consultation, as a way of bringing a confused or rambling patient to order and at the beginning of a counseling session as a way of recalling previous important issues.

6. Reflections of feeling
mean labelling the patient's emotions and putting them into a context. When feelings are subtle or the doctor is unsure of the accuracy of the label it is preferable to soften the reflections with a stem such as 'You seem to be upset when talking about your son'. It is best to reflect feelings expressed in the interview ('here and now'). It is crucial to note non-verbal communications of feelings and mixed or 'double messages'. These are contradictory communications often with the patient saying one thing, e.g. 'I'm not worried', but non-verbally indicating another, e.g. hand wringing.

Techniques for developing specific interviewing skills:

1. Didactic presentation using mixture of methods as outlined earlier.

2. After the first session ask students to summarize material from previous session for one another. Arrange students in pairs and ask that they allocate labels A and B to themselves, then ask A to present material to B; and next time reverse the order.

3. Demonstrations of skills are vital. The more varied the methods of demonstration the better, viz:

   (a). live real patient interviews by teacher;

   (b). live simulated patient interviews by teacher or student;

   (c). videotape real patient interviews made by a teacher or student in a studio or of a clinician in real life;

   (d). videotape simulated patient interview by teacher or student in studio;

   (e). tape of television interview from news or talk show;

   (f). any other good idea.

4. Demonstrations of how *not* to use certain skills can be provided by:

   (a). analysis of tapes of real life clinical interviews;

   (b). students 'hamming it up' in front of the group;

   (c). videotapes of the teacher or an interview exaggerating bad interviewing skills.

Such caricatures of bad interviewing skills forcefully bring the information to the student and are a lot of fun.

5. Warm up exercises help before role plays (see below). Try to break up set groupings by asking students to pair with someone they know *least* well. Very many warm up exercises are available (Pfeiffer & Jones, 1974). For example, here are some exercises to demonstrate the importance of eye contact.

First, ask pairs of students to stare at each other without talking for a full minute. A second exercise is to ask student B to think of a happy, sad, angry or frightening incident. Then ask student A, by looking at student B's eyes and without talking to ascertain about which of the four categories of incident student B is thinking.

A third exercise is to ask the pairs of students to sit back to back as close as possible without talking. Now ask student A to tell B a story for two full minutes, e.g. an incident from the weekend, without B giving ANY response. Discuss the students' feelings after each exercise.

6. Classroom practice of interview skills. Role plays are difficult for many at first. Arrange students in threesomes and ask them to call themselves, A, B and C. In the first role play A is patient, B is the doctor and C the observer. Next time, B is the patient, C the doctor and A the observer. The roles change each time. Students learn much that extends beyond interviewing skills from role-playing patients. As mentioned earlier, scripts or protocols for the role play are very helpful. The teacher(s) can circulate among the groups of students and assist the observers who need pen, paper and instructions on what to observe. Allow sufficient time, about 10–20 minutes, depending on the situation, for each role play; about 10–15 minutes for de-roling and small group discussion; and about 10–15 minutes for large group or whole classroom discussion. Role plays should be clinically based and present a challenge.

7. Follow-up exercises — written

Vignettes of interviews can be presented as tapes or transcripts and students asked to write down possible responses, what they would actually say, and label the response as a summarization or paraphrase, open question, minimal encouragement, reflection or feeling. Written responses can then be discussed by students in pairs or in small groups.

Example: Nurse to intern (about patient with leukemia): 'I really get hassled by Mrs Smithers and I just don't know how to handle her. I don't know if it's her or me. Also, she is getting worse and worse. Nothing works in her treatment. I feel terrible that I can't get on better with her, Sister James will probably say something too'.

Response 1:

_____

_____

_____ Type: _____

Response 2:

_____

_____

_____ Type: _____

Response 3:

_____

_____

_____ Type: _____

Response 4:

_____

_____

_____ Type: _____

8. Follow-up exercises — in vivo.

Ask students to practise the skills learnt after each training session while seeing patients. This can be monitored by a colleague or better still, by making an audiotape recording. Patients almost always give permission for interviews to be taped especially if they are informed that the tapes are anonymous and confidential, that they are for the student to develop his or her interviewing skills, and that the tapes will be erased next week (or whenever it will be that they are reviewed). Tapes can be reviewed by the student alone or in small groups.

Where possible, students can use videotapes; these provide much better feedback than audiotapes but are often impractical or too difficult to organize for daily use. If available, allocate special studio times for students to interview patients, and for teachers to review tapes.

9. Empathy and sensitivity training

Students can improve their ability to understand their patients' feelings by training with 'stimulus videotapes'. These videotapes can be bought or borrowed (e.g. Kagan, 1975) or can be prepared oneself using actors or others. Actors portray feelings such as anger or sadness, often in complicated life situations; students are asked to identify the feelings and to say how they would respond. Controversial issues and subtle feelings usually provoke a good discussion; for example, a woman with a breast lump denying the effects of a planned mastectomy and being seductive to the doctor to collude with the denial.

COMMON PROBLEMS IN INTERVIEWING

How do I ask possibly embarrassing questions?

Sometimes questions are more embarrassing to the interviewer than they are to the patient. Patients may be sensitive to questions about sexual preferences and practices, alcohol intake, illicit use of drugs, or the presence of psychotic phenomena such as hallucinations; but some students, particularly those who are immature or from different cultures, may find such topics even more difficult. These inhibited students may completely omit particularly sensitive questions, or ask about them in such an inadequate way that it is unlikely they will receive an accurate response.

Time and staff limitations usually preclude deep examination of such issues. One can, however, usually make students aware of how their inhibitions may reduce or distort the information they elicit, encourage them to discuss these issues (in small groups), and introduce them to some useful techniques. The principles of techniques are:-

1. *Universalization*: Give the patient permission to have an undesirable symptom or behaviour by pointing out it is acceptable or even common; e.g. 'most mothers have negative feelings to their children at some time but feel guilty. I wonder if you have ever felt like that? e.g. 'People often have strange experiences when their nerves are bad, like hearing voices or seeing things. Have you noticed anything like that?'

2. *Flanking*: Approach sensitive topics obliquely by asking about related safe topics first. The interviewer then proceeds to the sensitive topic and then, if appropriate, returns to another safe topic, e.g. menarche-menses-sexual intercourse; cigarettes-alcohol-marijuana-other drugs-medications.

3. *Creeping*: Approach the sensitive issue by degrees, e.g. fed up with everything — no point to life — not worth living — thoughts of doing away with yourself — plans for suicide.

Techniques for learning to ask:

(a). Didactic. These interviewing strategies are straightforward, easily integrated and require little practice.

(b). Videotapes to illustrate these stragies are helpful and should take only about 2 or 3 minutes each.

Difficult patients

Students can be taught strategies for dealing with difftcult patients:

(a). Rambling, circumstantial patient: directed interview; closed questions; permission at outset for frequent interruptions; frequent summarizations.

(b). Threatening, aggressive patient: deflect anger; ally oneself with patient and alliance position if seated; do not hem patient in; calm voice; reflect feeling of anger.

(c). Violent, berserk patient: prevention — re-channel anger before it becomes explosive; call for help, plenty ofmanpower — police if necessary; a show of force can be reassuring to a person terrified of his own lack of control; not too close — do not violate patient's territory; interviewer closer to exit than patient; calm, comforting voice; sedative chemicals, seclusion room, restraints may be needed.

(d). Malingerer: confrontation usually ineffective; diagnosis by inconsistencies in history and examination.

(e). Seductive patient: deal with issue underlying seductiveness; what does patient really want; be aware; doctor's fantasy or needs for omnipotence.

(f). Mute non-comatose patient: non-verbal communication is necessary (hold hands); do not talk *about* mute patient in his or her presence; patient sometimes can respond by nods or eyelid movements to closed questions.

(g). Psychotic or thought disordered patient: closed questions; directed interview; simple short sentences; concrete rather than abstract questions; avoid colluding with patients about delusions or hallucinations (neither deny nor agree, if possible).

(h). Organic brain impairment: as for (g); talk more slowly; give patient plenty of time to respond.

(i). Migrant: use interpreter; look at patient not at interpreter when talking; do not talk loudly.

(j). Elderly: if necessary ensure hearing aid or spectacles are available; talk more slowly; wait for replies; allow more time; sit face to face with patient; do not talk loudly; do not patronize; touch can be reassuring.

(k). Children: stay at same level as child with language and physically — do not sit at a higher level; distraction or mutual task while talking can be helpful.

(l). Doctor as patient/the very important patient (VIP): danger of interviewer not asking certain questions or assuming the VIP will volunteer essential information; danger of having strong, positive or negative feelings; often unconsciously towards the VIP; danger of managing VIP differently.

(m). Own family: conscious and unconscious biases preclude the interviewer properly assessing family members as patients.

Techniques for learning to interview difficult patients:

(i). Didactic and discussion. Students usually have many examples of difficult patients which they enjoy discussing.

(ii). If students have insufficient clinical experience have live or videotape demonstrations of good interviewing techniques on which they can model themselves as well as of bad interviewing techniques for students to criticize, e.g. doctor at end of bed shouting at elderly patient.

HOW DO I FINISH THE INTERVIEW?

Doctors terminate interviews in many ways: writing a prescription, arranging follow-up, making a referral, pressing the buzzer for the next patient, abruptly standing up, or saying goodbye. Few ask the patient for permission to finish — 'Is there anything else?', 'Shall we stop there?'. Seeking permission to finish pre-empts the situation where a patient who has a 'shopping list' of items for consultation, leaves the most sensitive item until last, just as the patient is at the door and just as the now frustrated doctor is preparing himself or herself for the next patient.

Much of what is said in the interview is forgotten by the patient by the time they leave the consultation room. Summarization is important at the end of the interview particularly with respect to instructions for treatment which are best written out for the patient (Ley 1977).

Techniques for learning to finish:

(i) Didactic and discussion. Students can recount their observations of termination of interviews.

(ii). Students can be given research assignments whereby they are to observe as many interviews as they can and count the different styles of termination they observe. This exercise can also be done for introductions or other aspects of the interview, e.g. how many times the interviewer touches the patient other than during the examination.

(iii). Demonstration of terminations by teacher, role-plays or videotapes.

(iv). Viewing of naturalistic interviews. Prepare a composite videotape of the ends of several clinical interviews from real life settings.

WHAT DO I DO WITH THE INFORMATION?

Students are routinely taught how to present case material during their clinical work and this aspect needs little attention, viz: identifying data, referral, presenting symptoms, history of the present illness, symptoms review, past history, family history, personal and social history, examination, formulation, diagnosis and management.

FEEDBACK

Interviewing courses evolve with the students and teachers; no teaching program is set in stone. Students can be encouraged to provide feedback on the course by having written evaluations throughout the course preferably, or at the end. Group discussion can be a lively way to obtain comment. It is best to warn students before the last session that time will be spent asking them for comments.

BIBLIOGRAPHY

Barrand J 1982 'Teaching Interviewing Skills' in Cox K R and Ewan C E (eds) The Medical Teacher Churchill Livingstone, Edinburgh.

Fine V K, Therrien M E 1977 Empathy in the Doctor-Patient Relationship; skills training for medical students. Journal of Medical Education 52: 752–757

Goldberg D P Stebble J J Smith C E, Spivey L 1980 Training family doctors to recognize psychiatric illness with increased accuracy Lancet,2: 521–526.

Ivey A E, Gluckstern Norma B 1977 Basic Attending Skills: An Introduction to Microcounseling and Helping. Leader Manual Second Revised Edition. Microtraining Associates Inc., Box 641, North Amherst, Massachusetts, 01059.

Ivey A E, Authier J 1978 Microcounseling. Innovations in Interviewing, Counseling, Psychotherapy and Psycho-education. Second edition. Charles C Thomas, Springfield, Illinois.

Kagan N 1975 Interpersonal Process Recall. Instructor's Handbook. Michigan State University, Ch 2 pp 20–81, Ch 3, pp 82–108

Korsch B M, Negrette V F 1972 Doctor-patient communication. Scientific American, August, pp 66–73.

Ley P 1977 'Communicating with the Patient' in John C Coleman (editor) Introductory Psychology. London: Routledge and Keenon, pp 321–343.

Ley P 1977 'Psychological Research on Doctor-Patient Communication' in S. J. Rachman (Editor) Advances in Medical Psychology. Oxford: Pergamon Press.

Magarey C J Whaite E A, Pigott B 1976 An academic course in Human Communication for first year Medical Students. Australian Family Physician 5: 976–980.

Maguire G P, Rutter D P 1976 History taking for Medical Students; 1- Deficiencies in Performance. Lancet 2: 556–558.

Pfeiffer J W and Jones J E 1974 (eds) A Handbook of Structured Experiences for Human Relations Traning, Vols, I–IV. University Associates Publishers Inc. San Diego.

How to teach clinical reasoning

Preview

What is clinical reasoning?
What is the nature of the clinical reasoning task?
Steps in the clinical process
Strategies for clinical reasoning
Learning diagnostic strategies

WHAT IS CLINICAL REASONING?

Clinical teachers have always spent considerable time helping students to search for the most useful evidence, to interpret what they have turned up, and to amalgamate the evidence into a diagnosis and management plan. Such teaching has been strongly empirical, distilling the lessons from experience, often expressing them as anecdotes and clinical impressions.

The past decade or so has seen the expansion of research into the processes of clinical reasoning, and the development and testing of optimal strategies for exploration and decision making.

The state of knowledge in these areas is still minimal. Most studies are descriptive, and hypotheses about the clinical process are tentative. Descriptions of what doctors actually do (even experienced and respected doctors) may not be picturing the ideal. Even if we understood the process, it is not yet clear whether it is teachable in the sense that knowing the concepts improves practice. Nevertheless it seems worth teaching students strategies of 'how to look' as well as 'what to look for', particularly if the empirical experience of clinicians is able thereby to be translated into lessons about how to tackle the clinical process.

WHAT IS THE NATURE OF THE CLINICAL REASONING TASK?

The student's task is not simple.

First, the problem to be managed is not a given, but must be sorted out from within the patient's concerns. The patient's often ill-defined presenting problem has been termed 'open' or 'undifferentiated'; the doctor's task is to narrow the focus to a 'closed' or 'defined' problem statement, such as 'A 28 year old man presenting with purulent urethral discharge for one day.' Indeed, the facets of the problem to be dealt with are selected or 'chosen' by the doctor who is seeking only the 'medical' problem suggested by the patient's complaints. The doctor is deciding which problems can be 'accepted' as within the doctor's responsibility and which cannot.

Second, the data available to solve the problem may be few in number, low in specificity, unreliable and inconstant. Or the data may be hidden, and revealed only by special investigations (or even not until the patient has died).

Third, the illness may be early, or mild, or recovering, so that the clinical picture may be only faintly delineated.

Fourth, working from effects back to causes is a focusing task (like the game of Twenty Questions in which a limited number of questions is allowed to find out, say, someone's job) without a set of rules, but with a set of possible strategies available to heighten efficiency.

Fifth, the end point of the diagnostic task is a name; that is, the task is one of classification, of assigning the case to a category. Diagnostic classifications, however, have no category rules, no agreed sets of necessary and sufficient criteria, no taxonomy, and not necessarily fixed names.*

Sixth, the task is not only naming the illness, but also establishing the extent, severity, effects, and even the cause; further, other co-existing nasty diseases must be excluded. In hospital settings, the 'diagnostic work-up' must be sufficiently extensive to protect the student from criticism; thoroughness protects the student/doctor more than the patient.

Unfortunately, these 'rules of the game' are never made explicit to the student. Quite the reverse. The student is socialized strongly into the importance of 'getting the diagnosis right'. The diagnosis is regarded as a form of 'truth', even though it represents only an agreement on the use of words about a pathological state and an illness.

The medical teacher must consider very carefully how 'honest' to be with the students about these matters. The line of frankness lies delicately close to cynicism when students see that senior clinicians clearly have not studied these underlying concepts of diagnostic reasoning, although they may have a shrewd, empirical skill with high accuracy. The medical teacher has the responsibility to help each new generation of students to construct an understanding of clinical process which goes beyond an empirical art.

STEPS IN THE CLINICAL PROCESS

Clinical interaction has three major phases
    sorting out what is the problem to be dealt with,
    working out a sufficient explanation of the problem, and
    deciding what to do about it.

These phases are not clear-cut, or necessarily sequential. The teaching of the fiirst phase is largely covered in Chapter 13 on interviewing skills. As was noted at the beginning of this present Chapter, however, the choice of which problem will accepted by the doctor reflects beliefs about what is the role of the doctor and what is not, about what the doctor is capable of handling, and feelings about what illnesses the doctor is comfortable in dealing with. Many doctors define psycho-social problems as outside their province. Many surgeons are unhappy managing patients with advancing cancer, and transfer them to the care of others.

The medical teacher can help students clarify these choices through group discussion of Who does what? within a particular illness, and then subsequently as an additional point within all such illnesses (since the answers to the questions raised determine who will manage the care of the patient). Asking who does what leads into many further questions about who currently does what, with what training, how adequately, at what cost in time, money and facilities. As specialization of practice increasingly differentiates care among a range of different health workers, students (and graduates) may need explicit training in team work with other health professionals.

The medical teacher can assign different students to find what the physiotherapist, social worker, or community health nurse would expect to do with such a patient, and how they see their roles integrated with the medical care.

This Chapter deals with the second phase of working out an explanation or diagnosis of the problem.

The third phase of deciding what to do about it is dealt with in Chapter 16.

STRATEGIES FOR CLINICAL REASONING

What clinicians actually do can be summarized under three principal cognitive strategies.

1. Pattern recognition (intuitively)

When a picture is strongly pathognomonic (the limp of a stroke, the stare of exophthalmos, the colour and shape of a melanoma, the slump of depression, the facies of Parkinsonism), the recognition from a pattern stored in 'clinical memory' is so immediate as to be called 'intuitive'.

---

* Some diagnoses are based on organs (eg. appendicitis) and pathological processes (eg. myocardial infarction, fistula in ano), some are symptoms (eg. pruritus ani), some describe manifestations (eg. diabetes mellitus) or behaviour (eg. depression), some indicate the cause (eg. infectious hepatitis, peptic ulcer), some define severity (eg. fulminant ulcerative colitis) or time relationships (eg. chronic relapsing pancreatitis), some are eponymous (eg. Paget's disease) and some retain their historical nomenclature (eg. stroke).

2. *Exploration of provisional diagnoses (deductively)*

When the features suggest a possible diagnosis, an 'if-then' deductive search begins for the other features expected to be present, the other characteristics of that diagnostic category. Exploration is guided by that tentative explanation or diagnostic hypothesis. When more than one hypothesis is plausible, search may alternately pursue the positive features of each. Or, the search may focus on the features which would discriminate between hypotheses.

3. *Systematic scanning (inductively)*

When the clues available are few and non-specific, each body system in turn is questioned and examined, hoping to turn up evidence which would suggest an explanation.

LEARNING DIAGNOSTIC STRATEGIES

Each of these approaches requires a different form of learning. None is better or worse than the others. None is right or wrong. All are useful and are used, but in different patients, and at different phases within the exploration of the patient's illness.

1. Pattern recognition

To re-cognize patterns one must have first experienced the pattern.

How does the teacher ensure such experience? The quantitative response is to arrange for clinical experience to begin as early as practicable. Since different examples of disease arrive ad hoc, it is necessary to provide the maximum time to increase the number of patients seen and felt, and the probability of covering the widest range.

The variety of patterns seen can, however, be limited by the nature of the teaching institution, if specialization brings into the hospitals only those on whom procedures are to be performed. To ensure the quality of experience, teachers must consider all available sources of patients eg. mental health institutions, oncology wards and clinics, physiotherapy departments for nerve injuries, pediatric orthopedic departments for congenital bone maladies, registers for 'interesting' examples.

Seeing the patients is necessary, but is not sufficient. Guidance in both seeing, examining and interpreting the relevant features is needed. The sensory experience must be clarified, explained and consolidated at a conceptual level by discussion and reflection, so that it can be fitted with other knowledge, categorized and filed. The clinical pattern is thus reinforced mentally and can be remembered through its category flle name (diagnosis) or 're-cognized' next time it is seen.

If students are unable to see sufficient real examples, the medical teacher must collect colour slides, photographs, films and videotapes of such patients to ensure visual comprehension. Word pictures in textbooks fall far short of pictures of real patients in the building of pattern recognition.

2. Diagnosis-directed search

The first step is to think of the possible diagnoses. Students and doctors (in common with other humans) jump to explanations of what they see; observably those provisional diagnoses are thought of within the first minute of the clinical encounter, and are based on very few data (Elstein, Shulman & Sprafka 1978).

The medical teacher's tasks are to help students to interpret the patient's initial clues in terms of the possible diagnoses they suggest, and to avoid closing prematurely on too limited a set of possibilities.

If the correct diagnosis is not thought of in the first minutes, it is unlikely to be thought of later (Barrows, Norman, Neufeld, Feightner, 1982). The teacher must, consequently, help the student build accurate associations between clinical features and diagnoses.

Each clinical feature has a measurable association with one or more diseases, countable as sensitivity and specificity (Cox 1984). Most clinicians have only scant understanding of what those terms mean, let alone how to incorporate them into clinical practice (Berwick et al, 1981).

Medical teachers will do their students a disservice if they fail to guide them in calculating the quantitative strength of a clinical feature or test result in relation to a diagnosis. Without doubt, such calculations will be central to clinical practice in a decade, as they already are in computer-assisted diagnosis. Students who do not comprehend how these associations have been counted cannot question the quality of the data set on which they are based, nor the appropriateness of the calculations.

The second step of looking for the features of the provisional diagnosis and its near competitors requires knowledge of what those features are likely to be. That knowledge comes from book learning initially, then from clinical experience. Knowing what is most likely to be found means knowing the sensitivity of the clinical features in that diagnosis (Cox, 1984).

The third step of interpreting the collected evidence takes considerable judgment, and consequently comprises a large component of bedside discussion among teacher and students. The various pieces of strong and weak evidence must be combined somehow to create a coherent picture. But how does the student know what is strong and what is weak evidence?

How can the teacher guide the student here? The teacher can invoke personal experience; but hopefully the student would then ask 'How many patients is that opinion based on? How alike were they? How like this patient?' and so on; in which case the teacher realizes that clinical impressions may not have sufficiently thorough substantiation. The teacher can invoke the 'literature', but medical writings turn out to have little quantitative information in a form usable in this clinical task of combining the multiple probabilities of different features, and no reference to the very extensive research on judgment in other fields.

The teacher has two functions. One is to help the student learn the empirical strength of each piece of evidence, since that is the 'state of the art' in clinical practice. The second is to show how to record and cumulate clinical data in their relation to disease, so that in the future clinical impressions will be tempered by more exact counting and locally accurate prevalence data. Personal computers have simplified this latter task.

Within this hypothetico-deductive strategy, the exploration can pursue all the possible features of the provisional diagnosis, and then those of its reasonable competitors, finally comparing those cumulated sets of features for best fit with the different diagnoses. Cumulation is an inefficient strategy, however, compared with discrimination, in which only those features are sought which will separate competing diagnoses. Discrimination is much more demanding intellectually than the relatively mindless collection of components of a text book list of possible features. Discrimination draws on quantitative estimation (eg. of likelihood ratios of how frequent a feature is in one diagnosis compared with another). The most discriminatory items can be grouped as the optimal sub-set worth collecting in such patients (Neutra, 1977).

These approaches guide the student into the most efficient strategy to answer the diagnostic questions. If the diagnostic strength of each clinical feature or test is known, the student/doctor can avoid investigations which may reassure the clinician but will not affect the management decision to be taken.

3. Systematic scanning

Traditional teaching of physical examination embraces a series of drills designed to check the most frequent evidence of abnormality of function or structure in each organ system. These drills will not be repeated here. What are touched on are some of the implications of the method, and what happens in practice. The teacher's responsibility is not to demand a single, favourite 'right' style, but to help the student understand when to use different styles appropriately.

Systematic scanning has an important place when systems are being checked before some intervention, such as surgery; or in a 'routine' screening examination; or in a search for clues when no clear picture is apparent; and also in keeping the mind open to possibilities in differential diagnosis to avoid premature closure on one chosen provisional diagnosis.

Thorough scanning of all body systems takes close to an hour. This much time is not usually available in clinical practice. If the few clues supplied by the patient seem vague or non-specific, the immediate decision is how much time to devote to this patient.

What is the teacher's task when thoroughness competes with available time? One task is to have the students choose where and when to apply a limited focus, and to justify that judgment. Discussion of this choice opens a very wide range of pragmatic and ethical questions.

A second task is to foster *efficiency* in rapid but *effective* scanning. Most of the drills for physical examination are schemes for revealing the most potent evidence. The drills suffer, however, from a desire to be all-embracing, and from a 'routine' approach to the whole system rather than an optimally efficient approach for rapid scanning. What are the 'best' questions? In what sequence? Here the teacher can have students analyze what information could be obtained from each question or clinical test in a drill. From the results they obtain, students can develop their own optimal sequence for general or focused scanning.

A third task lies within the phrasing used by students, particularly in questioning. Negatively phrased questions are the rule rather than the exception. 'You don't have any shortness of breath, do you?' is a statement, not a question. The patient must disagree with the student/doctor to reverse the statement. If the doctor doesn't expect shortness of breath, perhaps it shouldn't be there! Phrasing may be critical to obtaining evidence about which the patient feels guilty or embarrassed or fearful. 'Do you have any vaginal discharge?' may receive a (socially more acceptable) negative answer, where 'What colour vaginal discharge do you have?' produces a different response by having accepted the possibility.

A fourth task relates to ensuring routine hands-on examination. Surprisingly many students hang back in bedside teaching, not through fear of being questioned but through embarrassment at handling other people's bodies. I am not sure how to handle this in busy tutorials, save to ensure that all students rotate in opportunities for physical examination. Discussion within a safe group may allow these inhibitions to be surfaced, but I am uncertain whether that eliminates them or whether they carry through into practice later. I suspect the latter. Some progress in open discussion of these feelings was made within a study in which we admitted all our beginning clinical students to hospital as patients with different simulated maladies, with regular group discussion of the multitude of feelings evoked (Magarey et al 1975).

A corollary of routine physical examination is that embarrassing questions are often raised by the patient only when undressed. Avoiding touching the patient can result in the most significant information being missed.

The teacher's task is to help students find these lessons out for themselves, to share the learning experience of each student among the group, and to help them build some level of routine physical examination into all patient contacts.

The teacher's task is to help students to try different strategies in exploring clinical problems, to consider the strengths and limitations of each, to find which works best when, and to develop their own styles.

It is critical that the medical teacher does not confuse effectiveness and efficiency of exploratory strategies with 'right' and 'wrong' or correct and incorrect. Ability to reason and to solve problems does not grow from being forced to follow a particular sequence that a teacher prefers. The clinical process is too complex and too little studied to allow such dogmatism.

A wiser teaching strategy is to confess this poverty of theory and research, and to unleash the students' curiosity. By exploring the clinical processes they will use twenty times every day in practice, they are more likely to illuminate their (and our) understanding.

REFERENCES

Barrows H S, Norman G R, Neufeld V R, Feightner J W 1982 The clinical reasoning of randomly selected physicians in general medical practice. Clinical and Investigative Medicine 5: 49–55

Berwick D M, Fineberg H V, Weinstein M C 1981 When doctors meet numbers. American Journal Medicine 71: 991–998

Cox K 1984 How well does a test predict the diagnosis? Aust New Zealand Journal of Surgery 54: 379–383

Elstein A S, Shulman L D, Sprafka S A 1978 Medical

Problem Solving Cambridge, Harvard Univ. Press

Magarey C, Cox K, Hunt D, Jacobs P, Knight S, Piggott B, Pryor D, Salek A, Todd P and Williams J 1975 Learning by experience. A student residential workshop in hospital Medical Journal of Australia 2: 516–518.

Neutra R R 1977 Indications for the surgical treatment of suspected acute appendicitis; a cost-effectiveness approach 277–307 in Bunker J P, Barnes B A & Mosteller F(Eds) Costs, Risks and Benefits of Surgery Oxford Univ Press, New York

How to teach at the bedside

Preview

WHAT IS SPECIAL ABOUT CLINICAL TEACHING?

WHAT ARE YOUR GOALS IN BEDSIDE TEACHING?

HOW DO YOU TEACH STUDENTS TO SEE, FEEL, HEAR AND SMELL?

    Clear understanding of the task
    Supervised practice
    Direct experience
    Knowledge of results
    Persistence

WHAT IS SPECIAL ABOUT CLINICAL TEACHING?

Clinicians become so accustomed to their setting they frequently fail to recognize what is unique about clinical teaching, such as:

1. The setting

Physically, the ward has beds, patients, nurses, smells, busyness.
Psychologically, the task has responsibility plus fear of failure, threats within the disease and in the risks within interventions, emotional needs of patient and family (and less frequently acknowledged within students, nurses and doctors).
Socially, the staff have complex relationships with overlapping roles, functions and responsibilities. Authority and control are remarkably peripheral.

2. The clinical task

The patient care responsibility is real world activity before the student's eyes.
The task of observing, interpreting and deciding is intellectually demanding and exciting.
Whole patient management embraces clinical, psychological and social dimensions.

3. The student learning task

Voyeuristic observation of patient, teacher and setting is the first experience.
Apprentice participation in asking questions and feeling bodies follows.
Manual procedures and skills are then learned.
Learning takes place within small groups at the bedside or in a side-room.

4. The teaching task

Teaching is based on a series of individual patients chosen ad hoc from those available at the time.
Concepts, principles and decision rules are derived empirically.
Good practice is modelled by the teacher, including courtesy, communication skills and thoroughness.
Methods and evidence are demonstrated within the highly complex clinical task.
Student performance is supervised with progressive responsibility allowed.
What are the implications for teaching of all these dimensions? Given that the students are adults, and will be independent professionals in

a few years, what is the most effective relationship the teacher can create to facilitate learning? How would you like to have been treated when you were a clinical student?

WHAT ARE YOUR GOALS IN BEDSIDE TEACHING?

What is the clinical teacher to do at the bedside? What can be done at the bedside which cannot be done anywhere else? Therefore, how are you to spend this very precious time? What are you trying to achieve in clinical teaching?

Unfortunately these goals are not always made explicit, or carried through to detailed planning. Clinicians are so accustomed to the constraint that teaching is linked with practice and the availability of cases, that the teaching becomes *ad hoc* rather than systematic. Worse, the fascination with the questions which could be discussed about the malady exemplified by a particular patient can cause the bedside session to focus on management discussions, for which the presence of the patient is often seen as an embarrassment rather than the purpose. Even worse, the clinical teaching session can move away from the bedside to a teaching room wherein clinical learning can be disembodied, and treated as an exercise in interpretation of data.

Clinical practice requires the application of an immense fund of bio-medical knowledge to the illness of a person and the manifestations of a disease. Application requires the exercise of many skills. Those skills are the stuff of 'bedside' practice, whether in the hospital, the clinic, the office or the home.

Clinical practice requires the application of:

1. Communication skills, in building confidence and trust, in listening effectively, in eliciting and verifying the story of the illness, and in probing the understanding and expectations of the patient

2. Perceptual skills, in seeing, hearing, touching, and smelling the available evidence of disease

3. Reasoning skills, in interpreting findings, in generating and testing explanations, in choosing what further data to seek, and in integrating the available information into a coherent picture

4. Manual/procedural skills, in probing more deeply with tubes, needles, mirrors and 'scopes, and

5. Management skills, in planning a sequence of investigations, in optimizing the patient's care within the limits imposed by the disease and the social situation, in coordinating care among many colleagues, and in recording and referring with full information.

Communication skills are covered in Chapter 13, reasoning skills in Chapter 14, and some aspects of management skills in Chapter 16. This Chapter addresses only the learning of perceptual skills, the lessons for which appear to apply very largely to the learning of manual skills.

HOW DO YOU TEACH STUDENTS TO SEE, FEEL, HEAR AND SMELL?

We often confuse observation, perception and interpretation (Heath 1980). None of us has 'immaculate perception'. Our observations are always tempered by what we are looking for; we perceive what we are capable of comprehending, what we can 'understand'.

Karl Popper expressed this clearly in relation to scientific hypotheses.

'The belief that science proceeds from observation to theory is still so widely and so firmly held that my denial of it is often met with incredulity. But in fact the belief that we can start with pure observations alone, without anything in the nature of a theory, is absurd; . . . Twenty-five years ago I tried to bring home the same point to a group of physics students in Vienna by beginning a lecture with the following instructions: "Take pencil and paper: carefully observe, and write down what you have observed." They asked, of course, *what* I wanted them to observe. Clearly the instruction "Observe!" is absurd . . . Observation is always selective. It needs a chosen object, a definite task, an interest, a point of view, a problem. And its description presupposes a descriptive language, with property words; it presupposes similarity and classification, which in turn presuppose interests, points of view, and problems.' (Popper 1972).

Perception is a complex process involving the

sensory stimulus, its processing, and its interpretation as patterns or symbols or meanings. Since perception is central to health care, Hooker (1981) has developed a taxonomy of perceptual ability as a guide to teaching and testing the skill.

1. Clear understanding of the task

It is the teacher's responsibility to spell out exactly what the sign or discrimination comprises, and consequently, what the task is in perceiving it.

Students must know what they are looking for, and what devices help them look more efficiently. Remember, however, that telling students about a clinical finding cannot teach the perceptual concept before they have experienced it. Experience of the phenomenon is essential for learning the concept. Describing the phenomenon increases the efficiency of identification, but does not determine it (Furth 1961).

If the sign is jaundice, the student must understand that bile pigments circulate normally, that the task is to make a discrimination on intensity of those normal colours, and consequently a good white (not yellow) light on the normally white sclera is needed. If the feature is side to side movement of the middle finger as a test of interosseous muscle function, and thus of the ulnar nerve, the task requires isolation of that movement from other movements and control of proximal joints to eliminate trick movements. Consequently, the feature is observed with the whole hand flat and the fingers splayed. If the feature is the behaviour of a psychiatrically disturbed person, the task requires patient observation and sensitive listening to allow the features to be displayed, followed by discrimination of their intensity or pattern to distinguish them from normal behaviour.

Clinical teaching is full of devices to assist perception — adequate illumination and exposure of the area to be examined, tangential light to reveal pulsation, relaxation of the patient with soothing words and a sequence of taking the tension out of various muscle groups, relaxation of the doctor by sitting and by support of proximal joints before beginning palpation, use of specific sensory areas such as the dorsum of middle phalanges for testing temperature, or the volar proximal phalanges for palpating breast lumps.

When the task is clearly understood, the teacher can demonstrate how to elicit the feature most efficiently, and how to discriminate certain from uncertain evidence. Gagne & Gibson (1947) studied the training for recognition of aircraft; the best results were achieved by teaching distinctive features, such as a tapered wing or a short nose. It was not necessary to memorize a full description, but only the distinguishing features.

How we learn to detect the fine details of clinical abnormalities has been little studied. Nor is the study of human perception in general well advanced: '. . . much more thinking and research will be necessary before we can say how the perceptual process uses distinctive features for discrimination' (Gibson, 1969).

Studies on the perception process in radiology show a fast component, detecting abnormalities in one fixation of the eyes (Kundel & Nodine, 1975), and a slower component dependent on a systematic search which begins with the high yield areas and then moves peripherally (Christensen et al, 1981). While most abnormalities were detected by fast reading, slow systematic search was necessary for finding subtle or peripheral abnormalities.

Perception is an active exploration and search to extract information. Our subjective uncertainty is an important motive for such exploration (Berlyne, 1966). Clinicians actively seek positive information to fit an hypothesized diagnosis. Consequently, we also run the risk of finding what we're looking for when its not truly there, and of overlooking other evidence which doesn't fit what we're wanting to find. That our perception is influenced by what we expect is illustrated by the increasing number of false negative diagnoses when the observer is presented with an increasing number of normal radiographs, and by the increasing number of false positive diagnoses with an increasing number of different radiographic views (Potchen & Sierra, 1981).

Learning to discriminate requires discovery of what is different. During training the emphasis should be on distinctive features, especially by showing graded examples of contrasts between normal and abnormal. Enhancement of the features, as in a cartoon, brings out what is identifiable about an individual. It has been shown that accented drawings were more easily recognized than the real object, followed by photographs and then outline drawings (Gibson 1969).

We learn to *abstract* distinctive features out (e.g. in recognizing someone's voice, or their handwriting, or the first bars of a tune, or the origin of a wine) from which we categorize the observation.

We learn to *filter* out irrelevant noise, but respond to important stimuli (such as hearing one's name mentioned some distance away at a cocktail party). Teaching needs to identify the specific 'signals' of clinical significance within the 'noise' of non-specific observations.

Teaching perceptual skills, then, has two components. First, the student needs to know *what* to look for or to feel. While words can direct the student to a recognition of the sign, direct sensory experience is critical to 'know' the sign. Second, the student needs to know *how* to go about that perceptual task most effectively. The technique must isolate and preferably amplify the 'signal' while reducing the 'noise' from other sources which can mimic the signal.

Students can devise for themselves how to set about these observational tasks within the teaching of normal human anatomy. I believe strongly that no medical student should leave the Anatomy Department without an (examined) ability to examine living human anatomy in all its systems. I would add the ability to detect loss of continuity of nerves, bones, tendons and joints.

Some medical schools (e.g. Limburg University at Maastricht) have created a Skills Laboratory to ensure the proper learning and certification of a sequence of observational and measurement skills, rather than leaving them to chance (which in so many medical schools results in the skills not being firmly in place at the time of graduation!).

Given a clinical tutorial of two hours with eight students, not all students get to practise the skill on the patient. Given about ten tutorals to learn all physical signs, not all signs can be covered. Given that appropriate patients may be unavailable, some signs are never taught. Given that some clinical tutors use a side room and blackboard to *talk about* clinical signs, rather than ensuring direct experience on patients, many student learning opportunities are lost. Given that teaching the collection of clinical evidence competes with teaching the interpretation of the evidence collected, skills learning may be overlooked. It is salutary for each clinical tutor to have an independent recorder to note how much time is spent in various activities — tutor demonstrating, explaining and supervising, students examining, and tutor talking about pathology, diagnosis and management.

The limited possibilities for learning skills at the bedside underline the necessity for thorough understanding and skill learning *before* entering the wards.

These skills of physical examination are taught, and more or less remembered as drills or routines. Students are especially anxious to be 'trained' in these drills, and often reluctant to be 'educated' in comprehending any principles involved. If a 'right' way to do it is available, students can be most reluctant to work out a method of their own. Teachers similarly have 'right' ways which they teach and examine.

The questions for thoughtful medical teachers are: How do I know that this method is effective, if I cannot be sure exactly what the student has actually felt or heard? What is the anatomical/physiological/pathological basis for this drill? Is that basis valid? What are my assumptions? Can I test them? What different approaches are used? What is their basis? Can we, as a learning group or as a group of teachers or examiners, develop an agreed set of effective procedures? Can we record those procedures, e.g. on videotape or film, for agreement among ourselves, and for self-directed learning by the students?

2. Supervised practice

Two phases must be taught here. The former is the learning of the routine methods. The methods may be for feeling an organ (such as the liver or the dorsalis pedis artery), hearing sounds (e.g. of heart, lungs or gut), or testing function (e.g. of ankle reflexes or cranial nerves). The latter is the delineation of the abnormal feature and its characteristics (e.g. for an ulcer its site, size, shape, edge, floor, base, surrounding tissues and draining lymph nodes). A thorough and detailed description is a necessary component of the examination and the verification of its accuracy.

The students must begin to practise the skills for themselves under the teacher's guidance. Since the abnormal clinical features cannot be provided on demand, much practice of methods is on the normal (patient or fellow student).

The logistic difficulty in providing patients with abnormal signs has led to creation of 'simulations', such as models of breasts which contain silica gel and various lumps, or models of the female pelvis with various replaceable organs containing different swellings, or models of the optic fundus with different pictures, or recordings of heart sounds or breath sounds (Griffiths 1979). Simulations run the risk that the real feature appears to be simulated (i.e. the simulation has 'face validity') but that the subtle characteristics of feel or sound present in real life are not included or are different.

Supervision provides an essential feature for learning perceptual skills. The teacher/observer can advise students when they are right and when they are wrong, how to interpret the features they are perceiving, and what diagnostic labels to put on them, both for memory and for communicating them to others. In pelvic and rectal examinations the teacher does not know exactly what the student is feeling, except by the student's description. Trained simulated patients used for teaching pelvic examination can give students accurate feedback on their palpation of ovaries and uterus (Holzman, 1978).

3. Direct experience

No instruction, practice on normals or simulations can substitute for direct personal experience of the abnormality in the flesh. The range and variety of signs to be learned in clinical medicine are extremely large. Obtaining direct, personal experience of these signs needs years of exposure to clinical medicine. Such years of clinical exposure must begin early if the experiences are to be discussed with teachers.

Students recognize the need for extensive, personal experience in eliciting clinical features, but are inhibited by many personal uncertainties in approaching patients. An understanding teacher can lead insecure students to many experiences they might otherwise miss. Within a clinical teaching session the teacher may need to ensure that diffident students do actually feel the lump or hear the murmur.

Some teachers organize learning sessions in which up to twenty patients with abnormal physical signs are collected for an intensive experience for a larger group of students.

Despite these efforts by teachers, students are likely to have limited personal experience and incompletely developed skills if learning is restricted to scheduled formal teaching sessions. Since only three or four patients will be seen in a two-hour session, and a block of teaching may include only about ten sessions, the number of maladies seen falls far short of those the student should recognize. The teacher must help students to gain confidence in their capacity to search out cases for themselves, to visit the wards regularly, to use resident doctors and nurses as sources of information, to scan admission lists, and to seek other sources of patients (even within overseas elective studies).

4. Repetition

Skills are not acquired instantly, but require practice. The clinical features to be perceived are presented differently by each patient, and to varying degrees.

Observations from learning of perceptual skills under experimental conditions show that improvement in ability to detect differences and make fine discriminations increases rapidly with supervised experience, and the threshold of perception is lowered (Gibson 1969). The learning curve (the percentage correct or of progressively finer discriminations with increasing attempts) shows a sharp rise with an early plateau. The curve flattens after about ten attempts. If a gap in learning follows for, say, a month, then testing begins again, the skill resumes at the level to which it had been learned; that is, the perceptual skill is retained. The lessons for teachers are that students must tackle about ten examples before their skills are maximal, but that once properly learned, the skills are not forgotten.

Learning takes longer the more complex the activity. Recognizing an abnormality (such as inguinal hernia) takes a short number of repetitions, fine discrimination (such as direct from indirect hernia) more, and a complex skill like judging whether the rectal mucosa showed early ulcerative colitis considerably longer. The sequence can be compared with recognizing cars, distinguishing models from one another, and driving a car.

The teacher should be available through all phases.

5. Knowledge of results

Some learn accuracy quickly. Some seem to make the same mistakes all their life. Many stay in a haze of uncertainty, like students who 'think there is a possible, vague swelling'.

The observations under experimental conditions are not clear. Intuitively, it seems obvious that we can't improve without knowing if we're 'getting it right'. Research does not support this intuition about the effectiveness of feedback (McBurney & Collings, 1977). Teachers may wish to explore this under-studied field.

Humans are, however, capable of remarkable discrimination. Eskimos can distinguish eleven different varieties of snow. Wine judges pick the country, the area and the year. We can distinguish 160 colours. We can spot birds, 'planes and trains. We can spot diagnose a wide range of disease manifestations. We assume that we are unable to make these clinical distinctions accurately unless we can check whether our choices are correctly labelled.

To provide this feedback, a second person (usually the teacher) is necessary, or a system which provides information on the true state of affairs. If a teacher is not available, the student must be guided to seek another 'expert', such as the resident doctor or even a senior student. Perhaps as important as the feedback is the attitude of verifying one's findings with another observer.

6. Persistence

In clinical diagnosis, detection of faint evidence can be important. If the evidence is present, however slight, it can be used. If the capacity to discern that evidence has never been fine-tuned, no certainty exists whether slight evidence is present or not, and the diagnosis can be missed or unnecessarily delayed.

Further, the capacity for self-appraisal must be developed. Without a critic, habits can become sloppy, and standards fall. For independent professionals, the only available critic is oneself. Teachers have an important role in modelling self-critical behaviour, and in modelling tenacity at repeating observations on clinical features until it can be confidently stated that a sign is present or not, even if only of slight degree.

Teachers must also model tenacity of purpose in seeking features, even if the system places disincentives in the way. Busy clinics generate pressure for rapid overviews of patients. On one hand, the ability to detect abnormal features in a quick scan is highly valuable and efficient; but, on the other hand, time must often be taken to listen patiently and to examine meticulously, if clinical features are not to be overlooked. The teacher's example of persistence is seeking information while under external pressure to hurry is a valuable lesson for subsequent independent practice.

REFERENCES

Berlyne D E 1966 Curiosity and exploration. Science 153: 25–33
Christensen E E, Murray RC, Holland K, Reynolds J, Landay M J, Moore J C 1981 The effect of search time on perception. Radiology 138: 361–365
Furth H G 1961 The influence of language on the development of concept formation in deaf children. Journal of Abnormal Social Psychology 63: 86–389
Gagne R, Gibson J J 1947 Research on the recognition of aircraft in motion picture training and research. Army Air Force Aviation Psychology Program. U S Government Printing Office, Washington DC
Gibson E J 1969 Principles of perceptual learning and development. Prentice Hall, New Jersey, p 103
Griffiths D A 1979 Use of 3-D models in medical education. Medical Teacher 1(2): 76–81
Heath T 1980 Observation, perception and education. European Journal of Science Education Vol 2, 155–160
Holzman G B 1978 Pelvic examination instruction. Journal of Medical Education 53: 227–228

Hooker E Z 1981 The perceptual domain: a taxonomy for allied health educators. Journal of Allied Health 198–206, August.

Kundel H L & Nodine C F 1975 Interpreting chest radiographs without visual search. Radiology 116: 527–532

McBurney D and Collings V B 1977 Introduction to sensation perception. Prentice Hall Englewood Cliffs, New Jersey

Popper K R 1972 page 46 Conjectures & Refutations: the Growth of Scientific Knowledge, Routledge and Kegan Paul, 4th Ed London

Potchen E J and Sierra A E 1981 Value judgments in diagnostic radiology. Radiology 138: 501–504

How to teach clinical decision making

Preview

INTRODUCTION

WHY TEACH CLINICAL DECISION
MAKING?

WHEN TO TEACH CLINICAL DECISION
MAKING?

HOW TO TEACH CLINICAL DECISION
MAKING

Doctors discuss clinical decisions at all opportunities, and do their best to pass on to students a
series of working rules which will guide them on
what to do under different circumstances.
Teaching usually centres around what to do about
a particular disease in a particular patient; the
choices made in one case are used to illustrate how
to apply those general working rules to different
particular cases.

These working rules are, however, empirical
guidelines distilled from experience which is both
personal and passed down from previous
teacher/clinicians.

Clinical practice is currently entering a phase of
more searching analysis which requires substantially more quantitative justification for each decision made. Preparing students for a practice based
on a clinical science of decision making, as much
as on a clinical art of judgment, requires teaching
in new areas with few precedents in a sparse
literature.

When a particular decision is analyzed at length
with a clinician, many factors emerge which have
clearly entered the equation before a final yes/no
choice was made for some particular option.

Looking at *how to decide* can reveal as much
complexity within medical thinking as working
out *what to decide*. Discussion by teachers about
the decision is usually limited in practice,
however, to what to do, and how to justify that
course of action. Despite this frequency of
discussion about actions, the *processes* of decision
making are rarely addressed.

This Chapter attempts to bring out some of
those influential factors as a preliminary to helping
teacher/clinicians plan how to help student/doctors
make optimal choices. Much of the difficulty in
discussing and teaching this subject lies in the
'built-in' or intuitive aspect of decision making.
If students ask a surgeon how he decided to
operate on a patient with acute abdominal pain,
he may struggle to recollect exactly what factors
he took into account. The surgeon may be unable
to explain his reasoning in a way that relates
directly to what he has been teaching students
they 'must do'.

Much of our decision making as experienced
clinicians, in other words, is 'intuitive' in the same
sense that driving a car requires a succession of
choices and actions of which only some appear to
be conscious calculations.

Decision making is not to be denigrated because
it has a large intuitive component. Our intuition
(for want of a better word) incorporates a host of
experiences (seeing, reading, hearing, trial and
error) which we are unable to remember clearly.
Even if we could remember them all, we could not
handle them simultaneously within the sharply
limited information processing capacity of our
'short term memory' or mental 'problem space'.

Clinical practice requires the doctor to extract
from a huge volume of biomedical knowledge

through a mental problem solving mechanism of extremely limited capacity and slow processing. Such a task would be impossible without some mechanism for decision rules based on similar situations from our past. We could not start afresh with each case to work out what to do from first principles; yet we cannot unreservedly apply a fixed set of rules to all cases. Our intuition provides us with a mechanism for 'knowing' what to do which is not always rational in the sense of being fully describable in words, and examinable and testable intellectually. We have 'gut-feelings' or hunches, and we have decision rules which we have difficulty accounting for. This is what we mean by our intuition.

Such intuitive ability is actually being tapped to be the (misnamed) 'artificial intelligence' of 'expert' computer systems. That is, the decision rules developed by experienced and expert clinicians are being collected to create sets of *if-then* rules for computer programs which can guide other clinicians in similar cases.

While it is observably true that we operate at 'subjectively intuitive' as well as 'objectively rational' levels, teacher/clinicians have been slow to study the former, that is, to study the processes of 'doctoring', and they have often made unwarranted assumptions about the objectivity of the latter.

What do students need to know about what decisions to make? What are decisions based on? What do students need to understand about how decisions are made? What skills must students learn? How can students best learn such knowledge and skills? How shall we know whether students have learned to use these skills sufficiently to make effective and efficient decisions?

WHY TEACH CLINICAL DECISION MAKING?

1. To make the steps of clinical decision making explicit

All clinicians use rules to make decisions. The rules go under different names, such as indications and contra-indications, axioms, protocols, unit routines, flow charts, decision trees and algorithms (algorisms) and heuristics.

At the simplest level, a clinician will request an intern to measure the blood glucose in a diabetic patient; based on the test result the dose of insulin will be raised or lowered by a certain number of units according to the prediction of the outcome of the blood glucose level as a result of that much insulin.

The teacher's task is not necessarily to teach exactly how much insulin to prescribe, but to teach the logical and numerical basis of the rule by which the insulin dose can be worked out.

2. To help new decision rules be developed.

Changes in disease patterns, or the arrival of new technology, alter opportunities and probabilities. Is chest radiography or electrocardiography obligatory before surgery? How does the CT scanner affect investigation of headache? What is the logic and what is the evidence?

Until decision rules are explicitly set out, they cannot be tested for safety, effectiveness or efficiency (Balla et al 1985).

3. To reveal the value judgments within the decision

No matter how pragmatic we see ourselves to be in basing our decisions on probable outcomes, every decision leads to some gains and some losses. Even a decision as apparently simple as whether to prescribe antibiotics for a patient with an inflamed throat entails intended gains, such as a shorter illness with earlier return to work, to be balanced against the possible losses, such as the cost of the antibiotic and the risk of induced side-effects.

Teachers can engage students in listing the full range of possible gains and losses with each treatment and without treatment. Which outcomes are most important? Who is deciding priorities among outcomes? How are 'importance' and 'priority' decided? By whom?

4. To reveal the probabilities on which the decision is based

Decisions are based not only on what is important, but what is most likely to happen. How likely is the sore throat to respond to this antibiotic? Or the length of illness to be materially shortened? How frequent is each possible side-effect of the antibiotic? How serious the consequences of no treatment?

Teachers can help students reveal how these probabilities are implicit in the decision, but are usually unstated explicitly (or may be unknown or based on inaccurate or out of date beliefs).

WHEN TO TEACH CLINICAL DECISION MAKING?

Undergraduate teaching

It is not clear when clinical decision making should be best taught to students. In the University of Otago, teaching in the third year is effectively integrated with applied epidemiology and biostatistics. In the University of New South Wales, teaching by lecture during third year, but not linked into current clinical learning, fails to reinforce or extend the skills. In Monash University, Australia, teaching in the context of clinical learning at the bedside demonstrates direct application (Balla & Edwards 1986).

As with any other skill learning, it would be expected that practice in application, and in transfer to other similar problems, would be most effective, but we have too few samples of teaching from which to generalize, and too few teachers who understand the field.

Postgraduate teaching

Demonstration and discussion of decision analysis at hospital clinical meetings can raise considerable interest, but usually with little follow through in seeking help with application, indicating that clinicians may not see analysis of their decision rules as of immediate or practical significance.

Pressures for accountability, effectiveness and efficiency may alter the climate for acceptance of these analytical frameworks for justification of clinical procedures.

For undergraduate teaching to be effective, students need reinforcement by different clinicians in varied settings. Decision making is (we assume) best taught within the context of the individual cases managed by different clinicians.

HOW TO TEACH CLINICAL DECISION MAKING

1. How to structure the problem

What series of decisions is entailed in the management of a particular patient is often quite unclear to students and many factors remain unrevealed. Students hear opinions expressed for and against certain forms of treatment in individual patients. Opposing views may be put with equal conviction by respected and senior clinicians. A great deal of subtle reasoning and judgment may have preceded the opinion. But if that reasoning and judgment remain unexplained to the student, the student's learning task appears to be to memorize opinions, not the underlying strategy, values and probabilities.

Students can be given the task to dissect the problem into a sequence of critical questions; or to draw up a flow chart or decision tree; or to work out what information they require before coming to a decision about a patient they have just seen in the ward; or to set out the goals of management, and then the means by which they may be able to get there.

The process of working out such a structure teaches students what are the essential elements in management of the problem, what must be done first, and what information will be needed.

A 'critical questions' sequence fits clinical thinking easily. For example, given a patient with hematemesis and melena, the most urgent question would be 'Is the patient hypovolemic?' which leads to the underlying questions of 'What evidence do I need to answer that question?' then 'Given the evidence I have been able to collect, what is my judgment about hypovolemia?' then 'What action do I take on the basis of my judgment?' Having dealt with the urgent first question, eg. by transfusion, the second critical question would be 'Is the patient still bleeding?' followed by its set of underlying questions.

The sequence becomes one of Question, Evidence, Judgment, Action, followed by the next Question, Evidence, Judgment, and so on. What is the appropriate next question depends on the answer to the previous question. The sequence consequently branches according to the findings at each stage (Cox, 1975).

A more formal layout is provided by a decision

tree, which sets out the choices of action quite explicitly. Having set out all the options and possible outcomes, probabilities can be assigned to each of the outcomes. The likely results of one course of action can then be compared with another. This structured approach is called decision analysis (Weinstein et al, 1980).

The teacher can pose the students the management problem of someone they have just seen in the ward, eg. with transient ischemic attacks in the carotid territory, and for whom two treatment options are available — carotid endarterectomy or aspirin. Given the first task of identifying what information is required before reaching a decision, students soon recognize the need to ask questions about the likely outcomes of the disease with either form of treatment, and the risks of surgery versus aspirin therapy. They can then draw a simple decision tree. The probability estimates can be provided by the tutor.

2. How to decide what tests to order

Choosing investigations requires knowledge of the diagnostic power of the various tests available, particularly their sensitivity and specificity. From these test characteristics the predictive value of the test can be inferred, given the prevalence of the possible diseases under investigation. Most students will have heard terms such as sensitivity and specificity, but few will understand what underlies their use in any operational way. They see multiple tests ordered in the ward, but have little comprehension of how the results will contribute to the final diagnosis and to management decisions. Explanations are now timely about prevalence of disease, predictive value of positive and negative test results, and the prospects of false alarms when prevalence is low and false positive rates are high (Cox. 1984).

Teachers can give students a take-home exercise for working through such concepts. For instance, a patient with head injury may have developed a sub-dural collection for which a CT scan as soon as possible will make the diagnosis and thus reduce the possible morbidity. Students are asked to decide what information they require before recommending CT scans on all head-injured patients coming to a Casualty Department. Students are also informed that about one third of patients with sub-dural collections suffer undue delays in diagnosis.

Students need to work out that, for an informed decision, they need to know the prevalence (prior probability) of sub-dural collections in an unselected series of head-injured patients, as well as the true positive and true negative rates of CT scans in that population. Given the very high true positive rate about .96 and the true negative rate about .98, they tend to choose routine CT scans for all cases. Some will, however, be able to calculate from a 2 × 2 table that, in view of the rarity of sub-dural collections (.003 in such a population), falsely positive results will outweigh truly positive results by about 6 to 1 (Balla & Elstein, 1984).

It is impressed on them that a value judgment is now required. Is the expense of routine investigation plus the patient morbidity from unnecessary surgery plus the waste of neurosurgical and operating room time and resources worthwhile, when counted against the morbidity from delayed diagnosis in a few patients with sub-dural collections? What factors enter such a trade-off? Whose values are paramount?

3. Where do the probabilities come from?

Students become anxious because the probability estimates needed for such calculations are not available from textbooks which are arranged descriptively around disease states, not calculated around the illnesses with which patients present.

To some extent specialists are becoming more aware of the availability of probability estimates in journals. Some specialists are compiling their own databases from personal case records using personal computers.

Nevertheless, most clinicians will not be able to provide exact probabilities, and may even denigrate their necessity, despite the implicit inclusion of the same probabilities in the clinical decision they are currently making. The task for the teacher is to help the students compile whatever data can be found which provide successive approximations to the figures needed. When estimates vary, collating local figures shows how closely or not local experience coincides with published figures from other populations.

Students can be encouraged to devise how they

could set up a personal database for their own practice in the future.

4. How much do the figures matter?

When the decision is finely balanced, the accuracy and comparability of the sources of data may be critical. In such a case, students can recognize the tentative status of any protocol, and the necessity for their maintaining a careful and critical approach to any claims for the superiority of one treatment over another. Particularly important will be their scrutiny of where the probabilities came from.

The layout of the problem and the figures allows the decision to tested in theory by inserting different figures to see how far they have to be altered before the decision would be changed. This testing of the decision is called sensitivity analysis, (Weinstein et al 1980 p. 61), testing how sensitive the decision is to such different estimates. Showing in which areas the data will be critical identifies where more work needs to be done, and perhaps other criteria drawn upon.

Teachers have many opportunities to guide students into skills of critical thinking in extracting usable probabilities from journal articles, and how to apply those probabilities to clinical decisions.

5. How do we decide what's important?

Students have little conception of the importance of value judgments when choosing among treatment strategies. Unfortunately, most clinical teachers also have no clear framework for clarifying these issues with patients or students.

Teachers can begin by helping students to identify the full range of possible outcomes of a treatment and to consider their personal priorities. Taking our earlier example of transient ischemic attacks, the decision whether to operate will depend to a large extent on what risks are involved in the surgery. One can take it further by asking the students to nominate the level of risk they

would be willing to take before choosing surgery. Some will accept only minimal risks, say, no more than 2 to 3% morbidity, as opposed to the high risk takers who will accept even a 10 to 20% chance.

Students can now be helped to understand how low risk takers are likely to want to postpone risk, while those accepting the chance of high morbidity may not wish to accept the uncertainty involved in non-surgical treatment.

Students are relatively homogeneous educationally and socially, yet their values on risks and goals of treatment usually differ. They can now see how their values could differ quite widely from patients who have a very different understanding of the disease and its implications. This leads into discussion of how to involve each patient in the decision. What does the patient expect will happen, and what is the patient most concerned about?

The obvious next step for the teacher is to have the students return to the patient to check the patient's understanding and to elicit priorities. Before doing so, the students need some tools for calibrating as well as ranking those priorities among outcomes. For example, take a patient with suspected secondary cancer of the spine. The treatment options are laminectomy or 'blind' deep X-ray therapy. Laminectomy may result in death or substantial morbidity, but with the (transient) relief of symptoms if successful. Deep X-ray therapy may miss an occasional benign and treatable tumour. Most people have no difficulty placing their preferences on a scale (Iansek et al 1985) and students can devise different ways of presenting patients with choices.

The interest in teaching clinical decision making is increasing as shown by the large number of University courses (Elstein, 1981) and the increasing number of articles in leading journals. Clinicians are at the beginning of their learning curve in understanding the discipline, yet they are critical to its teaching around the individual patient. The field will be burgeoning within five years, and students need preparation now.

REFERENCES

Balla J I & Elstein A S 1984 Skull X-Ray Assessment of Head Injuries: A Decision Analytic Approach. Methods of Information in Medicine 23

Balla J I & Edwards H 1986 When Students Learn Numbers: Evaluation of a course in Clinical Decision Making. Medical Education

Balla J I, Iansek R & Elstein A S 1985 Bayesian Diagnosis in the Presence of Pre-Existing Disease. The Lancet 1: 325–329

Cox K 1975 How do you Decide what it is and what to do?. Med J Aust 2: 57–59

Cox K 1984 How well does the test predict the diagnosis? Aust & N Z J Surg 54: 379–383

Elstein A S 1981 Education Programs in Medical Decision Making. Medical Decision Making 1: 70–73

Iansek R, BallaJ I, Harrison M 1985 Decision Tree Analysis of management of suspected metastatic Spinal cord Compression. Abstract 7th Annual Meeting of the Society for medical Decision Making, in Medical Decision Making

Weinstein M C, Fineberg H V, Elstein A S, Frazier H S, Neuhauser D, Neutra R R and McNeil B J 1980 Clinical Decision Analysis, Saunders, Phil

Including bioethical decision-making in the undergraduate course

Preview

TRENDS

   Increase in bioethical problems
   Teaching bioethical decision-making

PURPOSES

   Prerequisite
   Teacher
   Student

GUIDELINES FOR CONDUCTING THE SESSIONS

RESOURCES

TRENDS

Increase in bioethical problems

As a response to the complexities of bioethical problems in health care there is a demand for increased understanding of bioethical issues and increased skills in resolving bioethical dilemmas. The issues arise not only in clinical problems but in institutional, community and political debates. Conflicts occur when a decision has to be made between alternatives, neither of which will result in a desirable outcome. The moral conflict occurs when acting on one moral conviction to resolve a dilemma may mean breaking another. Therein lies the complexity of ethical decision making.

Teaching bioethical decision-making

Most health profession courses include professional ethics; few have developed fully fledged courses in bioethics where ethical reasoning, ethical reflection and ethical decision-making are taught.

The aim of this Chapter is to suggest guidelines and resources for teachers who have the responsibility for conducting short courses, one-off seminars or ad hoc sessions after clinical rounds.

PURPOSES

One-off sessions tend to give students what Hicks (1981) calls a 'quick ethical fix'! Admittedly, single separate sessions are less than ideal, nevertheless, the opportunity to sensitize students to the importance of the influence of ethics in health care is not to be dismissed out of hand. Furthermore, if the session is to be followed by discussion (e.g. after a clinical round) the initial session can be structured to lead into issues to be taken up when specific clinical conflicts arise.

You might have several sessions in mind and a sequence is therefore desirable. Alternatively, your opportunity may be limited to one or two session. Clear goals for each session are essential so that the issues and discussions are focused and manageable.

The following suggested goals would allow for a sequence, or one or more could be selected for separate ad hoc sessions:

to increase awareness of the significance of ethical issues in health care practice.

to identify ethical issues and ethical dilemmas in everyday practice.

to recognize own values and their underlying basis.

to develop skills in ethical reasoning.

to analyze an ethical dilemma.

PRE-REQUISITES FOR THE TEACHER

Although interest in bioethics has grown (texts, films, printed case studies are increasingly available) there are few guidelines to assist teachers to manage the teaching session. Recognizing this, the Harvard University's new program in Professional Ethics is designed to prepare teachers who have a health professional background but no philosophy, and philosophers without a medical qualification, for addressing current ethical principles and practices in bioethics.

You may be fortunate to have on hand a philosopher, ethicist, theologian, behavioural scientist, or humanities teacher who could join you in planning and conducting the session. If not, you will need to have at the very least, a nodding acquaintance with terms such as moral philosophy, values, utilitarianism and deontology and should have access to texts on ethics, ethical theories, values and human rights. (A list of resources is given at the end of the chapter).

Teachers who accept ethics teaching in addition to their usual responsibilities of a clinician, researcher, lecturer, colleague, counsellor or administrator, may sometimes wonder why they have committed themselves to an extra demand on their time and skills. Although some knowledge of ethics as a subject is desirable, it is well to remember that the aim of the teacher is not to be an authority on all things ethical, but to encourage students to develop their awareness and skills in recognizing ethical dilemmas and to engage in ethical reasoning as preparation for their role as graduates.

PRE-REQUISITES FOR THE STUDENTS

Previous knowledge

Although ethics is a basic component of the dealings in everyday life, expressed as 'I should'; 'I ought'; 'I have to'; 'I really must'; in their daily encounters health professionals enter another dimension of ethical responsibility. Moral bonds, obligations and duties are involved. Human rights and values also have a special emphasis in health care.

Many students have some knowledge of these components and relate fairly easily to issues of moral responsibility, students' rights and values. Take, for example, the graffiti on any campus, or the topics of student meetings with invited speakers, or the slogans adopted by lobby groups. Students' knowledge of these issues provides a direct lead into clarification of values and considerations of moral obligations and ethical conflicts in health care.

Previous experience

Bioethical decision-making occurs within the context of health care policies and practice. Students need to have had some contact with patients and other health professionals if the subject is to ring true. Probably the optimal time for introducing ethics is when the student has had personal responsibility involving patients and can relate to the conflicts occurring around them.

Intellectual skills

The intellectual approach to the resolution of an ethical dilemma (reflection, ethical reasoning) differs from that required in most pre-clinical subjects where learning of content and achievement in examinations clearly directs students' goals and dictates their priorities.

In ethical decision-making the intellectual demands on students are more likely to arise from working with unfamiliar concepts from the humanities and behavioural sciences. For many students, deciding which horn of the ethical dilemma is to be preferred, and for what reason, will be a confrontation with their own values. A certain degree of intellectual frustration accompanies the steps in ethical decision-making especially when there are ambiguous signals from patients and professionals.

GUIDELINES FOR CONDUCTING THE SESSIONS

General goal for all sessions:

To increase awareness of the significance of ethical issues in health care practice

General guidelines:

Before the Session(s)
  Find out what students already know
  Accumulate examples of ethical issues and community attitudes and reactions to topical issues in health care
  Structure a few questions to direct students to identify examples of ethical conflicts they have met

During the session(s)

Act as a facilitator of student involvement rather than an assessor of student attainment as there is rarely a 'right' answer to an ethical dilemma
Point out to students that ethical reasoning takes time and contrasts with the often very speedy decisions required in life-threatening clinical situations
Involve other disciplines and professions in issues requiring multi-disciplinary discussion
  Include an ethicist when ethical theories are discussed
    If a single session, try to summarize by obtaining group consensus on the meaning of terms such as ethics, ethical dilemma, ethical decision-making and reasoning
    Provide access to readings or a case study or a problem with questions for follow-up for individual students.
    Suggest students keep a log of ethical issues they have observed or experienced for discussion later

Goal: To identify ethical issues and ethical dilemmas

Guidelines:

Request that students keep a diary of newspaper cuttings of resolved and unresolved ethical dilemmas for discussion Organize a debate on one or more of the issues so that students raise details on each horn of the dilemma
Lead students to identify whether a moral issue is involved; what is it? Would acting on one moral conviction mean breaking another? Does an ethical dilemma really exist? Are there two equally undesirable alternatives making up the horns of the dilemma?
Be prepared to allow the time needed for reflection with students on ethical situations, issues and dilemmas. Confirm that time spent in reflection is legitimate.
Summarize by asking students to define: an ethical issue in non-technical words (e.g. when a right or a value esteemed by society or a person is threatened); an ethical dilemma (e.g. the choice between two alternatives neither of which is desirable in all respects)

Goal: To recognize own values and their underlying basis

Guidelines:

Recognize the trap of 'moralizing' about values
Resist the urge to give a mini-lecture in an attempt to control the session
Instead, begin with a global issue, then follow with a professional issue and lastly a personal issue
Choose a specific provocative statement for debate e.g. capital punishment should be re-introduced for terrorist crimes
Ask students to declare their position and to state the value supporting their stance
Proceed to a professional issue, e.g. health professionals should 'blow the whistle' on a colleague for malpractice or 'all health professions should have the right to strike'
Lastly take an issue requiring an intensely personal decision e.g. deciding whether a close relative should survive or be allowed to die (after an accident causing possible brain damage)
Summarize by asking students to distinguish between societal values, institutional values, professional values (as listed in codes) and personal values and their underlying foundation

Lead the group to identify (in clinical rounds, later) the conflicts arising between e.g. institutional values, and patient's personal values; between professional values and institutional values, and so on

Guide the group to observe values conflicts in their own clinical practice and to identify their own value system

Goal: To analyze an ethical dilemma

Guidelines:

Use a written or videotaped case study or preferably a case presented by a student from clinical experience

Purtilo & Cassel (1981) has identified a four-step process that anyone facing an ethically perplexing situation should engage in.

Steps	*Process*
1. Gather all information	Students suggest all relevant sources of information in addition to the medical problem
2. Identify the dilemma	Students weigh up the moral obligation, rights and duties involved, and decide whether a dilemma exists
3. Decide what to do	Students discuss who should decide; What values are involved; Whose values; Whose rights; What complications follow a decision
4. Complete the action	to act in one way or another? What ethical theory could assist the decision?[*] Decide a strategy that could be used for carrying out the decision rather than leaving it as an intellectual exercise

Encourage students to tolerate frustration during ambiguities and lack of certainty in the analysis of an ethical dilemma

Goal: To develop skills of ethical reasoning

Guidelines:

Arrange for students to see 'experts at work' by inviting a multiprofessional panel to analyze and resolve an ethical dilemma

Analyze the process of reasoning reported by experts in their resolution of an ethical dilemma

Recognize that ethical reasoning is the keystone skill in resolvlng an ethical dilemma; choose a teaching method to provide students with opportunities for practice

Use case studies, ethical rounds, role play and small groups to develop a pro and con position for resolution

Provide access to ethical Iiterature case studies and ethical theories as students show 'readiness'

---

[*] Involve ethicists and other disciplines and professions in the analytical process where access to further reasoning is required.

BIBLIOGRAPHY

Abernethy V (ed) 1980 Frontiers in Medical Ethics: Applications in a Medical Setting. Ballinger Publishing Co. Cambridge Mass Contains verbatim reports of simulated medical ethical rounds.

Applegate M L, Entrebin 1984 Teaching Ethics in Nursing. A Handbook for use of the Case-Study approach. NLN New York Contains a list of educational resources, films, texts, journals and resource centres.

Beauchamp T H, Childress J F 1979 Principles of Biomedical Ethics Oxford University Press. New York

Childress J F 1981 Priorities in Biomedical Ethics. Westminster Press, Philadelphia

Issues in Ethics. 1981 Community Health Studies. Centre for Human Bioethics, Monash University

Purtilo R, Cassel C K 1981 Ethical Dimensions in the Health Professions pp 27–29. Saunders, Toronto

Varga A C 1980 The main issues in Bioethics Paulist Press, New York Gives select bibliography of resources under 14 categories of ethical concerns

Teaching counseling skills

THE PHYSICIAN AS PATIENT
COUNSELOR AND PATIENT EDUCATOR

Medical educators consistently endorse teaching patient interviewing to medical students. Most educators also endorse the importance of patient education. When it comes to counselling, however, differences of opinion appear about the physician's role. One point of view is that the physician can make an important contribution to a patient's lifestyle and attitudes. Others would define the role of the practitioner in more strictly biological terms of diagnosis and treatment of disease. For those who do conceptualize the medical task as including patient counselling, the work summarized in this Chapter provides one model for teaching patient counselling.

A basic consideration in the decision to imple-

ment training in patient counselling is an answer to the questions: 'Can physicians influence patient behaviour?' and 'Is there time in the course of a normal medical practice for such intervention?' I believe the answer is 'Yes'. Patients usually have high regard for their physicians. The very nature of the relationship is such that the physician is permitted to know and see a patient in ways permitted to no one in society, but in ways which are reminiscent of parent/child transactions. In addition to this high degree of intimacy inherent in doctor/patient interactions, physicians often see patients during crises. Crises typically enhance patient readiness for personal change, and therefore much more than one would ordinarily expect can be accomplished by a medical practitioner in a relatively short time. The issue is not one of opportunity or of role but how to educate physicians reliably and efficiently so that they are able to help patients deal with emotionally changed issues; how to teach medical students enough patient counselling so that they can be effective, and yet to design such instruction so that it can be accommodated in an already full curriculum.

The course outlined below is one of the products of research begun in the early 1960s (Kagan, 1984). The course has been offered to first year medical classes with as many as two hundred students. Ordinarily, one or two primary instructors can teach the course with the help of small group leaders or preceptors with one preceptor for every 16 students. It is assumed here that each preceptor can lead two groups of eight students, requiring approximately eight hours of time commitment each week. Preceptors are also required to attend a three day preceptor-training workshop which precedes the course. The

---

* IPR methods and research findings have been reported in numerous publications beginning in 1962. Many of the ideas reported here appear in Temoshock L Zegans L & Van Dyke C (Editors) Emotions in Health and Illness: Applications to Clinical Practice. Grune and Stratton, New York. 1984

preceptors can be recuited from various sources, depending on availability and instructor goals. If the instructor wishes to influence colleagues in other departments, then preceptors might be recruited from among the faculty. If the instructor wishes to influence the medical community, preceptors can be recruited from among practising community physicians. A third source of preceptors is second year medical students, who have themselves recently completed the course.

THE GENERAL GOALS OF THE COURSE

It is important to help students understand clearly the purpose of the program. The following has been an effective introduction to the course:

We want you to be able to relate to a patient in such a way that you can elict from the patient important and complete information which you need for a valid diagnosis, and in order to formulate an appropriate management plan. We want you to be able to relate to a patient in such a way that your manner and questions do not exacerbate the patient's illness by adding unnecessary stress to what is already a painful or frightening condition. We want you to be able to relate to a patient in such a way that patients are encouraged to cooperate in the treatment effort rather than to sabotage the treatment plan. We want you to be able to relate to a patient in such a way that that patient is not angry and eager to retaliate.

We will teach you to review tapes for each other and to share certain concerns with each other because we want you to begin a process through which you will learn to rely on each other for support and counsel to prevent professional isolation, loneliness and depression.

These are our minimum expectations, but there are many among you who believe that patient counselling and patient education are a core part of medical practice.

There are those among you who are interested in helping patients understand the impact that environmental stress has on their lives. There are many among you who want to help your patients live, not just in the absence of disease, but in health and vigor. For those of you who see medicine in these terms, this course will offer you some of the basic tools you need. We expect that you will see the experiences provided and the skills taught as an important part of your medical knowledge.

One may ask, 'Can these techniques not be used to control the patient? Do not advanced skills in interpersonal communication give the physician one more powerful tool which can be used to impose the physician's will on the patient?' The answer, in general, is 'yes'. Any skills which are powerful enough to make a difference in the lives of people conceivably could be perverted or misused; but as you go through the various units of the course, we think you'll find that the most repeated exercise involves engaging patients as active participants in the medical process, an exercise which should actually mitigate against encroaching on the patient's power within the medical process.

BASIC STRUCTURE

During subsequent sessions basic concepts are presented, usually on videotape or film, and students are given opportunities during the lecture to discuss the concepts or practise the skills. The skills required for patient interviewing and those required for patient counselling overlap considerably. Weekly sesions are devoted to practice interviews with actors serving as patients, and in later weeks with fellow students presenting concerns they themselves have. In the final lab sessions, students interview volunteer patients who have had a long- term chronic illness and who are willing to share their experiences with first year medical students. Students also interview a mother who has recently experienced childbirth.

ELEMENTS OF THE COURSE

1. The affective sensitivity scale

During the first class session students take the Affective Sensitivity Scale (Kagan and Schneider, 1986). The Scale requires looking at candid scenes in which a teacher and a student, doctor and patient, counselor and client, family units or group or dyad were filmed in unrehearsed interactions. At the end of each brief scene students are required to choose from among three statements the one that they think each participant would actually say about what they had experienced at the moment the scene ended. Students are told that the scores will be used to provide them with a profile of their sensitivity to men, women, children and adults and the student's tendencies, if any, to favour or avoid specific emotions. Students are asked to keep in mind that all scenes are of actual interactions and to treat the scale not as a test but as an opportunity to practise identifying the feelings of others. Students are assured that the results will not be entered into their medical school record or be used in evaluating their work.

Two full-day sessions are then scheduled in which many of the basic skills and concepts of the course are presented in workshop format. The course instructor presents material, usually on film, and students are asked to discuss the ideas or practise the skills with their group. The first workshop begins with instructions on how to understand one's Affective Sensitivity Scale profile which has been distributed. If the results do indeed seem to represent validly a student's interpersonal strengths and weaknesses, it is suggested that the student use the profile as a guide to improve skills and sensitivity.

2. Elements of facilitative communication

The first skill unit delineates four characteristics of facilitative communication: 'exploratory', 'listening', 'afffective', and 'honest labeling'. The behaviours are explained by the class instructor and by a woman narrator on film.

After each skill has been described and illustrated, students are asked to practise the new response made with a series of simulated patients on film who look directly at the viewer and make statements varying in complexity and intensity.

3. Interpersonal stress simulation

The second unit is not devoted to skill training in the usual sense. The purpose of the unit is to help students identify, think through and become less

threatened by interpersonal situations that cause them stress, to overcome their own 'interpersonal allergies'. Students are told that if they are to help patients talk about important personal stresses in their lives then the students themselves must be helped to overcome any of their own resistance to becoming involved in a psychologically intimate and meaningful way with other human beings.

A series of simulation exercises is introduced to help students become better able to label feelings and to help them deal with factors that might otherwise interfere with thelr effectiveness in human interactions. They are asked to look at vignettes in which a person on film will look directly at them. They are asked to try to imagine that they are alone with the person on the screen, to pretend that they have been talking with the person, and to allow this person to have an impact on them.

After each vignette, the preceptor invites anyone in the group to volunteer a reaction to the vignette viewed. The preceptor encourages elaboration and does not interpret or make judgments about student reactions. Often, students find that listening to another student's reactions helps them identify their own reactions more clearly. Students are often surprised to find themselves stressed by situations that they had not thought would be problematic.

After the preceptor has led the debriefing of a few vignettes, each member of the small group is asked to serve as group facilitator for at least one vignette to have the experience of encouraging one's peers to describe their reactions to an emotionally stimulating event. In another exercise using the vignettes each student selects a partner. The student leaves the room, and the partner views a vignette. On return, the student's task is to debrief the partner.

4. The recall process

The recall process is one of the unique characteristics of the course. To learn counseling processes within this model, the students study their own covert behaviour and that of their patients by means of a stimulated recall process after each of their patient interaction sessions. Each of the sessions, whether with actor, fellow student, or patient is recorded on videotape. Students then have an opportunity immediately after the interview to review the tape. The first such review session is conducted by the student's preceptor and only student and preceptor are present during the recall session. The student is told to stop the videotape whenever the playback helps the student remember any thoughts, feelings, goals, impressions, or images the student had during the session as well as anything the student was tempted to say or do. Students are also asked to try to recall how they thought the actor perceived them, how they wanted to be perceived, and how satisfied they were with their own behaviour during the time of the interview.

The process does not include evaluation, advice or critique by the person serving as debriefer or inquirer. The student is asked to describe to the inquirer whatever the student can of the interview. Before turning on the tape again, the inquirer may ask for elaboration on comments or may ask the student to talk about any other area of related content. For instance, if the student said, 'At that moment the patient really confused me. I couldn't understand what he was trying to tell me,' the inquirer might ask, 'How did that feeling of confusion affect your behaviour?', or, 'Was there anything you were tempted to do or say?'. The inquirer asks only non-interpretive, non-judgmental questions. The inquirer does not offer suggestions, critique or feedback.

Student recall

The purpose of the individual recall sessions is to enable students to make explicit their own covert processes; to state in words that which they intuitively sense in their interactions with others but do not ordinarily put into words. The recall session also gives students an opportunity to hear the sound of words they may have been tempted to utter, but did not in the interview — a sort of behavioural practice, difficult to achieve in other ways.

Concurrent with this course, all students attend a three hour lecture on human sexuality. The regular lab session which follows requires that each student interview a patient model, an actor or actress who is well rehearsed to speak with

students about a sexual concern. The interview is videorecorded but not watched by anyone other than the preceptor. Immediately after the interview, student and preceptor review the tape. For this session, none of the other lab classmates is present. The student is given control of the playback switch and encouraged to stop the tape (a) whenever any thoughts, feelings, expectations, images or impressions that she or he had made or wanted to make are remembered; (b) If there are ideas, goals satisfactions, dissatisfactions, or bodily reactions, that she or he wanted to express but couldn't find the words for, or (c) if anything else is recalled. The preceptor serves as inquirer for each student.

Patient recall

Feedback to the student *is* provided in subsequent sessions not by the preceptor but rather by the patients themselves. First, students are taught the inquirer role and given practice sessions using film simulation and interviews with each other.

Mutual recall

One of the inevitable student discoveries in patient recall sessions is a realization that, regardless of the content of the interview, a considerable amount of patient attention is focused on the interaction with the interviewer. Teaching people to use the process of an interaction as part of the explicit content of the interaction is ordinarily a difficult and very time consuming process, well beyond the time afforded in a medical program. Mutual recall is a process which facilitates the rapid learning of this complex skill.

After a student/patient interview has been recorded a second student, in the role of inquirer, joins patient *and* student during the recall phase in a so-called Mutual Recall session. At that time both student and patient are encouraged to stop the playback and tell each other what they had experienced at each moment during the interview session, what each wanted of the other, how satisfied each felt with her own or the other's behaviour; risks and disappointments as well as pleasurable or satisfying moments.

The first lab session on mutual recall is focused

on counseling with patients suffering with loss or grief. In conjunction with this lab unit a three hour seminar is given to the entire class on loss and grief by a guest lecturer. The lab assignment which follows requires that students form pairs and that each student presents an incident of loss to the other. As defined in the lecture, 'loss' can be as obvious an event as a death or as subtle as the loss which accompanies a promotion or relocation. The student in the peer counselor role is asked to be as helpful as possible, using any of the skills learned during the course which seems appropriate. Each pair makes a tape of approximately ten minutes duration and the recall sessions are kept to approximately thirty minutes. A mutual recall session follows in which students serve as inquirers for each other. The inquirer receives feedback from the participants whose tape had been reviewed and then from the other students and from the preceptor.

The second lab session using mutual recall is focused on childbirth and its impact on families. A three-hour class session on new families is presented by a member of the Department of Paediatrics. The lab session which follows requires each student to interview a woman who had recently given birth. The situations are candid and the women are volunteers. In some instances, the mother has the infant and any older siblings with her. The session which follows is a mutual recall with students serving as inquirer for each other and the woman. No other students are present during the recall.

The final mutual recall lab session is one in which each student interviews a patient who has suffered with a long-term illness. Students are encouraged to discuss with the patient the history of the illness. If appropriate, students also are asked to consider with the patient how the illness has affected the patient's life, how the medical system was experienced by the patient, the patient's coping techniques (both physical and social-emotional), and the patient's aspirations, expectations, joys and fears.

This feedback through patient recall is usually experienced by students and patients as highly instructive and not especially stressful. It is the single most powerful learning experience in the course.

Evaluation

Evaluating individual student change in interpersonal sensitivity and behaviour is difficult. Such basic attributes as warmth and genuine concern are often communicated subtly and can only be measured reliably through evaluation by patients after several sessions with a counselor (Kurtz and Grummon, 1972).

The Affective Sensitivity Scale can be administered at or near the end of the course. Because reliability of such instruments is not high for individuals and can be affected by student mood and context, it is recommended that the Scale be used for group evaluation only until we learn how to improve its reliability for individuals. Student profile, rather than total score might be of interest to instructor and student.

It is possible to measure reliably the students' ability to use the specific behaviours taught in the first unit of the course by rating one of the recorded student interviews made during the course. One might assume that the final interview would be the most appropriate; however, an examination of the interviews with patients reveals an incredible variability in openness among patients. New mothers posed a similar problem. In our experience the sexuality interview with actors provides the most uniformly difficult task for each student. The first twenty statements by the student in the interview are each rated as exploratory or non-exploratory, listening or ignoring, affective or cognitive, and honest or avoiding. If even greater precision in measurement is required, as for instance when evaluating a relatively small modificaion in the course content, then it is possible to have each actor interviewed by a single interviewer and rated on degree of openness prior to having students interview the actor. Openness score can then be co-varied to further equalize the interview difficulty for each student.

Long term evaluation would be highly desirable but seldom is attempted. One exception is a study conducted at the University of California at Los Angeles (Kauss, Robbins, Abrass, Bakaitis, and Anderson, 1980). Physicians about to begin an internal medicine residency were evaluated. Those students who had taken a *full* course in patient counseling during their previous medical training scored significantly higher than did students who had not had such a course or who had been given only superficial instruction as part of another course.

INNOVATION

We wondered if there were experiences which might stimulate in medical students a better understanding of the connections between mind and body. Would such learning be evident in the ways in which students would then interact with patients? Would they be more inclined to look for mind-body interactions in patients, if we enabled them to discover such connections in themselves? After years of preliminary work the following procedures were developed.

Each student is scheduled for an appointment at a special lab site which is equiped with physiological recording devices. A research assistant explains what will happen during the lab and the goals of the experience. The assistant is especially careful to point out that the physiological recordings, polygraph and videotape feedback, and computer analyses are all in the service of helping the student recall and define the meaning of the experience; that the student is in charge of the technology, not the reverse. The assistant then attaches to the student's arms and hands electrodes to record heart rate, and left and right hand skin conductance and a rubber bellows is attached to record respiration. The student is asked to pretend to be alone with each of the people presented on the motion picture screen and to give emotions and thoughts 'free rein', in much the same way students did when similar vignettes were used in class. As before, in each film vignette a person looks directly at the student and says things which have a high likelihood of evoking emotional reactions. The initial vignettes are obviously medical, but the subsequent ones are more general in nature. For instance, in one of the early scenes a woman, mid-fifties, wearing a white medical coat with a stethoscope hanging out of her pocket says 'Oh, don't give me that crap! You were in charge, dammit. *You* were responsible. Just don't give me that crap.' There is a rest period between scenes in which blank film leader appears and then a neutral but mildly distracting scene is viewed. The rest period lasts a minute and is then followed by another evocative vignette.

As the student watches each scene a video camera records the student, the films presented and the polygraph pens as physiological reactions unfold. The polygraph is wired to a laboratory computer.

After viewing twelve vignettes, the student is joined by the assistant and together they watch a videotape which contains a recording of the student, the material viewed and the corresponding physiologlcal behaviour. The student is encouraged to stop the playback as often as possible to describe particular thoughts and feelings at each moment of viewing the scene. The assistant gives the student the controls for the playback and asks only exploratory questions after the student has stopped the playback to comment. None of the assistant's open ended questions are judgmental or interpretive. By pressing a button the student can also have displayed an *intra*-personal statistical analysis of her or his physiological behaviour in the form of the number of standard deviations that each physiological reaction to each vignette deviated from her or his average reaction to all vignettes. The student may also request that a pattern analysis of clusters of vignettes to which there were similar physiological reactions be computed and displayed on the screen.

After viewing the entire playback, the student is given the paper polygraph record, a typescript of the vignettes viewed, and an audio-cassette recording of her or his recalled reactions to each vignette. The student is asked as a 'homework assignment', to try to identify patterns, if any, of the interaction between mind and body; in essence, to write a self-theory.

A second lab session is then scheduled a week later in which the student will view twelve new vignettes and study reactions to this new material. It is also an opportunity for the student to find out if the patterns of mind/body interactions identified in the self-theory homework assignment are replicated.

Student enthusiasm for the procedures was high; and based on data collected at the end of the year we concluded that, when first year medical students review a videotape of their own physiological reactions to interpersonal messages as an extra-lab experience in a patient counseling course, students offer to coached patients more statements related to the affective components of the patient's concern than do students who have not had the extra-labs. It seems reasonable to infer that studying their own mind/body interactions helped students to seek similar information from patients.

The potential of such procedures for helping students recognize the meaning to them of some of their more subtle or even suppressed reactions is immense. It may be possible within the time constraints of a medical curriculum not only to teach patient counseling but to enhance the interpersonal health of students as well.

Not all programs have the equipment or the personnel to carry out such procedures. Some of the same student gains may be achieved by encouraging students to focus their attention on their various bodily reactions while viewing stimulus vignettes or engaging in a recall session. Especially useful might be to train inquirers to occasionally respond to the statement, 'I was feeling 'X' at that moment, with, where in your body did you feel that emotion most clearly?' and to follow the next response (If affirmative) with additional questions about the feeling.

CONCLUSION

Primary care physicians are not expected to practise counseling and psychotherapy instead of medicine; however, they have numerous opportunities to offer counseling. They can have an important therapeutic impact in the lives of patients, and they can help patients deal with the emotional concomitants and consequences of illness. Lack of time for such functions is more than compensated for by long term contact, interaction at times of stress, and physician status. Within their proper and traditional roles physicians can make important contributions as psychotherapeutic agents if we can develop efficient and valid methods to provide them with the knowledge and skills necessary to make such contributions.

This chapter outlines a structured course of study supported by films and a manual which is designed to help students learn the basic skills and attitudes essential for patient counseling. Information on availability of materials may be obtained from the author.

REFERENCES

Kagan N 1984 Interpersonal Process Recall: Basic methods and recent research. In Learsen D (Editor) Teaching Psychological Skills Monterey, California: Brooks Cole

Kagan N, Schneider J 1986 The Affective Sensitivity Scale Journal of Counseling and Development (in press)

Kauss D R, Robbins A S, Abrass 1, Bakaitis R F, Anderson L A 1980 The long-term effectiveness of interpersonal skills training in medical schools. Journal of Medical Education 55: 595–601

Kurtz R R, Grummon D L 1972 Different approaches to the measurement of therapist empathy and their relationship to therapy outcomes. Journal of Consulting and Clinical Psychology 39: 106–115

Preparing students for a consumer education role

This chapter deals with teaching students the knowledge and skills that they will, in turn, use when educating consumers.

EDUCATION FOR BETTER HEALTH

The World Health Organization states that education for health is 'aimed at encouraging people to want to be healthy, to know how to stay healthy, to do what they can individually and collectively to maintain health, and to seek help as needed.' (WHO 1985)

To implement this concept many activities need to be undertaken. These include patient education, health promotion, and community development. Such activities involve all health professionals in a multidisciplinary approach, and often professionals from sectors other than health. Moreover, this approach raises expectations that health professionals will become more active in their fight against ill health, and not remain service providers only — that is, not waiting to be asked by individuals to provide help, when a disease process has become disabling. Thus, the learning outlined in this chapter will be relevant not only to the doctor's role, but to other health professional roles too.

THE CONTEXT OF CONSUMER EDUCATION

Two specific factors differentiate consumer education from either teaching in an institution, or practising as a clinician in an hospital setting.

1. Education in institutions is bound by formalized procedures and policies which affect both students and teachers. Examples of these include — academic entry standards, lengths of courses, accreditation procedures, student-staff ratios, and the provision of physical facilities. Some of these policies are set by law, and others by individual institutions.

In contrast, when the learners are consumers, each time a new course is commenced each decision has to be made anew — where? when? how long? how many teachers? how many learners? No ongoing commitment can be guaranteed from learners in the community as it can be from learners in institutions.

Thus, while some of our time as teachers in institutions is spent providing informal touches in formal settings, much of the time of community educators is spent providing structure in an unpredictable environment. Thus the skills required in each setting are related, but different.

2. Further, the community educator needs to understand the grounds on which decisions can be

and are being made. Each time a program is developed, priorities must be chosen, and therefore the community worker requires an understanding of different models of resource allocation, of different cultural expectations, and of ideals and norms within a given society.

EDUCATIONAL STRATEGIES FOR SPECIFIC GROUPS

1. Within community settings three distinct groups can be defined — each requiring different approaches:
   a. individual patients
      e.g. assisting a patient after a myocardial infarction to change his diet
   b. small group of people with the same risk factor or condition
      e.g. providing mothers with the information and skills to use oral rehydration therapy if their infants become ill with diarrhea.
   c. cohorts or populations
      e.g. raising the awareness of the community at large about the health risks associated with cigarette smoking.

Within each of these groups many subgroups can be identified. The educational strategy chosen will depend not only on the number of people in the target audience, but on the age, sex, religion, lifestyle and educational standard of the participants. A strategy will be chosen to match the target group.

As consumer education is time consuming all clinicians in practice must choose for themselves what their involvement in consumer education should be.

Some of the questions that can be asked to help make this decision are the following:

1. Will an educational intervention have any effect on the outcome of their patients' condition?

2. Is an individual or group learning method more appropriate for this condition, and this patient?

3. Is the clinician's role to be a counsellor, a facilitator, a transmitter of knowledge, or a support person?

4. If an educational program is appropriate, should it be organized or implemented by the doctor or by another health personnel [e.g. diabetic nurse educator]?

5. Should the learning be informal and spasmodic]i.e. when the patient initiates visits], or should it be organized and a program set out from the beginning [e.g. a 10 week night program]?

6. What time span will this learning program require. Will it be for 30 minutes once [e.g. explaining about an operative procedure] or will it involve interaction for more than one year [e.g. rehabilitation after spinal injuries]?

A MULTIDISCIPLINARY APPROACH TO TRAINING FOR COMMUNITY EDUCATION

That education is part of community health care — both preventive and therapeutic — is no longer questioned. However, the breadth of knowledge, and the skills that are required to support good community education are often underestimated. The experience of WHO illustrates the problem:

'As this training in health communication is a relatively new area of work for WHO, involving a combination of background and experience in health, communication and pedagogy, it has taken much more time and effort than was foreseen to make a start. The dearth of qualified trainers is a very serious problem, to which there is no quick and easy solution' (WHO, 1985).

What are the abilities for which training is required? The following list illustrates the comprehensive nature of knowledge, skills and attitudes consumer educators require.

They need:
— A basic knowledge of the normal and abnormal structure and function of the human body.
— A knowledge of human mental processes, how people learn, and how and why people change their behaviour patterns.
— A knowledge of how human beings relate to one another in families, groups and communities.
— A knowledge of disease patterns, and health risks in a give community.
— Skills in running small group activities.
— Counseling and communication skills.

— Organizational and planning skills, expertise in conducting meetings, workshops and seminars.

— Skills and knowledge about different media for communication, including the advantages and disadvantages of written material, television and radio, posters, books and one to one communication.

— Managerial skills to coordinate other workers or volunteers.

— An understanding of the cost of various parts of programs, and the ability to analyze their effectiveness.

— Ability to evaluate and document programs for funding agencies, or for other community groups to enable them to adopt successful strategies.

— Understanding of one's own personality, and a knowledge of the importance of attitudes in such health promotion programs, to allow non-judgmental communication, and to allow for cultural, age-related and socioeconomic differences in other people's attitudes.

— A knowledge of political processes, and organizational structures.

Much of the knowledge outline above is the same or similar to the knowledge required by the medical teacher.

In other words the content of a course preparing students to be consumer educators is 'educational process' as is outlined in other chapters of this book.

This is learning about:

— How people learn. Why people will or will not change their behaviours.
— Small group process
— Self Directed Learning
— Using audiovisual materials
— Communication skills
— Counseling and interviewing skills
— How human beings relate to one another in faculties, groups and community.

The most effective methods to help students learn these process skills are through experiences, simulations, and practice — in fact through the processes that are being taught. The objectives need to be embedded in the process, by providing real world work experiences as far as is practical.

SUMMARY

Doctors have an important part to play in consumer and community education, but will be successful only if they initiate a closer coordination with other professionals and consumer groups, and broaden their skills in education.

REFERENCES

World Health Organization 1985 The work of WHO 1984–1985 Biennial Report of the Director-General Chapter 13 Public Information and education for health.

Bibliography

Helping health workers learn — David Werner

Preparing students for continuing education

Preview

WHY PREPARE STUDENTS FOR
CONTINUING EDUCATION?

HOW DO ADULTS LEARN?

Basic principles are that:-
Adult learning is largely self-initiated, self-
motivated, self-managed and self-evaluated
Different people prefer different kinds of
learning experiences
Adult learning is most effective when it is
related to perceived needs
Adults tend to build on what they already
know
Motivation for learning is a complex process
depending at least partly on environmental
pressures

HOW WELL DO MOST
UNDERGRADUATE CURRICULA
CONFORM TO THESE PRINCIPALS?

HOW MANY STUDENTS BE PREPARED
FOR CONTINUING EDUCATION?

INFLUENCING ATTITUDES OF
TEACHERS AND STUDENTS:

Strategies include —
Setting explicit curricular objectives to prepare
students for lifelong learning
Admitting appropriate students
Teaching about the need for CME, providing
information about CME opportunities and
assessing student attitudes to it
Teaching elements of the undergraduate

curriculum in conformity with adult education
theory

PROVIDING SKILLS AND TECHNOLOGY:

Strategies include —
Practice with self-learning methods and self-
paced learning
Practice in self-assessment and identification of
learning needs
Introduction of technology to assist with
information retrieval and analysis
Developing skills in critical assessment of
clinical evidence
Teaching management skills and effective use
of time
Involving students in CME research

WHY PREPARE STUDENTS FOR
CONTINUING EDUCATION?

Lifelong learning is increasingly acknowledged to
be a characteristic of professionalism. Houle has
written 'Every occupation that lays claim to the
distinction conferred by the term *profession* seeks
constantly to improve itself in certain distinctive
ways. These characteristics — such as increased
competence in solving problems, a capacity to use
more complex knowledge, and a more sensitive
awareness of ethical problems — are related to the
entire life career of the individual practitioner and
to the stature of the occupation to which he or she
belongs. Therefore, a lifetime of learning is
required to establish, maintain or evaluate the

level of accomplishment suggested by each of these characteristics'. (Houle 1978).

New information is being generated with increasing rapidity and doctors must be able to cope with it. It is estimated that the biomedical literature is expanding at a compound rate of 6–7% per year (Price 1980); thus it doubles every 10–15 years and increases tenfold across the 35–40 years of an individual's life in practice. Furthermore, society's needs are undergoing rapid changes and doctors need to be flexible and able to change with them.

Even where mandatory requirements for continuing education exist, practising doctors have to take the responsibility for initiating their involvement in the educational programmes of their choice, whether these lectures are seminars or periods of journal reading, listening to tapes, watching videos, or using interactive computer programmes in personal study. It is a matter of concern to their colleagues and to professional bodies that a proportion of doctors is known to be out-dated in knowledge and practice, and that some are using hazardous practices. Directors of continuing medical education (CME) recognize a wide spectrum in the priorities doctors give to CME and the time they invest in it (Richmond et al, 1984)

Doctors, then, ought to be concerned as part of their professional obligation about the quality of care they provide. Accountability for quality should be seen as a professional obligation and not just as a response to the pressures of consumerism (Hunter 1981). Concern about quality of care will lead inevitably to the conviction that lifelong learning is an obligation which doctors cannot refuse to accept.

HOW DO ADULTS LEARN?

Knowles (1973), in arguing that most of the scientific theories of learning have been derived from the study of animals and children observes that "the theory and technology on which most of our graduate education is based are at least a generation behind what we know about learning". Interest in the process of adult learning has, however, been increasing in recent years. Tough (1978) surveyed research into adult learning and

showed that the basic situation is remarkably consistent from one population to another. Approximately 90% of persons conduct at least one major learning effort per year. Of these learning projects, in excess of 70% are self-planned, 10–15% are group projects and the remainder are discussion-type projects on a one-to-one basis with either peers, a professional assistant, or a non-human resource such as a computer. Studies such as those by Manning and Dennison (1979), Ellsworth and Graeber (1971) and Guptill and Graham (1976) illustrate the importance of self-learning in the field of medicine.

Preferences for learning methods differ from person to person. Houle (1978) notes that 'In all curricula . . . attention must be given to individual differences. In continuing education particularly, where the establishment of individual ways of work, of specialization of practice, and of various settings of employment all accentuate diversity, special efforts must be made to avoid a monotonous uniformity of training activities. . . . a much greater indvidualization than at present must be provided so that the whole program does not rest on a single process, however established its traditions or intriguing its novelty may be'. Thorpe (1979), reporting exercise designed to discover the learning styles of medical practitioners, found what he believed to be differences in the approach to CME by medical specialty; psychiatrists, for example, tended to learn best by abstract, introspective reasoning through literature and encounter groups, surgeons from one to one instruction or personal preceptorship. Whether or not these generalizations hold true for the specialties, there is no doubt that there is a wide range of preferences for learning styles between individuals.

Research indicates that adult education is most effective and interesting when it has relevance to the professional needs of the individual. As Houle (1978) summarizes it, 'The chief lessons learned by a professional during the years of active service are the intentional or unintentional products of the work itself . . . . . when the professional enters the service, the problems presented by particular cases become the absorbing centre of attention. The confrontation of these problems is the most significant stimulus for continuing education throughout the whole course of an active career' Margulies and Raia (1976) asked 290 scientists and engineers 'What was the most fruitful learning experience you have had over the past year or two?' The most frequent response was "on the job problem solving". Tough (1971) was interested to determine what motivated adults to begin a learning project and found that his subjects 'anticipated several desired outcomes and benefits to result . . . . some of the benefits were immediate, e.g. satisfying their curiosity, enjoying the content itself, enjoying practising a skill . . . . . others longterm; producing something, imparting knowledge and skills to others, understanding what will happen in some future situation, etc.'

In this theory of adult learning (andragogy) Knowles (1973) makes several assumptions about adult learners. One of these is that, as an individual matures, 'his readiness to learn is decreasingly a product of his biological development and academic pressure and is increasingly the product of the development tasks required for the performance of his evolving role. Andragogical theory assumes that learners are ready to learn those things they 'need' because of the developmental phases they are approaching in their roles as workers . . . . .' Another assumption is that 'the adult . . . . . comes into an educational activity largely because he is experiencing some inadequacy in coping with current life problems. He wants to apply to tomorrow what he learns today'.

The basis of B.F. Skinner's theory of behaviour (Skinner 1971) is that behaviour is determined by its consequences, and that the way to change behaviour is change the consequences and therefore rearrange the 'contingencies of reinforcement'. According to his theories, behaviour which has reinforcing consequences (rewards) is more likely to occur again; and behaviour which has aversive consequences (punishments) is less likely to recur. In a sense, the latter could be characterized as 'learning from one's mistakes'. In the world in which doctors live, the 'rewards' for developing and practising 'good' behaviour has thus far proved to be extremely difficult; and where rewards have been given for 'good' behav-

iour (e.g. The American Medical Association Physicians' Recognition Award), they are based on behaviours which, although easily measured (e.g. attendance at CME programs), have not been proven to effectively improve clinical performance or the quality of care practised by physicians. However, active monitoring of doctors' behaviour with a view to applying sanctions or recommending remedial actions where needed, is capable of altering it (De Dombal et al, 1974; Lembke, 1956; Sanazaro & Worth, 1978). This is one rationale for quality assurance and peer review activities. From the viewpoint of continuing education it is important that quality assurance activities be linked with CME because the methods of determining where current standards of practice fall short can also be used to identify educational needs. Relevant CME may then be prescribed (Sanazaro, 1976). In summary, principles of adult learning emphasize that:

Many learning efforts are self initiated, managed and evaluated

Learnig is most effective when based on perceived needs

Individuals differ in their preferred methods for learning

Work-related problems often determine topics for learning, and such learning builds on existing knowledge

Both potential rewards and the realization of the need for remedial action may induce further learning activities.

HOW WELL DO UNDERGRADUATE MEDICAL CURRICULA CONFORM TO THESE PRINCIPLES OF ADULT LEARNING?

Many constraints on undergraduate curricula militate against conformity to these principles. Some are as follow:

An apparent disproportion exists between the mass of information which 'must' be taught and the relatively short time available for teaching. This leads to an emphasis on lecture formats (often even during small group work) and a tendency to dogmatic assertions about biomedical 'truth'. Students are faced with four to six years of intensive cramming in order to accumulate 'facts' Could it be that the sheer intensity of this learning process suppresses forever the joy of learning?

The need to evaluate student progress. The danger here is of an examination-oriented curriculum encouraging examination-oriented student approaches to learning. Unfortunately,it is also a problem which has dogged many CME programs because their organizers are biased towards undergraduate-type evaluation methods.

Many medical school teachers have no experience of life as an isolated practitioner out in the world. Most have regular exposure to hospital-based learning and peer review programs and ease of access to colleagues for informal discussion. Hence they may not be able to coach students in effective self-initiated learning methods.

Medical school teachers may be unfamiliar with technological advances in information retrieval and delivery systems which are going to alter radically the world of informatics in the near future.

Students are seldom able to observe their teachers in the role of learners in CME, peer review and quality assurance type activities, and therefore, have no role models to follow

Despite increasing time spent in clinical activities, and in electives, projects and essays, students still have little involvement in deciding what they need to learn and the rate at which they must learn. Hence, personal responsibility for planning lifelong learning is not fostered.

There are penalties for admitting ignorance as a student. Does this suppress the ability to honestly evaluate one's learning needs at a later date?

HOW MAY STUDENTS BE PREPARED FOR CONTINUING EDUCATION?

Two aspects must be considered:

Developing positive attitudes

It may be more important to begin by attempting to influence the teachers' attitudes to CME rather than the students'. Strategies which may be helpful include:

1. Setting as an explicit curricular goal the preparation of students for lifelong learning, and ensuring that each department evaluates how its teaching seeks to meet that goal.

Awakening Interest in CME Within the School.

Why not:

* ask each department to describe the way its programs specifically prepare students to be life-long learners?

2. A commitment by medical school administrators to encourage teachers to use continuing education opportunities themselves.

3. Involvement of university faculties of medicine in responsibility for organizing CME.

Strategies aimed at students' attitudes could include

1. Selecting students with appropriate attitudes. Psychological testing may allow medical schools to select students who have 'enquiring minds' (Gunzburger [1980]; Finestone et al [1981]) but whether this will lead to greater involvement in CME as well as, for instance, interest in research is not entirely clear.

2. The introduction of teaching information on the theory and practice of CME including teaching about adult education theory, the need for continuing education, information about opportunities for continuing education and a discussion of students' attitudes to it. Caplan (1977) has reported the limited knowledge which medical students have about opportunities for and methods of CME.

3. Planning undergraduate courses which are consistent elements of adult education theory and practice. These could include providing students with opportunities for self-assessment of progress — including developing their own criteria for achievement — encouraging them to take part in peer review techniques, allowing them to observe their teachers' involvement in peer review and CME as learners, requiring students to obtain increasingly substantial amounts of information from sources such as the library and journals rather than from lectures and handouts and a switch in the philosophy of teaching to encourage 'evolutionary thinking' by emphasizing what is not

yet known, and what is likely to change; and the recognition that most of today's biomedical 'truth' may yet be subject to challenge. At every level of the medical course, it must be clear to students why these approaches are being taken. Approaches to try

Developing positive attitudes to CME

Why not:

* organize discussion groups on selected cases from the annual reports of medical defence agencies, medical disciplinary bodies or legal publication where sub-optimal practice was an issue?

* prepare information on areas of medical practice in which knowledge and/or techniques have changed so much in the last 20 years as to alter the clinical management of patients radically — e.g. trends in management of angina pectoris, myocardial infarction

Encouraging interest in peer review.

Why not:

* during small group clinical instruction, have students observe one another's techniques of history-taking and physical examination and critique them, the teacher monitoring the process?

* have students mark each other's case histories and comment on them according to guidelines drawn up in collaboration with the teacher?

Providing skills and technology

Appropriate strategies might include:

1. Providing practice with self-learning methods and self-paced learning in some areas of the undergraduate course, for example, reading about clinical cases, developing skills in using audiotape, videotape, and computer-based intruction.

2. Practice in self-assessment and identification of learning needs. A recent review of the curriculum in my own Faculty reveals how little formative evaluation exists and how little of that involves student self-assessment.

3. Emphasis on technology which will enable students to discover more easily Information they lack, e.g. computerized literature searching, developing personal filing systems, or skills in data

transmission. Medical schools must increasingly be involved in the developing computerized information networks both within the hospital and in the wider community medicine.

4. Developing skills in critical assessment of clinical evidence and the medical literature. Faced with the burgeoning literature the practitioners of the future must have skills In deciding what is worth reading and assimilating (Dept of Clin. Epid & Biostats., McMaster University 1981). Courses in critical assessment ought to be mandatory as part of every curriculum.

5. Teaching management skills and the effective use of time.

6. Involving students in CME research or in projects relating to CME so that they begin to get a 'feel' for involvement in it (Jewell & Schneidermann 1978). Approaches to try.

Providing experience in self-learning. Why not:

* require that with every case-history written, the student also provides a minimum of two pages of referenced discussion on some aspect of the patient's problem, from sources other than textbooks?

* organize sections of the course to include self-paced learning as exemplified, for instance, by Brewer (1977)?

Developing Skills in the Assessment of Learning Needs. Why not:

* following written formative evaluations — including MCQs — have students use their marked exam scripts as the basis for listing areas of knowledge deficiency; and these in turn to determine the subject matter of a subsequent series of brief assignments?

ARE THESE APPROACHES SUCCESSFULL?

The literature on the motivation of students towards CME is sparse. So far there has been little evaluation of the effects of problem based learning and other relatively new curricular approaches on the behaviour of the graduate in terms of involvement in CME. This is mainly because the more modern schools which have opted for radically different curricular approaches have yet to graduate enough classes to be able to evaluate the outcome on a longterm basis. It will be important for those schools to investigate this question if the validity of the approaches they are taking is to be established. When validity is established, schools which have thus far opted for a more traditional curriculum, will have a greater incentive to consider other educational approaches.

REFERENCES

Brewer Ilma M 1977 SIMIG A case study of an innovative method of teaching and learning. Studies in Higher Education 2: 33–54

Caplan R M 1977 Relating undergraduate medical education to continuing medical education. Journal of Medical Education 52: 674–6

De Dombal F T Leaper D J Horrocks Jane C et at 1974 Human and computer-aided dignosis of abdominal pain. Further report with emphasis on performance of clinicians. British Medical Journal 1: 376–380

Department of Clinical Epidemiology and Biostatics, McMaster University Health Sciences Centre 1981 How to read clinical journals. Canadian Medical Association Journal 124: 377–81, 703–10, 869–72, 985–90, 1156–62

Finestone A J Brigham M P Strony J et al 1981 Can Medical School Admission Criteria Identify Life Long Learners? AMA Con Med Ed Newsletter 10: 2–6

Gunzburger C F 1980 Characteristics identified upon entrance to medical school associated with future participation in professional education. Annual Conference in Research in Medical Education 19: 117–22

Houle C O 1980 Continuing learning in the professions. Jossey-Bass, San Francisco

Hunter J D 1981 continued learning for the professional. New Zealand Medical Journal 94: 219–23

Jewell S E and Schneiderman L J 1978 Students in CME. Journal of Medical Education 53: 1008–9

Knowles M 1973 The adult learner — a neglected species. Gulf Publishing, Houston

Lembke P A 1956 Medical auditing by scientific methods, illustrated by major female pelvis surgery. Journal of the American Medical Association 162: 646–655

Price D S 1980 Warren K S Coping with the biomedical literature, Praeger, New York

Richmond D E Hannan S and Hunter J D 1984 A survey of the participation of physicians in continuing medical education. New Zealand Journal of Adult learning 16: 164–79

Sanazaro P J 1976 Medical audit, continuing medical education and quality assurance. Western Medical Journal 125: 241–52

Sanazaro P J and Worth R M 1980 Concurrent quality assurance in hospital care: Report of a study by private initiative in P.S.R.O. New England Journal of Medicine 298: 1171–1177

Skinner B F 1971 The adult's learning projects. Ontario Institute for Studies in Education, Toronto Tough

A 1971 The adult's learning projects. Ontario Institute for Studies in Education, Toronto

Tough A 1978 Major learning efforts: recent research and future direction. Adult Education 28: 250–63

Thorpe J H 1979 Learning Styles in CME. American Medical Association Continuing Medical Education Newsletter 8: (8) 9

Assessment

Introduction

Recognizing the continuing dissatisfaction among medical teachers with available assessment methods, we have attempted to extend our ideas in new chapters describing 'free response' written tests, and we comment upon the management questions of MCQ banking. Patient management problems have continued to develop, and are covered somewhat differently.

International interest has grown rapidly in Structured Clinical Examinations. This area has been expanded by one of the technique's most vigorous developers.

Performance assessment continues to present problems because of its extraordinary complexity, and for the necessity for judgment in choosing what to look at, and how to calibrate it. The chapter perhaps raises more questions than it answers.

A chapter has been added on self assessment, which we see as about to grow very rapidly in importance. The two last chapters deal with scoring, particularly attempting to expose the assumptions under many of our practices. Clearing this ground seems to be a prior step to freeing up the scoring process.

What type of written examination should I use?

The common written examination methods (pen and paper tests) can be separated into four categories for comparison

1. Essays
2. Short answer questions
3. Modified essay questions (MEQs)
4. Multiple-choice questions (MCQs).

This chapter is directed to the usefulness and the relative advantages and disadvantages of each. None of the methods meets all the criteria of the perfect test. It is for the teacher to decide which mix of features,on balance, meets the needs best. Practical steps in their construction and improvement will be set out in subsequent chapters.

The two most popular forms, essays and multiple-choice questions, represent the two ends of the spectrum from free to fixed response within which the others fall

ESSAYS VS MCQs

1. An essay question tests the student's store of information and tests ability to organize ideas, plan an answer and express it lucidly. An MCQ item requires the student to choose among a fixed set of alternatives.

2. An essay can sample only a small number of areas using relatively general questions calling for extended answers. Students can be shrewd or lucky in studying towards those areas.

An MCQ test can sample a broad range and variety of facts using specific questions requiring a choice among responses

3. Students spend most of their time thinking and writing in essay tests. Students spend most of their time reading and thinking in MCQ tests.

4. Essay tests permit a position to be expounded and qualified. Examiners can reward the student's reasoning.

MCQ tests provide no opportunity for qualifying the choice made. Answers are right or wrong, with no credit for partial information.

5. Essay tests permit, and occasionally encourage, bluffing. MCQ tests permit, and occasionally encourage, guessing (Ebel, 1972).

6. Essay examinations are easy to set, but extremely time-consuming in their marking.

MCQ examinations are extremely time-consuming in construction, but are rapidly machine-scored, and economical for large groups.

7. The quality of an essay test is determined largely by the skill of the reader of the students' answers. Examiners are not, however, consistent on the criteria used, and correlations within and among examiners are low (Bull, 1956). The standards are implicit within examiners, not explicit within the student's task.

The quality of an MCQ is determined largely by the skill of the test constructors. Examiners often take considerable time and discussion to reach agreement, but this difficulty is not reflected in the single choice format. The student's task and the basis on which its achievement is judged are, however, explicit with MCQ tests.

8. In essay tests no cues are given to the 'correct' answers.

With MCQ tests the 'correct' answer is provided for recognition, a situation not equivalent to real practice.

9. Essay tests are not usually returned to students with extensive comment; educational feedback is limited or absent. Teachers receive negligible data on areas of weakness in the students as a group or the examination as a whole. That is, the bulk of words generated by a class of students is indigestible and very difficult to analyze except by impression. Some highlights might be noted, but no quantitative information is available.

MCQ tests can be computer analyzed to provide detailed feedback to examiners, teachers and students; this feedback is, however, rarely given to students.

10. With essay tests, the distribution of scores is strongly affected by the beliefs of the examiner. Some examiners mark within a narrow range of 45 to 75 per cent, and others from 0 to 100 per cent. Some are marking by comparison with other students. Some mark by comparison with specialist knowledge.

With MCQ tests, the distribution of scores is determined by the test (the correct answers for which are determined by the beliefs of examiners).

11. With essay tests, the standards for scoring vary with the group of examiners.

With MCQ tests, the standards for scoring can be kept constant for years.

12. Essay tests are usually created and marked independently by specialist professionals who are not trained in examining and who do not often collaborate on studying the examination.

MCQ tests are usually created jointly by specialist professionals who collaborate in constructing the questions, and who may learn something of examining in the process.

13. The human scoring of essays is subjective and unreliable. The machine scoring of MCQ tests is objective and reliable.

SUMMARY

Use essay tests when
1. the student group is small

2. the purposes include encouragement and testing of abilities in written self-expression
3. the examiner is satisfied that a few questions in depth provide a sufficient sample of the content to be tested
4. the examiner feels more proficient as a fair and critical reader of essays than as a writer of MCQ tests
5. objective and reliable marking is not regarded as critically as the need to allow free expression.

Use MCQ tests when
1. the student group is large
2. the purposes include testing a broad range of facts and concepts
3. the examiner feels more proficient in constructing sound MCQ items than in marking essays fairly and consistently
4. impartial, fair and reliable scoring is critical
5. time is available for test preparation.

The practical preparation and use of essays and MCQ tests will be set out in subsequent chapters.

SHORT ANSWER QUESTIONS

Some of the disadvantages of essays can be reduced if precise, limited questions are posed with only breif responses expected.

The advantages of short answer questions are that
1. questions are easily set
2. the range of subject areas tested is increased
3. examiners can more easily agree on what answers are acceptable, and how to score them
4. the objectivity and reliability of marking increase sharply (Mowbray & Davies, 1967; Wakeford & Roberts, 1979)
5. cues to correct answers are not provided.

The disadvantages of short answer questions are that
1. the range of subject areas tested is still limited
2. marking still requires the time of specialist professionals, and some subjective judgements for 'nearly correct' answers
3. the responses sought are often the recall of key words, rather than reasoned discussions; questions can often be trivial
4. given the limited extent of the questions and the response, MCQ tests are far more efficient for the same purpose.

Correlations of scores on short answer tests with MCQ test scores are high (Ebel, 1972), demonstrating that the outcome will be similar whichever test is used, and implying that similar characteristics are being measured.

Use short answer tests if examiners do not accept MCQ tests, but still wish to sample more broadly and score fairly.

MODIFIED ESSAY QUESTIONS (MEQs)

The format is based on a case history which is presented in successive stages (see Ch. 36). The candidate is presented with description of a clinical scenario followed by one or two questions on interpretation of signs and what actions should be taken. Having answered those questions, the student passes to the next phase in the patient's illness, with a further three or four sentences of scenario followed by questions.

The advantages of the MEQs are
1. the use of clinical descriptions raises the validity of the test as a measure of clinical competence
2. practical management responses to an undifferentiated problem can be tested
3. areas of clinical weakness for individuals and the group can be identified for teachers
4. management can be tested through the phases of diagnosis, investigation, treatment and counselling.

The disadvantages of the MEQs are
1. marking requires professional time and judgement. Examiners must test the question, agree upon the expected answers, and use judgement on whether the response are acceptable

2. each case requires extensive time to prepare and test; once used, it may become known to examinees
3. each case represents an examination in itself; to the extent that the content area is familiar or not, candidates can be more or less lucky
4. the information provided at each step is limited, which can frustrate candidates
5. candidates have difficulty allotting time among the various steps.

The MEQs can be seen as a structured form of the Case Commentary, in which a clinical story was set out in extenso, and the candidate could choose reasonably freely which areas upon which to comment. The MEQ, however, requires the candidate to describe what to *do*, rather than allowing the liberty to avoid decisions.

SUMMARY

To repeat, no written examination method is perfect, and each method has different attributes. The teacher's task is to choose the method which is capable of testing for the purposes for which this examination is intended, which is appropriate for the particular subject matter, which the other teacher/examiners accept and are skilled in, and which is understood and handled satisfactorily by students. Sometimes more than one method is needed (Lipton & Huxham, 1978). Multiple Choice Question and Modified Essay Question methods require considerable preparatory work ahead of the examination, and the solving of associated logistic problems. Essays and short answer questions are often used because few teachers had the energy for that preparatory work.

REFERENCES

Bull G M 1956 An examination of the final examination in medicine. Lancet 2: 368–372
An early paper revealing inconsistencies which stimulated much subsequent analysis
Ebel R L 1972 Essentials of educational measurement. Prentice-Hall, New Jersey
A thorough lucid textbook embracing the whole field
Lipton A, Huxham G J 1978 Examination design and preparation. Medical Education 12: 159–167 A review of rules to guide examiners
Mowbray R M, Davies B M 1967 Short note and essay examinations compared. British Journal of Medical Education 1: 356–358
Wakeford R E, Roberts S 1979 A pilot experiment on the inter-examiner reliability of short essay questions. Medical Education 13: 342–344

BIBLIOGRAPHY

Hubbard J P 1971 Measuring medical education. Lea and Febiger, Philadelphia
A review of the test procedures used by the National Board of Medical Examiners in the USA, the agency which has done most to advance MCQ testing in medicine.

How to manage written tests: short answer, modified essay and long essay questions

Preview

WHY USE WRITTEN TESTS?

HOW CAN WRITTEN TESTS BE IMPROVED IN DESIGN?

HOW CAN WRITTEN TESTS BE BETTER CONSTRUCTED?

HOW CAN WRITTEN TESTS BE IMPLEMENTED EFFECTIVELY

HOW CAN MARKING, ANALYSIS AND FEEDBACK ON PERFORMANCE BE FACILITATED?

SUMMARY

WHY USE WRITTEN TESTS?

For this paper, written tests are those requiring an extended answer (i.e. paragraphs, sentences or lists of words). The features of these tests have been summarized and compared, in Ch. 34, The Medical Teacher (Cox & Ewan, 1982). The collective advantage of Short Answer (SAQ), Modified Essay (MEQ) and Long Essay Questions (LEQ) is to allow examinees more time to think (than do viva or clininal methods), a and better chance to express their answer (than do multiple choice questions).

By opting for these kinds of open-ended question it is clear that examiners do not expect a singular, or word-perfect answer. This more flexible approach suggests that consideration of *how* the answer is derived or presented by the examinee may modify *what* is expected in it and the mark given.

Unfortunately, this feature is also open to abuse. Some questions may be too ambiguous, which is frustrating to students keen to do well. Some answers may be deliberately vague in return, or difficult to read. Consequently they become more inefficient to mark, less reliable in scores given or less popular for examiner use.

Rather than reiterate the distinct merits of each type of written test (Cox & Ewan, 1982) this paper focuses on how to design, construct, implement, and analyze them with a view to obtaining a more valid and reliable measure of examinees' competence.

HOW CAN WRITTEN TESTS BE IMPROVED IN DESIGN?

Examiners can take more advantage of these tests to see how well examinees can *integrate* and *apply their knowledge* to solve and/or manage clinical problems. Even if diagnoses or management decisions are tested by multiple choice question (MCQ), the written part of that answer might require the examinee to justify or explain it in terms of basic mechanisms of disease or management. Here are some suggestions for each kind of test.

Short Answer Questions (SAQ)

SAQ could begin with a brief scenario or clinical problem, such as given in Figure 22.1. By requiring only a short answer this method enables wide sampling of knowledge by using many items, meanwhile reducing unreliability in scores due to cuing and guesswork in answers.

Suppose you are an intern in the Casualty Ward of the Royal Newcastle Hospital. Using the information provided, answer as follows:

1. For the following patient problem indicate the order in which you consider the possible management steps should be carried out:

    A. Resuscitation
    B. Diagnosis i.e. Relevant History + Examination + Investigations
    C. Specialist Referral
    D. Definite medical and/or surgical treatment
    E. Patient/relatives/friends explanation

YOU DO NOT NEED TO RECOMMEND ALL MANAGEMENT STEPS

2. Beside each step indicate the time frame in seconds, minutes, hours, days you consider appropriate for implementation of each step

3. List 1-3 diagnoses you consider are the most likely (Provisional Diagnoses). YOU DO NOT NEED TO LIST 3

	Management Step Order	Time Frame
EXAMPLE		
A 25 year old female presents	A	minutes
to Casualty complaining of severe	B	minutes
lower abdominal pain and vaginal	C	minutes
bleeding. Her pulse is 120, BP 70/20.	D	hours
	E	hours

Provisional Diagnoses

Ruptured ectopic pregnancy
Incomplete abortion

* Extracted from third-year student assessment (1985) at the University of Newcastle, New South Wales
This item was developed by Professor Robert Burton

Fig. 22.1 An example of a Short-Answer Question* using a simple multiple choice and written response in solving and managing a medical problem

The Modified Essay Question (MEQ)

MEQ presents a logical sequence of short answer questions, relating to an initial scenario or clinical problem (Hodgkin & Knox, 1975). New data may accompany successive items, which test the integration of relevant knowledge in examinees' intended action or its justification. Items must be attempted in strict sequence, page by page, without previewing the outcome of the problem or turning back to change previous answers in the light of subsequent information. If a wide sample of medical problems or skills is desirable, MEQs can be limited to a few items each. Some MEQs could then focus on management (emergency or subsequent) and others on information-getting (from history or examination) or diagnosis (including interpretation of laboratory test results). A more extensive treatment of the MEQ is given by Feletti & Smith (in press).

The Long Essay Question (LEQ), unlike the MEQ presents the whole problem initially. It then

Mr J. Lewis is aged 26 and has recently diagnosed mild essential hypertension. Since his hypertension is mild and he is not keen to commence drug therapy, you decide to commence a trial of dietary therapy.

Question	a)	Discuss the role of dietary sodium restriction in the treatment of hypertension
	b)	Include epidemiological data supporting or refuting its use as well as evidence (or lack thereof) of its therapeutic effect.

Model Answer	a)	Treatment: - several studies showing that mild, moderate and severe dietary salt restriction reduces BP - others that don't - evidence that increasing salt intake to people with essential H/T does not alter BP
	b)	Epidemiology - Dahl's graph of increasing BP with increasing salt intake in different communities - lack of good evidence within communities - evidence that population groups that move from low salt to high salt diet develop an increase in BP - recent US evidence that people with a high salt intake have a lower BP when compared to those with a low salt intake
Mandatory Level of Competence (MLC) for this item	a) b)	2 of 3 points 2 of 4 points

* Extracted from third-year assessment (1985) at the University of Newcastle, New South Wales
This item was prepared by Dr Shane L. Carney

Fig. 22.2 An example of an MEQ item*, Model Answer and MLC split into two 5-minute parts (of equal value), testing examinees' understanding of basic science in relation to a clinical problem

requires a more comprehensive answer in terms of the most relevant aspects, and at an adequate level of explanation within the given time. Organization of thought and clear expression of ideas are inseparable in this kind of test.

For all three forms of written test both the answer and its marking can be facilitated by including instructions to examinees on which aspects to discuss, and how the response time should be apportioned (see Figure 22.2). This practice should lead to their answers being a more accurate measure of performance, given a valid set of questions.

HOW CAN WRITTEN TESTS BE BETTER CONSTRUCTED?

The actual test(s) chosen will depend on the desired areas of competence (*see* Feletti et al, 1983), the extent of sampling needed (i.e. wide area or focused), and the time and other resources available (to design, implement and mark items). Unfortunately no simple formula exists for choosing the best balance of tests. While the SAQ, MEQ and LEQ each have separate advantages, they also share certain features of construction. A common checklist is presented in Figure 22.3,

1. What is the main emphasis (e.g. recall, understanding, application) or rough balance of skills to be tested?

2. How many areas are to be tested? What extent of sampling is required? (Therefore, how much time per item?)

3. Is it desirable to test examinees' integration of subject areas, discipline-based knowledge, or different skill domains?

4. What kind of written test(s) will best satisfy 1. to 3. (above), given other factors such as: number of students, staff and time available?

5. Develop a simple, realistic scenario or problem (which includes: a local setting or common context, the examinee's simulated role, the immediate task, available resources).

6. If integration is intended, draft a skeleton outline of each problem which initially incorporates items in those areas. Plan for and encourage contributions from relevant staff (as potential examiners) at a very early stage.

7. Identify (small teams of) examiners for each test. Check their availability for item construction and marking. Nominate one person with overall responsibility for collating and checking items, model answers and scoring systems.

8. Develop procedures and deadlines for ensuring progress and quality control checks on each test, and the overall examination (e.g. by correspondence or regular meetings).

9. Identify special procedures, facilities and timescales needed a) for the examination itself; b) for marking and reliability checks; and c) for decision-making in relation to progress or re-examination, and any remediation.

Fig. 22.3 A checklist for constructing written tests in a given subject, discipline or skill domain

aimed to improve the choice of test and minimize difficulties in construction.

These procedures can be facilitated by having an academic coordinator of examinations (for a given year), who initiates steps 1–4 (above) in consultation with a handful of key (subject) examiners. The drafts (steps 5 and 6) of these tests are made available, at a set location and for a brief period only, to relevant other staff members (e.g. discipline heads) for their inspection and interaction, resulting in step 7. The coordinator then completes steps 8 and 9 by passing on administrative needs and duties to the designated non-academic or clerical staff. For example, the specific nature of the MEQ requires special instructions to examinees on how to answer, additional guidelines to invigilators about closer supervision, and an extra back page for various examiners to record their item-specific judgments

and make recommendations for further attention by the examinees.

HOW CAN WRITTEN TESTS BE IMPLEMENTED EFFECTIVELY?

The effectiveness of any test should relate as much to its educational value as its judgment of competence. This can require a considerable change of attitude by examiners, but needs little additional effort of organization to initiate the following actions.

1. After the examination, allow examinees (as a group) to review the questions, model answers and pass standards.

2. Timetable such a review session *before* marking occurs, and allow examinees to submit constructive suggestions for varying the marking on any item.

3. Allow examiners sufficient time and opportunity to review these suggestions and include acceptable ones into their pre-set scoring system (and adjust the marks accordingly).

4. Allow time for staff to debrief students (as a group) about the accepted marking changes, as well as collective strengths and weaknesses in performance.

5. After marking and notification of results, allow students to review their own papers, and to use them for remedial purposes. (A more comprehensive description of these five steps in operation is given by Leeder et al, 1979).

HOW CAN MARKING, ANALYSIS AND FEEDBACK ON PERFORMANCE BE FACILITATED?

The time available, and the effort required to mark written tests manually, can be a major disincentive (rather than disadvantage) to examiners. For Short Answer and Modified Essay Questions, marking should be easiest for items testing factual recall. Correct answers may only involve key words, phrases or sentences.

Items testing understanding of principles or the integration and application of knowledge, however, present more of a challenge to examinee and examiner. A model answer should always be developed for these kinds of item, but the marking should be figuratively rather than literally based (see Figure 22.2 for example).

To ensure mark equivalence between items, and hence to make scores more valid and reliable, examiners are encouraged to develop their items and marking schema based on a notional 5-minute unit (for 1 mark). Thus, each SAQ may be of 5 minutes' duration (each with a simple pass standard which scores 1 mark). An MEQ may contain several 5 and 10 minute items. Satisfactory answers for those items would get 1 and 2 marks respectively. An LEQ with a recommended time limit of 25 minutes should have corresponding criteria for marking that answer, as if it contained five 5-minute items (each worth 1 mark). Not only does this simplify the addition of marks from various written tests but also it should facilitate marking and analysis of performance based on item-type or representation (e.g. by discipline). The reliability of scoring can then be tested by having two or more examiners score blindly each student's paper, particularly with the LEQ. Scoring differences in excess of 10% suggest that examiners are expecting different answers. Such differences may be reconciled by discussion with discipline heads and/or a conference of examiners.

It is fairly simple procedure to categorize items prior to examination. This enables a check on the relative balance of skills or knowledge (mentioned in Figure 22.3), as well as providing a uniform basis for making overall judgments of competence on the written test, and identifying particular areas for further remediation or re-examination (see Bobula, 1974, for a useful general schema for item categorization).

SUMMARY

Written tests such as the SAQ, MEQ and LEQ have a common advantage to medical teachers interested in measuring how well examinees can integrate and apply clinical knowledge without the patient or examiner being present, or time pressures. Short Answer Questions are perhaps the most versatile to set; they provide comprehensive sampling of knowledge, and are easiest to mark. Modified Essay and Long Essay questions, however, have the capacity to present and/or require a systematic outline of an examinee's approach to solving or managing a simulated problem. Procedures have been recommended for the construction of these written tests which should make them more valid and reliable. A system is also described which, if implemented conscientiously, will improve the educational value of any written examination for both examiner and examinee.

REFERENCES

Bobula J A 1974 Examinations and decision-making, in Educational Strategies for the Health Professions. WHO, Geneva, Public Health Papers No 61
Cox K R, Ewan C E 1982 The Medical Teacher. Churchill Livingstone, Edinburgh
Feletti G I, Saunders N A, Smith A J S 1983 Comprehensive assessment of final-year medical student performance based on undergraduate program objectives. Lancet, July 2, 34–37

Feletti G I, Smith E K M Modified essay questions: are they worth the effort? Medical Education (in press)
Hodgkin K, Knox J D E 1975 Problem centred learning. Churchill Livingstone, Edinburgh
Leeder, S R, Engel C E, Feletti G I 1979 Assessment — help or hurdle? Journal of the Association for Programmed Learning and Educational Technology 16: 308

Writing multiple choice questions

Preview

PLAN THE QUESTION

Ensure that the question deals with an important aspect of the subject
Test knowledge around the central theme in each question
Decide on what ability you wish to test
Consider how the 'fact' should be presented

WRITE THE QUESTION

Use simple and clear language
Write the stem as a question
Keep the reading time of the question to a minimum
Make responses clear and concise Avoid clues to the correct answer
Use only plausible and logical distractors
Do not include eponyms, acronyms or abbreviations
Specify units of laboratory investigations precisely
Minimize negatively phrased statements
Beware of asking two questions at the same time

TEST THE QUESTION

Multiple choice questions are increasingly used in the assessment of medical students. Controversy about them, however, is as old as their use. When the arguements against the use of multiple choice questions are examined closely, many of them relate to their inappropriate use or deficiencies in construction (Pickering, 1979). This chapter sets out guidelines for construction of multiple choice questions to maximize the validity and reliability of student assessment using this form of question.

Multiple choice questions are of various structures (Hubbard & Clemans, 1961). The guidelines which follow generally apply to most of these types, but specifically to Type A (one-best response type).

PLAN THE QUESTION

1. Ensure that the question deals with an important and useful aspect of the subject

Too many questions are written around minutiae or trivia of inconsequential knowledge, or about rare conditions, or about decisions that examinees would not be called upon to make. Each question must justify itself as dealing with an issue which is common, or which is serious, or where misunderstandings are frequent and important, or where the knowledge tested is essential to understanding some other concept of importance. The question should be appropriate to the level of knowledge expected of a student at that stage. Test your question out by writing the idea as an explicit statement, proposition or principle. If this would have formed an important part of your instruction, it is worth testing.

Common problems are not easy to write testing questions around. A question such as:

Example 1

The most likely variety of anaemia in a 38-year- old woman is

   A. ....

   B. iron deficiency anaemia
   C. ....

   D. ....

   E. ....

is dull, and tests only recall of information.

Ability to interpret data can be added, e.g. by rephrasing such as:

Example 2

In a 38-year-old woman with the following blood count,

		Normal range
HB	8.9 g/dl	$(14 \pm 2.5$ g/dl)
		Normal range
MCHC	29 g/dl	$(33 \pm 2$ g/dl)
		Normal range
MCV	80 fl	$(85 \pm 8$ fl)
		Normal range
ESR	10 mm	(0–7 mm)

the most likely diagnosis is:
   A. ....
   B. iron deficiency anaemia

Similarly the question:

Example 3

Mild iron defiency anaemia is best treated by:
   A. ....

   B. oral iron supplements

can be combined with the above, finishing with a question such as:

Example 4

In a 38-year-old woman with the following blood count,

		Normal range
Hb	8.9 g/dl	$(14 \pm 2.5$ g/dl)
		Normal range
MCHC	29 g/dl	$(33 \pm 2$ g/dl)
		Normal range
MCV	80 fl	$(85 \pm 8$ fl)
		Normal range
ESR	10 mm	(0–7 mm)

the most appropriate treatment would be:
   A. ....
   B. oral iron supplements
(Example by David Hunt).

2. Test knowledge around a central theme

The examiner should be clear about exactly what fact, concept or generalization is being tested. Otherwise the question is likely to be unclear, and the students will not be sure exactly what is expected of them. This central theme or idea which the question seeks to test should be clearly defined in the stem, and all options within the item should refer to this theme or idea.

3. Decide on what ability you wish to test

Ask yourself the question: 'Do I wish to test recall or recognition of facts and concepts, ability to interpret a set of data, or ability to solve a problem?' While MCQ examinations can test all three (Cox, 1976; Anderson, 1979), papers restricted to factual recall are dull to answer, and do not draw on the intellectual capacity of the brighter students. Nor do they test the ability of the student to apply knowledge to novel or practical situations, e.g. testing anatomical knowledge via clinical questions in questions such as the following.

Example 5

A child has gashed the palmar aspect of her wrist from falling against a window. Which of the following would be evidence of damage to her median nerve?
A. inability to flex the distal interphalangeal joint of the index finger
B. inability to flex the inter-phalangeal joint of the thumb
C. loss of sensation on the palmar aspect of the little finger
D. inability to oppose the thumb to the little finger
E. inability to abduct the index.

4. Consider how the 'facts' of the data should be presented

They could be presented as photographs, radiographs, tracings (e.g. visual fields), diagrams (Hunt, 1978) (e.g. anatomical diagrams) or word descriptions for large numbers of examinees. Movie films and amplified sounds (such as heart and breath sounds) can be used for small groups.

WRITE THE QUESTION

1. Use simple and clear language

When a question or statement is clear to us, we often assume it is also clear to others. But words and sentences can be interpreted differently, especially by anxious examinees who imagine traps set for them (Cox et al, 1973). Avoid using technical terms or unusual words which may not be familiar to examinees. Each question must be 'answered' and subsequently discussed by a group of examiners before anyone can be confident it is unambiguous. Preferably all questions should be tried on a student group, followed by discussion of each with the students. Only thus can one determine what the question is actually testing.

Multiple choice questions provide excellent stimuli within a lecture to test the grasp of principles you have just taught. The opportunity can be used to check for ambiguity with the whole group.

2. Write the stem as a question, if possible

This layout will make the task clear for the examinee. The stem can be an incomplete statement but, if so, ensure that each response follows grammatically and logically from the stem; i.e. the stem plus each response must be a complete sentence correct in syntax and grammar. Items which use just one or two words in the stem are better avoided.

Example 6

Hair:
A. growth in man shows the phenomenon of asynchronous cyclic growth
B. ....

3. Keep the reading time of the question to a minimum

Include only material or explanations necessary for the solution of the question.

Example 7

In considering your management of a 28-year-old fashion designer with bleeding from the nose, you would be aware that the most frequent cause of epistaxis at any age is
A. ....

4. Make the responses as clear and concise as possible

The more words in a response, the more oppor-

tunities arise for semantic confusion. If a response needs a large number of words in order to qualify what is meant by it, the question is probably too complex for a multiple choice format. All common elements in the responses should be included in the stem.

Example 8

The third part of the duodenum
A. is anterior to the uncinate process of the pancreas
B. is anterior to the common bile duct
C. is anterior to the right ureter
D. is anterior to the superior mesenteric artery
E. is anterior to the inferior mesenteric vein.

The phrase 'is anterior to' is better included in the stem.

5. Aviod clues to the correct answer

Some common ways in which clues are provided are:

a. The use of stereotyped or standard phraseology e.g. the pituitary gland is the master of the endocrine orchestra.

b. The unequal length of alternatives. If one response is clearly longer than the others, it is usually the 'correct' answer, which has been excessively qualified so that it is unambiguously 'true'.

Example 9

An intercostal tube may be placed in a patient with a flail chest but without a pneumothorax or haemothorax to
A. remove air
B. remove blood
C. prevent onset of pulmonary contusion
D. prevent development of a tension pneumothorax when the patient is placed on positive pressure ventilation
E. eliminate paradoxical movement of the flail segment.

c. Obvious inconsistencies between the stem and a response. Responses A and B in Example 9 are obviously wrong as the stem indicates there is no air or blood in the pleural cavity. This inconsistency would be obvious even to an examinee who does not know why an intercostal tube is placed in such a patient, but who knows the definition of 'pneumothorax' and 'haemothorax'. This is also true of response A in Example 10, as paralysis of a vocal cord cannot be *bilateral*.

d. Using the opposite of the correct answer as a distractor.

Example 10

Paralysis of a vocal cord in a patient with bronchogenic carcinoma is most likely to be:
A. bilateral
B. on the right side
C. on the left side
D. due to metastasis to the larynx
E. due to cigarette smoking

The question is virtually reduced to a 'true false' type on one alternative such as: 'Paralysis of a vocal cord in a patient with bronchogenic carcinoma is commoner on the right side than on the left'.

e. The use of absolutes such as 'always', 'only' or 'never'.

Example 11

Adamantinomata of the mandible
A. never metastasize
B. usually metastasize to lymph nodes
C. are predominantly locally malignant
D. usually metastasize to the lungs
E. are benign.

f. The use of synonymous or overlapping alternatives

Example 12

Antidiuretic hormone is synthesized in
A. the anterior lobe of the pituitary gland
B. the posterior lobe of the pituitary gland
C. the pars intermedia of the pituitary gland
D. the pars nervosa of the pituitary gland
E. the hypothalamus.

Since response B response C + response D, an examinee who eliminates C and D will obviously eliminate B.

g. The use of distractors of very similiar form so as to make the correct response more conspicuous, as with response E in Example 12.

6. Use only plausible and logical distractors

Distractors should be equally plausible to the naive candidate. If not, they would be disregarded and the question effectively becomes one from 2, 3, or 4 rather than from 5. A good way to derive distractors is to think of the common errors students make, and the common misconceptions they hold. If legitimate distractors cannot be found, consider re-casting the question in a different MCQ format.

7. Eponyms, acronyms and abbreviations

Do not include these without some qualification after each special term. Terms in pathology, for instance, have many synonyms, and do not necessarily carry the same meaning, even in the same university.

8. Specify units

When laboratory investigations are quoted the units must be precisely specified. The normal range for that laboratory should also be quoted (see Example 2). Laboratories can vary substantially, and students from one hospital could read a set of results differently from those from another hospital.

9. Indicate opinions

If a question is based on opinion or authority (where the present state of knowledge is such that the question deals with what has not been established as a fact), indicate whose opinion or what authority it is based on.

Example 13

According to the passive equilibrium model of Kokko (1975) the main factor responsible for the concentration of urine in the loop of Henle is:
A. the relative impermeability of the descending limb of the loop of Henle to sodium chloride
B. the movement of urea out of the apex of the loop of Henle
C. ....

10. Minimize negatively phrased statements

Avoid double negatives, particularly in the stem of the question.

Example 14

Haematemesis is not unexpected in each of the following, expect ....

Such statements confuse examinees, and could become more a test of language comprehension than of the subject matter. Where it is absolutely necessary to use negatively phrased questions, emphasize the words conveying the negative aspect by using capitals and /or underlining, so as to break the examinee's normal positive set. Such questions are best grouped together within the paper.

11. Beware of unintentionally asking two questions in the same option

Never ask two questions in the same option, especially if the answer to one is 'true' and to the other 'false'.

Example 15

Psychological process and gastointestinal fuction are:
A. clearly separable and rarely correlated
B. ....

12. Avoid 'all of the above' and be very careful with 'none of the above' as an option

Example 16

After partial gastrectomy, gastric emptying is abnormal because
A. the pylorus is removed
B. there is interference with the pacemaker
C. the gastric remnant is smaller
D. all of the above
E. none of the above.

An examinee who recognizes any one of the options A, B or C as false would not choose option D. On the other hand, the examinee who recognizes that any two of these options are true would choose option D since only one option is to be chosen. An examinee who recognizes that even one of the options A, B or C is true would not choose option E. 'None of the above' is appropriate only when it is important to conceal the correct response for fear of recognition. Then, every distractor must be unequivocally incorrect.

TEST THE QUESTION

Fellow examiners must agree that the question is worth asking, that it is clearly and unambiguously stated, that they agree on the correct answer, and that the distractors are reasonably plausible alternatives which test common student errors. Students, however, are the best critics, for they can represent the differing interpretations which can be placed on the question, can reveal what the questions was actually testing, can discuss whether the question was testing an important and validly demonstrable proposition, and can indicate the question-answering strategy for dealing with the distractors.

REFERENCES

Anderson J 1979 For multiple choice questions. Medical Teacher 1: 37–42
Cox K R, Ludbrook J, McCarthy W H, Dunstan M 1973 National comparisons in a trial examination in surgery. British Journal of Medical Education 7: 21–24
Culls Australian observations to reveal inconsistencies of interpretation of questions
Cox K R 1976 How did you guess? or What do multiple choice questions measure? Medical Journal of Australia 384–386
Exposes inconsistencies among examiners, and how risky it can be to assume how someone else thinks

Hubbard J P, Clemans W V 1961 Multiple choice examinations in medicine; a guide for examiner and examinee. Lea and Febiger, Philadelphia
Sets out the range of formats for multiple choice questions, together with guidance on construction and many examples (now somewhat out of date)
Hunt D R 1978 Illustrated multiple choice questions. Medical Education 12: 417–420
Presents an interesting study of the same questions posed with and without illustrations
Pickering G 1979 Controversy: against multiple choice questions. Medical Teacher 1: 84–86

How to construct a fair multiple choice question paper

Preview

PLAN WHAT THE EXAMINATION IS TO TEST

CHOOSE THE MCQ TO BE USED

ASSEMBLE A REVIEW TEAM OF FOUR OR FIVE EXAMINERS

LAY OUT THE QUESTION PAPER

PREPARE THE STUDENTS FOR THE TEST

Multiple choice question examinations provide an opportunity for broad sampling across a syllabus, for ensuring balance among the subject areas tested, for efficiently using the limited time of the examination period, and for adjusting the level of difficulty (see Ch. 21).

To the extent that the examination fails to match the subject matter and the teaching emphasis, so it can be unfair. If an examination is too difficult, or poses too many questions for the time, it is unfair. If the examination uses multiple choice questions to test attributes it cannot measure (such as skills in physical examination) it is unfair.

A number of steps should be followed to ensure that the test is fair.

PLAN WHAT THE EXAMINATION IS TO TEST

1. Lay out the syllabus the examination will test. Separate the subject areas or regions, such as respiration, circulation and digestion. Considering the size and importance of each subject, and the emphasis each was given in teaching, allocate a proportion of the examination to each subject.

2. Consider which components are suited to MCQ examination, and which are not. Clear-cut situations with generally agreed solutions are suitable. Ambiguous situations requiring substantial quanlification are not. After separation of components to be tested by other methods, allocate the total number of MCQ among the remaining subject areas so as to ensure broad sampling and a balance which reflects teaching emphasis. Clinical subjects can be cross-divided also e.g. as diagnosis, laboratory investigation, management, therapeutics, prognosis, so that balance across these categories can be ensured. These subdivisions lead to a matrix layout of clinical processes along one axis and subject areas along the other (Fig. 24.1); the layout immediately reveals gaps in coverage, perhaps requiring new MCQ to be written and tested.

3. The total number of questions is determined by the number of subject areas to be sampled, as above, the time available, and the reliability necessary for this examination (see Ch. 25). Allow one minute for each question, then add extra time. For example, for 120 MCQ allow two hours, then add half an hour. Some examinations test how many MCQ students can cover in a short time; examinations in medicine should concentrate on accuracy rather than pace.

CHOOSE THE MCQ TO BE USED

1. Collect the existing MCQ available to you in each of the subject areas to be tested.

	Etiology & pathogenesis	Diagnosis	Differential diagnosis	Investigation	Management	Complications	Rehabilitation	Prognosis
Anesthesia								
Eye								
Ear, nose, throat								
Gut								
Hepato-biliary								
Chest								
Heart								
Peripheral vascular								
Endocrine								
Trauma								
Cold orthopedics								
Plastic & reconstructive								
Neurosurgery								
Urology								
Circulation and resuscitation								
Fluid balance								

Fig. 24.1 Sample matrix for planning a surgical examination

2. Determine whether the available questions are testing the important principles in that subject area. If not, MCQ must be written to embrace what has been taught as important.

Too often questions have been written around rarer aspects with scant attention to common problems which form the core of the subject. At the same time, it is true that questions on common topics can be so obvious as to be trivial. For example, the principle for testing may be that bile salts emulsify fats. A question such as:
The principal function of bile salts is:
A. ....
B. emulsification of fats
is dull to set and to answer.

The principle can be tested by addition of a few other principles, e.g. of absorption and of application of that principle as:
Absence of bile salts in the small bowel results in:
A. ....
B. reduced absorption of vitamin K

The principles can be taken further by linking with clinical application, and by looking at a further consequence, as:
Obstruction of the common bile duct results in:
A. ....
B. reduction in prothrombin concentration

For the physiology student, the recall of a simple principle has been extrapolated to something of a problem-solving exercise without departing from core material.

3. Given sufficient appropriate questions, consider the data on the previous performance of each question. Was it too hard or too easy? Was it marked correct more by the high scorers or low scores in the test, i.e. was it positively discriminatory?* Were two .possible correct answers implied by the analysis? Did the distractors

distract, or were they ignored (see second half of this chapter)? Rewrite unsatisfactory questions.

4. Review each question meticulously searching for errors of grammar or syntax, for ambiguity of phrasing, for eponyms, acronyms and abbreviations, for laboratory data without explanation of the units used and their normal range, for negatives and double negatives, and for spelling errors.

ASSEMBLE A REVIEW TEAM OF FOUR OR FIVE EXAMINERS

1. The team should be familiar with what students are taught, and with the common errors students make.

2. The team should, as individuals, read each question in silence and choose the 'correct' answer. These answers are now compared, and the reasons for differences explored. Differences about what the question was asking are settled by re-editing the phrasing. Differences about matters of fact should cause the question to be set aside. If examiners differ about 'truth', then students are likely to have received differing teaching. If the 'correct' answer is not the same for examiners, which is the 'correct' answer to expect of students? Of course, examiners are capable of reaching consensus if the team is no greater than five. But that eventual consensus among examiners is disregarding the fact that each student is facing the same dilemma that examiners faced. Such questions should be tested out and discussed with student groups to find out exactly what is being tested, before the questions are used within formal examinations.

3. Since this sequence of events takes so long, start preparing next year's examination now!

4. Recognize that not all examiners can write comprehensible MCQ; that learning to write good MCQ takes time — at least a year; that understanding the computer feedback of item analysis data comes slowly — at first, examiners are likely to resent its 'criticism', and to cover their feelings by scoffing; that it is wise to keep an experienced team of MCQ writers and examiners together for some years, and to replace only one at a time in order to preserve the corporate experience.

---

* Students who know the subject well should score more questions correct than students who know the subject less well. Each question can be analyzed by comparing how many of the high scorers (say, the top 25 per cent in this exam) chose the answer keyed as correct compared with the low scorers (say, the bottom 25 per cent in this exam). From this comparison a 'discrimination index' for that question can be derived, counting how effectively the question 'discriminates' between high and low scoring students. If the discrimination index is negative, low scorers had chosen the correct answer more frequently than high scorers. The question should be examined for explanations of why high scorers have not chosen the 'correct answer'.

LAY OUT THE QUESTION PAPER

1. Decide if subject areas are to be grouped, or deliberately mixed through the paper. Students prefer questions grouped and dislike shifting their thinking from one area to another. Examiners often prefer mixing so that each question is handled on its own merits, not as a result of a set approach.

2. Check the phrasing of the instructions to students on how to answer questions. Ensure that the correct set of instructions for that MCQ format has been used. If possible, arrange that the instructions appear at the top of each page of questions.

3. Separate negatively phrased questions with 'not' or 'except' in their stem. Group these questions together. Ensure that the 'not' and 'except' are in capitals and/or bold type and/or underlined. Ensure that the directions at the top of the page draw attention to the group.

4. Start the paper with a few easier questions. The examination is fairer if students are not 'rattled' by difficult questions before they have built up confidence.

5. Check the paper for typing and transcription errors, and arrange for two other examiners to do the same.

6. Check that the answer sheets are compatible with the letter (or number) designation of responses on the question paper; that is, if the paper lists them as A, B, C, D, E, so should the answer sheet.

7. Check the correct answer for each question against the key list of correct answers that will be used for scoring.

8 Arrange for a few extra copies to the examination paper to be at the place of examination in case some pages are poorly printed or missing.

PREPARE THE STUDENTS FOR THE TEST

1. If the students know when they'll be tested, and what the test will expect to cover, they can pace their study more efficiently. Surprise tests are unfair, since students are not equally prepared.

2. Students need to learn basic skills in taking MCQ tests

to read each question carefully

to practise answering different MCQ types

to pace themselves through a paper a little ahead of the time allocated

to check from time to time that they are entering choices on the correct line of their answer sheets, and not smudging their answer sheet (which can affect the machine scoring)

to avoid cramming the night before.

3. Students need to learn basic strategies to avoid lowering their possible score by being familiar with scoring procedure (some true/false styles subtract a mark for incorrect answer: thus uncertainty is often better dealt with by leaving an answer blank than by marking an incorrect answer). If right answers only are scored, always guess. In the one-from-five format, a guess has 20 per cent chance of being correct; and, anyway, the scores are being 'corrected' by deducting that 20 per cent in setting the pass level (see Ch. 39) by skipping difficult questions first time through, marking them for latter attack by not changing their choice unless confident an error has been made — first guesses are more likely to be correct by recognizing clues, such as longer and more carefully qualified responses as probably correct by eliminating responses known to be incorrect, and those never seen before by cultivating a low rather than high level of anxiety and by gaining confidence that examiners are not attempting to trick candidates and thus accepting that a straightforward interpretation will be correct.

BIBLIOGRAPHY

Cox K R 1976 Quality control in the Part I FRACS examination. Australian and New Zealand Journal of Surgery 46: 269–278

This paper reviews briefly the sequence of procedures in setting up a multiple choice examination in basic surgery

What can teachers and students get out of multiple choice examinations?

Preview

WHAT ARE THE STUDENTS' SCORES?

IS THIS EXAMINATION EASY OR HARD?

HOW DO I SET THE PASS MARK?

WHO SHOULD FAIL?

HOW WELL HAVE STUDENTS PERFORMED IN DIFFERENT CASES?

HOW CAN TEACHERS BE INFORMED HOW WELL THEIR STUDENTS HAVE LEARNED?

HOW CAN STUDENTS GET FEEDBACK ON THEIR PERFORMANCE?
HOW GOOD ARE THE QUESTIONS?

Multiple choice questions, or any test with a fixed set of responses for students to choose among, are scored by a mark on an answer sheet. Those marks can be read by an optical sensor, and the scores analyzed by computer programs (Fig. 25.1).

These analyses can provide teachers with a rich source of feedback data on candidates, on the examination, and on the effectiveness of teaching. Similarly, the computer can provide candidates with a precise specification of their performance in different areas, their comparative performance vis-à-vis other candidates, and even specify sources of information for further study.

Consider what you, as a teacher, need to know about the performance of your students, about particular subject areas and about the individual questions.

WHAT ARE THE STUDENTS' SCORES?

The computer printout gives each student's name, number and score. The score can be provided as a 'raw' total, that is, the number of answers scored correct. The raw score can be recorded as a percentage of the total possible mark.

The frequency distribution of scores for each exam paper can be set out numerically or graphically, showing what proportions performed strongly or weakly. Frequency distribution curves on scores of medical students are usually skewed towards the left (Cox et al, 1973), showing a good grasp of the subjects by the majority (Fig. 25.2).

Examinations certifying the students are competent should show students clumping at the upper end. A normal frequency distribution curve can be intepreted as a failure of teaching to influence a random distribution of scores.

IS THIS EXAMINATION EASY OR HARD?

The overall difficulty of the examination is calculated as the mean score achieved on all questions. The mean score may be higher or lower than previous examinations. Possible explanations are that the students were better or worse, or that the mix of questions contained less or more difficult questions.

The second explanation can be checked in two ways. First, the frequency distribution of difficulty of questions is inspected; that is, the numbers of students scoring 100 per cent to 91 per cent, 90 per cent to 81 per cent and so on are compared with previous examinations, to see if a disproportionate number of questions fall into

ROYAL AUSTRALASIAN COLLEGE OF SURGEONS

Dear Dr . . . .
Here are some details concerning your Part I Fellowship examinations on . . . . The questions in the examination were classified according to discipline, system and section of the manual, and for each subclassification area, the number of questions asked is stated, together with the range within which your percentage score fell.

Scores by discipline

Number of Questions	Percentage Score Range	Area
113	66–70	Anatomy
149	66–70	Physiology
76	56–70	Pathology
22	66–70	Clinical

Scores by system

Number of Questions	Percentage Score Range	Area
3	66–70	Adrenal
2	51–55	Biostats, computers, clinical trials
3	66–70	Bone marrow and blood production
13	61–65	Brain, cranial nerves & cerebrospinal fluid
10	51–55	Coagulation and hemolysis
..	....	....
..	....	....
6	66–70	Trauma, incl. wound & bone healing
5	76–80	Veins incl. thrombo-embolism

Scores by Section of Surgical Manual

Number of Questions	Percentage Score Range	Area
2	51–55	History of Surgery
6	81–85	Clinical Genetics
27	66–70	Musculo-skeletal system and skin
3	66–70	Intro. to statistics & information theory

Dr
Cand. Number:

Fig. 25.1 An example of a computer printout available to examiners and candidates giving details of candidate performance on a multiple choice examination

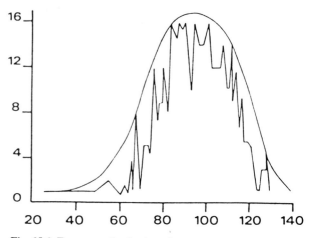

Fig. 25.2 Frequency distribution of raw scores from 150 questions by 721 final year students

tions. Question difficulties are remarkably stable from year to year (Cox & Royle, 1980; Royle, 1980). If this student group has scored higher on re-used questions, it is a reasonable interpretation that they have learned their work better (although examiners are always anxious that students may have 'cracked the bank' of questions).

HOW DO I SET THE PASS MARK?

While the computer sets out the scores with numerical precision, setting the pass mark is always a matter of judgement by examiners. Custom makes 50 per cent the score separating the sheep from the goats. Examiners must consider what is the purpose of the examination (Is a competence level of 50 per cent, or some other figure, appropriate to what I am certifying?), how difficult or easy is this particular examination (as above,), and what would be consistent with standards of previous years.

A consensus among experienced examiners achieves stability in expected standards.

Remember that one-from-five questions have a 1 in 5 (20 per cent) chance score of being correct, irrespective of the student's knowledge. The zero score is thus 20 per cent, not 0 per cent, and the range is 20–100 per cent, not 0–100 per cent. Choosing half the items correctly achieves a score of 60 per cent. With true/false items, the random

easy or hard categories. A batch of hard questions can pull the mean score down. Second, the scores achieved on previously- used questions are compared with previous experience on those ques-

score is 50 per cent; getting half the items correct yields a score of 75 per cent.

WHO SHOULD FAIL?

If a pass mark is fixed, students are competing with a standard of an acceptable body of knowledge. If a proportion of the bottom 'tail' of the curve of frequency distribution of scores are cut off (marking on the curve), students are competing with one another.

A sharp cut off, which passes one candidate but fails another with one mark less, is applying a precision which few examiners believe any examination can warrant. That precision is measurable. The computer calculates the reliability coefficient of the examination, in effect the probability that the same scores would be achieved on repetition. All certifying examinations should have a reliability above 0.7 (Schumacher, 1971). Examinations with a reliability below 0.6 are unfair. Reliability of an examination increases with the number of questions in the test, the homogeneity of questions, from questions of high discrimination and of average difficulty, and from having a wide range of ability among candidates (Ebel, 1972).

Given the reliability, the standard error of measurement can be calculated.* Going down two standard errors below the cut off level covers the lower half of the 95 per cent confidence limits of the 'true' score. Students in that grey zone can be judged in the light of other available data before automatic failure (Cox & Royle, 1980).

HOW WELL HAVE STUDENTS PERFORMED IN DIFFERENT AREAS?

Consider what you, as a teacher, wish to know about the performance of your students. For example, you may want the scores compiled

according to the components you used in putting the examination together (see Ch. 24 on how to construct a fair MCQ examination), such as diagnosis, laboratory investigation, management, prognosis. Scores can be set out in the computer printout under any number of categories in which questions have been classified. Scores can be counted by discipline (e.g. anatomy, microbiology), by practice sub-specialty (e.g. urology, allergy), by body system (e.g. cardiovascular, endocrine) or by clinical process (e.g. differential diagnosis, management). Questions can be classified on whether the material is essential core knowledge or relatively esoteric; or by whether the question appears to test recognition of facts, interpretation of data, or problem solving.

Set out the features you are interested in as a classification, and allocate the examination questions accordingly. The rest is handled by the machine.

HOW CAN TEACHERS BE INFORMED HOW WELL THEIR STUDENTS HAVE LEARNED?

The classifications above provide an analytic framework which informs teachers how well students have performed in each category. The computer can set out the results according to each classification, spelling out for teachers which regions or facets students have learned well (e.g. scored more than 70 per cent) and in which they have performed poorly (e.g. scored less than 30 per cent).

Item analyses reflect the questions on which good students are confused, and which students did not attempt.

Teachers, consequently, can examine the amount of time allocated to these areas and/or the clarity of teaching.

Remember that teachers will hear what areas students are confused about only if they listen to their students. Work through a set of multiple choice items with your students telling you how they respond. You will learn a deal more about your teaching than you anticipated, and can improve those MCQ items in the process.

---

* Standard error of measurement
= standard deviation of test scores $\sqrt{(1 - \text{reliability coefficient})}$

HOW CAN STUDENTS GET FEEDBACK ON THEIR PERFORMANCE?

While the total score is the most critical measure in the student's eyes, that score gives no precise guidance to students on their performance in different areas. Since every question can be classified in one or many ways, the individual's score can be added up within each classification (Cox, 1976). Students can be given their scores in, say, obstetrics, surgery and so on; and, classified in a different way, they can have their scores on pancreas and parathyroid (see Fig. 25.1).

In each component, students can be told the number of questions, the percentage each has scored correct, and the percentage scored correct by all those sitting that examination.

In a short examination, each score can be followed by a journal or textbook reference which deals with that subject matter.

The computer prints out the entire individual student letter with all these data. The student has now been given precise guidance to enable self-learning to proceed efficiently.

HOW GOOD ARE THE QUESTIONS?

Every question (item) is analyzed individually. This item analysis records how many students chose the correct answer, how many chose the other distractors, and how many omitted to answer the question. Some distractors are ineffectual; some clearly attract many students.

The student group is divided into high and low performance groups by the computer on their score in this examination. The proportion of each of these groups choosing each possible answer is set out, revealing in each question whether 'good' students chose the correct answer more frequently than 'bad' students. A question scored correct more frequently by 'bad' than 'good' students should be examined carefully to clarify why 'good' students are not choosing the correct answer. Perhaps the question is out of date, perhaps it can be interpreted in more than one way, or perhaps the teaching differs on what is correct. The computer calculates a discrimination index (see Ch. 24) for each question by comparing the performance of 'good' (high scoring) with 'bad' (low scoring) students on the question. The question should discriminate positively in favour of 'good' students.

The printout can list separately questions which seem too easy or too hard, those which students omitted, those with ineffectual distractors, those with low or negative discrimination indices, and those which seem to have two or more possible answers. These lists trigger examiners to review the question in the light of the computer's 'criticisms'.

Examiners, then, have a rich source of analytical data from which to review the examination to ensure that its fairness and accuracy are as impeccable as their science in their own discipline.

In summary, machine marking and analysis can provide quite specific feedback on the class and the individual, on the examination as a whole and on each question, and on teaching and learning of areas and single principles. Teachers have no excuse if they continue with bad examinations to students to whom they are not providing feedback on their performance.

REFERENCES

Cox K R, Ludbrook J, McCarthy W H 1973 National comparisons in a trial examination in surgery. British Journal of Medical Education 7: 21–24
Describes the use of an MCQ examination across 8 medical schools with 14 teaching hospitals to test the comparability of 'right' answers in different places
Cox K R 1976 Quality control in the Part I FRACS examination. Australian and New Zealand Journal of Surgery 46: 269–277
Reviews the setting up, administration, analysis and feedback from a substantial MCQ examination

Cox K R, Royle J P 1980 Measurement plus judgement. Medical Education 14: 424–427
Scrutinizes a number of decisions examiners may have to make with an MCQ examination, and how these link with examination analysis
Ebel R L 1972 Essentials of educational measurement. Prentice Hall, Englewood Cliffs, New Jersey
Provides a sound and direct review of the use of examinations
Royle J P 1980 The re-use of multiple choice questions in the Part I FRACS examination: an analysis of the results.

Australian and New Zealand Journal of Surgery 50
4: 438–439
Looks at the effect of publishing and re-using MCQ items
Schumacher C F 1971 Scoring and analysis. In: Hubbard J P
(ed) Measuring medical education, Lea and Febiger,
Philadelphia

Reviews the procedures of the National Board of Medical
Examiners in measuring reliability and establishing grading
standards

How to organize multiple choice question banks

Preview

WHO SHOULD CONSTRUCT QUESTIONS?

HOW CAN QUESTIONS BE IMPROVED?

HOW CAN QUESTIONS BE STORED?

As anyone who has attempted writing a multiple choice question would have realized, the creation of good questions is not an easy task. How much more difficult is it, then, to construct a fair multiple choice question paper? In the first edition of this book some guidelines for writing good questions (Bandaranayake & Cox 1982) and for constructing a fair paper (Cox, 1982) were given. This chapter deals with a strategy for creating a bank of multiple choice questions in an institution or department, so that the effort that goes into the construction of good questions is put to use repeatedly when examinations are set.

The practice of creating new questions each time an examination is due, and discarding these questions after the examination is over, is a waste of effort and an inefficient use of an academician's time. Banks of questions increase efficiency in the use of multiple choice questions and improvement of their quality.

WHO SHOULD CONSTRUCT QUESTIONS?

The construction of a multiple choice question is an individual task. A group of five teachers focusing their attention on the construction of one question could easily spend five times as much time as each of the five teachers focusing attention on one question. While brainstorming in a group could produce a better question, opportunity for this occurs later (see the next section). Initial construction of a question, even if it is in an incomplete or draft form, should be carried out by an individual. The best time to undertake this activity is while preparing for a lesson or immediately after it, not just before an examination is due. The best way to derive distractors for a question is to use students' incorrect responses to questions in class, or their misconceptions evident in answers to essay questions.

HOW CAN QUESTIONS BE IMPROVED?

While initial construction of a question is an individual activity, clarification and improvement of that question takes place best through group discussion. This is the first step in question improvement. The more diverse the group the more likely that the final version of the question is both relevant and important. For example, when discussing questions in anatomy, the presence of physiologists and clinicians, could increase both functional and clinical significance of the questions.

As constructors of questions are painfully aware, one of the most difficult aspects of construction is to think of an adequate number of plausible distractors. Group members can often provide suggestions for distractors and help complete a question which has originated from one member.

The second step in question improvement is

pre-testing. Useful feedback for question improvement, by actually trying it out on a group of students, is obtained in two ways: by discussing the question with students after they have answered it, and through item analysis.

1. Discussing with students: Teachers are reluctant to discuss questions in a test paper with students, ostensibly for reasons of security. While it is possible that students keep a record of questions discussed, and often do so in practice, the advantages of discussion outweigh the disadvantages. Many are the ambiguities, errors in content and in construction, instances of contradictory teaching and of triviality of content pointed out by students in such discussion.

One practical way of doing this is to display each question on an overhead transparency to students assembled in a lecture theatre, and invite comments from them. They could, of course, remember questions and note them immediately after the session; but that is possible even after an examination. Use these discussed questions next year. As the size of the bank of questions increases, however, the need for security decreases.

2. Item analysis identifies deficiencies in questions, as a prior step to improving them. Questions which are either very easy or very difficult can be looked at closely to determine if they test important content; if so, they are retained. If they do not, they could be revised to achieve a desirable level of difficulty.

Questions which, through item analysis, have been identified as discriminating between good and weak students in a negative direction (i.e. more weaker students than better students answering the item correctly according to the key) should be scrutinized carefully for keying errors, or for ambiguous and misleading statements, and corrected as necessary.

Item analysis can conveniently be carried out by those with access to computers programmed for such a procedure. Those who do not have this convenience can still train clerical or other staff in the department to carry out item analysis manually, time-consuming though such a procedure would be. In the latter case the format of the student response sheet can be designed to make manual item analysis easier.

HOW CAN QUESTIONS BE STORED?

The first step in question storage is to decide on one or more systems of classifying questions. Several classifications, each on a different basis, may be used for a given bank of questions. For example, a bank of anatomy questions could be classified according to:

i. subdivisions of the subject (gross, histology, embryology etc.);

ii. body systems (cardiovascular, respiratory, renal etc.);

iii. cell or tissue type (epithelium, muscle, blood vessel etc.);

iv. level of knowledge possibly tested (recall, understanding, application etc.);

v. type of item (single-response, true-false, assertion-reason etc.). The classification(s) used should be appropriate to the subject, and such that selection of a fair sample of questions for an examination is facilitated.

The next step is to assign a number to each question. If the bank is a large one, the accession number assigned to each question could include a code to identify the nature of the question. Thus a four digit number could be assigned in such a way that the first digit refers to the type of question, the second to the body system, and the third and fourth digits assigned in series.

The most convenient way of banking questions is computerized banking (using an appropriate database program such as D-base III.) This permits easy access to a given question via any of its classifications, addition of item analysis data each time it is used, and opportunity for correcting the question when necessary. For those who do not have such a facility, storing questions on sorter cards (Figure 26.1) is very convenient. The perforations along the borders of the sorter card are cut to the edge (as in Figure 26.2), to indicate the relevant category according to each classification used. When all the questions of a particular category are required, if a long needle is passed through the cards, all those in that category will fall out. Further categories can be selected from the ones so separated using the same procedure. This is a simple and convenient way of separating questions of different categories to select questions for an examination.

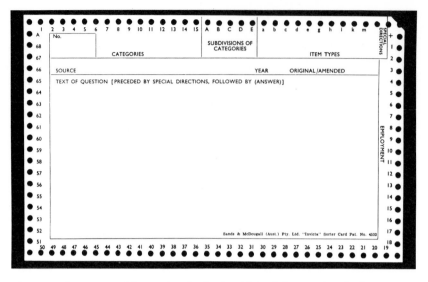

Fig. 26.1 Front and reverse of a sorter card for use in a bank of multiple choice questions in Anatomy

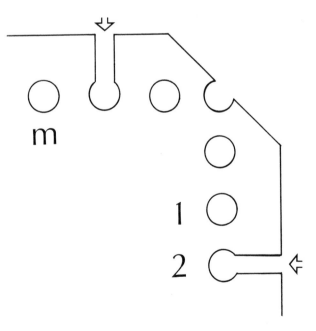

Fig. 26.2 Part of a sorter card (enlarged) to show how question category is indicated according to two classifications

The reverse of the card (Figure 26.2) is used to enter item analysis data each time the question is used. Thus, a permanent record of the question and its performance is easily maintained and readily available. The cards can be securely stored in a card index box or filing cabinet which can be kept locked.

The manner in which questions can be selected for an examination, using a grid, has been previously described (Cox, 1982).

The creation of a bank of multiple choice questions in an institution or department is not a task to be undertaken lightly. In the initial years it requires the cooperation of all the staff in the department, and the commitment of one, the 'bank manager', who encourages his/her colleagues to create questions, arranges regular meetings for discussing questions, supervises staff responsible for the item analysis and ensures that records are kept meticulously. The reward for such painstaking work in the initial years is the ease with which questions can be used, fairly, in future examinations. As medicine advances rapidly, however, the need to update the bank constantly by revising existing questions, and adding new questions cannot be over-emphasized.

REFERENCES

Bandaranayake R C, Cox K R 1982 Writing multiple choice questions. In: Cox K R, ·Ewan C E (eds) The Medical Teacher. Churchill Livingstone, Edinburgh (Chapter 37), pp 206-210
Provides guidelines for the construction of multiple choice questions, with examples of some of the more common errors made by constructors.

Cox K R 1982 How to construct a fair multiple choice question paper. In: Cox K R, Ewan C E (eds) ibid (Chapter 38) pp 211-214
Provides guidelines for selecting and reviewing questions for an examination, laying out the question paper and preparing students for the test.

How to design and use patient management problems

HISTORICAL

Patient Management Problems (PMPs) were developed in an attempt to produce a test format which would be capable of measuring knowledge at a 'higher level' than pure recall of facts. It is now some 25 years since Rimoldi (1961) produced his card pack as a test of diagnostic skills. An adaptation of this by McGuire and Babbott (1967) and by Hubbard (1971) provided pen and paper versions of the technique. These PMPs provided a series of options concerning history, examination, investigation and treatment based on initial presenting complaints. The options available proceeded in a step by step fashion with information concealed by invisible ink or ink blocks which had to be uncovered. As such they provided a linear model of the PMP with a limited number of options available at each situation. In this way they bore some relationship to the simple completion case history type of multiple choice question and there are certain similarities to the

linear format used in the later development of the modified essay question (*see* Chapter 22).

Many other versions of the PMP have been produced, the variety of techniques used being a reflection of the inability of most to produce a test which could consistently measure a higher level than recall of factual knowledge. This has unfortunately produced a situation where many widely differing techniques are classified under the same heading of Patient Management Problem, resulting in problems related to one technique being unconsciously transferred to all.

OBJECTIVES

The type of patient management problem to be described here was developed in an attempt to produce a test which was consistently capable of measuring 'the degree of success in providing a satisfactory solution to an undifferentiated presenting problem, using a standard considered adequate for the discipline, in an economy of time, at minimal expense and causing least inconvenience' (Marshall 1983). The test, which uses a branching rather than a linear format, has been described in detail elsewhere (Marshall & Fabb 1981). The following is a brief description.

TECHNIQUE

It is essential to state in detail at the outset what the test attempts to measure and, dependent on this, to explain the scoring system if this is to be used as an assessment for examination purposes. Practice cases are essential to ensure that any deficiency in performance is not a reflection of unfamiliarity with the technique.

The test begins with a brief statement concerning the problem, giving the age and sex of the patient involved. A description of the setting and the facilities available is necessary. An example would be:

> Mr Eric Thompson aged 35 years, a new patient to your practice, presents at your office with a history of having had a severe headache for the past 2 hours. He is obviously distressed. You are practising in a city suburb adjacent to a community hospital with general medical and surgical facilities. All radiological and laboratory facilities are readily accessible with consultant support as necessary. A major teaching hospital is located 5 km away.

Following this introduction a series of pathway options is presented.

Opposite each pathway choice information is concealed using a technique such as invisible ink, ink overlay or coloured over-print. Where the test result is used for decision making a permanent record of each choice is needed, thus entailing a permanent method of exposure of the information. Where the test can be reused, coloured over-print can be used with a plastic strip of the same colour as the over-print to reveal information. In this case a pencil mark may be made opposite each choice for later self-assessment if desired. In this way the material is reusable.

Exposure of information in the pathway section provides a direction to one of the clinical sections of the patient management problem with a further direction as to what should be done when sufficient information has been obtained in that particular section. For example see Figure 27.1.

Each of the clinical sections, history taking, examination etc. contains an alphabetical listing of all possible options regardless of the nature of the problem. This standardized list is used to prevent cuing as far as is possible in a pen and paper test. The performers are advised to write down their initial thoughts about the case and the first questions they wishes to explore. Having done this they look up the items alphabetically before revealing the relevant information. As little information as is immediately required should be extracted as, once any clinical section has been entered, it can be re-entered at any stage up to completion of the problem. In this way the performance of the PMP simulates to a large extent the real life consultation.

When the relevant information has been obtained the next pathway choice is made which directs to the next clinical section required. In this way, information is gradually gathered until the participant feels the problem has been completed.

The final pathway section ensures that this has in fact happened (Figure 27.2).

At this stage diagnoses are recorded.

TEST CONSTRUCTION

1. The general and specific objectives of the problem must be initially defined. This will entail deciding what audience the test is aimed at, and what level of knowledge is expected. Such consideration allows general objectives and some specific objectives to be formulated before proceeding.

2. A suitable problem should be selected. This is best done by selecting a case from practice. Such cases have an air of authenticity which is difficult to create in producing an artificial case based on textbook information. At the same time a combination of two cases may be used if the test

---

Section A1

10. Take detailed history	10. Go to Section B and on completion select from A2
11. Perform detailed physical examination	11.
12. Take brief history while making rapid assessment of patient	12.
13. Perform rapid preliminary assessment	13.
14. Perform office/domiciliary investigations	14.
15. Order investigations	15.
16. Give emergency treatment	16.
17. Call in consultant	17.
18. Send to hospital as a private patient	18.
19. Refer to hospital as a public patient	19.

Fig. 27.1 Example of exposure of information in pathway section of a PMP

Section A6

Select from the list below what further action you wish to take. Unless otherwise instructed, select ONE only. Do not select any previously chosen.

60. Take a detailed history	60. Go to Section B and on completion select again from Section A6
61. Perform detailed physical examination	61. Go to Section J and on completion select again from Section A6
62. Perform domiciliary investigations	62. Go to Section H and on completion select again from Section A6
63. Order investigations	63. Go to Section D and on completion select again from Section A6
64. Commence elective treatment	64. Go to Section D and on completion write your diagnoses in the boxes below. *End of problem*
65. Refer to consultant	65. Write your diagnosis in the boxes below. *End of problem*
66. Refer to local hospital	66. Admitted. Select again from Section A6
67. Refer to hospital as a public patient	67. Write your diagnoses in the boxes below. *End of problem*
68. Review patient in 48 hours	68. Sister requests review. Select again from Section A6.
69. Review patient in 2 weeks	69. Patient seeks treatment from another doctor. Write your diagnoses in the boxes below. *End of problem*

Fig. 27.2 Final pathway section of PMP

is meant to test several clinical areas at the same time.

3. When the specific case has been chosen the next step is to work out the sequence of management, in other words, the main pathway choices and their ordering. This will entail deciding whether a detailed history is taken initially or whether, because of an emergency situation, a brief history only is necessary at the beginning. This strategy is necessary where marks are allocated to the sequence of pathway selection. Special care must be taken in the final management section that the opportunity is given for the problem to be completed no matter which of the options is selected.

4. The presenting conditions of the test must be given in detail.
These will include
  i. The physical setting
  ii. The presenting features of the case
  iii. The role and task of the performer
  iv. The resources available
  v. The initial instruction.

5. The clinical choices must then be selected, which involves providing a response to each of the alphabetically listed items in each of the clinical sections. This task is best attempted by filling in initially the positive responses for the case involved. Most of the remainder of the responses will entail merely single words such as 'not, no, present, absent, negative or positive'. Care is also required to ensure that different information is not given under a similar heading. This involves cross-referencing item of the test such as 'blood in urine' which should be compatible with 'haematuria'. This cross-referencing is most easily handled by providing an answer to the first alphabetically listed option and for any subsequent identical option, listed under a different alphabetical heading, referring to the number of the first response. This ensures that not only is the correct information given each time but allows only one mark to be picked up in the scoring for the particular item.

6. The test should not be scored. Scores are allocated to each of the pathway options, to each individual item of information under the clinical sections and to the diagnoses concerned. The total of all these scores will be the maximum score for the problem. It is essential to determine whether or not one will reward efficiency in performance of the test. If this is the case then the items of information necessary for the successful performance of the test should be looked at in detail, and these items should be regarded as the optimal items to be selected. As such the score allocation

for all these items should provide 100% of the test mark. In the clinical sections, the sum of marks for such items should also provide the maximum positive score available within each section. This will prevent a rather obsessive data gatherer, who collects many minor scoring marks, from achieving a better score than an efficient performer who selects only the information vital to solve a particular problem, thus avoiding unnecessary expense, inconvenience and time.

7. When all the above have been completed the only step to be carried out is pre-testing of the PMP. In order to achieve this a panel of people conversant with the technique should be given the test to perform. Subsequent to such performance discussion can take place about any possible problem areas or any areas where there tends to be a conflict in opinion. A consensus opinion will determine the final score allotted.

ADVANTAGES OF THIS FORMAT OF PMP

1. The construction of this test allows for individual approaches as would occur in the clinical situation.

2. Complete freedom is given to follow any sequence of data collection up to completion of the problem.

3. By avoiding short lists of options, cuing is removed as far as is possible in a paper format.

4. The allocation of individual marks for each item of information provides an objective test.

5. The allocation of a maximum score for each clinical section prevents less efficient problem solvers scoring on a higher level than efficient problem solvers. This is particularly necessary if a test is meant to measure efficiency. By allowing negative marks up to −50, appropriate penalties are incurred for choices which could be life threatening in a real life situation.

6. The same problem may be used to test the ability at different levels, for example, medical student, general practitioner or specialist. By altering the maximum marks allowed for each clinical section a different total may be set dependent on the expected problem solving ability of the group concerned.

USES FOR THE PMP

The test has several potential uses.

1. In summative assessment

Initially the test was designed to measure problem solving ability in a pass/fail examination. The objectivity of the test allows this to occur yet at the same time provides little information to candidates who have not been successful. This is one of the defects of the test.

2. In formative assessment

This is a more useful function for the test which can be used to identify potential problems in clinical reasoning ability. Feedback allows such areas to be addressed. In a similar way the test may be used at the beginning and at the end of a specific learning period to provide a measure of any improvement in problem solving ability after such a period.

3. In group learning

Possibly the most important role for the PMP is in the group learning situation. By appointing a group leader who has access to the exposed copy, the remainder of the group can problem solve by 'thinking out loud', debating each choice before the information is requested. In this way those with less well developed 'critical thinking skills' have the opportunity to learn from peers by discussion as to why certain choices were made at specific times.

4. In computer learning

A further application of a group process is computerization of this type of PMP. The paper test is directly transferable onto computer. Cuing is even further reduced on computer than in the paper model and all members of the group can participate in the process as the answers are provided by the computer itself and no group leader needs an exposed copy. Storage of the problem on a mainframe computer allows virtually unlimited access.

5. In critical thinking

An extension of the process being looked at currently is designed to examine in detail the thought processes used in problem solving. This is being explored in an attempt to determine whether a computer will eventually be used to analyze pathways taken and in such a way identify any specific problems in the clinical reasoning ability of individuals. If this proves to be possible, programs could thus be designed to allow individuals to identify and correct specific problem areas.

SUMMARY

A brief historical account of the development of patient management problems is provided followed by a description of one specific type of patient management problem designed to measure efficiency in problem solving.

The steps necessary in the construction of a patient management problem are outlined briefly. This is followed by a short discussion on the advantages of the type of patient management problem described and finally some other potential uses of this type of test are discussed.

REFERENCES

Hubbard J P 1971 Measuring medical education. Lea and Febiger, Philadelphia, Pennsylvania

Marshall J R 1983 How we measure problem solving ability. Medical Education 17: 319–324

Marshall J R & Fabb W E 1981 The construction of patient management problems. Medical Education Booklet No 12. Association for the Study of Medical Education, Dundee.

McGuire C H & Babbott D 1967 Simulation technique in the measurement of problem solving skills. Journal of Educational Measurement 4: 1–10

Rimoldi H J A 1961 The test of diagnostic skills. Journal of Medical Education 16: 137–142

How to plan and run structured clinical examinations

Preview

WHAT IS A STRUCTURED CLINICAL
EXAMINATION?

HOW DOES ONE PLAN A STRUCTURED
CLINICAL EXAMINATION?

— Location
— Length
— Content of stations
— Design of stations
— Selecting patients
— Appointing examiners
— Other practical details

HOW DOES ONE RUN A STRUCTURED
CLINICAL EXAMINATION?

HOW TO FIND OUT MORE ABOUT HOW
TO PLAN AND RUN A STRUCTURED
CLINICAL EXAMINATION?

WHAT IS A STRUCTURED CLINICAL EXAMINATION?

Contrary to popular belief a structured clinical
examination is not a method of assessment as
such. Rather it is an organizational framework
into which can be incorporated a variety of test
methods. Nor, it must be said, is it new, having
been used for many years, for instance, to assess
students' abilities in gross anatomy. Interest was
rekindled, however, in the approach as a way of
overcoming problems associated with the traditional clinical examination (Harden et al 1975).
Several medical schools have used the structured
clinical examination for long enough for it to
become the new convention (Cushieri et al 1979,
Newble & Elmslie 1981) and it now appears likely
that it will be adopted in an enthusiastic way in
North America (Hart et al 1985).

The objective structured clinical examination,
or OSCE as it is often called, consists of a series
of stations around which students rotate. At each
station the student is required to undertake a well-
defined clinical task. The criteria on which
performance is to be assessed are carefully
defined. Structured marking sheets and examiner
rating forms are prepared in advance. In some
OSCEs, each station is followed by one requiring
the answering of questions about the previous
station. The length of time spent at a station is
usually short (5–10 minutes).

The flexibility of this approach allows a wide
selection of tasks to be assessed, the range being
largely limited only by the ingenuity of those
constructing the test. However, there are some
practical limitations. It is certainly easier, for
instance, to construct stations to assess technical
skills, laboratory skills, test interpretation and
physical examination performance than it is to
construct stations which test validly the interpersonal and attitudinal components of competence.

HOW DOES ONE PLAN A STRUCTURED CLINICAL EXAMINATION?

The organizational aspects depend very much on
local circumstances. This description, therefore,
relies heavily on the procedures which have been

in successful operation for seven years at the University of Adelaide.

Decide on the location for the examination

It is preferable that the examination be conducted within a hospital to allow ready access to patients. Some have used the wards (Cushieri et al 1979) but our preference has been to find an area which can be isolated from routine hospital traffic for the duration of the examination. For this we have used the hospital's lecture and tutorial rooms and, where necessary, the corridors. The facilities themselves are likely to influence the format of the examination to some extent, but a satisfactory compromise should be possible.

Decide on the length of the examination

The length of the examination may be decided by others or be influenced by the available time and facilities. Our own circuit has been set at 90 minutes, which allows us to assess approximately 120 students over two days. Preliminary psychometric data suggest this time ought to be considerably longer if we are to achieve truly reliable estimates of our students' competence. Once the length is agreed the time must be apportioned. We have used fourteen five-minute stations. However, these were arbitrary decisions which suited our particular circumstances.

Decide on the content of the stations

Choice of content is probably the most critical aspect of the organization of an OSCE. The selection of content will be based ideally on sound educational principles. In other words, the sample to be included must be one which is truly representative of the defined objectives of the course. In Adelaide, the Departments of Medicine and Surgery have agreed on a statement of clinical learning objectives which are both general (e.g. to be able to obtain a history, perform a physical examination etc.) and specific (e.g. to be able to *perform* injections, stool examinations, ophthalmoscopy, endotrachael intubation etc.; be able to *interpret* common ECG abnormalities, biochemical profiles etc.). The selection of skills to be tested

is made by an appointed working party charged with constructing the examination. An example of the content of the stations in one of our examinations is shown in Figure 28.1. It demonstrates the breadth of skills that can be tested.

Designing the stations

Each station must be designed to fit the time available and to measure objectively the skill to be tested. This process may cause some problems initially. Stations designated to measure interpretive skills (e.g. ECG tracings, X-ray films, biochemistry results) are relatively easy construct (see Figure 2 for an example).

Those designated to measure clinical skills are more difficult as patients may be involved and structured rating sheets must be prepared (*see* Figure 28.3 for an example). In an institution where OSCEs have not previously been used, a pilot test should always be conducted to familiarize both staff and students with the procedure.

Selecting patients for clinical stations

The use of real patients provides some difficulty as even the most cooperative may grow weary of being examined by a new student every few minutes throughout the whole day. As a rule we do not ask patients to stay for more than half a day and break up the time with tea-breaks and rest stations. Changing patients during the test potentially interferes with its objectivity, but it is usually not too difficult to obtain replacement patients with reasonably equivalent clinical features. It is more important not to change examiners during the examination.

Another option is to use volunteers, such as friends and relatives! This is a good solution if the main aim of the station is simply to assess technique rather than to elicit and interpret signs (e.g. ability to examine the chest or knee joint). If one ventures into the more difficult realm of history taking and other areas of interpersonal skill, volunteers can quite easily be trained as simulated patients.

Station 1: Pleural aspiration technique (5 minutes)
Location of site for aspiration on a diagram. Answer questions about technique and tests to be performed on specimen.

Station 2: Location of spinal cord lesion (5 minutes)
Interpretation of sensory signs indicated on a chart. Answer questions about cause and other likely features.

Station 3: Interpretation of X-ray films (Barium meal) (5 minutes)
Identification of procedure and interpretation of films. Answer questions about diagnosis, symptoms and other diagnostic procedures which would be advised.

Station 4: Fluid balance chart (5 minutes)
Make calculations about fluid and calories from a balance chart. Comments about inadequacies of the treatment and measures required to restore balance. Instructions to nurses.

Station 5: Interpretation of ECG tracing (5 minutes)
Report and interpretation of ECG. Advice on management of the arrhythmia present.

Station 6: Interpretation of haematology report (5 minutes)
Report and interpretation of CBP. Answer question about likely causes of the anaemia present.

Station 7: Anticoagulation (5 minutes)
Outline procedure for heparinization.

Station 8: Interpretation of X-ray films (IVP) (5 minutes)
Identification of procedure and interpretation of films. Answer questions about differential diagnosis and further investigations.

Station 9: Interpretation of clinical chemistry report (5 minutes)

Report and interpret biochemical screen. Answer questions about likely diagnosis and clinical symptoms relating to the jaundice present.

Station 10: Interpretation of clinical photograph (5 minutes)
Identify the type of ulcer and the likely associated symptoms and signs.

Station 11: Performance of arterial puncture (5 minutes)
Selection of needle, heparinization of syringe, demonstration of technique (short of insertion), post-puncture procedure, treatment of specimen. [Volunteer; two examiners]

Station 12: Advice to patient regarding breast lump (5 minutes)
Advice to patient about management options following a needle biopsy which has shown a malignancy. [Simulated patient; two examiners]

Station 13: Cardio-pulmonary resuscitation (5 minutes)
Demonstration of mouth-to-mouth resuscitation and external cardiac massage. [Manikin; two examiners]

Station 14: Rest (5 minutes)

Station 15: Examination of the abdomen (10 minutes)
Full examination of the abdomen on patient with polycystic kidneys. Assessment of examination, technique and interpretation of findings. [Patient; two examiners]

Station 16: Examination of patient with thyroid disease (5 minutes)
Examination of patient with some features of hyperthyroidism. Assessment of examination technique. [Patient; one examiner]

Station 17: Rest (5 minutes)

Fig. 28.1 Example of a final year structured clinical examination conducted by the Departments of Medicine and Surgery at the University of Adelaide

Station 5: This 42-year-old patient presents with palpitations which started one hour ago.
a. *Report on this ECG*
   A: Regular (1/2) tachycardia of about 190/min (1/2).
   P wave not visible (1/2) but QRS normal (1/2).
   Diagnosis — supraventricular tachycardia (1)
   (Total 3 marks)
b. *What specific questions would you ask the patient?*
   A: Any precipitating factors (1/2)
   Past history of previous episodes (1/2) (Total 1 mark)
c. *What would be your first step in the specific management of this patient?*
   A: Try Valsalva or carotid sinus massage (1/2) under ECG control (1/2) (Total 1 mark)

Fig. 28.2 Station designated for interpretive skills

Appointing examiners for clinical stations

Surprising as it may seem, clinical teaching staff appear to be remarkably tolerant of the repetitive task of rating students on a structured marking sheet. It is important to brief the examiners carefully on their task prior to the day of the test. This includes familiarizing them with the task and the rating form they will use. Some advocate a period of training but studies indicate that this offers little additional benefit (Newble et al 1980). We have always used two examiners rating independently but if there is a shortage of examiners it is preferable, from a reliability point of view, to have more stations with one examiner rather than less with two examiners.

Attending to other practical details

The smooth running of any examination often depends on the ability of the organizer to anticipate and deal with a wide variety of apparently minor, but nevertheless essential, practical details.

These include arranging for patients to attend; providing nursing staff to look after the patients; organizing refreshments for examiners, patients, helpers and students; ensuring facilities are booked well in advance and so on. A good rapport with a wide section of the hospital community is essential for success.

HOW DOES ONE RUN A STRUCTURED CLINICAL EXAMINATION?

'There's many a slip twixt cup and lip' is a good adage for those appointed to run such an examination. Unlike any other examination, a breakdown in organization leads to immediate disaster akin to the chaos caused in a car factory should one machine malfunction. Thus an obsessional attention to detail and a team of reliable assistants is essential for success.

What to do on the day prior to the examination

All test materials should have been in the organizers' hands well before this. The main task of the day ought to be the final arrangement of the facilities. This will entail furniture removal, screening of areas for patient examination; labelling of stations and so on.

What to do on the day of the examination

The organizer and his or her assistants should arrive early. All test materials should be distributed to the relevant stations. Patients should arrive next with their nurse attendants, followed by the examiners who will wish to examine the patients and settle into the station environment.

Students will have been instructed to report to a suitable venue close to the examination setting. They must be briefed and, as the time to begin arrives, allocated to a starting position on the circuit. Ingenious arrangements must have been made to prevent students who have completed the examination from coming into contact with those yet to participate later in the day.

When all are ready, the timekeeper rings the bell and the examination is underway. At the agreed interval (say 5 minutes) the bell is rung and students move on to the next station. Any lagging by examinees must be corrected immediately and vigorously. Materials may be required at strategic points to ensure the smooth passage of students from station to station.

Space precludes a full account of the many other minor and major difficulties which may arise. Suffice to say that the organizer must be constantly alert and prepared to take instant and firm decisions to ensure that the examination proceeds in a smooth and calm manner.

What to do about marking

There will be a variety of marking tasks depending on the types of stations being used. Those involving examiners will take care of themselves in sense that structured rating forms, like the one in Figure 28.3, will be completed at the time the student passes through the station. Those which do not need examiners will have required the students to generate a written response of some kind, either by answering a series of multiple choice questions (a popular approach in Dundee [Harden & Gleeson 1979]) or by writing free responses in a structured answer book (which is our own preference [Newble, Baxter & Elmslie 1979]). In the latter case the acceptable responses and marks are determined in advance by those constructing the stations. After some clinical stations, a case write-up may be required.

By far the most satisfactory and efficient way of completing the various scoring tasks is to organize a team of markers to work throughout the day of the examination. Answer sheets are collected after the completion of each circuit and passed to the markers who finish their task before the next circuit concludes. In this way it has been possible to have all marking completed within one hour of the departure of the last student. When examinations extend beyond one day, and when the Faculty is pressing for overall results, this approach has much in its favour.

The only task remaining is for the coordinator to collate all the results and present them for decision making. This is not the time to deal with the very important issue of whether results should be prepared as a single mark or as a profile. Nor

Arterial blood sampling
Student's name

(Surname) (*Block letters*)   (First Name)

Greet the student then give the following information:
'Assume that this patient has presented as an emergency and for good reason you wish to obtain an arterial blood sample. Demonstrate how you would do this up to the point of inserting the needle. Describe what you are doing as you go along'.

	Performed adequately	Attempted but not adequate	Not performed
1. General approach to patient	1/2	0	0
2. Approaches to radial A (if approaches a brachial or femoral redirect to radial)	1	0	0
3. Selects the appropriate syringe (heparinized) and needle	1	1/2	0
4. Prepares the skin with antiseptic	1	1/2	0
5. Palpates artery and locates it between two fingers	1	1/2	0
6. Directs needles between fingers at 45° with intention to transfix	1	1/2	0

Now say: 'Assuming you have obtained the blood, what are you going to do now?'

7. 'Press a swab over the puncture site for at least five minutes'	1	1/2	0
8. 'Cap syringe, mix and immediately place in ice then deliver to lab'	1	1/2	0

Total   Signed

Examiner

Fig. 28.3 Station designated for clinical skills

is it the time to grapple with the problems associated with setting standards.

HOW TO FIND OUT MORE ABOUT HOW TO PLAN AND RUN A STRUCTURED CLINICAL EXAMINATION

The listed references will provide more information on the educational justification for introducing structured examinations as an integral part of clinical assessment. Unfortunately, there are few articles or books which deal with the details of how to organize and run an OSCE (Harden & Gleeson, 1979). Every effort should, therefore, be made to visit an institution in which such examinations are conducted regularly. Such institutions are not common but at least one should be identifiable in most countries.

REFERENCES

Cushieri A, Gleeson F A, Harden R M, Wood R A B 1979 A new approach to a final examination in surgery. Annals of the Royal College of Surgeons of England 61: 400–405

Harden R M, Stevenson M, Downie W W, Wilson G M 1975 Assessment of clinical competence using objective structured examination. British Medical Journal 2: 447–451

Harden R M, Gleeson F A 1979 Assessment of medical competence using an objective structured clinical examination (OSCE). ASME Medical Education Booklet No 8. Medical Education 13: 39–54

Hart I R, Harden R M, Walton H J (eds) 1985 Proceedings of an International Conference on Newer Developments in Assessing Clinical Competence, Ottawa (to be published)

Newble D I, Baxter A, Elmslie R G 1979 A comparison of multiple choice tests and free-response tests in examinations of clinical competence. Medical Education 13: 263–268

Newble D I, Hoare J, Sheldrake P F 1980 The selection and training of examiners for clinical examinations. Medical Education 14: 345–349

Newble D I, Elmslie R G 1981 A new approach to the final examinations in medicine and surgery. Lancet 2: 517–518

How to assess performance

Preview

We constantly assess the performance of others, and they assess us. Our purposes are not always clear, even to ourselves. Our criteria are not usually spelled out, and we may not be sure what assumptions and values underlie the judgments we make.

When we assess our students and our junior colleagues, we are unable to escape from our habits. We trust our judgment. We know what we have seen. Our assessment is based on that reality.

We don't, however, trust the judgment of others to the same extent. We know that they may be biased; and they have not seen what we have seen.

The assessments of our students and juniors can have profound effects on their lives and their careers. Our capacity to understand what we are actually judging in their performance, what importance we attach to each component, and how we amalgamate the evidence and our values into a decision, is, however, still only shallowly comprehended.

This Chapter, consequently, touches not only methods for assessment of real life performance, but tries to dig into the first layer that underlies our methods to see on what assumptions they are based.

WHY ARE YOU ASSESSING?

Some of our purposes in assessing performance are
  to certify — as pass/fail
  to promote — to the next level
  to select — for admission to a training program
  to appoint — to a job
  to rank — for prizes or jobs
  to predict — for future increased responsibility
  to diagnose — learning needs
  to analyze — performance problems.
Each purpose calls for a different role for the assessor, a different focus of attention, and different criteria.

WHAT IS YOUR ROLE?

For the first six purposes the role is as judge or examiner. The focus is on valid measures of job performance, on quantifiable outputs of performance which can be scored objectively, and on standardization to ensure consistency and fairness.

For the diagnostic purpose, the role is as teacher or coach. The focus is on the skills learned, on experiences gained and those still needed, on deficiencies requiring specific training, and on feedback on observed behaviour.

For the analytical purpose when performance seems sub-optimal, the role is as colleague or mentor or counselor. The focus is on joint analysis of the job, of the context and colleagues and self, on achievement of goals, and on an approach of listening, open-ness and sharing of points of view.

Since teachers fill each of these roles at different times, the roles can become confused. Students have difficulty confessing inadequacies and difficulties to 'teacher as supportive colleague' when next week the relationship will be vertical rather than horizontal with 'teacher as examiner'.

Students are shrewd enough to recognize that most teachers cannot keep those role separations watertight. They dare not jeopardize their scores by revealing their confusion or ignorance unless trust in the teacher has been carefully nurtured over a long period.

Given the power within the examiner role, the student cannot change the relationship with the teacher. Only the teacher can change such a power relationship with the student.

Yet clinical students are adults, soon to be responsible doctors, who will be performing independently. Teachers who wish to shift from an authoritarian, Parent/Child, paternal relationship with their students to a colleagueal, Adult/Adult, fraternal relationship must recognize that the shift must come from themselves. Building acceptance and trust requires open-ness and discussion more than criticism and judgment.

Many teachers expect students to metamorphose at the moment of graduation from knowledgeable, but inexperienced, observers to effective clinical performers. After graduation, however, the teachers will be supervising that performance only a minute fraction of the time. Clinical performance is, in the long run, assessed only by the performers themselves. The most critical question for the teacher is whether the student will graduate as a capable assessor of personal clinical performance as well as a capable clinical performer.

WHAT TO ASSESS

Clinical performance can be assessed at increasingly deeper levels of complexity and responsibility, which correspond with the career stage of the student — doctor.

Levels of performance

Level 1. Clinical knowledge. Pen and paper tests (essays, modified essays, short answers, multiple choice questions, patient management problems on paper or on computer) create verbal simulations of clinical reality. The unit of study is knowledge about clinical states, expressed in words. Manipulation of this verbal knowledge is a pre-requisite for clinical performance, but cannot be equated directly with real life.

Knowing is not equivalent to doing. In no way can verbal tests, written or oral, be called clinical performance. Talking a good game is not equivalent to playing a good game.

Level 2. Component skills of clinical performance can be separated out as partial tasks and assessed individually. Here the unit of study is a task prescribed by the examiner, such as taking a urological history, or examining a hip joint, or interpreting a radiograph.

Being brief activities, each can be reduced further to a set of constituent steps. The sequence of steps can be spelled out in a check list. The quality of performance of each step may be scored on a rating scale. Since the criteria of performance have been agreed in advance, and make up the check lists, scoring is objective with little opportunity for examiner bias. Such assessment has been developed as Objective Structured Clinical Examinations or Assessments (OSCE or OSCA) [see Chapter 28].

This format for assessment sets out to test a drill, an obedience to a predicted routine, and is particularly useful for testing the acquisition of a set of clinical skills. Since the student's options are limited and the expectations sharply prescribed, the format tests the outcome of training more than the outcome of education.

Failure to develop reasonable accuracy and efficiency in these clinical skills has been a common concern at the time of graduating examinations. A contributing factor may have been the lack of a barrier examination earlier in the course within which students demonstrated their grasp of the skills. The formal testing of the drills within an OSCE has provided a framework for such testing. The necessary discussion and agreement among teachers on criteria and expectations has been valuable within Faculties in making more coherent what have often been idiosyncratic craft skills.

Level 3. Clinical competence is assessed in the student's clinical performance with a patient. The unit of study is the whole patient and illness.

The assessment usually has a limited focus of diagnosis plus a verbal management plan in a selected patient with sufficiently evident disease for substantial findings on physical examination.

Nevertheless, the examination does require the student to select what to ask and what to look for, to be skillful and accurate in revealing the data, to interpret the evidence collected, and to combine the evidence into a diagnosis. The examination usually incorporates the process of clinical exploration, the products of the process which are the diagnosis and management plan, and the testing of clinical knowledge as it would apply to this patient.

When a patient is the unit of study, the task is not fixed and identical for all candidates. Not only do cases differ in the complexity of the clinical problem, but in the ease of obtaining historical and/or physical information from the patient. The clinical process is a fleeting interaction between student and patient. Time and efficiency are important, as well as protection of the patient.

Level 4. Clinical performance embraces habitual behaviour within the complexity of responsible clinical practice. The unit of study expands from the single patient to the care of many patients in the wards, to the sequence of patients in the clinic, to the priorities among patients such as emergencies, to the relationships with other health workers, to referral to other doctors, to long term maintenance, and so on. The skills include management, communication, and efficiency, as well as effectiveness as seen in the outcomes of care. Medical schools vary in whether such a range of (supervised) responsibilities has been part of the educational program.

Assessment at Level 1 is covered in Chapters 22 to 27. Assessment at Level 2 is dealt with in Chapter 28. This chapter focuses on only Levels 3 and 4.

HOW TO DEVELOP CRITERIA OF GOOD/BAD PERFORMANCE

As we have worked down through the increasing complexity and responsibility of those four levels of clinical knowledge and skills, two aspects of measurement at Levels 3 & 4 have become obvious. First, too many events are taking place for any assessor to be able to fill in check lists or rating scales. Second, the events are unpredictable, in that the student/doctor has choice in selecting what to do, in what order, and to what degree.

What is the examiner looking for? Unfortunately for the student, the examiners' expectations are rarely explicit. Unless they are carefully drawn out, each examiner's mental check list of criteria will not be clear. Further, the weighting assigned to different actions by the student ('I'd always fail a student who can't pick a femoral from an inguinal hernia!') reflects a range of standards of expectation.

Clinical performance contains so many possible (and legitimate) actions by the student that no single 'true' approach can be expected. The 'rules of the game' are rarely fully spelled out; students check the rules with questions such as 'May I ask the patient questions?' In assessing performance examiners exercise considerable judgment, but are not necessarily choosing the same actions to judge. Even if they choose the same actions to score, they are not necessarily scoring to the same expected standard, or giving those actions the same importance or relative weighting as another examiner.

Examiners must, consequently, choose what to concentrate on. The choice should link directly to the purpose of the examination, and what is most important within the performance. Deciding 'what is important' is not a simple task. A pragmatic view would emphasize outcomes, a professional view would ensure competent and ethical behaviour, an economic view would look for effectiveness and efficiency, and a consumer view would incorporate interpersonal style and delivery of the services sought. Which questions will you ask about the performance?

1. Did s/he do it right? or DIAGNOSTIC PROCESS
    = following a logical and efficient process for collecting clinical data accurately
2. Did s/he know it right? or CLINICAL KNOWLEDGE
    = using appropriate knowledge for exploring and explaining this specific problem
3. Did s/he get it right? or ACCURATE, COMPLETE DIAGNOSIS
    = interpreting, weighing and integrating clinical data
4. Did s/he plan it right? or MANAGEMENT PLAN
    = fitting treatment options to this patient and situation
5. Was the patient satisfied? or PATIENT SATISFATION
    = ensuring effective communication and an acceptable solution
6. Was s/he efficient? or EFFICIENCY
    = using minimal resources, investigations, time
7. How did s/he behave? or BEHAVIOUR
    = listening carefully, showing respect, being honest
8. Was his/her judgment sound? or CLINICAL JUDGMENT
    = balance in trade-offs among competing values and outcomes
9. Did s/he arrange referral well? or TEAM RESPONSIBILITY
    = choosing appropriately, transferring clearly, organizing care
10. How did it turn out? or EFFECTIVENESS
    = achieving best results, least complications

Many assessors waste considerable time testing knowledge which can be measured more efficiently and reliably in other ways. Such testing may be based on the unproven assumption that knowledge will predict performance, or on an underestimate of the necessity to explore exactly how that knowledge is being applied. That is, performance represents active application of knowledge; the clinical assessor's task is to assess application in action, not to revert to testing the

pre-requisites to application. The clinical examination is too fleeting an opportunity of seeing the candidate in action for time to be spent on lists or key words.

At this level of performance by students soon to graduate as independent professionals, issues of the teacher's philosophy arise. Medical teachers must consider whether the virtue of fairness to students via examiner uniformity simultaneously extinguishes openness to accepting lateral thinking or creative behaviour. Do we stifle spontaneity? Is our current approach to patient care 'right'? Are we helping our students become better than us if we demand that they be exactly the same as us? What if the student and the patient define the illness differently from us as examiners? Are we right, or are they, or are we both? If we are to help clinical medicine evolve, we cannot stick to one view of correct behaviour.

The medical teacher must choose which of these facets of clinical performance are to be assessed to meet the purposes for which the assessment is being mounted. Given the facet to assess, criteria must be chosen which represent what can be agreed upon as important by those involved.

CRITERIA FOR CHOOSING CRITERIA

The criteria chosen for measurement may derive from habit or tradition. It is useful to check the qualities of each against the purposes of assessment to be sure they are worth using.

1. Relevance to the decision

Eventually the results will be used to decide something about the student/doctor (otherwise the assessment is wasting everybody's time). Is every criterion you have chosen relevant to the decision? If not, discard it.

2. Accuracy/validity re performance

Each criterion should accurately reflect the performance being assessed. Look at each. Don't measure personality traits, for example, if they are not related to getting the job done; and don't leave them out if they are.

3. Reliability across assessors

Each criterion should be consistent and stable from one assessor to the next. Is the criterion understood in the same way by all, and acknowledged to be reasonably objective?

4. Sensitivity to differences

Assessment must discriminate between effective and ineffective performance. Is the criterion sufficiently sensitive to reveal significant differences?

5. Acceptability to all concerned

Criteria must be accepted by teachers, students and those making decisions or the procedures will be treated as meaningless and a waste of time, or worse, unfair.

A critical decision for every clinical examiner is whether to be present during the clinical interaction. The dilemma is often resolved by leaving the student alone with the patient in the 'long' case, and looking over his or her shoulder during the 'short' cases. The issue within this is whether it is necessary to observe the clinical process, or whether a satisfactory account of the findings can be interpreted as satisfactory process.

Criteria of clinical process

The process is a series of events happening; and to be assessed, must be observed in action. Why do you want to observe what the student is actually doing? What are you looking for?

Most teachers say that they're looking at the approach to the patient, at the ability to take a history, and to examine for physical signs.

At this stage it is necessary to separate the levels of performance referred to above. If the assessment is to observe whether 'drills' have been learned for each component skill, then an OSCE or its variations will best meet the criteria of accuracy, reliability, and so on above. If the assessment is to observe how the student sets about an unknown situation, how pertinent is the questioning, how efficient the process, how gentle yet direct, or how appropriate the level of thoroughness, then the criteria for measuring each

of those abilities will require considerable thought and discussion among examiners.

Criteria of clinical outputs

The outputs or products comprise the immediate results of the performance, and can usually be stated in words without having to be observed. If those products are accurate and appropriate, the process can usually be assumed. If, for example, one product being sought is the accurate collection of a complete clinical history, then a (mental) check list of all the positive and negative points in the history can be relied upon without watching the process of history taking. If patient satisfaction with the consultation is to be assessed, however, then an output measure (such as asking the patient) may not be sufficient or reliable evidence of the quality of the process.

If basic skills have been verified at an earlier stage of clinical learning (eg. by an OSCE), examiners can more confidently assess performance on the products without observing the process.

Criteria of clinical outcomes

The outcomes of care are measured in the medium to longer term. Outcomes may not be used for student performance, if students do not carry clinical responsibility. Outcomes can, however, be used for assessing performance of graduates. We shall, in the future, see progressively more attention to the results of on-going practice as clinicians become accustomed to personal computers and adequate practice records, and as pressures mount for recertification of clinical capacity.

WHO ARE THE EXAMINERS?

We noted above that the number of events within a clinical performance was so great that choices must be made about what to focus on, and on what aspects to give weight. Choices involve judgment based on values, on what is 'important'.

Whom do we appoint as the judges? Do we appoint them because of their ability as examiners, or because of their position in the clinical hierarchy? Where do their criteria come from? What do we know of their criteria and values?

The task (and responsibility) for the chief teacher/examiner is to convene the clinical examiners to elicit what criteria of good and bad performance they are using. We are likely to use the same words but with different meanings. Considerable discussion may be needed to be sure what each other really means. Since our assumptions are often difficult to reveal, having the examiners 'blindly' score a clinical performance (or, more conveniently, a videotape thereof), and having them note the criteria on which their scoring was based, reveals what was important to each. The informal approach to performance assessment by many clinicians which assumes that 'everyone knows what's good clinical performance', is demonstrably untrue as soon as their criteria are spelled out. Each pointer can be judged for validity, relevance etc. [see above], and the most useful set chosen.

Examiners must accept that judgment is essential in assessing performance, that 'subjective' is not a dirty word but part of everyday life, including practice life. The task becomes one of aligning judgments so that they are based on the same criteria and weighting. To do this, teacher/examiners must estimate the extent of scatter, and the sources of variation, among scores in the examinations for which they are responsible. The techniques are simple:

— retaining the scores of examiners allows calculation of their individual means, range, mode and variance
— blind double marking establishes the variance of examiners on the same performance
— analysis of class scores identifies the variance within each component of the examination, and across components (see Chapter 33 for elaboration of how to handle the scores).

If it is decided that examiners are allowed to be free to apply different criteria and standards (as a result of thorough discussion about different perspectives, not because of failure ever to have communicated effectively),and/or if we accept the existence of an irreducible diversity among judges, we must increase the sample of judges and the sample of performances observed until we can be confident we are approximating the candidate's 'true' score.

Constraints of logistics and resources related to the availability of patients, time and examiners, however, sharply limit how many performances can be formally certified. We really have too few experienced judges available; therefore, the task becomes one of tidying up their inconsistency. Other solutions are possible using informal settings and other examiners (such as self, peers, residents, nurses, and even patients), but experience with their use has been only sparsely reported.

The criteria, once clarified, should be set out on a convenient form.

FORMS FOR PERFORMANCE ASSESSMENT

Formalization by using 'forms' can effectively
1. Structure the processes of observation and judgment
2. Help minimize bias in assessment
3. Provide standardized information
4. Record observations for subsequent feedback
5. Reduce the administrative burden

The number of observable events in any performance is so many that forms must allow summary judgments by examiners. Judges/examiners choose critical incidents which illustrate good or bad performance, and use these anecdotally to persuade other examiners to their judgment on an individual. Forms can ensure that a broader range of observations are included in the judgment.

HOW DO YOU MINIMIZE BIAS?

Performance assessment always involves judgment. Judges differ in their assessments, even when presented with identical evidence. Performances differ, even when student/doctors deal successfully with identical patients or problems.

The teacher/examiner must consider how to increase the reliability of examinations. What responses to assessment variation are practical? Current responses within clinical examinations are:

1. To standardize the clinical cases so that all students face the same test.

(a). Standardization can be achieved by limiting the clinical task to be performed (as in OSCE, see Chapter 28) to a procedure for which a check list, or 'correct' answer can be agreed upon in advance of the examination. In this way both the task, and the criteria for scoring performance on the task, are identical for all students. The unit of study is necessarily a component skill for which a 'drill' or routine can be specified. To this extent, the test is of training rather than of judgment.

(b). The task can also be standardized by using simulated patients (Barrows & Tamblyn, 1980) who are either patients who have recovered from the malady, or actors trained to simulate the story and even many of the physical signs. Here the unit of examination is a whole patient. Compared with the usual clinical examination, however, the clinical picture is maintained reasonably constant for all candidates.

(c). Rarely do examiners attempt to organize the relative difficulty of cases in clinical examinations, but usually leave to chance who will see what cases in what sequence. In my experience examiners make insufficient adjustment of scores according to the ease or difficulty of the cases seen by each candidate, or to the effect on subsequent performance of a very difficult first case.

2. To standardize examiners to ensure consistent scoring. This standardization has both consensus and training components. Examiners must work towards consensus on

(a). the criteria being sought

(b). the standard expected in performance on each criterion

(c). the relative weighting assigned to the score on each criterion

We have discussed above how identification of criteria, standards and weighting is readily undertaken by a group observing and scoring a video-taped clinical examination performance. Little data are available about the effectiveness of such training.

(d). means, modes and range of scores Examiners can receive feedback on their personal scoring patterns, and where they differ from other examiners. What is the 'right' pattern?

Every score is a judgment. Every score contains a decision about written or practical performance which assesses this performance against an implicit set of performance standards, and allocates the candidate to some category or level in the examiner's mind.

Humans appear to judge events in category terms, not numerical terms. The performance is first placed in a category, such as Just Pass or Clear Fail and then fine-tuned to produce a number such as 51 or 36.

Examiners make these subsequent numerical allocations on the basis of an agreed system as to what the numbers mean. Fifty per cent has no 'reality' as the sum of marks at which someone passes, but is a number to which examiners agree to mark (in many countries, but by no means all). Many use a 'close marking system', say, 9, 10, 11, 12. Of these, 11 is a pass, 10 just fail but able to be helped up by a 12, and 9 an irremediable failure. The numbers are irrelevant in a mathematical sense; but they provide a language for a four category scoring system.

Many of these difficulties disappear if the student must 'master' a sequence of abilities derived from the objectives of the course. First, the abilities are defined. Second, the criteria for acceptable performance are set out and made available to teachers and students. Third, when the student feels ready, the performance can be arranged under supervision, and certified if satisfactory. If not, another opportunity is arranged after further learning, and testing is repeated until mastery is demonstrated.

Mastery systems can embrace all the core abilities, diminishing the uncertainties about graduating a '50% doctor' who may have never satisfactorily learned all these core abilities.

(e). training to minimize the common evaluation biases of halo, central tendency, and leniency.

i. *Halo* describes the (good or bad) impression a student/doctor carries from one task to another, or from one attribute (such as knowledge displayed in tutorial discussion) to a different task (such as interpretation of physical signs). Performance on the first case is unconsciously extrapolated to the next cases.

Halo lowers the variance of the individual's

score; yet studies of scores on performance reveal consistently that students and doctors show a low correlation and a high variance among their scores on different performances, even when the doctors are performing within their own practice specialty.

Halo is diminished if candidates are not previously known to examiners, if easy and difficult cases are seen, if a larger number of cases is seen, and if examiners record scores separately for each patient the candidate examines.

ii. *Central tendency* describes the incapacity of examiners to discriminate among candidates, putting the majority into a single category or level. The tendency may reflect low confidence in one's judgment, or expectations about the probability of all being at that level, or the use of very few scoring criteria, or lack of thought or skill in the evaluation process. Central tendency bias lowers the variance of all scores, and lowers their discriminatory capacity. Examiners are usually unaware that such low variance decreases the impact of that component of the examination compared with components with wider variance in their scores, such as written examinations (see Chapter 33).

Examiners need to agree to use the full range of scores, and to be given regular feedback on the scores they actually give.

iii. *Leniency* inflates scores, particularly scores at or below the borderline.Leniency is commoner in face to face examinations. Leniency may reflect a desire to be kind, a failure to think through the consequences, inexperience in examining, or difficulty in justifying a negative evaluation which always takes more explaining. An examiner's modal score and pass rate can reflect leniency when compared with other examiners.

3. To standardize the scoring procedure.

Consistency in scoring is assisted by creating scoring forms containing check lists and rating scales devised around the chosen criteria and standards, so that observed performance will be recorded as objectively as practicable in a given framework. Devising such scoring forms entails discussion and clarification of behaviour which exemplifies good and bad performance; such ident-ified behaviour can act as the top and bottom ends of the rating scale, with 5 to 7 points between on which a candidate can be placed.

Unfortunately, while such lists and scales can be created in discussion, clinical examiners often have great difficulty using them in practice. Partly, all attention is directed to the details of the performance being observed. Partly, most examiners are involved in formal examining only once a year, and may never gain familiarity with the format.

While these approaches increase the reliability and visible fairness of the scoring, some of the 'face validity' of 'reality' is lost by too many constraints. Once a standardized format is chosen for any examination, both teachers and students may learn to operate within the 'rules of the game'. Every rule places boundaries on choice; to that extent the examination measures the level of obedience to group choice rather than individual expression.

I prefer to increase the number of samples tested,that is, to accept that variation exists within reality and within approaches to explaining reality. Therefore, extensive and repeated testing are needed to yield a fair assessment.

What is a sufficient sample in a statistical sense turns on the reliability of the examination and its consequent standard error. Such calculations usually suggest that at least ten cases should be seen; but this is not logistically feasible in most medical schools, and competency examinations usually cover only three or four cases in each discipline.

Staff are usually not available for such a task. Who better, then, than the students (about to metamorphose into doctors) to conduct a series of self-assessments? Or their colleagues (who will be informally assessing them later out in practice) to undertake a peer assessment (eg. Smith et al, 1984)?

SELF ASSESSMENT

Self-assessment has many strengths. (*See also* Chapters 27 & 31)

1. Comparison with teachers' scores can show high correlation (Morton & Macbeth,1977;

Henbest & Fehrsen,1985), but not necessarily so (Sclabassi & Woelfel,1984).

2. New information is provided, particularly on non-cognitive aspects of performance (Arnold, Willoughby & Calkins,1985)

3. The task has a positive effect on the student, engendering new insights into performance (Henbest & Fehrsen,1985)

4. The transfer of trust to the student can be seen by students as a very strong statement about relations among colleagues (Henbest & Fehrsen,1985).

5. Students can develop their own criteria and rating forms with guidelines from teachers, moving progressively to independent responsibility as a practising professional.

FEEDBACK TO IMPROVE STUDENT PERFORMANCE

Does the teacher/supervisor communicate to the student/doctor all the information within the assessment of performance? Usually not. Most people find it difficult to give unwelcome messages about what someone else did badly. Despite their training and practice in communication and patient education, doctors often also prove reluctant in practice to sit down and discuss the situation openly.

How can we as teachers organize our review of performance to make it most constructive, and to elicit the least defensiveness and resentment? Immediately we run into our assumptions about the role of the teacher.

How do we train people to do what they should do? We know what they ought to do, and how they ought to do it. Should we simply tell them where they went wrong, and show them or tell them how to do it properly?

Or should we tell them, and then discuss their point of view as well? At least that way they can explain what happened, and express their defensiveness.

Or should we arrange frequent opportunities to discuss this and other performances, to share our different perspectives, to find explanations for the events, and to work out together what additional learning should be arranged?

These three approaches to feedback have been called Tell and Sell, Tell and Listen, and Joint Problem-Solving (Maier, 1958). The approaches reflect training at one extreme and education at the other.

Whichever view of the teacher role is adopted, frequent meetings are likely to improve both the flow of information and the teacher's information base for judgment. The halo effect may, however, 'give a dog a bad name'.

A critical, authoritarian style in the teacher can inhibit the student who will conceal ignorance or uncertainty, rather than express it in order to get advice and guidance. The criticism seems often to meet the needs of the teacher more than those of the student/doctor, without seriously considering whether the student's learning from the experience may be blocked by feelings of anxiety, resentment and frustration. If the criticism is felt as a put-down of the student/doctor's self-esteem, the recipient may become angry, and the messages are no longer heard.

REFERENCES

Arnold L, Willoughby T L & Calkins E V 1985 Self-evaluation in undergraduate medical education: a longitudinal perspective J. med. educ. 60: 21–28

Barrows H S & Tamblyn R S 1980 Problem-based learning: an approach to medical education Springer Series on Medical Education #1, Springer, New York

Henbest R J & Fehrsen G S 1985 Preliminary study at the Medical University of Southern Africa on student self-assessment as a means of evaluation J. med. educ. 60: 66–67

Maier N R F 1958 Three Types of Appraisal Interview Personnel, March–April,

Morton J B & Macbeth W A A G 1977 Correlations between staff, peer and self-assessment Med. Educ., 11: 167–170

Sclabassi S E & Woelfel 1984 Development of self-assessment skills in medical students Med. Educ., 84: 226–231

Smith H, Chan S S Chalmers T C, Reitman D, & Sacks H S 1984 Peer review using a paired-comparison technique Med. Care, 22: 412–417

Professional behaviour — how can it be assessed?

The aim of this chapter is to explore further some of the difficult issues inherent in assessing *'clinical performance'* as defined in Chapter 29. In particular it deals with the assessment of those behaviours related to values and beliefs about health, illness and health care. One of the reasons that assessment in this area is difficult is that, unlike teaching in other areas of medicine, teaching by specific objectives is difficult or inappropriate because it is difficult to define exactly what it is that students should learn.

WHAT DO WE WANT STUDENTS TO LEARN?

Students enter the medical course with different relevant knowledge, personality traits, values, and personal goals.

Certain academic prerequisites are always laid down, and certain knowledge and skills are assumed to have been acquired before admission. This is not so in the affective area, although some schools try to ascertain attitudes through interviews or comprehensive selection procedures (*See* Chapter 3).

All individuals, however, come to the program with their own cultural, social, family and individual backgrounds which have influenced their personalities and value system. Thus, with wide ranging and divergent 'basic information' to build on, the training program cannot teach a definite set of attitudes, or behavioural responses. Nor would it be appropriate for it to do so.

On the other hand, it is unrealistic to suppose that a program does not impart to its students some values and beliefs. Every time one area of content is selected for inclusion in the syllabus, another is selected to be excluded. The examples we provide, the teaching methods we employ, and the places in which we teach, all influence the students' interpretation of what we are teaching.

The educational program provides the link between the student's past experience and future role, and should encourage adoption of those behaviours which reflect the program goals. Assessment of those behaviours is, therefore, highly desirable but assessment requires that criteria of acceptable performance be defined.

Defining criteria for assessment of behaviour

The first questions to be asked when defining criteria are the following: What are the characteristics required for acceptable performance in the working role? That is, what are the objectives of the training program, what tasks do they reflect and what qualities do we wish to encourage in students which will enable them to perform those tasks effectively?

These questions usually give rise to responses such as:

— above all to respect other people, and in so

doing tolerate differences among groups and understand the right to individuality

— [as a corollary to the above] to be aware of their own personality traits, beliefs and value systems
— to respect human life, not only in the physical sense but in a psychological and social sense
— to be willing to give to others, but also respect themselves and their own needs
— to have the ability to solve problems and make decisions in a systematic, humanitarian way, with regard to the patient as a whole person, and with regard for the expertise of others in the health team
— to have a positive attitude to life-long learning
— to have a commitment to the profession they are part of, and a willingness to enable it to change to meet changing needs in society.

This list constitutes both objectives and criteria for assessment of professional behaviour. The next task for the teacher is to determine how to provide a training program which encourages such values, beliefs and attitudes and which provides opportunities for valid assessment of their development.

ENCOURAGING DESIRABLE BEHAVIOURS TO DEVELOP

Explore values

Firstly, the goals of the program should be clearly defined, and the values and beliefs upon which those general goals are built should be made explicit. The teacher's task is to facilitate constructive debate about those values and beliefs so that students become experienced in the process of clarification of value issues (See Chapter 17). At the same time students become aware of the inherent subjectivity of decisions concerning the definition of the doctor's role. The teacher can also help the students to understand that subjectivity is not a problem in itself although it may become a problem when people choose to deny its influence. To deny subjectivity is to deny one's own value system, whereas to be a role model of one's own values and to help students

to recognize their own values may be the greatest contribution a teacher can make.

Impart information

The more information one has about an issue or topic, the more likely it is that a rational judgment can be made about its value. For example, a teacher may wish to plan an adolescent health program for medical students, emphasising attitudinal components. However, a prior task may be to provide the students with basic knowledge about drugs, alcohol, sexual maturity and the psychological pressures of adolescence. This prior step ensures that core information is shared and enables more wide ranging discussion which can then encompass attitudes and values. Thus, while it is essential to teach more than just knowledge, it is also essential when exploring the affective domain not to forget that knowledge is a basic component contributing to an individual's value system.

However, what is and what is not factual or core information, is not always easy to decide. In other words what one person 'knows' may not be what another person agrees to. For example 'Surgery is the best treatment for coronary artery insufficiency' may be more or less acceptable to different experts. Knowledge is relative. Interpretation of facts is coloured by beliefs, and beliefs are the result of the way we interpret our experience and fit it into our existing conceptual frameworks. Part of this process involves valuing certain pieces of information above others, that is, we give weighting to certain 'facts' and ignore others, in adding to our store of knowledge and beliefs.

Thus, while providing information is an essential part of the process of developing desirable behaviours we must not lose sight of the fact that knowledge, beliefs and values exist in a dynamic relationship with each other.

Provide practice in using desirable behaviours

Students need opportunities to practise coping with difficult situations in order to develop appropriate professional behaviour. Teachers can facilitate this practice in a relatively low risk environment by providing simulation exercises.

Such exercises can act as a trigger for discussion of values and behaviours and also as an opportunity for feedback on performance (See Chapters 13 and 18). Examples of use of simulation exercises are:

— Using a trigger film of an interview with an angry patient followed by discussion of the responses and emotions the film evoked and the ways in which students could cope with those feelings.

— Role playing a conversation with a terminally ill patient in order to explore appropriate responses to the patients' needs.

— Using a film about health problems in another culture, to facilitate an analysis of inherent beliefs about health and illness.

— Using experiential exercises and learning 'games' to illustrate interpersonal communication skills.

Provide practical experience

Teachers should provide opportunities for field visits in which the student becomes a participant observer (See Chapter 9). Suitable sites for field visits can range from the home of one family to a market place, a health clinic or shopping centre or a hospital.

Provide opportunity for reflection

Lastly, but most importantly teachers can provide opportunities for students to reflect on and discuss their experiences in the training program (See Chapter 10). Skilful development of the student learning group and of a colleague relationship between teacher and student can provide necessary affective support for students when they take responsibility for patient care for the first time. It is important to remember that the behaviour which the teacher models will be a strong influence on the learning that takes place.

ASSESSMENT OF PROFESSIONAL BEHAVIOURS

Professional behaviour can be assessed on three levels:

1. Knowledge
2. Knowledge, and the ability to value important components of knowledge
3. Knowledge, valuing important components and carrying out defined desirable behaviours.

At the first level students may be expected to *know* that surgery is the treatment of choice for acute appendicitis. At the second level interns may be expected to know the surgical procedures involved in appendicectomy but also to *value* the goal of aseptic techniques and the necessity to work as part of a surgical team. At the third level a surgical registrar may be expected not only to know and value the appropriate techniques and performances but also to demonstrate that he or she can *perform* the procedures safely.

All of these levels of performance can be assessed using methods which are described in Section 4 of this book. There is, however, still a fourth level which should be assessed. That level seeks to answer the question 'How would the student *tend to behave* in a particular context?'

We do not expect the same behaviour in every situation; we expect the appendicectomy patient to be discharged from hospital when it is appropriate for his physical state, his home circumstances and his age. This 'tendency to behave' parallels the psychologists' term 'attitude'. Much of the confusion about assessing attitudes can be removed if we ask the questions:

Do we want standard behaviour?

Do we want the graduates to tend to behave in a certain way, but expect them to show discernment in any particular context?

Do we only want graduates to know about a certain topic or do we want them to value specific aspects of it in specific ways?

Methods of assessment appropriate to each level of learning goal can then be organized. Standardized attitude scales have little or no role to play in assessment when attitudes and behaviour are placed, as they should be, in the broader context of professional performance. Assessment of professional behaviour is most appropriately conducted as part of the students' experiential learning. Each of the methods for encouraging development which were discussed earlier in this chapter can have assessment components incorporated into it. Some of the techniques for encouraging self-assessment (See Chapter 31) may be useful in the context of field work or simulation exercises, for example. Components of attitudes and 'tendency to behave' can be assessed in Objective Structured Clinical Examinations, oral examinations or even Patient Management Problems which have been designed to incorporate valuing as well as knowledge components of the problem solving process.

Viewed in this light assessment of attitudes and professional behaviour does not require teachers to develop and use a specialized assessment technology. What it does require is that teachers clarify their goals in the affective area, define them as specifically as possible in terms of tendencies to behave in certain contexts, and incorporate opportunities to assess those tendencies in the course of routine clinical learning and examinations.

How to facilitate self-assessment

Preview

WHAT IS SELF-ASSESSMENT?

HOW CAN SELF-ASSESSMENT BE
INTRODUCED INTO EXISTING COURSES?

WHEN SHOULD SELF-ASSESSMENT BE
INTRODUCED?

ARE INCENTIVES NEEDED?

CONCLUSION

WHAT IS SELF-ASSESSMENT?

Self-assessment is not an additional technique in
the repertoire of assessment methods; it is
different in kind from other forms of student
assessment. Although self-testing can be regarded
in some senses as a technique for assessment in
which students test themselves and check their
own answers, self-assessment amounts to rather
more than this. It involves students taking responsibility for monitoring their own learning: establishing appropriate criteria for their learning, and
making judgments about the nature and extent of
it. It is primarily a means whereby students can
develop the ability to become independent
learners, not needing the continuing presence of
a teacher or examiner in order to check their own
progress (Boud & Lublin, 1983).

It is undesirable that students should engage in
self-assessment in isolation from others, especially
peers and those who may be more experienced
practitioners. While responsibility for assessment
should reside essentially with the learner — for it
is the learner alone who must apply the results of
assessment to lead to improved performance —

the learner must be able to draw upon the expertise of others to form his or her judgment.

Self-assessment is:
the involvement of students in establishing
standards and/or criteria to apply to their work, and
their making judgments about the extent to which
they have met these criteria and standards.

Self-assessment assists students to reflect on
their learning. It engages them in thinking actively
about the problems which they meet, how they
define them and react to them, and what the
implications are. The importance of reflection in
learning is being increasingly recognized, especially
in areas where students are exposed to complex
experiences (Boud et al, 1985). Self-assessment
can introduce aspects of reflection without the
need to make more substantial changes to existing
courses.

Although self-assessment may in some circumstances be used to supplement or replace teacher
assessment it is primarily used to assist students
to be more effective learners. It can be incorporated into courses of any kind at any level. The
particular approaches which can be adopted vary
greatly depending on the type of course, the
nature of the subject, the degree of sophistication
of students in working independently, and on the
particular reason for introducing self-assessment
into the course (Heron, 1981). For some examples
see Table 31.1 (Boud 1986).

Although each type of self-assessment can be
used in many different contexts, the first types
(A, B) have been commonly used in introductory
courses where the emphasis is on learning new
ideas and assimilating information, or where the
content is primarily technical. Types C and D are
of particular value where students are involved in

Table 31.1 Types of self-assessment

Self-assessment may involve student in both establishing criteria and making judgments about their learning. If students are involved only in the latter aspect it is usually termed self-testing.

A. Self-testing using multiple choice or short answer tests

Students test themselves by completing the tests and checking the answers for themselves. Sufficient information is provided about incorrect responses to enable students to understand where they have gone wrong and be directed to reference material for them to study further. Sometimes model answers may be used.

B. Self-testing with peer feedback

This is a similar approach to A except that students work in groups and discuss their answers with their peers.

C. Setting individual criteria for assignments and projects

Students work through a series of questions which help them focus on the criteria which should be used in assessing their performance in any given area and in giving priorities to them. These criteria are used as a check-list for students to assess their work prior to submitting it for staff assessment.

D. Setting group criteria for assignments and projects

The criteria which are produced by individuals can sometimes be quite limited, and it is often desirable to involve a group of students in reaching consensus on the criteria to be used. This can be done in groups of up to about 30 students using a nominal group technique. Students are briefed in advance to think about the issue and bring a few criteria with them to the meeting. At the meeting the person running it records one criterion from each person in turn without comment until all items have been listed. The items are clarified and grouped under major themes suggested by the group. Priorities may be given to some of these by the group or all may be used. The final list is used as a check-list against which students judge their work.

E. Self-generated criteria wlth peer feedback.

Individual students generate criteria as in C above and give feedback to each other on their work using these. It is helpful to provide guidance to students on ways to give useful feedback — *See* Table 31.2

F. Retrospective self-assessment schedules.

At the end of each term or semester students prepare a self-assessment document for a given subject including the following: their goals for the course (both initial goals and those which have emerged during the course), activities in which they have engaged which pursued these goals, evidence they have accrued which demonstrates the extent to which the goals have been met, and judgments about the extent of their learning in each area. If further study is to be made in a similar area the schedule may also include a set of plans for future action.

---

the synthesis of ideas in practical projects or more extended written assignments. Types E and F can be used in more complex learning situations such as clinical placements or project work. To become fully autonomous learners, students should be able to develop their own self-assessment criteria and tools for assessing themselves. The introduction of self-assessment activities into courses should be directed towards this ultimate goal.

HOW CAN SELF-ASSESSMENT BE INTRODUCED INTO EXISTING COUSES?

Although effective students have always used their own informal forms of self-assessment, it is sometimes a challenge to introduce the idea into a conventional course. Students often become very dependent on their teachers and become anxious when they are expected to take more responsibility

for their learning. Of course, they have to become independent at some time, but it is common for them to exhibit an initial resistance, especially if it appears to be creating more work for them to do. To minimize the problems which may be expected in any new approach it can be helpful to consider the following:

1. Choose a form of self-assessment which fits well with the aims of the course and the final assessment requirements. If students see the activity to be directly relevant to the major concerns of the course and the formal assessment requirements they are more likely to accept it.

2. Provide a clear rationale for self-assessment. Explain not only why it is important for effective learning both in the course and for future learning, but what practical benefits are likely to accrue to students. The type of self-assessment described in D in Table 31.1, for example, has improved the final quality of students' project

Table 31.2 Giving and receiving feedback

Good and bad feedback

It is important to distinguish between those forms of feedback which are helpful to others and those which may be unhelpful, or in some cases harmful.

We all know what it is to be on the receiving end of bad feedback. We feel 'got at', 'attacked', 'put down' and generally invalidated as a person. We become more preoccupied with what we perceive to be an affront than with the specific content of the message; we feel prompted to defend ourselves. Such feedback arises from the needs of the person giving it rather than from the receiver.

Useful feedback, on the other hand, affirms our worth as a person and gives support whilst offering genuine reactions to the work being displayed. The person providing the feedback shows that he or she values us and is sensitive to our needs. This does not mean that feedback should only be positive, but that criticism should occur in an overall supportive context, in which all parties should be able to trust one another.

Offering feedback

Worthwhile feedback has many characteristics but the most important aspect is the manner in which it is given. The tone, style and the content should be consistent and provide the message that 'I appreciate you and what you have done and whatever else I say should be taken in this context'.

Helpful feedback should be:

Realistic, that is, directed towards matters about which the person can do something.

Specific and direct, that is, it should provide sufficient information for the receiver to pinpoint the areas which are referred to and have a clear idea about what is being said about those areas.

Sensitive to the goals of the person, that is, it needs to relate to the intentions of the person not the giver's intentions. Those giving feedback may share their reactions so long as they recognize the goals of the recipient.

Prompt and timely. It is no use offering feedback if the time has passed for when it might be used.

Descriptive, not judgmental. Personal views should be given, but in such a way that they are presented as such and not as if they come from a great authority (even if the person is one). Use the first person: 'I felt . . . when . . .'.

Receiving feedback

There is no point in someone seeking feedback unless they are open to it and are prepared to consider comments which differ from their own perceptions. The person asking for feedback should be:

Explicit, making it clear what kind of feedback would be appreciated and what would not. If this does not occur then the seeker of feedback should not be surprised if it does not meet expectations.

Aware, of their own reactions both intellectual and emotional particularly any reactions of rejection or censorship. The most useful feedback can often be that to which it is hardest to listen.

Silent, not responding to the comments provided either at the time or at all. This is a particularly important point. It is difficult to listen to feedback and assimilate it effectively whilst also attempting to frame a response. Listening without responding can be frustrating at first until the benefits are realized.

---

work through providing them with a much more explicit set of expectations than could be normally gained by any of them individually or even supplied by a staff member.

3. Provide an opportunity for students to discuss the idea and raise any misconceptions which they may have. There are many misunderstandings about self-assessment; for example, that it is a substitute for teacher assessment (it usually is not), that it could lead to a pooling of ignorance rather than understanding (this should not arise if it is done systematically and is monitored by staff), that students do not have the ability to assess themselves (studies have shown that they can do this in a much more sophisticated manner than they imagine) (Boud., 1986).

4. Develop clear and explicit procedures and brief the students on them, preferably in writing. Experience with self-assessment has shown that success with it is dependent on paying attention to the details of the procedure. A good self-assessment procedure needs to be carefully planned and refined. Student acceptance can be greatly increased by small modifications to detail. In particular, students often find it difficult to think in terms of criteria; it can be useful to use expressions such as 'what are the characteristics of good work in this area?', or 'what distinguishes competent from less than competent performance?'

5. Establish a positive climate towards self-assessment through demonstrating one's own commitment to it and introducing it as a valuable activity.

WHEN SHOULD SELF-ASSESSMENT BE INTRODUCED?

We know that it is difficult for students to change their habits and attitudes towards monitoring their own learning if the idea is introduced towards the end of a course, or at a late stage in the academic year. We also know that it is difficult for students entering higher education direct from secondary education to change the habits acquired there. However, it is in the early stages of any course or of any year that students should ideally encounter the concept of self-assessment if it is to be taken seriously and applied effectively. The forms of self-assessment introduced should be consistent with the degree of student dependence on staff: the examples in Table 31.1 are listed broadly in terms of the degree of student independence required for their use.

ARE INCENTIVES NEEDED?

Although self-assessment can be regarded as primarily an approach to help learning, there are occasions on which marks or grades might be associated with it. In some situations the constraints of the formal assessment system are so powerful that students are unwilling to take seriously any activity which is not associated with grades. While this is not a desirable state of affairs for any course, the individual teacher wishing to introduce self-assessment may have to consider the need to provide an incentive over and above the intrinsic interest of the task. This can be done by building it in as a course requirement, by assigning class time for the activities, or by awarding marks for its successful completion. In the latter case the weighting need not be great, but even a small allocation of, say 4–5%, can have an influence on student attitudes and demonstrate to them that staff take the activity seriously. The amount of time required to introduce self-assessment need not be great, but the formal recognition of it which does occur when it is a part of the normal student load is important for its acceptance by students.

CONCLUSION

The importance of continuing professional education is being increasingly accepted. For this to be effective all professionals need to be able to take responsibility for and direct their own learning. Self-assessment is a vital component of this and the foundation for it needs to be provided in all courses (Boud & Kilty 1985).

REFERENCES

Boud D J, Lublin J 1983 Student self-assessment: educational benefits within existing resources. In: Squires G (ed) Innovation through recession. Society for Research into Higher Education, Guildford, Surrey p 93–99
Discusses the idea of self-assessment in undergraduate courses and gives some examples from different disciplines.
Boud D J, Keogh R, Walker D (eds) 1985 Reflection: turning experience into learning. Kogan Page, London
Provides a model to guide learning from experience and presents strategies for debriefing, using writing to reflect on learning, helping others to learn from experience, and the use of computers to aid reflection.
Heron J (1981) Assessment revisited. In: Boud D J (ed) Developing student autonomy in learning. Kogan Page, London p 55–68
A critique of existing assessment practices which proposes ways in which students can take greater responsibility for assessing themselves.

For an annotated bibliography on self and peer assessment see:
Boud D J (1983) Self and peer assessment in higher and continuing professional education; an annotated bibliography, Revised edition, Occasional Publication No 16, Tertiary Research Centre, University of New South Wales
Boud D J (1986) Implementing Students Self Assessment Higher Education Research and Development Society of Australasia, Sydney.
A report of the implications for teaching of a program of research and development on self-assessment in professional subjects.
For an application on self-assessment in continuing professional education see
Boud D J, Kilty J M (1985) Self-appraisal: an approach to academic staff development. In: Cryer P (ed) Training activities for teachers in higher education, Vol Two, Society for Research into Higher Education and NFER-Nelson, Guildford, Surrey p 33–44.

How did you score?

Preview

MULTIPLE CHOICE QUESTIONS

FREE RESPONSE QUESTIONS

RELIABILITY OF EXAMINATIONS

How do you arrive at a mark in an assessment? How do you actually mark an essay or an assignment report or a clinical performance? What assumptions underlie scoring? What do you know about your own scoring behaviour? How does your scoring relate to that of your colleagues?

Examination scores can make or break careers. Whether as numbers or grades, scores are recorded in academic transcripts and become part of the currency of selection and promotion. As such, scores should have the accuracy and precision which academic scientists apply to their own work. Do they?

Let us work through some scoring tasks to test that assumption of accuracy and precision. While we can attempt to deal with the issues as measurement questions, it soon becomes apparent that the whole philosophy of professional education is intimately and inextricably entwined with questions of purposes and roles.

MULTIPLE CHOICE QUESTIONS

1. The examination scoring of mcq is 'objective' in the sense that the 'right' answers are chosen in advance, and each candidate's right choices are added up by machine or visually.

But who chose which was the right answer? Either one examiner or a small group of three or four. If you have worked in such groups, you know how examiners disagree, and must persuade one another to consensus. A group larger than six is unworkable because differences take too long to resolve.

What does that say about the 'objectivity' of the 'right' answer? For example, when an mcq examination was conducted among seven medical schools (Cox et al, 1973), the mean scores within questions across schools, and even across teaching hospitals within medical schools, often differed so widely that, clearly, different 'right' answers were being taught. Truth turned out to be regional.

These observations demonstrate that 'national' examination results should be treated with great caution. While the machine scoring is objective, the diversity of views among examiners has been submerged; yet that diversity of view will be expressed within the teaching of each, and within the different responses chosen as 'correct' by different knowledgeable students.

The task for teacher/examiners is to clarify the issues impeding consensus, to find where agreement among examiners lies, and to ensure, as teachers, that the agreed principles are uniformly taught. If that agreement cannot be reached, the question should not be used.

2. For fair comparison of student performance from year to year, the difficulty of the examination is assumed to be constant. If not, in some years good students will be penalized, and in other years weak students will be inappropriately promoted. With mcq examinations in which new questions are introduced each examination (and which vary in their difficulty) the assumption that difficulty

is constant is unsound, as any review of an item analysis of the examination demonstrates.

3. Negative or penalty marking is often introduced into the scoring of multiple choice examinations of the multiple true/false statement type in order to 'reduce guessing', which may be regarded by some as inappropriate behaviour by doctors. That is, assumptions are being made about the relationship between how a candidate decides what choice to make to maximize the score in an mcq exam, and the same candidate's behaviour in clinical practice. To the best of my knowledge, that assumption has never been tested.

Marking the same paper with and without penalty marking can change rank order of students substantially. Yet there has been no difference in the knowledge held by those students, only a difference in the marking procedure after the exam. That is, the effect of penalty marking can be profound, even without introducing the effect on the candidate's strategy of the risk of losing marks, an effect whose rationale is totally speculative.

4. Does the examination fit with the amount of time and attention given to each part of the curriculum? The distribution of questions across subject areas is assumed to parallel the distribution of teaching, but this assumption is rarely tested. It is unfair to students if the examination questions include much material which has received little or no attention during the course.

The task for teacher/examiners is to categorize the examination questions used, say, by discipline and/or by body system and/or by stages of disease — such as etiology, pathogenesis, modes of presentation, symptoms and signs, and/or as essential 'core' knowledge, interesting but not essential, and esoteric and/or as requiring recall of facts, or interpretation or problem solving. The emphasis of the examination on each category is established by a simple count.

Does the emphasis reflect the objectives of the curriculum? Or the proportion of teaching time in each area? What objectives or areas have not been tested at all? Why not?

Examiners can set up lists of categories and the approximate number of questions to be asked from each category, or a matrix from two categories with expected numbers of questions in each cell of the matrix. Such an exercise immediately reveals large gaps in the breadth of examination coverage, and the redundancy of questions in some areas.

FREE RESPONSE QUESTIONS

(such as short answers, modified essays, long essays, assignment reports).

1. Since students are expressing responses in their own words, the examiner's task is to interpret those words and the concepts they explain, then to match them against the concepts and explanations the examiner was expecting.

The expectations can be made explicit in model answers upon which teachers agree. As mentioned above, the examiners' expectations should correspond with both the extent of curricular coverage, and what are perceived as correct answers. (For detail on developing a framework for model answers, *see* Bandaranayake, Chapter 35 in the first edition of *The Medical Teacher* (1982) and Feletti, Chapter 22 in this editionl). Students may even be allowed to argue their interpretations of the question before marking begins [see Chapter 22].

Even so, small matters, such as the choice of words and style of expression, the neatness of writing, and the layout of the answer, all influence examiners, producing inter-examiner variation.

2. The expectations of examiners usually centre on subject matter to be mentioned within the answer, with a clear expectation that a 'right' answer exists. Students recognize these expectations, and aim to provide what the examiner wants. Answers are frequently tailored to suit different examiners, or different disciplines which may be asking questions about the same area.

Medical teachers must decide whether this is what they wish to find out about their students. Is the examination intended to test whether the student can give back to the teacher what the teacher has previously given to the student? Such a relationship maintains the teacher's control (in transactional terms, maintaining the Parent/Child or paternal relationship), and also meets the teacher's responsibility for asserting that the student has mastered the subject matter in that field.

The rules of the game can, however, be rewritten, if the roles are. Teachers accepting a role as 'more experienced colleague' (in an Adult/Adult or fraternal relationship) can respond to students as thinking, growing individuals, rather than as obedient "little, living libraries". The examination can then embrace additional criteria of critical analysis, imaginative problem solving, appropriate thoroughness, depth of understanding, and of independent learning from sources other than textbooks. Chapter 8 (Hegarty-Hazel) demonstrates such an approach within microbiology in the laboratory.

The aim of the examination can be to allow the maximal freedom for exploration and expression of ideas, rather than a sharply bounded regurgitation of 'the facts'. Scoring on areas outside knowledge and its application necessitates the acceptance by teachers of unorthodoxy, imagination and lateral thinking, and often some uncomfortable criticism.

Such examinations cannot, by definition, be standardized. A similar situation applies with 'open book' examinations, in which students may bring any book they wish into the examination; the memorization of knowledge ceases to be a determinant of success or failure. If an examination cannot be standardized, should it be used at all? I like Maslow's paraphrasing of an old homily: 'If a thing's worth doing, its worth doing even if we don't do it very well'. If we don't start down the path of assessing these important but difficult qualities, we shall remain prisoners of the present and the past.

The task for the teacher/examiners is first to be clear on the qualities to be fostered in the students. What do you really want? Memorization of facts is easy to assess relatively unambiguously. But if other important goals of student learning are stifled thereby, the whole approach to examination must be reviewed.

What the examiner scores turns very much on the examiner's values about what are the important goals of the course. If the goals of examiners do not coincide, chance can affect which students score well and which poorly. Thorough debate until consensus is reached is

clearly obligatory for examiners, but sadly is not always undertaken. Without such debate we shall not expose the untested assumptions and judgments on which the examination scores rest.

Such concerns are particularly serious in assessments of a fleeting performance, such as a clinical examination, in which the responses are not available for second thoughts or for review by a panel of examiners. Scoring of performance is dealt with in Chapter 29.

RELIABILITY OF EXAMINATIONS

Having achieved consensus on *what* is to be assessed (the accuracy of the examination in measuring what it was intended to measure), how can the examination be made as reproducible (that is, as precise) as possible so that it is a reliable measuring instrument?

The first step is to measure the variance of the examination scores. The technique is based on dividing the examination into two halves and comparing the halves.

Calculations of the reliability (reproducibility, precision) of an examination show what weight can be placed on each candidate's score in reflecting his or her 'true' score. The foolishness of pseudo-precision in arguing over a few marks determining an individual score as Pass/Fail or Credit/Distinction is obvious when the variance of scores is looked at statistically.

Ebel (1972) has identified a number of different aspects of reliability of examinations, particularly written examinations, which help us to recognize exactly what we are talking about.

1. Reliability is the coefficient of correlation between one set of scores and another obtained independently from the same group.

2. Examinee reliability indicates how consistently examinees perform on the same set of tasks.

3. Examiner reliability indicates how closely examiners agree on the same performance.

4. Test reliability indicates how similarly examinees perform on different but (supposedly) equivalent tasks.

5. Test reliability (particularly mcq tests) increases with

    i. test length

ii. homogeneity of test

iii. discrimination of items

iv. questions of medium difficulty

v. a wide range of variability of performance in the test group

The medical teacher's responsibility in scoring fairly is to acknowledge the many sources of variance, to seek cooperation among examiners to develop a coherent and consistent system of marking, and to maintain a surveillance over the judgments made and the figures allotted.

REFERENCES

Bandaranayake R C 1982 Setting & marking essay questions Chapter 35 in Cox K R & Ewan C E Eds The Medical Teacher Churchill Livingstone, Edinburgh

Cox K R, Ludbrook J, McCarthy W H, Dunstan M 1973 National comparisons in a trial examination in surgery British Journal of Medical Education 7: 21–24

Ebel R 1972 Essentials of Educational Measurement Prentice Hall, Englewood Cliffs

What did you do with the scores?

Every set of examination scores contains information useful to both teachers and students. Surprisingly, little more is usually done with the scores than to provide students with their individual results as a single score or grade. Yet simple analysis of scores helps to provide a sounder basis for the many judgments which teachers must make about students and examinations.

HOW DIFFICULT WAS THIS EXAMINATION?

To be consistent, and to be fair to students across years, the difficulty of examinations should be kept uniform.

How do you know if this examination is as hard as last year's? Or easier? What information can you use?

The variables are the students, the examination tasks, and the examiners.

Class scores

Start with the scores of the class as a whole. What is the class mean? How does that compare with previous years? Has the class mean been consistent across the years? What is the standard error of the class mean (that is, how widely have scores varied from year to year)? If the class mean is lower than expected, does that imply that this class is weaker, or that the examination is more difficult, or that the examiners have imposed tougher standards? Is any explanatory evidence available?

To find such evidence, we must inspect other areas.

Students' scores

Look for data about the students. How many passed, how many failed, and how many were awarded high grades? What is the frequency distribution of the scores? How do the characteristics of the frequency distribution compare with previous years? Have the scores of a particular batch among the students shifted the distribution and the mean? Were the scores of individuals as predicted (from teachers' reports or other tests during the year)? If not, what were the directions and sizes of the discrepancies? What explanations are available?

Examination analysis

If no explanation is evident among the students'

scores, analyze the examination. Did the scores drop in one part of the examination? Could that relate to the questions posed, or to the coverage of that field in the curriculum, or to a particular examiner?

Multiple choice examinations are particularly easy to analyze in these ways, especially by computer. Each question can be analyzed for its difficulty. The frequency distribution of difficulty can be set out for the examination as a whole. Questions can be grouped by subject matter, enabling performance to be examined in each subject. The 'correct' answers can be checked. When students differ widely from examiners on what is the correct answer, the teaching given and the examiner's answer must be carefully compared.

Multiple choice questions usually show a remarkable consistency of performance from examination to examination. If this consistency pertains in your examinations, the performance of previously-used questions can be taken as a bench mark against which to assess each batch of examinees. If the percentages correct among the subset of previously-used questions within an examination are lower than expected, the students sitting this examination can be regarded as weaker.

The task for teacher/examiners is to analyze performance on a sub-set comprising previously-used questions within the examination. If the class mean on the whole examination is low, but class scores on previously-used questions are normal or higher, then the rest of the examination (particularly the new questions) is presumably more difficult, and to a measurable degree (Cox & Royle, 1980).

To respond to the varying level of difficulty across examinations, the cut-off level for passing or failing may be allowed to 'float' up or down according to the difficulty of each examination. The criteria of difficulty used are the class mean on this examination compared with the expected mean, and the performance of these students on the previously-used questions within the paper compared with the performance of previous students on those questions (Cox & Royle 1980).

Examiners' scores

Examiners may be 'hawks' or 'doves'. Blind scoring (that is, independent scoring recorded before any discussion about the candidate) by individual examiners (eg. on essays or in oral examinations) allows the mean, mode and range of each examiner to be determined.

Subsequent comparison of the individual marks against the finally agreed mark identifies the influence of one of a pair of examiners on the other.

Some mark across a wide range (0 to 100) while others mark within a narrow range (eg. 45 to 75). Identical performances could thus win quite different scores. Low scores can be the result of examiner idiosyncrasy.

Face to face examinations are subject to 'leniency error', and typically fall into a narrower range of scores than scores on written examinations, particularly multiple choice questions, which impose no 'judgment' on the scores. The effects on ranking of students as a result of a narrow or broad range of scores is dealt with below.

WHAT IS THE PASS MARK?

Teachers operate within conventions about what a particular score 'means'. Pass marks of 50% are most frequent, although it is not clear that the public would wish to accept doctors with only 50% knowledge or performance.

Table 33.1 contains a useful exercise which

Table 33.1

The following set of examination scores (set out as percentages) were received by a (hypothetical) student group. Typically, the multiple choice written paper had a wider spread of scores than the clinical examination. Scores in face to face examinations usually fall in a narrower range.

The ward clerking was marked on a Pass/Fail basis. Passing candidates were awarded 60% (which was chosen to coincide with the usual class mean over all examinations of close to 60%).

Student	Written	Clinical	Ward clerking
A	90	45	60
B	80	50	60
C	70	55	60
D	60	60	60
E	50	65	60
F	40	70	60
G	30	75	

Who should pass and who should fail?
Who came top?
Which component of the examination had the greatest effect on rank order of the students?

brings out the range of views which can underlie apparently simple decisions. I suggest that you put this set of scores in front of a group of fellow examiners, and ask them to write down who should pass, and who came top.

Discussion among teachers of such a set of figures surfaces a wide range of assumptions and values. Examiners differ on the weight they would give to different parts of the examination. Many of these differences may never have been discussed before, yet they would clearly have affected the original scores given to different student performances.

Similar discussion is needed to establish what are expected standards of performance, irrespective of what percentage number is chosen to represent that cut-off point.

If teachers define some areas as core or essential, the performance expected may be 'mastery', or close to 100%, or a Pass/Fail mark on that area with testing repeated on it until the student eventually passes.

HOW ACCURATE ARE THE SCORES?

We make many assumptions about what the scores we generate 'mean'. Accuracy represents the extent to which the method measures exactly what it was that you wanted to measure (the term 'validity' is also used for accuracy, but is so often mis-used that I prefer not to use it). A prior condition, consequently, is to define exactly what that is.

Many of the characteristics which teachers say they wish to measure are at the level of intangible concepts (such as 'critical thinking' or 'problem solving') which are often difficult to operationalize. Examiners then are likely to retreat to measuring grasp of knowledge, even though the relationship between knowledge and the characteristics may never have been empirically demonstrated.

The most usefully 'operational' approach is to test the characteristics expressed as *abilities* to do something for which those characteristics were a prior condition. If the characteristic were critical thinking, for example, the ability tested could be the critical analysis of a journal article.

Ebel (1972) has identified characteristics of examination scores which help us understand what the scores 'mean' or don't mean.

1. Numerical marks emphasize the attempt to measure educational achievement.
2. A single examination score cannot convey serious meaning about the multitude of factors entering into its production.
3. Marks can report reasonably accurately on a student's success in learning required knowledge.
4. Marks do not predict success in life.
5. Examination scores lack clearly defined, generally accepted, scrupulously observed definitions of what the marks mean.
6. Little relevant, objective evidence is available to use as a basis for scoring.
7. What a test measures is defined by the tasks that compose it, not by the characteristics the test is supposed to measure.
8. Accuracy (validity) is a property of the inferences and uses of a test, rather than a property of test content.
9. Decisions based on test scores are made judgmentally, not statistically. Judgments are based on both numbers and values.
10. Values are not 'valid'. Values are held. Values are not 'true' in any objective sense.

HOW PRECISE ARE THE SCORES?

Precision relates to the reproducibility (or reliability) of a set of scores (*see* Chapter 32). Reproducibility or precision is measured by the closeness of a series of measurements of the same phenomenon. The examination scores of individual students show considerable scatter. Each examination is not, however, identical in content or in the tasks to be performed. The number of samples on each student is low.

The use of different methods of examination also reduces reproducibility of scores, partly because each calls on different aspects of student performance, and partly because each method carries its own sources of imprecision.

Teachers usually fail to perceive the impact of this scatter on ranking; yet a superficial glance at Table 33.1 shows that the examination method with the highest variance has the greatest effect on ranking. An effect at the ends of the ranking is to influence who fails and who comes top as a result of characteristics of the examination format rather than of performance. Shrewd students know that scores on 'the writtens' will do more for their overall score, and consequently 'bash the books', which may not be what teachers intended.

When scores from different subjects (or different components within one subject as in Table 33.1 above) are to be combined, teachers may aim to render scores as equivalent as possible.

Scatter (or variance) can be 'controlled' in different ways. The commonest method is by 'scaling' all scores to a common mean and standard error; that is, an assumption is made about the 'best' mean and shape of the frequency distribution, and all scores are converted to fit. Scaling does not change rank order of students. By giving all subjects the same mean and scatter, high-scoring subjects are placed on a par with low-scoring subjects.

Or the scores with a lower variance can be given greater effect on ranking by weighting the scores until their variance is approximately equal; that is, if the clinicals had half the variance of the writtens, the clinicals could be given double weighting (say, measured out of 200 while the writtens were out of 100) so that their effect on ranking would then be equal.

Or clinical examiners can be encouraged to mark across the same range as written examinations, as well as the same range as one another. Such exhortations may be insufficient, however, especially with the large numbers and turnover of clinical examiners.

This effect of different scores on ranking, and even on failing, becomes critical when individual Departments seek the authority to fail students who have not passed their subject.

First, teachers in that subject may not recognize that their scoring pattern differs from other subjects. Second, they may not be aware how widely the scores of indvidual students vary across different parts of the examination, and even across components within subjects. Recognition of such large variance reduces the significance which should be given to any particular score.

WHO CAME TOP? WHO GOT THE HONOURS?

Examinations in medicine are widely used for ranking graduates. Since rank and awards (prizes, gradings of Distinction/Honours) are key criteria of hospital placement and subsequent career choice, examination scores are seen as importantly competitive by both students and teachers. The value system of this medical Darwinism of 'selecting the best' is so strongly entrenched that attempts to discuss its implications produce only puzzlement.

Scores are used to define the boundaries of these grades. The definition of performance is, however, not as tidy as those sharp boundaries. The reliability (reproducibility, precision) of examinations is estimated by techniques of comparing one half of the students and examination with the other. This 'split-half reliability' is easily performed with computer-marked multiple choice examinations, and may lie between 70% and 95% which is the probability of getting the same score if the examination were repeated. The standard error of MCQ examinations (which are by far the most precise form of examination, although not necessarily the most accurate) is not often below 5%. An individual's 'true score' (significant to the 5% level) on that segment of the examination could thus be 10% above or below the score actually given. Other formats of examination have far lower precision, as separate blind marking by examiners easily demonstrates.

FEEDBACK TO TEACHERS

The most frequent flaw in management of the medical curriculum is inadequate communication. Failure to analyze the examination results (by subject area, by teaching segments, by areas of responsibility such as tutorials or laboratory) and to inform teachers accordingly is a typical example. Yet the results can show how well an area was learned, where confusion persists, and generally how well a teacher is doing.

At the least, teachers can easily be given a set of class scores displaying the frequency distribution, plus mean, mode and median to summarize the scores.

FEEDBACK TO STUDENTS

For students the critical evidence on which progress is monitored is their scores. Those scores can easily be reported as a personal score, together with the class mean and standard error, and the reliability of the test.

Greater detail on subject matter can be provided if the components of the examination are separated and reported upon individually. Such analysis is simple with multiple choice examinations. Students can receive (computer-generated) reports on as many subdivisions as are made of the subject matter. Each batch of subject matter can not only be scored, but a list of references given back with each to turn the examination into a learning opportunity.

PLAN FOR UTILIZATION OF EXAMINATION SCORES

A. Routine examination management

1. Inform Faculty on results in each subject
   a. class mean and standard error
   b. pass/fail rate
   c. reliability of examination
2. Inform each Department on each component
   a. class mean and standard error in each
   b. pass/fall rates
   c. reliability of each test
3. Inform students on
   a. personal score overall
   b. personal grade overall
   c. personal score in each component
   d. class mean and standard error
   e. reliability of examination
   f. if practicable, areas of strength/weakness + references appropriate to areas of need.

B. Flow chart if results unexpected

If the class score and/or the pass/fail rate are outside the expected range, then the examination scores must be dissected according to their possible sources of origin — students, subject matter and questions asked, and examiners.

1. Students

(a). examine the frequency distribution of students' scores to find Who? and By how much?

(b). examine other evidence available about those students, such as previous performance in different years, different subjects, different components (eg. laboratory, clinical, assignments), scores across year within progressive assessments, different teaching hospitals.

2. Subjects, components, questions

(a). dissect the scores across and within subjects to find whether the effect is general, or specific to parts.

If the effect is general, the explanation is likely to be with the examiners or the students.

If the effect is partial, the explanation is likely to lie with the teaching, the questions asked, or the examiners.

(b). examine the component parts to check their match both with the 'approved' curriculum and with what was actually taught. Was the teaching equivalent among teachers/teaching hospitals? Are the 'correct' answers identical among teachers? Do they coincide with the answers expected by these examiners?

(c). examine the questions or tasks required to be performed. Were the specific questions or tasks reasonable with respect to the curriculum and expected standards?

3. Examiners

(a). survey the examiners. Are any new examiners being used? Does any new examiner relate to any unexpected set of scores?

(b). identify the scoring pattern of each examiner by counting their mean, mode and range. How does each examiner's pattern compare with colleagues and with the overall pattern of scores for the class?

(c). explore the criteria on which any 'abnormal' examiner is scoring; explore the standards to which such an examiner is scoring. Has that examiner been properly apprised of Faculty's criteria and standards? Does that examiner raise inappropriate questions in written, oral or clinical examinations?

REFERENCES:

Cox K R & Royle J P. 1980 Measurement plus Judgment in examinations Medical Education 14: 424–427

Cox K R 1969 An analysis of students' scores on 6 essay questions in the Final MB BS examinations showed that 35% of students failed at least 1 essay question; the overall failure rate in the examination was 6%. Unpublished study, University of Melbourne,

Ebel R 1972 Essentials of Educational Measurement Prentice Hall, Englewood Cliffs

Resources

Introduction

The following chapters describe the design and use of some of the more commonly used teaching and learning resources. We have not attempted to be comprehensive in this section because many of the principles of resource use are unchanged since the first edition of the Medical Teacher was written. This edition contains only those aspects of resource usage which benefit from an updated consideration. The absence of renewed consideration of computer aided instruction may be conspicuous to some readers. However, the problems created by the multiplicity of systems available and the rapid development of the field render detailed consideration impossible within the scope of a book of this type. The chapter detailing the principles of computer aided instruction in the first edition of Medical Teacher remains a useful resource.

The first chapter in this section is an overview of the design process which can be applied to almost all forms of audio-visual resource. The second and third chapters in the Section deal with the preparation of graphics and, for those who do not have access to a specialized audio-visual unit, provide an introduction to the technical aspects of the production of 35 mm slides. The chapter on use of the overhead projector is an update of the same chapter in the first edition but incorporates the production of overhead transparency originals using micro-computer generated graphics and text. A chapter on the design and use of handouts is included because of the importance of handouts as a teaching aid, particularly in lectures.

A wealth of information and expertise in the production and use of resources is available in specialized books and in the many medical illustration, photography and audio-visual units which exist in most medical education institutions. This Section should be regarded as an introduction for medical teachers which will help them to make best use of the resources available to them.

How to design effective audiovisual resources

Preview

INTRODUCTION

WHAT ARE THE STEPS IN DESIGN?

HOW TO PUT WORDS AND VISUALS TOGETHER

THE TEACHER AND THE MEDIA PRODUCER

SUMMARY

INTRODUCTION

The effective use of audiovisual resources for learning depends on detailed design and planning in order to ensure that the audiovisual resources produced are in fact an integral part of the overall learning program.

Audiovisual resources are not cheap to produce and require a commitment in time and effort, both for the content specialist and for the audiovisual producer. It is not worth expending time and money producing a program unless it is designed to meet the overall objectives of the educational program. Audiovisual resources used in a constructive manner can stimulate the learner.

The following principles apply to the design of a range of audiovisual media including illustrated booklet, tape-slide, audiotape, videotape and film.

WHAT ARE THE STEPS IN DESIGN?

Begin the design of audiovisual resources by posing a series of questions. The answers to these questions will assist the teacher to structure a program which will meet the educational objectives.

What is the program about?

What is the program trying to get across to the learner? Is it a summary of techniques which have already been taught? Is it to demonstrate a new technique? What is the learner expected to achieve after use of the program? A clear definition of the objectives of the program is essential if the teacher is to be able to convey the message, firstly to the media producer and then via the program to the learner.

For whom is the program intended?

The form of the instructional message will depend upon the teacher's knowledge of the target audience. Will the program be aimed at nurses, medical students, health professionals, patients or the general public? What prerequisite knowledge, skills or attitudes will the learner have?

A knowledge of the characteristics of the target audience is therefore important for the teacher and establishes what is to be incorporated into the program.

Characteristics such as age, education levels, previous knowledge of the subject will all have a bearing on the treatment of the subject. By asking 'WHO?' the teacher determines whose needs are to be met. This knowledge assists in the definition of the objectives of the program.

Where does the program fit into the overall educational program?

Is the program designed as an introduction to a concept? Is it meant to reinforce certain principles already taught? Is it to demonstrate a technique? Is it designed to summarize previous learning?

These questions assist the teacher in determining the content required in the audiovisual program. For example, if the program is designed as an introduction to a concept the teacher will need to be aware that the learner has no previous knowledge and will need to take this into consideration when planning. If the program is designed to summarize previous learning, however, the content can be limited to essential information only in order to reinforce previously learnt principles.

Which medium best suits the educational message?

Is motion required? Is colour important? Is sound essential? Or could the message be conveyed with visuals alone or even as a printed handout?

Colour transparencies or prints, for example, would be better suited to a program on dermatology or histology than use of a videotape. If motion is important, for example, to demonstrate the abnormal movement of the eyes, the use of videotape or film would be the obvious choice.

The limited research as to which medium best suits an instructional message has not provided adequate guidelines on how to select the best medium to fit particular instructional messages. The task of selecting appropriate media is complicated by the number of audiovisual resources from which to choose (photograph, graphic, audiotape, videotape, film, tape-slide, overhead transparency, booklet, poster, etc.). If motion is important videotape or film would be the logical choice. If motion is not important, materials which are easier and less costly to produce should be considered.

Many teachers tend to select media on the basis of what they are familiar and comfortable with

and, importantly, what media facilities are readily available to them.

What audiovisual replay equipment is available for the learner?

Is there equipment readily available for the learner to use the program? Is there enough replay equipment? Can the learner use the equipment?

Prior to producing an audiovisual program, it is important to be sure that the learners have access to, and are familiar with, replay equipment.

Will the learner participate actively during the program?

Can the learner participate in the program? Can questions be raised which require active participation by the learner?

Active participation improves learning (Kemp 1980). In order to stimulate participation by the learner it is necessary to build into the program some form of activity or exercise which requires a response. This would require the program to be stopped at given points so that the learner could answer questions or carry out some task.

The learning process is more interesting and effective when the learner participates actively, rather than passively absorbing information. Many types of participation may be possible. Appropriate activities will depend on the purpose of the program. For example, a program on 'How to measure blood pressure' could be stopped after demonstration of the technique and the students asked to practise the technique before returning to the program.

Will the program be used by individuals or groups?

The learning of basic principles or techniques using a question and answer sheet in conjunction with an audiotape would suit an individual better than a group. When the object is to stimulate discussion within a group, defining a problem and leaving it open-ended will allow the program to be stopped at given points for group discussion before proceeding further.

Will the program be used during practical sessions?

Will the program be used in conjunction with the learner's practical work? Will the practical require the learner to have 'hands on' experience with other equipment while participating?

For example: A program on learning to use the microscope in which the student is required to use both hands, would be better presented by using an audiotape rather than a videotape. Visual input is already provided by the microscope itself, so an audiotape could prompt the learner leaving the hands free to operate the microscope.

Is the program intended to act as a 'trigger' for discussion?

The program can be constructed to act as a series of structured 'trigger' segments which will stimulate discussion in a group. This technique is particularly effective in helping students to learn to solve problems. The target audience can be guided through a problem-solving process by a series of problem presentations which act as 'triggers' to stimulate discussion.

These 'trigger' segments are structured to present information in small amounts. The program is stopped after the presentation of each segment of information to permit the group to hypothesize, brainstorm and eventually to solve the problem.

Will a tutor be available to answer questions prompted by the program?

Is it possible to divide the program into sections? Each section might then conclude with questions designed to prompt group discussion, or pose a problem to be worked through after presentation of the principles presented in the program, or perhaps provide a self-assessment for individual learners.

Can the target audience assist in the design of the program?

When planning the program, input from the target audience can be invaluable. After completion of a rough outline a small group of the intended audience should be given the opportunity of assessing the content. This assessment may highlight deficiencies in the proposed program and may highlight concepts or principles which the target audience may find difficult to understand.

How to evaluate the program?

Some form of evaluation of the effectiveness of the program is desirable. This evaluation should result in some kind of action or decision; therefore, it is important to have a clear idea of its purpose. A videotape, for example, could be evaluated by a pilot group in order to assess its effectiveness. This evaluation may highlight deficiencies which would require a decision to modify a part of the program in order to meet the objectives.

The appraisal instruments used in the evaluation process could include questionnaires, interviews or assessment results. The criteria to be evaluated in relation to audiovisual media would include presentation of content; relevance of the presented content to the aims of the program; the organization of the content; the technical quality of the program, for example, legibility of visuals or quality of sound.

HOW TO PUT WORDS AND VISUALS TOGETHER

Prepare an outline

The answers to the above questions provide a guide to the overall structure of the program which should meet the instructional objectives. The next step in the process is to prepare an outline which will show the direction the program will take, in particular, how the information will be put together. This outline is an essential part of the scripting process as it ensures a logical flow of the content.

The outline should be a logical progression of the sequence of the instructional message. A well thought out, organized and concise outline is easier to understand than a lengthy document.

Develop a storyboard

The script for an audiovisual program will be

changed and refined even during the production. However, it is essential in order to meet the instructional objectives that the instructional message is committed to paper in some form as early as possible to ensure that the message, not the production, becomes the dominant aspect.

The design of audiovisual programs depends on careful and detailed planning of both auditory and visual components. Where visuals are used the visuals are usually the primary stimulus and for this reason they need to make an impact. The sound reinforces and complements the visual message.

The use of a storyboard (Figure 34.1) will assist the teacher to begin to think in terms of both visuals and sound together. The storyboard helps to get away from the normal habit of thinking only in words and instead to think in terms of visuals. The storyboard emphasizes that the visuals make the initial statement and the sound makes the statement more specific. The use of the storyboard in planning the program ensures maximal harmony between both visual and auditory channels of communication.

The storyboard can take two forms, either individual cards or simply a page divided for words and visuals. When using storyboard cards, each card will represent a sequence in the program. The card includes a description of the sequence and the accompanying dialogue. Space is available for a simple sketch detailing the visual.

The other storyboard method is simply a page divided vertically which has the script typed on the right side of the page and outlines or rough sketches of the visuals on the left side. When typing the script use double spacing, and leave ample spacing between paragraphs for alterations to the script. The storyboard makes it easier to see the program as a whole, and to balance the visual content with the spoken word. It also ensures that the visuals complement rather than compete with the commentary.

The storyboard has three main advantages. Firstly, it ensures that the educational message is conveyed correctly and in its proper sequence. Secondly, the storyboard can be discussed with colleagues or members of the target audience to assess the effectiveness of the program before production commences. Thirdly, it ensures that the media personnel, who will be responsible for translating the script into a cohesive audiovisual program, understand precisely what the teacher requires in the completed production.

Refine the script

Writing the script is not like writing a paper. A script should be direct, conversational and informal as if talking to a small group. As the script is developed ask 'Is that point clear? Should a question be asked? Is this a suitable place to stop the program for discussion? Does that segment explain the technique?'.

Revision of the script with colleagues, media production personnel and, if possible, the target audience will clarify the message and rectify any problems. This process will ensure that the program will meet the educational objectives.

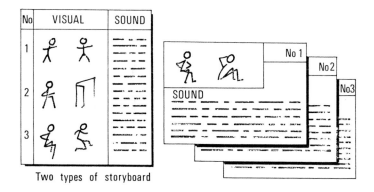

Two types of storyboard

Fig. 34.1 Storyboards help to plan the verbal and visual aspects of the program together

Design a handout

Information in an audiovisual program, unlike a book, cannot be referred to easily. The preparation of a handout for distribution to groups or individuals has a number of advantages. The handout can summarize information presented in the program, it can give an outline of the content, and it can provide a bibliography of references for further study by the learner.

The preparation of the handout will assist the learner by stimulating recall of concepts presented in the audiovisual, and therefore should be part of the design of the program.

THE TEACHER AND THE MEDIA PRODUCER

The production of effective audiovisual resources depends on close cooperation between the teacher and the media producer. The teacher is not an expert in audiovisual techniques and equally the media producer is not an expert in all branches of the health sciences. The ultimate effectiveness of the program will depend on close liaison between the teacher and the media producer right from the initial proposal.

It is important that both have a clear idea of what the proposed program is about. By following together the guidelines suggested in the design and planning of the program each will be able to contribute — the teacher in the content of the message and the media producer suggesting the most appropriate media technique to convey that message.

The development of the storyboard between teacher and media producer will ensure that the message is conveyed effectively using the most appropriate media techniques. At this stage the producer is able to begin to schedule the production. Close liaison between teacher and producer will ensure that teaching staff required to appear in a program, the resources required, and the relevant production crew and equipment are all available at the given times and locations.

Close involvement between teacher and media producer throughout the planning and design of the program, will also mean that postproduction of a program, for example, editing of a videotape, can be left to the producer, the teacher being called upon only if any problems arise.

The use of audiovisual resources in teaching involves the teacher and the media producer. The effectiveness of audiovisual resources in the learning process is dependent upon cooperation, respect, and an understanding of the contributions each can make to the design and production of audiovisual programs.

SUMMARY

The design and production of effective audiovisual resources relies on careful and detailed planning by the teacher. This planning needs to be based on an understanding of how people learn and of the effectiveness of well-designed audiovisual media programs in communicating concepts, techniques and information. Detailed planning of audiovisual resources which become an integral part of the overall educational program can stimulate and enhance the learning experience.

REFERENCES

Kemp J E 1980 Planning and producing audiovisual materials. 4th Edition Harper & Row, New York pp 3–6

BIBLIOGRAPHY

Brain E A, Bidwell C M 1979 Construct an audiovisual programme. British Medical Journal 1: 394–396
Engel C E 1971 Preparation of audiotapes for self-instruction. Medical and Biological Illustration 21: 14–18
Evans E M, Eldridge WS 1978 Audiovisual media: a combined operation. Journal of Audiovisual Media in Medicine 1: 140–142
Discusses the interface between teacher and media producer and suggests guidelines relevant to the design of effective audiovisual programs.
Graves J, Graves V 1979 Designing a tape-slide programme. Medical Education 13: 137–143
The design, planning and production of audiotape and tape-slide programs are discussed. The basic principles discussed apply to the design and production of other audiovisual media e.g. videotape and film.
Gray D E 1980 Planning visual media for self-instruction. Journal of Biological Photography 48: 117–137
A detailed review of audiovisual media and learning theory within the context of the design of effective audiovisual resources.

Film in medical education. Production and use 1973. Published jointly by the Council for Educational Technology and the Department of Audio Visual Communication, British Life Assurance Trust for Health Education with the British Medical Association. Discusses the design variables as applied to film. These design variables are applicable to the planning and production of video programs.

Preparing graphics for projection slides

Preview

INTRODUCTION

How often have you sat at the rear of a darkened auditorium and strained your eyes trying to decipher what some learned speaker was attempting to show on the screen with a 35 mm slide? How often have you been that learned speaker, probably unaware that you were creating the same problem for a section of the audience unfortunately occupying the rear seats? How often have you heard a speaker say, 'You probably can't see this from where you're seated, so I'll read it out to you'? One of the surest ways of losing the attention of an audience, particularly in teaching, is by projecting material which is illegible.

The majority of offending slides are due not so much to poor photography as to careless preparation of the original artwork. A few simple guidelines followed in the preparation of the original will ensure legibility and considerably enhance the quality of a presentation. This Chapter offers such guidelines.

Medical teachers have variable access to facilities producing graphic teaching material. For the majority, the preparation of this material turns out to be a 'do-it-yourself' task. Those with access to a well-equipped illustration unit should begin by seeking advice as to what material aids are available from that source, and determine at the same time what 'local' variations exist in relationship to the information given here. For those without a photographic service, Chapter 32, 'Producing 35 mm Slides', may be helpful.

THE PHYSICAL SETTING

Whenever possible, the setting in which the presentation is to be made should be inspected before use.

A well-designed teaching area should have a square projection screen to accommodate the rectangular images from horizontal and vertical 35 mm slides without cut-off. Some screens are of the horizontal type and thus unsuitable for upright images. Illustrations which have a naturally vertical form therefore either have to be redesigned or photographed not filling the 35 mm frame, thus losing valuable magnification.

For the content of the projected material to be legible to all viewers, the rear seats should be no further from the screen than six times the longest dimension of the projected image. Additionally, no one should be seated at more than a 30° angle to the projection axis.

Population trends

Year	1976	1926
Sydney	3094	1071
Melbourne	2672	944
Brisbane	986	274
Adelaide	912	316
Perth	820	184

Population, thousands

Table for publication

CONTENT OF THE SLIDE

A lecture is concerned with the communication of concepts and facts through the spoken word. Projected images should therefore supplement, support and integrate with the verbal message.

Overcrowding the slide with words and figures should be avoided. A common mistake is to include material which is not referred to at all. The speaker who says, 'I want you to concentrate on this area and ignore the rest of the slide' could have done better without the 'rest of the slide'. Similarly, excessive notes and explanations which can be communicated orally are better omitted.

One of the most important, yet often ignored, rules is to limit each slide to just one central idea. It is better to build one's message by showing several slides, rather than let only one or two carry all the information.

It is difficult for the audience to concentrate on a complex image and, at the same time, listen to the lecturer. Long rows of figures, for example, make the point more readily and elegantly if they are transformed into comparative curves or bar charts (Figure 35.1). If illustrations have to be taken from books, simple ones should be chosen, and legends eliminated.

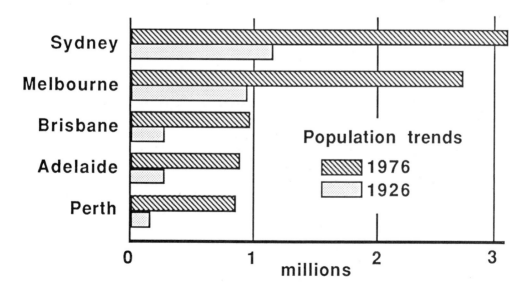

... redesigned for projection

Fig. 35.1

ARTWORK DIMENSIONS

As long as the limit acceptable to one's photographic department is not exceeded, the actual linear dimensions of original artwork are not critical, being determined by personal preference, size of lettering to hand (see Table 35.1), and such factors as the need to trace from existing material. The proportion of the artwork is of great importance. To gain maximum use of the rectangular 35 mm image area, it is necessary to achieve, as far as possible, the same 2:3 proportion in the artwork. It may thus be necessary, for example, to re-draw an existing graph, extending one axis in relation the other.

LINE AND TONE ORIGINALS

Line originals

Illustrations in which only the pure whites and blacks are to make up the image, as in ordinary text, tables and graphs. These are the easiest to prepare and photograph, and may be altered by such means as white-out fluid and by 'cutting and sticking'. Faint marks, joins in the paper and transparent adhesive tape do not show in the final result. (Adhesive tape, however, should not cross lines or lettering, as it degrades their quality for photography).

Continuous-tone originals

Often called simply 'tone' originals, these are illustrations consisting of varying densities of grey, including white and black. Examples are black and white photographs, scans, radiographs, and most traces (EEG, ECG etc). Continuous tone material is photographed on a low contrast film, which picks up any faint markings in the original. For this reason, tone work must be prepared on plain white paper and kept free of all blemishes.

Half tones

A term sometimes incorrectly used to describe 'continuous tone'. Half tones are the result of converting a tone illustration to a series of black dots, varying in size according to the grey tone values of the original. In this way, it can be handled as line work for printed reproduction.

LINE-DRAWING AND LETTERING METHODS

Artwork prepared for camera reproduction must have as high a contrast as possible, that is, the paper must be perfectly white and the lines and lettering perfectly black. To achieve this end, line originals are traditionally prepared in Indian ink using technical drawing pens (e.g. Kern, Rotring, Staedtler) in conjunction with rules, French and flexible curves, lettering stencils, and templates for geometric shapes. This method has the distinct advantage of almost zero cost, once the basics are assembled. Unfortunately, some workers find ink-drawing messy and time-consuming, and opt for other more convenient (but more expensive) methods. These include the use of self-adhesive graphic tapes (e.g. Letraline) for constructing straight and curved lines (Figure 35.2), dry transfer (rub-down) sheets (e.g. Letraset) for lettering and symbols, and self adhesive tone shading film (e.g. Letratone) for large area differentiation (Figure 35.3).

Whilst the graphic tapes represent a significant advance over pen-and-rule, dry transfer lettering is not a particularly fast way of producing text in quantity. (Its use is, however, a necessity when making up certain originals, as explained later).

Text may be produced more quickly by using one of the many lettering machines now on the market, although the cost of these may restrict their purchase to the School or Faculty level.

These desk-top machines fall into three groups:

1. Electromechanical devices which impress carbon images of letters and numerals, correctly spaced, onto a transparent, self-adhesive carrier tape. An example is the 7204 from 3M Australia Pty. Ltd., costing about A\$1400 (plus 20% sales tax if applicable).
2. Computerized versions of the above, which have typewriter-style keyboards instead of lettering discs, and 'microchip' memory storage. The Merline from Gestetner Pty Ltd., is an example, and costs approximately A\$3500 (plus tax).

Fig. 35.2 Graphic tapes are available in a variety of forms to provide different line widths and patterns. Some tapes are flexible and can be used for constructing curved lines.

Fig. 35.3 Some examples of tone shading patterns available in sheet form. To preserve the 'line' qualities of the illustration, tone shading must be bold relative to the size of the original.

3. Photo-mechanical machines (phototypesetters) which give very high lettering quality by means of exposing photographic paper to lettering negatives, and then developing the paper internally. The Varityper Headliner from AM International is the least expensive of the these, although in this case 'least expensive' means about A$4300 (plus tax).

The ongoing expense of additional lettering discs and carrier tapes should not be overlooked when considering the purchase of one of these machines.

Going beyond lettering machines, there is a natural temptation to use the even greater speed and flexibility of computer-linked printers and pen plotters for making up originals for slides.

Unfortunately, the quality of the results from most of these peripherals is generally very poor for reproduction purposes. The images tend not to be black enough to record well on high-contrast copy film, and lettering styles leave much to be desired. A notable exception, though, is the laser printer, the output from which is of excellent quality.

CHOICE OF PAPER

If pen and ink is the preferred method for preparing the original, the use of proofing chroma paper (also known as baryta paper) is highly recommended. This material is available only from a printer or specialist graphic-art supplier, but is superior to other papers in whiteness and in its ability to give clean-edged ink lines. The surface may be scraped with a sharp blade to correct errors, and it is also suitable for typing. A transparent grid or sheet of graph paper tapes to the back, and transilluminated on an X-ray box, facilitates data plotting and alignment of letterig on the otherwise blank surface.

Bristol board, CSIO and Schoellershammer paper from art supply outlets are good alternatives. Tracing paper and films also produce clean ink lines, but are not perfectly white, and therefore best avoided for illustrations destined to be photographed.

It is rare to find graph paper with a surface suitable for drawing ink. If the direct use of graph paper is for some reason unavoidable, then line originals (never continuous tone) may be prepared on faint ('drop-out') blue or very faint grey grids which do not record on high contrast copy films. One may also use drop-out blue or 'non-repro' pens for roughing out work and making notations which are invisible to the copy camera. Other grid colours and densities can create problems for the photographer. It is possible to filter out yellow, orange and red grids, but only when using a lower-contrast film, which gives an inferior result on the remaining line work. Green, brown and dark blue grids cannot be successfully filtered out, and should never be used.

If the original is to be constructed entirely using graphic tapes and dry transfer or machine lettering, then virtually any white paper may be used. If it is necessary to use graph paper in conjunction with these materials then the colour and density of the grid should conform to the specifications just outlined.

PREPARING TONE ORIGINALS

Continuous tone originals must be prepared and handled with much more care than line work. To preserve the complete tonal range of the artwork, low contrast copy films are used. These pick up such faint artifacts as fingerprints, transparent adhesive tape, white out fluid, joints in the paper, and even the edges of lettering strips. Such blemishes should not be allowed to appear in continuous line work. These types of originals should be prepared on plain white paper not graph paper); and if lettering is required, it should be dry transfer. The latter is particularly valuable when annotations are to be added to the image area of radiographs, scans, and black and white photographs.

In continuous tone originals, the paper should extend far enough around the artwork to prevent its edges showing in the slide. Also it is worth protecting each tone original by means of a flap-over piece of paper, taped to one edge, especially when the original incorporates dry-transfer lettering, which is easily abraded.

COLOUR ORIGINALS

Coloured artwork is of course photographed onto colour film, which faithfully records every last detail in the original. All colour work must therefore be prepared and handled with even more care than (other) continuous tone originals.

The availability of graphic tapes and dry transfer lettering in various colours greatly simplifies the construction of effective colour graphics, although one should bear in mind that the presence of colour raises additional legibility factors.

Briefly, it is necessary to use strong colours, such as pure reds, oranges, greens and blues for text, graph lines and simllar elements, and contrasting, pastel colours (not white) for backgrounds.

LEGIBILITY FACTORS

The factors affecting the legibility of projection slides have been well researched. The size of the lettering and the thickness of lines on a slide are the most important considerations, yet these are the ones most often neglected. Lettering style is also important. Letter forms which have serifs (finishing or decorative strokes to the ends of letters) or are condensed, expanded, too thin or too bold should be avoided. The most suitable typefaces for slides are: Helvetica Light, Helvetica Medium, Univers 55, and the Micronorm series.

The lecturer may feel confident that a slide will be legible under average projection conditions if these simple rules have been followed in the original artwork:

Minimum capital letter height artwork divided by 400	= overall long dimension of
Minimum thickness of lines artwork divided by 600	= overall long dimension of

Table 35.1 gives practical translation of these limits for different artwork sizes

Some useful legibility rules to follow when using tone shading are:

Minimum line thickness artwork divided by 600	= overall long dimension of
Minimum spacing between lines thickness	= four times the line
Minimum dot size artwork divided by 500	= overall long dimension of
Minimum space between dots diameter	= not less than one dot

When the original is finished, a final check on legibility may be carried out simply by viewing the artwork from a distance of six times its longest dimension. All of the information should be easily visible.

GENERAL DESIGN CONSIDERATIONS

Written Information

- Text slides should be kept short and concise. 35 words (say five lines of seven words each) is a good upper limit. Sixty words would still be legible, but this number is most undesirable in practice.
- The main body of words on a slide is more easily read if the words are in lower case ('small') lettering rather than capitals. The variation in height of lower case lettering gives each word a characteristic shape, which is important for recognition. Short headings, however, may be in capitals for emphasis.
- Use a line separation about equal to the height of the capital letters. Badly spaced lines of text are difficult to read.
- Listed material is made more understandable when each new subject line is preceded by a marker (as here).

Table 35.1 Letter heights and line thickness in relation to artwork sizes

Artwork size (note 2:3 ratio)	10 cm × 15 cm	15 cm × 23 cm	20 cm × 30 cm	25 cm × 38 cm
Minimum capital letter height	4 mm	6 mm	8 mm	10 mm
Nearest lettering point size	12	18	24	30
Minimum line thickness	0.25 mm	0.4 mm	0.5 mm	0.6 mm
Nearest Micronorm* pen size	0.25	0.35	0.5	0.7

* ISO drafting standard

Tables

- Tables are more easily read and have a less 'solid'appearance if vertical ruling is omitted.
- Column headings are often longer than the data to which they refer. Extensive abbreviation and laying the headings at a 45 degree angle can help solve this problem
- Tabular information is only suitable for slides if it is simple. The information embodied in a complex table is better shown in graphical form.

Graphs

- Remember that for projection purposes, a graph should represent trends, rather than make accurate, individual values available to the audience. It should include only the mininum of information necessary to make the point.
- Data points and lines should be drawn bolder than the axes.
- To retain maximum image size on the slide, it is usually necessary to label y-axes vertically (i.e. reading sideway).

Diagrams

- Diagrams should be kept as simple as possible.
- Follow the legibility recommendations when using tone shading. Very fine hatching or tone dots may appear to the copy camera as a continuous grey and reproduce as a patchy, uneven area.

- Where graphic tape lines are to cross an area of tone shading, they must be placed on top of the shading.

All Originals

- It is undesirable to construct a frame or border around the artwork: the edge of the projected slide itself acts as a natural frame.
- Leave plenty of space around the illustrations for ease of handling during photography.

TYPED ORIGINALS

Typing is suitable for simple word slides, but for good results, note the following:
- Use a 'golfball' machine wherever possible, and keep the typeface clean using a plastic eraser.
- Use a plastic ribbon for maximum transfer of carbon onto the paper.
- Place a reversed sheet of carbon paper behind the typing paper to increase the density of the image. (Interleave the finished work with tissue or paper to prevent smudging).
- Do not type continuous lines, or use felt-tipped pens: only Indian ink in a technical pen (or a narrow graphic tape) gives an even, black line.
- 35 words is the maximum recommended for one slide (e.g. five lines of seven words each).
- To retain legibility, the overall typewritten area for one slide should not exceed 7.5 cm $\times$ 11 cm. (13 cm $\times$ 20 cm if using the larger Directory, Orator or Bulletin typefaces).

BIBLIOGRAPHY

Reynolds D and Simmonds D 'Presentation of Data in Science' 1st edn. 1981. Martinus Nijhoff P O box 566, 2501 The Hague, The Netherlands.
A comprehensive guide to producing illustrations for slides, publication, posters, overhead projectors and television, aimed at authors and teachers. The theoretical as well as the practical aspects of data presentation are covered.
Simmonds E and Bragg G "Charts and Graphs" 1st edn. 1980 MTP Press Ltd., Falcon House, Lancaster, UK
Covers a similar range of topics to the above publication, but in a more concise and less theoretical manner.

Producing 35 mm slides

INTRODUCTION

The production of high quality 35 mm projection slides from original artwork and printed publication ('flat copy') required some expertise. Once the basic concepts of flat copy photography are understood, good results can be achieved with relatively inexpensive equipment and non-darkroom types of film.

This chapter is intended as a brief introductory guide to the essentials of flat-copy photography, with much of the theory necessarily omitted. At the outset, it is assumed that the reader has a basic understanding of simple photographic terms, is aware of the different classes of flat copy, i.e. line and tone. (See Chapter 35) and has a 35 mm single lens reflex camera (Non-SLR cameras are unsuitable for this type of work) with through-the-lens metering and a standard lens (50, 55 or 58 mm).

Flat-copy photography (reprography) differs from normal, everyday photography in the following respects:

1. The camera is working very close to the subject, usually in the range from 80 cm down to 10 cm.

2. The camera must be aligned exactly straight-on to the subject, and be rigidly fixed in place.

3. Light distribution across the subject must be perfectly even.

4. Ordinary films are unsuitable for the type of flat-copy most often encountered, i.e. text, tables, graph and line diagrams.

5. The normal exposure-metering method usually gives incorrectly-exposed slides.

CLOSE-UP METHODS

The mininum focusing distance normally found on a standard lens is generally around 80 cm, meaning that the smallest area able to be photographed measures 30 × 45 cm. This is inadequate for photographing flat-copy, the size of which is usually smaller.

Four different methods are available to enable one to focus closer than the usual minimum given by a standard lens. These are listed below in order of increasing image quality and ease of use.

1. Supplementary ('dioptre') lens

These are positive, meniscus lenses which, when attached to the front of a standard lens via their screw-threaded mounts, act to reduce the minimum focusing distance, allowing artwork as small as 9 cm × 13 cm to be photographed. The advantage of this method is its low cost (about A\$25 for a set of three, i.e. +1, +2 and +3 dioptres), but it suffers from being inconvenient in that, when photographing orginals of different sizes, the lenses must be interchanged accordingly. Additionally, these simple lenses degrade the sharpness and definition of the standard lens, although this effect is reduced on stopping down the aperture.

2. Extension tubes

Extension tubes are inserted between the camera lens and body, either singly or in combination, to achieve a close-focusing capability. Extension tubes are equally as inconvenient as supplementary lenses, but do not degrade image quality to the same extent. The use of 'automatic' extension tubes are recommended, thereby retaining the automatic diaphragm action of the camera lens. These are available, in sets of three, for between A$80 and A$150.

3. 'Macro-zoom' lens

Wide-angle to telephoto macro-zoom lenses are now widely used in general photography, combining in one optic the attributes of wide-angle, standard and telephoto lenses together with a close focusing (macro) capability, ideal for photographing small, three-dimensional objects. Unfortunately, these lenses do less well in photographing flat-copy in three respects. Firstly, the minimum focusing distance is usually not enough to cope with small originals. Secondly, the macro facility usually operates at the wide-angle end of the zoom range, giving a very short working distance between the lens and the flat copy. Thirdly, a certain amount of linear distortion is usually present, such that straight lines in the original turn out to be noticeably curved in the final slide. Any macro-zoom lens should be given a practical test before it is considered for reprographic use.

4. Fixed focal-length macro lens

A fixed focal length macro lens is specifically designed for close-up photography and thus produces excellent image quality. All of the major camera manufacturers (and a few independent lens-makers, such as Vivitar and Elicar) offer 50 or 55 mm macro lenses, ranging in price from A$150 to A$400. (Note: These *focusing* macro lenses should not be confused with *bellows* macro lenses which must be used with a bellows unit. Bellows macro lenses are unsuitable for vertical reprography).

CAMERA STABILITY

It is impractical to photograph flat copy with a makeshift, horizontal set-up, for example, with the camera on a tripod and the artwork taped to a wall.

The only workable method is the use of a photographic copy stand, which consists of a horizontal wooden baseboard (for the artwork), a vertical column with a sliding camera support, and side-arms holding two or four copy lights, the latter being held some distance from, and at a 45 degree angle to, the centre of the baseboard.

Inexpensive copy stands may be purchased from photographic dealers from about A$100. The use of such a device ensures that three of the requirements for reprography are met, i.e. camera stability, camera alignment and an even distribution of light over the artwork.

A cable release for the camera's shutter, and a right-angle viewing attachment to fit over the eyepiece of the pentaprism, are the only further items needed to complete the copy set-up. The former is essential to minimize the vibration caused by direct contact with the release button, and the latter allows more convenient viewing through the downward-pointing camera.

TYPES OF FILM

The recently introduced Polaroid 35 mm Autoprocess system allows the user to develop and mount a 36-exposure slide film in ordinary room lighting in a matter of minutes. This has greatly simplified the rapid production of lecture slides and is ideal for the medical teacher with little time or inclination for darkroom work.

This system encompasses one colour and two black and white reversal (slide) films in standard cassettes to fit any 35 mm camera. It also includes a small, hand-operated processing unit, and a simple device for mounting the processed film into slide mounts. The cost of the hardware i.e. the processor and the mounter, is about A$120 (plus tax).

The HC Autoprocess black and white slide film is of very high contrast, intended for use with line original, whilst the CT film gives best results with continuous tone originals. The quality of these two films can only be described as excellent, easily as good as the traditional negative-positive methods. (The colour films would be better described as reasonably good in comparison with conventional colour reversal materials — see Colour Originals).

DETERMINING CORRECT EXPOSURE

Achieving correct exposure in reprography is a major problem area for the newcomer, made worse by the fact that the type of film being used (reversal) requires an exposure accurate to within half-a-stop to give acceptable results.

The problems are greatly minimized once the following factors are understood:

1. Camera exposure meters are suitable only for assessing exposure in reprography if a correction is applied to compensate for the nature of the flat copy. These meters are calibrated on the assumption that an 'average' scene is in front of the camera, i.e. one of just 18% reflectance. The meter measures only 'quantity of light' and ignores the *inherent* lightness or darkness of a subject. Thus, a pure white paper surface will be interpreted as a particularly *brightly-illuminated* 18% grey. The meter will compensate for this non-existent 'extra' light and reduce exposure, making the paper appear dark (and therefore underexposed) in the finished slide. This occurs when photographing line diagrams and graphs in which large areas of white predominate. In these cases, two stops more exposure should be given over the meter recommendation. On manual cameras, this means altering the shutter speed from say 1/4 second to 1 second. On automatic exposure cameras, the meter must be 'fooled' by use of the exposure correction control. (Further

information on this may be gained from the camera's instruction manual).

Increasing amounts of dark areas in line originals will necessitate a proportionately smaller exposure correction, until finally the meter reading may be used without correction, as in the case of black and white and colour photographs in books, and scans and radiographs containing equal amounts of dark and light areas.

2. Exposure varies with magnification, therefore do not assume that a small original will require the same exposure as a large one of the same type — it will need *more* exposure. 'Through-the-lens' camera meters, however, do compensate for this variable, so a new reading should be taken when there is a major change in artwork size.

3. Any exposure determination, however derived, should be taken as a *starting-point* only as there are many hidden variables in reprography. Exposures for critical work should be 'bracketed', meaning that two different exposures are made in addition to the one considered correct. These extra exposures should be half-a-stop over, and half-a-stop under the first exposure.

4. All conditions must be standardized when copying. This includes the lighting on the base-board (brightness, angle and distance of lamps always the same) plus other details, such as always turning off room lighting. If a high level of standardization is maintained, it is possible to speed-up copy work by using previously- determined exposures, rather than always using the camera meter. A simple 'artwork size (or height of camera) vs. exposure' table can thus be made up for each different film speed and kept near the copy stand. (Note: exposure does not vary with magnification when using supplementary lenses).

5. Shutter speed is irrelevant to the quality of the final image, whereas aperture (f number) is critical. Recommended minumum working apertures for the various close-up methods are: supplementary lenses, f/11; extension tubes and macro-zoom lenses, f/8; fixed focal length macro-lenses, f/5.6. Exposure bracketing, if needed, may be carried out by going half-a-stop either side of the recommended apertus, but any other exposure changes should be done by altering the shutter speed, even if this means ending up with

exposures of one second or longer. Such exposures are common in reprography.

OTHER CONSIDERATIONS

Final image quality depends not only upon the major factors already outlined, but also on a number of lesser ones, most of which are under the control of the operator. For example:

1. Large areas of extraneous white paper beyond the limits of the artwork should be avoided. Although outside the photographed area, it will cause 'flare' in the camera and degrade the image.

2. When copying illustrations from printed publications, a piece of black paper placed behind the page being photographed helps reduce 'show through' of text and other illustrations from the reverse side.

3. Sheets of unscratched glass in two or three sizes should be to hand for use over originals which do not lie flat or have 'cut and stick' corrections.

4. Legibility is a most important factor in projection slides; all artwork and illustrations should therefore *fill the 35 mm frame* (in one direction or the other) when photographed.

COLOUR ORIGINALS

The various recommendations given previously are all applicable to coloured flat copy. The one major difference between black and white and colour originals is that, in the latter case, the type of slide film used must be matched to the 'colour

Table 36.1 Wratten colour-temperature filtration

	Copy Stand Lighting		
	Photographic bulbs		Domestic bulbs
	3400 deg.K.	3200 deg.K	2900 deg. K
Daylight film	80B	80A	80A plus 82B
Tungsten film	81A	no filter	82B

Table 36.2 Colour reversal films suitable for reprography

Film type	Example	ISO/ASA Speed (comment 1)	Colour Balance	comments
'K14' process	Kodak Kodachrome 64	64	Daylight	2
	Kodak Ektachrome 100	100	Daylight	3,4
'E6' process	Kodak Ektachrome 50	50	Tungsten	3,4,5
Polaroid 35 mm Autoprocess	Polachrome CS	40	Daylight	6

Comments

1. Films faster than ISO/ASA 100 are unsuited to flat copy work.

2. Of those listed, this is the best film for reprography as it exhibits outstanding sharpness and colour clarity. Its only drawback is the slow turn-around time; this film must be sent to Kodak for processing. (No other manufacturer produces K14-process films).

3. Equivalent films from other manufacturers are equally as good.

4. E6 films may be processed by films other than the manufacturer. Professional colour processing laboratories usually have a two or three hour turn-around for E6 film.

5. A professional film, usually only available from a specialist photographic supplier. This film should be kept refrigerated before use and processed soon after exposure for best results.

6. Of lower brightness and sharpness than the K14 or E6 films, but its lasser technical quality may be acceptable when fast access and user-processing are the prime criteria.

temperature' of the lighting, otherwise the colour rendition will be severely distorted. It is sufficient for the present purposes to note that daylight has a colour temperature of 5600 degrees Kelvin (as has the light from electronic flash), photographic light bulbs are rated at either 3400 or 3200 degrees, and 100-watt domestic bulbs are around 2900.

Two classes of colour slide film exist: 'daylight' balanced for 5600 degrees Kelvin and 'tungsten' balanced for 3200. Either type of film may be used with any colour temperature of lighting provided an appropriate filter is used over the camera lens. These filters are designated by Wratten code numbers, and are available either in glass (in screw-in mounts) or in gelatin from, which can easily be cut to size. The filter to use for a given combination of film and lighting may be found from Table 36.1.

Any one of a number of different makes and types of colour film can be used in reprography.

Reference to Table 36.2 may help in choosing the film most suited to a particular circumstance.

RADIOGRAPHS AND SCANS

Radiographs and scans require transillumination for photography, so it is necessary to obtain a portable X-ray box, graphic-art or photographic light box for use on the baseboard of the copy stand. Once the original is illuminated from behind the photography becomes straightforward and most of the recommendations given for reflective flat-copy may be followed. It is particularly important to mask off any areas of the light box not covered by the radiograph, as these will create a large amount of image-degrading flare in the camera.

The recommended film for making slides from scans and radiographs is Polaroid CT Autoprocess.

How to use the overhead projector

Preview

THE PROJECTOR

1. Position of the projector
2. Use of the projector

THE TRANSPARENCY

1. Size of lettering
2. Use of transparencies

OTHER USES OF THE OVERHEAD
PROJECTOR

Have you ever sat in the last row of a lecture theatre and looked at your own overhead transparencies? If you have, you may have suffered a nasty shock. The overhead projector can be an exciting and valuable teaching aid; however, in our teaching we often use such poorly planned or prepared transparencies that student learning is actually inhibited. Use of the overhead projector is now widespread in the teaching of the health professions. In some auditoria the blackboard is a thing of the past. This Chapter offers a few hints that may be helpful to teachers who use this very versatile machine.

THE PROJECTOR

1. Position

In many lecture theatres or seminar rooms over-

head projectors are set up for use in the same way as conventional slide projectors. Teachers should ask for better positioning of the overhead projector so that transparencies can be manipulated during the lecture without the lecturer moving from the lectern. The best arrangement is to have separate screens for the two styles of projector which allows for simultaneous use of overheads and 35 mm slides. The slide might be a picture of a patient, for example, while the transparencies contain descriptions of clinical signs or symptoms. The screen for an overhead projector should be tilted forward to elimate distortion or 'keystoning'; screens for slide projectors are best kept upright. This is another good argument for a two screen arrangement.

In some smaller rooms the teacher has an opportunity to select the optimal screen-projector arrangement.

The speaker stands to the side of the screen to allow the audience an uninterrupted view. The best position in a particular room can be found only by trial and error. With the help of a colleague, move both screen and lectern around until there is an uninterrupted view of projected image and the lecturer from the most difficult seats.

Use of the projector

The projector should be switched on only when a transparency is being discussed. Switching the projector off between transparencies avoids the glare which will distract the viewer and also brings attention back solely to the teacher. A transparency left on too long can be a distraction, especially when the topic has been changed. The use of a pointer is recommended. The pointer should be placed on the transparency and left until the item has been discussed; it should not be waved around or pointed directly at the screen. Hexagonal pencils make good pointers because they do not roll around. Coloured acetate or cardboard arrows can be used. The lecturer should never face the screen but should look directly at the audience. This reinforces the need for adequate positioning and checking before the lecture so that speakers are completely confident that what they can see on top of the projector is clearly seen on the screen by everyone.

THE TRANSPARENCY

Size of lettering

Most of this Chapter concerns the preparation of the transparency, as this is the step which is most abused. The greatest abuse is the use of inappropriate letter size. The letter size used is usually too small. How many lectures or seminars have you attended in which the writing on the transparencies can be seen only by people in the first two rows? (The speaker has no problem; he or she can read it from the projector!) A few simple guidelines can prevent this problem.

A rule of thumb is that, if the material is readable with the naked eye at 2 meters, the transparency will have adequate visibility. Normal typewriter print and print from textbooks or journals is much too small. Another formula for legibility of projected material considers three factors: the size of the lecture hall, the screen and information on the screen. The average lecture hall is about 10 meters–18 meters long and the size of the screen varies accordingly from 1.5–3 meters, thus the length of the hall is on average about six times the width of the screen. A very rough way to check the legibility of transparencies is to view them from a distance of six times the width of the transparency. This simulates approximately the view that a student sitting in the far corner of the lecture hall will have of the projected transparency.

The Orator 'golf ball' element which can be used on all single element IBM typewriters is suitable for use in tutorial rooms. For lecture theatres, however, this type is always too small. Another

problem with Orator type is that it has only capital lettering which is difficult to read, especially when the whole text is in this type. An alternative to Orator type is the 'Bulletin' Olympia Model SG3 typewriter. The Bulletin type face has lower case letters and this should be used where possible, reserving the upper case type for headings, captions and keywords. Another good alternative is to use mechanical lettering machines to make the original, for example, the Kroy or Varityper. Flgure 37.1 is a reproduction of the various types described above. Two normal type faces i.e. the IBM Advocate and Letter Gothic are included for comparison. These should never be used for transparencies unless they have been enlarged.

Two relatively recent developments make it easier for the lecturer to produce quality transparencies with lettering of appropriate size in a hurry. Firstly, the introduction of photocopiers with an enlarging capacity; using these machines, even conventional typewriter font sizes such as Advocate and Gothic can be used to prepare transparencies, as the original can be enlarged on a photocopier until the type size is appropriate. More importantly, there is no longer any excuse for the transparencies made directly from figures or tables in journal articles or textbooks (if there ever was!) These same figures can be made clearly visible on the projection screen by using photocopier enlargements to make the transparencies. The other major advance that allows rapid production of large type transparencies is the advent of the personal computer, in particular, the Apple Macintosh. This is discussed in detail in a later section.

Preparation of transparencies

Direct transparencies

Using appropriate pens, usually felt-tipped, the material is drawn directly on to the acetate sheet. Often this is done during a lecture. The projector becomes a substitute for a blackboard. This has always seemcd to be an unimaginative use of a versatile teaching aid. It is said that students are given a chance to copy everything in their notes by the lecturer who actually writes material on the transparency; that is, previously prepared trans-

This is the Gothic Golfball, lower case.

THIS IS THE GOTHIC GOLFBALL, UPPER CASE.

This is the Advocate golfball, lower case

THIS IS THE ADVOCATE GOLFBALL, UPPER CASE

THIS IS THE ORATOR GOLFBALL, LOWER CASE

THIS IS THE ORATOR GOLFBALL, UPPER CASE

This is the Bulletin typewriter,
    lower case
THIS IS THE BULLETIN TYPEWRITER,
    UPPER CASE

THIS IS KROY 30PT

THIS IS KROY 36PT

This is Varityper V4873

THIS IS VARITYPER V4873

Fig. 37.1 Reproduction of various typefaces. Normal typefaces such as IBM Advocate and Letter Gothic should never be used for overhead transparencies

parencies project too much information too fast (Maddox & Loughran, 1977). The answer to this criticism is better use of prepared transparencies. Direct drawing during a lecture can be very effective, however, when it is done onto a partly prepared transparency e.g. highlighting points, or adding student commnents.

The use of rolls of acetate sheeting encourages the blackboard type usage of the projector. Rolls prepared beforehand are inflexible and cannot be readily changed around. Images are easily damaged by friction of the roller. These rolls of films offer nothing over single sheets and should be avoided.

If it is necessary to write on the transparency during the lecture or to prepare written shects before the lecture, the same rules of image size apply. *Normal handrwriting is too small for overhead projection.* Each letter should be at least 7–10 mm high.

Direct carbon transparencies

These transparencies consist of a piece of thin acetate film attached to a piece of carbon paper ('Riteon Copycraft, Sydney). This is very useful for last minute, once off, transparencies when used with the Bulletin typewriter. This product is economical, and has proven extremely popular with our postgraduate students for use in student seminars.

Heat-process tranparencies

This process uses machines like the 3M Thermofax, the Gestetner and Fordigraph thermocopiers. A master is prepared by hand or typewriter and passed with special heat sensitive acetate film through an infra-red light source. The print absorbs heat thus causing an image to appear on the transparency. This is a completely dry process, and takes only a few seconds. All marks on the original must be made with heat absorbing material, for example, Indian ink, soft lead pencil, or good typewriter ribbon. The more carbon, the darker the image. Ordinary ballpoint pens and coloured printing inks will not reproduce by this process. If an original does not absorb enough heat, a photocopy is excellent for use in these machines. A wide range of films is available with different image tones or coloured backgrounds. One of the clearest is the 3M film type 383/574 which gives a dense black image on a clear background. For variety, similar films with coloured backgrounds can be used (3M, type 389). Images can be made darker and thicker by a simple adjustment that slows the transit time of the original through the heat copier. This is important for the Bulletin type, as it is too thin for normal projection.

Even though transparencies can be made rapidly on this machine it takes practice to get high quality results. Extraneous black marks should not be tolerated and probably indicate that the drum needs cleaning or replacing. A degree of wastage is inevitable with this process as different originals require different light settings.

Dry paper copier transparencies

The availability of acetate sheets that can be used in conventional plain paper copiers has meant loss in popularity of the heat process transparencies, although I still find them very useful if my transparency master is stuck together with adhesive tape (as the tape shows up on the plain paper copier but not on the Thermofax). When making a transparency with a plain paper copier the acetate sheet is placed on top of the sheet of the normal copy paper and copied in the normal way. The Xerox product produces excellent results and 3M have a range of similar products. Paper copies of the original can be made at the same time for distribution to the students eliminating the need for students to copy it during the lecture. As most departments now have ready access to plain paper copiers, this material allows the production of legible (assuming the size is right) professional transparencies minutes before a lecture. This is a definite bonus for those of us who often have a good idea for an overhead too late to call in the Medical Illustration Unit.

Another useful product that can give the added dimension of colour to these prepared transparencies is sheets of coloured stickon acetate especially designed by Letraset for overhead projection.

Access to a thermal copier or plain paper copier machine, and a box of film is all that is needed to produce interesting transparencies. Photocopied tables or figures from books can be cut up and arranged appropriately on a piece of paper (stick with adhesive tape) to produce good images, but keep in mind that the legends on these figures are usually too small. If you do not have access to a photo-enlarging photocopier, legends should be cut off and re-typed using the Bulletin typeface mentioned above. The axes of tables may also need to be re-labelled. Copy machines are available to make transparencies direct from books, but, unless the letters on the figures are unusually large, they will be poor images for projection.

Newspaper headlines copy very well onto these transparencies and can often be used for effective composition as can black and white cartoons.

Vertical copying camera

A facility offered by many illustration units is the production of transparencies using the Vertical Copying Camera Repromaster 2001 (Agfa) or its equivalent. This system produces the best transparencies available and has the added advantage of considerable enlargement of the original. Thus diagrams from books and journals can be transformed into easily legible transparencies. Another advantage is that black and white originals can be changed into transparencies in a range of six basic colours. Many conventional typewriter type faces are suitable for this equipment as the final image is enlarged. A type that has proved very popular in our experience with this machine is the IBM Letter Gothic golf ball (See Figure 37.1). A useful tip when producing the original is to limit the area of typing to a 120 mm × 95 mm template. When this material is enlarged to transparency size, the 6 x width rule described above will be fulfilled. This equipment is too expensive to be available in individual departments and therefore, even though transparencies are of the highest quality, they must be planned well in advance of the lecture.

Commercially prepared transparencies

Transparencies of a very high standard can be produced by commercial companies. This is useful if teaching materials are being prepared for general distribution. An Australian company that has developed a new process is Clarendon Press Pty Ltd, Anzac Parade, Kensington. Using a special process, the images from up to six 35 mm slides can be reproduced on the transparency. Each picture is covered with a hinged flap which thus allows multiple disclosure.

The Macintosh

A revolution in overhead transparency making. The advent of the personal computer gives us as medical teachers a new capability in the rapid production of high quality text and graphics for our overhead transparencies. While many machines are available, my experience has been only with the Apple MacIntosh. At present it does appear to have a unique versatility beyond its competitors and being so portable remains my machine of choice. Using this machine has so completely revolutionized my personal teaching that many of the methods described above have, for me, become redundant.

For example, the Macpaint program has seven different font types. Each font can be used in sizes ranging from 9 point to 72 point and there are eight different type formats e.g. Bold, Italic, Shadowed. Thus there are many possibilities. Also the Macpaint graphics facility is so versatile that imaginative, high quality diagrams can be produced by a non-artist in minutes. The real way to explore the potential of this machine for your teaching is to try one out. Figure 37.2 gives some examples of the effects that can be produced simply and rapidly by any non-expert computer user such as myself. This page was printed by a Laser printer which produces images of very high quality. As the Laser printer works on the same principle as a plain paper copier, the image can be printed directly onto plain paper copier acetate sheets. Even without the Laser printer, however, the normal images printed out on the Imagewriter printer are of very good quality and transparencies can be made with them on either a heat process copier or a plain copier as described above. For transparencies with text only, I find it easier to use the Macwrite software and usually type in the NEW YORK or TIMES font type face with a 24 point size setting and the bold type style. This size and type is clearly visible in all lecture theatres using standard projectors.

A final comment on transparencies is that no matter how they are made, they must be viewed from the most distant seat of the lecture hall before they are included in the lecture. Let us stamp out unreadable transparencies!

Use of transparencies

Many techniques can result in a more effective use of transparencies.

The following are examples of types written with MacWrite:

This is Courier 24 pt plain

This is Courier 24 pt bold

This is Helvetica 24 pt plain

This is Helvetica 24 pt bold

This is Times 24 pt plain

This is Times 24 pt bold

Below are some of the styles in Helvetica 24 pt:

Helvetica plain

Helvetica italic

Helvetica outline

Helvetica shadow

Helvetica bold,outline,shadow

Examples of the graphics potential of MacPaint

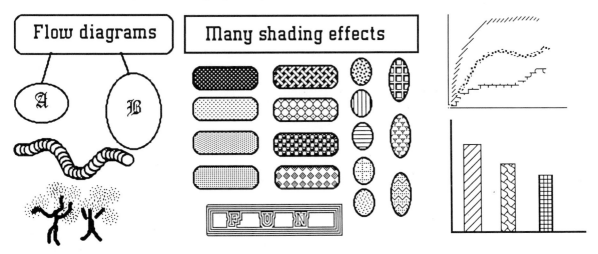

Fig. 37.2 Examples of computer generated letters and graphics

Overlays

The imaginative use of overlays can give the overhead transparency a dimension that can never be achieved with a 35 mm slide (McRae 1975). We all know how to use this method, but how often do we use it? An outline diagram, for example of a limb, is attached to one side with adhesive tape so that, when it is superimposed over the original diagram, the blood vessels become visible. Complex tables and diagrams would also be better produced on two or three transparencies and presented as overlays.

Frames

Transparencies are often better presented attached to a cardboard frame. Many commercial products are available. The frame allows more rapid lining up of transparencies when using overlays. Also notes can be written on the side of the frame which the lecturer can refer to while discussing the transparency. Indeed it is possible to have all the lecture notes written on the frames thus eliminating the need to return to the lectern. Frames allow better storage of transparencies and also protection, as they can be covered with clear acetate film.

Progressive disclosure

Information on a transparency should be limited to six words per line, six lines per transparency, and no more than two illustrations. While it is possible to get away with a little more than this, a problem occurs if more than one idea or piece of information is projected at once. The viewers immediately read and copy down all items while the first item is being discussed, and thus they miss important information. This problem can be effectively overcome by covering up all but the first point, and by progressively disclosing each item as it is discussed. Each point should be covered up by a hinged flap that is firmly stuck to the acetate. Moving a piece of paper on top of the transparency is very distracting. A useful tip is to use the original of the transparency for the cover sheet, each item is now clearly visible to the lecturer before it is disclosed. Teachers should use progressive disclosures much more than they do. Watch your students next time you project a transparency with more than one point on it. Then, try progressive disclosure; you will see the difference. Examination of the students' lecture notes in these two situations will reinforce this point.

A final comment on the use of transparencies is to stress the need for rehearsal of the lecture. Even if it is impractical to rehearse in the lecture theatre, a mental rehearsal in the office beforehand can be invaluable to ensure slides and transparencies are in the right order and the timing is right. If the same transparency is going to be used more than once, have multiple copies to ensure the flow of material during the lecture.

Student participation

Transparencies can be used to encourage active student participation, whether in large or small groups. A transparency of a laboratory request form could be distributed to students who are then given appropriate clinical histories and asked to fill in details of specimens to be collected and tests requested. This transparency is then given to the teacher who projects it on the screen, and commnents on the student choice. He or she can now put on an overlay which gives the laboratory results, and a discussion on interpretation could follow.

Use of handouts

One consequence of the increasing ease of making high quality transparencies is that we tend to make more. We thus create a problem for students as they then feel a need to write everything down in their notes. This is a waste of time and also detracts from the benefit of the lecture. *Copying time is neither thinking time nor learning time.* Frequently, students do not hear the pearls we cast in front of them because they are so busy copying down what is on the screen. Students should not have to copy material from the screen during a lecture; they should be provided with copies of all our transparencies. This might appear impractical, however, yet again advances in photocopier technology have come to our aid.

24

BACTERIAL GROWTH

Simple division.BINARY FISSION

Draw a typical growth curve for a culture of _Escherichia coli_ taken from a tube of serum broth and inoculated into a tube of nutrient broth.

CONC.
OF
BACTERIA
PER ML.

TIME OF INCUBATION

25

GASEOUS REQUIREMENTS FOR BACTERIAL GROWTH

AEROBIC   Requires oxygen

MICROAEROPHILIC Requires oxgen less than 20% atmospheric

ANAEROBIC   No requirement for oxygen

NB.Strict or obligate anaerobes
  eg.Clostridium spp.
  Facultative anaerobes
  eg.Escherichia coli
  Extremly oxygen sensitive

26   AEROBIC RESPIRATION

Catabolism

Glucose››››››CO_2 + H_2O

  eg.Citric acid cycle
Oxygen as the final electron acceptor
Oxidative phosphorylation

ANAEROBIC RESPIRATION

Organic or inorganic compounds act as final electron acceptors other than oxygen.

  eg.Nitrate ››› Nitrite.
     Sulphate ››› Hydrogen sulphide.
     CO_2 ››› Methane.

27   QUESTION:

Will a bacterial colony be larger or smaller when grown anaerobically compared to aerobically?

  NB:Glucose aerobically   ››...ATP

  Glucose anaerobically›...ATP

28 **CRITERIA USED IN THE IDENTIFICATION OF BACTERIA**

GRAM STAIN

MORPHOLOGY

CULTURAL CHARACTERISTICS

BIOCHEMICAL CHARACTERISTICS

ANTIGENIC DIFFERENCES

29

BIOCHEMICAL TESTS

The need for pure cultures.

| | TEST | | |
	A	B	C
Organism 1	+	−	+
Organism 2	−	+	+
Organism 3	+	+	+
Mixed 1 & 2	+	+	+

Fig. 37.3 Handout containing photo-reduced copies of transparencies presented during the lecture

Figure 37.3 is a handout for students attending a lecture in medical microbiology which contains a copy of the transparencies presented during the lecture. The handout was made by sticking together photo-reductions of the transparency masters. Students are told that this is intended as a supplement to their lecture notes at the appropriate place, and to cut out and stick in the photo-reduced copy of the transparency after the lecture. This facility has proved very popular and is greatly appreciated by students.

OTHER USES OF THE OVERHEAD PROJECTOR

Often, use of the projector is limited to the display of transparencies, but many exciting visual effects can be created on the screen. Colonies of *Staphylococus aureus* on a Petri dish, for example, project very well, and the addition of a solution of hydrogen peroxide on the plate produces the most exciting example of biochemical reaction. Articulated models using acrylic materials can be constructed (Sturrock, 1976). Rotating polarizers can create the illusion of motion. The possibilities are endless, and the only limitation is our imagination. Indeed imagination and enterprise are the key to successful use of the overhead projector. With application of some of the ideas and principles described above it can be the most effective visual aid of all.

BIBLIOGRAPHY

Auger B Y How to run better business meetings. Visual Projects Division, 3M Company Appendix pp 173–191 are particularly useful in decribing the art of processing a good visual

Brown J D, Lewis R B, Harcleroad F F 1973 AV instruction technology media, and methods, 5th edn. McGraw-Hill A comprehensive reference for those interested in the practical asppects of AV technology.

McRae R K 1975 The overhead projector, Booklet 4. Association for the study of Medical Education, Dundee.

A simple discussion on the use of the overhead projector with selected examples from teaching in medical schools

Sturrock R R 1976 Two Perspex working models for use with the overhead projector to illustrate the actions of the intrinsic muscles of the larynx. Medical and Biological illustration 26: 97–101

Maddox H, Loughran R J 1977 Illustrating the Lecture: Prepared Diagrams vs Built-up Diagrams, Audio Visual Communication Review 25: 87–90

How to use handouts

The 'handout' is one of the commonest aids to learning used by the teacher. The question is to what extent it is used as such by the student. The transition from 'handout' to 'throwaway' is a rather easy one. This Chapter is aimed at helping teachers minimize the chances of this transition occurring, by paying particular attention to the manner in which the handout is prepared and distributed to the students.

WHY USE HANDOUTS?

Handouts are used for many purposes. As their format and distribution depend very much on the purpose, we should examine these various purposes first.

1. As a class outline or lesson summary. This is one of the commonest purposes for which a handout is used. It gives the student a preconception of what the class is about, and helps the teacher keep track of what he/she intends to cover. It also serves as a reminder to students of what was covered in a particular class.

2. As a guide to the student through a lecture.

It gives the student an accurate record of a lecture, with emphasis on major points within it.

3. To relieve the student of taking notes. Note-taking is not an undesirable activity. Many students find it a useful way of keeping themselves alert and active during a lecture. In addition, notes provide a lasting record of a learning, experience, which would be particularly useful if they are recorded in one's own words. Under these circumstances handouts should supplement rather than replace notes. In some situations note-taking is not practical, however, as in a darkened room or during a practical class. Handouts would then be a useful substitute for student notes.

4. To prepare students for a discussion. Students are informed about a topic to varying extents. A handout, if read beforehand, could help 'level' all students, and make subsequent discussion on the topic both efficient and fruitful for all students. Such handouts are also useful when students are required to solve problems based on their previous learning. Handouts prepared appropriately can be used to stimulate thought, raising issues for subsequent discussion, or even posing a problem to be worked out from the principles covered in the lecture.

5. As a guide to further reading and to supply additional information not readily available elsewhere.

The handout could, for example, include up-to-date information which has not yet been published.

WHAT SHOULD BE THE FORMAT OF
THE HANDOUT?

The format of a handout varies with its purpose.

Teachers need to pay particular attention to format if the objective of the handout is to be achieved.

If the handout is to serve as a class outline, it should include the objectives of the lesson, an indication of the teaching/learning methods planned, the nature of assignments and assessments (if any), and a list of appropriate readings. An example of such a handout is depicted in Figure 38.1.

Students learn better if they are aware of the objectives at the beginning of a lesson. The methods to be used in the lesson, however, should not be spelt out in too great detail, as that may take away the element of anticipation and surprise which makes learning enjoyable. Clearly stated assignments and specifically prescribed readings aid the student after the lesson.

If the handout is to be used as a guide to the student during a lesson, a useful format is that of the 'incomplete handout'. Here, headings and sub-headings are listed, with adequate space intervening, to give the student opportunities to note important points dealt with under each sub-heading. The student is thus encouraged to listen to, and process, the information, instead of passively transferring it to a notebook. Such handouts could also contain blanks for the student to fill in, questions to be answered, or diagrams to be labelled. An example of the last type is depicted in Figure 38.2. Sometimes, the basic outline of a complex diagram can be provided in a handout, which the student then proceeds to build on during the course of the lesson.

When handouts are used to stimulate thought before a lesson in order to facilitate discussion, the content of the handout should be in the form of questions or issues raised but left unanswered. Such questions must be really thought-provoking, and issues must lend themselves to differing points of view if the discussion is to be animated.

Handouts used as instruction sheets could be laid out as in Figure 38.3. Clarity of procedure and anticipation of problems (as well as instructions on how to deal with them if they arose) could save valuable teacher time during a practical class.

When reference lists are provided to guide and stimulate reading by students, to supplement their learning in a lesson, the list should neither be too long as to overwhelm them, nor too short as to offer no choices. Important readings should be

---

Topic: Movements of the Eye

Objectives:
   1. Name the movements of the eye
   2. Explain how each movement, and each combination of movements, occurs
   3. Test for eye movement in a normal person
   4. Determine effects of damage of certain cranial nerves on eye movement
   5. Identify cranial nerve(s) likely to be damaged in a patient with defective eye movement

Methods:
   Explanation (with models)
   Demonstration
   Supervised practice

Assessment:
   Solve a problem based on cranial nerve damage affecting eye movement
Reading:
   Last R J 1981 Anatomy, regional and applied, 6th edn. Churchill Livingstone, Edinburgh, pp 434–435

Fig. 38.1 Handout on class outline.

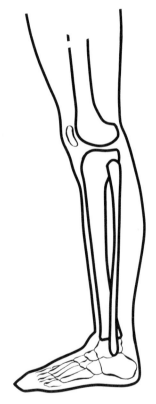

Fig. 38.2 'Incomplete handout' to increase active learning during a session.

INSTRUCTIONS SHEET
Title:

Purpose:

*Equipment/Materials
Required*:

Procedure:

Precautions:

Pitfalls:

References:

Fig. 38.3 A typical instructions sheet given as a practical class.

highlighted and annotated. Whenever possible, the level of difficulty of each and its library location should be indicated.

WHEN SHOULD HANDOUTS BE DISTRIBUTED?

Many teachers underestimate how important it is to time the distribution of handouts appropriately. Timing not only affects the use of a handout but, if inappropriate, could result in interference with other forms of learning.

The optimal time for distribution of a handout, in relation to the lesson it serves as an aid to, depends on the purpose and nature of the handout. Obviously, if a handout is to serve as a guide to the lesson, as a class outline, or as instructions to a practical class, it should be given out just before the class, and students given a few minutes to scan it before the lesson begins.

When a teacher decides that students need to pay particular attention to a lesson or part of it which requires concentration, and has prepared a handout to substitute for notes taken by the students, he or she should inform the students that a handout will be given but distribute it only after that part of the lesson is completed. Care should be taken to give the students a few minutes to scan the handout before proceeding to the next section of the lesson. Many students are inquisitive enough to read immediately what is handed out to them. This should always be remembered by the teacher when handouts are distributed just before or during a lesson.

Handouts used to prepare students and stimulate their thoughts for a discussion should be distributed well ahead of the class to give them adequate time for preparation, but not so far ahead as to result in their putting off such preparation.

Reading lists could be of two types: an initial list of important texts and references for the course given out at the beginning, and supplementary lists pertaining to each lesson given out throughout the course. An extensive list of all the references for the entire course handed out at the beginning of the course could be daunting to even the brightest student.

HOW MANY HANDOUTS SHOULD BE GIVEN?

This, of course, depends on the nature of the course and the purposes of the handouts. One should be careful not to overdo the distribution of handouts, as that would place the student in the position of having to read them all, select the more important ones, or not read any. When the number of handouts for each lesson has been decided on, there should be adequate copies of each for each student, a few extra copies for potential observers, and at least a couple extra for the teacher — one for filing and the other for use in class. The teacher should constantly draw the attention of the students to each handout during the class. Each handout should indicate its source clearly (if from a publication) so that the students can refer to the source if they wish to place the extract in context.

The handout is one of the most inexpensive and effective aids to learning. Its careful selection, preparation and distribution, with the needs of the students in mind, optimize its use by the latter.

Clinical simulation

Simulation can provide the bridge between the class-room and the environment in which the student will work. The class-room is ideal for the dissemination of knowledge; the instructor is able to talk to large numbers of students, to stimulate, motivate and explain. The integration of this knowledge along with the ability to use it in the real world ia an activity often left to the student, and it is not an easy task. Furthermore, the clinical environment, in the case of medical education, may not always be the place to have students practise new skills. As an educator having recognized and defined this kind of problem, one should consider the use of simulation. It must be emphasized that simulation is appro-priate for some, not all, educational encounters; that it should be used as a complementary method.

To illustrate the use of simulation consider a specific educational problem. Since the topic is simulation, the discussion will focus upon only those aspects of the problem relevant to simulation not on the total problem.

THE PROBLEM

Traditionally a student has been taught how to perform a pelvic examination by a physician working in a public hospital. The first exposure can be an emotional experience for the patient who is likely to become aware that this is an initial training experience, and for the student who is concerned about his or her ability to perform professionally. Guidance from the instructor is likely to be compromised, and the practice of interpersonal skills is frequently ignored. In short the learning experience may not be productive; it may even be counter-productive.

Three solutions are available. Each merits the definition of a simulation, an aspect of reality without all of its components.

Solution 1

Gynny® is a Special Task simulation available for pelvic exam instruction (Holzman et al, 1977). A special task simulation (simulator, or mannequin) is a model of some part of the body or body func-tion designed to allow students to practise psychomotor skills. Often there are interchange-able parts for different pathology or functions.

Gynny depicts the female abdomen and pelvis and provides a step between learning about the procedure and actually carrying it out on a person. The artificial material used as skin is firm and rather unyielding. Consequently some users find bimanual palpation different from reality, too difficult. This design decision was made realizing that the simulator would be roughly handled by hundreds of students. Still its useful life is only 3–5 years. The abdominal area is transparent and not skin coloured enabling the learner to see what he or she is feeling.

Reality has been altered to assist the learner. The incorporation of departures from reality is not without disadvantages although in this case it should be minimal. For example, the student could conceivably come to depend upon an 'abdominal window'.

Solution 2

Consent is obtained from women about to be anesthetized. Those selected are chosen because they are thought to have normal pelvic organs. Educators favouring this simulation point out that the student does not have to struggle with a simulator, that the uterus and ovaries are easy to palpate in a slender patient in whom the abdominal muscles are completely relaxed.

Solution 3

Both of the previous solutions focus upon cognitive and psychomotor skills. Kretzchmar (1971) has introduced a media dependent simulation — the use of professional simulated patients — that assists the student in the acquisition of psychomotor skills while reinforcing interpersonal skills learned elsewhere in the curriculum. Two students work with two professional simulated patients (PSPs). The PSPs introduce themselves, enumerate their educational background, and list the sessions' goals. A physician is not present. One PSP acts as the patient-instructor, the other the nurse-chaperon- instructor. One student performs the examination while the second observes. Upon completion of this examination the student-observer becomes the student-examiner and vice versa. The patient-instructor becomes the nurse-chaperon- instructor and vice versa. Everyone is encourage to comment and students are asked to repeat procedures until they reach some degree of proficiency. Women who are recruited have had past experience in interpersonal skill training and all are taught to perform a pelvic examination.

It could be argued that the use of simulation, particularly this simulation, is expensive. There is the recurring cost of the PSP. Patients in an out-patient department or under anaesthesia are not likely to be compensated. The use of a PSP does, however, free a physician, whose hourly wage is more than that of a PSP. This solution is less likely than the others to be approved by peers and central administration but such is the case with innovation. Approval comes with understanding. The major difficulty is recruitment. It takes time to find and train PSPs properly. Since graduate students in the social sciences usually form the applicant's pool, this becomes a recurring procedure, because they all eventually leave the university.

Advantages

'Noise' is an aspect of reality that makes a task more difficult or complex, and can be removed from the system without altering the educational objective (Table 39.1). A cantankerous woman is certainly not relevant to a student's initial pelvic examination experience and all three solutions eliminate this possibility. Time can be altered. In the simulations described the learners are allowed more time than they would have in an actual clinical situation. In simulations that involve chronic disease the developer may wish to contract time enabling the student to react to the entire course of the illness.

Table 39.1 Some advantages of medical simulations

'Noise' found in the real world can be controlled and/or eliminated
Tasks are relevant
Skills can be practised repeatedly
Retention and accuracy are increased
Risk to patients and to students is controlled
Availability of clinical entities is increased
Standards against which to evaluate student performance and diagnose educational needs are provided
Transfer of training from class-room to real situation is enhanced

Since the simulation is relevant to what a physician does in practice and since the PSP is a partner in the learning exercise, interest and motivation are usually high. The PSP is not only relaxed but encourages practice.In real situation it is not unusual for the student to feign understanding, to nod affirmatively, in an effort to avoid embarrassment considering further manipulation possibly painful to the patient. Furthermore, the PSPs provide the students with accurate feedback about their performance. A observing clinician usually cannot tell the examiner that he or she has just felt an ovary but the trained PSP can. Thus proponents argue that simulation promotes an increase in retention (improves memory) and accuracy.

Student involvement in patient care carries a risk to the patient and to the learner. The latter may be so humiliated that they may wish to withdraw from certain aspects of medicine or medicine entirely. Often such a tragedy could have been prevented if the learners had been faced with progressively more difficult steps instead of facing a complex real world situation first.

The use of PSPs ensures the availability of suitable patients, women who are slender, women who can relax. Likewise simulations are advantageous when the medical condition is rare enough not to be encountered, but important enough that the student should recognize the problem and be able to initiate management. The condition could be potentially fatal if unrecognized and easily treated if diagnosed early.

The simulations described herein have been educational, but simulations can be used also for testing purposes. Overlooking the problems of scoring, this is a standardized reproducible method of evaluation.

The intent of most instructional endeavours is not only the students' attainment of knowledge, but also their use of this knowledge in later life. This is called transfer of training which educators refer to as the transfer of learning to the real world and should ensure the greatest likelihood of transfer of training. But, as this chapter suggests, the real world is not always possible or even desirable. Theoretically, the closer the instructional method is to actuality the higher the probability of transfer of training.

OTHER TYPES OF SIMULATIONS

Teaching pelvic examination was chosen as an example for this chapter because it involved types of simulation readily available in many countries. Computer-controlled and paper and pencil simulations are discussed elsewhere in this book. Other types of simulation are briefly discussed below.

Games

Games are a rule-structured activity in which both skill and chance affect the outcome, and where the sense of winning or losing is communicated to the player. The simulation games currently available are not applicable to medical education at the undergraduate level.

Multi-task simulations

Multi-task simulations are models of the body which are supported by computer-controlled response mechanisms and which are programmed to react in a variety of ways to different stimuli. Examples are Harvey and Sim 1. These simulations are akin to aerospace simulations in their complexity, expense, and potential for instruction (see Abrahamson et al, 1969).

Media-supported simulations

In Media-supported simulations the choice and use of media are dependent upon the problem and the student. Usually a complete patient problem is simulated as a tutorial or in a small group setting. A student usually assumes the role of a physician. It is not unlike a viva, the main differences being the use of media such as video tape and a very specific scenario which directs the instructor in how to present the contingencies that the student encounters (Kagan, 1980).

CONCLUSIONS

Simulation is a solution to some, but certainly not all, educational problems. Many and varied types of simulations which can be adapted to local needs are commercially available. Furthermore, it is probably advisable to be a simulation user before becoming a simulation developer.

Simulations depict an aspect of reality. It is as though reality has gone through a series of filters and only the part essential to the instructional objective remains. Students are encouraged to respond. Their ability to process and apply knowledge can be assessed and directed using encourgement when the response is appropriate and constructive criticism when it is inappropriate. As such the method is used for instruction, practice, and evaluation.

REFERENCES

Abrahamson S T, Denson J S, Wolf R M 1969 Effectiveness of a simulator in training anesthesiology residents. Journal of Medical Education 44: 515–519

Kagan N 1980 Influencing human interaction — Eighteen years with I P R. In: Hess K (ed.) Psychotherapy Supervision: Theory, Research and Practice. Wiley, New York

Holzman G B, Singleton D, Holmes T F, Maatsch J L 1977 Initial pelvic examination instruction: the effectiveness of three contemporary approaches. American Journal of Obstetrics and Gynecology 129: 124–129

Kretzschmar R M 1971 Teaching pelvic examination to medical students using a professional patient. Newsletter No. 21 of the Steering Committee on Cooperative Teaching in Obstetrics and Gynecology, Department of Obstetrics and Gynecology, University of Utah, College of Medicine

BIBLIOGRAPHY

Maatsch J L, Gordon M 1978 Assessment through simulation. In: Morgan M K, Irby D M (eds) Evaluating Clinical Competence in the Health Professions. Mosby, St Louis 'Discussion centres on the value of the simulation in student evaluation; the key concepts, principles, and strategies involved in the design and use of simulations; and types of simulation technologies currently used for evaluation . . .

The techniques explored include paper and pencil, audio-visual, structured role play, the use of simulated patients and computers. Following the chapter is an annotated bibliography of 41 titles and these alone are worth reviewing. There are references to the many different types of simulations in current use in medical education for both instructional and evaluative purposes

Computer assisted instruction

Preview

COMPUTER HARDWARE

computer systems
1. shared central computer
2. shared small computer
3. dedicated small computer
4. microcomputer
terminals
printers

COMPUTER SOFTWARE

languages
source
1. computer patient management problems
2. simulation models
3. multiple choice questions
4. tutorial exercises
5. realtime problems

STEPS IN DEVELOPING COMPUTER
PATIENT MANAGEMENT PROBLEMS

AUDIO-VISUAL EQUIPMENT

CONCLUSIONS

Computers can be used to provide the basis for complete courses, or to complement material presented in other ways. They are particularly useful in facilitating self-assessment and this feature helps computer assisted programs to promote learning and reinforce material taught in other ways. Computers are at their best when formally integrated into the structure of the course, rather than when allowed to float alongside as an optional additional frill.

Three broad categories of programs can be defined:
1. Computer assisted instruction — CAI
2. Computer assisted assessment — CAA.
3. Computer managed instruction — CMI.

This chapter will deal mainly with CAI which could be defined as a mode of instruction in which students have an opportunity to learn by interacting with their teacher through a computer program presented at a terminal. Feedback from the teacher and self-assessment by the student are an inherent part of such CAI programs. CAA refers to formal assessment of student performance using programs presented at a computer terminal. CAA differs markedly from CAI in that feedback is deliberately omitted and there is no opportunity for continuing self-assessment. Computers can also be used to help administer the presentation of a whole course or part of it (CMI); programs of this type are not limited to presentation of academic material, but can be used to arrange timetables, make appointments between tutors and students, compile checklists of tasks completed by the student, record student's academic performance and manage a host of other functions.

CAI provides a medium for learning, free of the usual stresses that accompany student-teacher interaction. The students can learn at their own pace, in their own time, and can choose the material they wish to study. They can work alone or, if they prefer, in small groups of compatible friends. The main advantage of CAI if used properly is the vehicle it provides for constant feedback by the teacher and self-assessment by the student, in a quiet, non-threatening, non-competitive atmosphere.

COMPUTER HARDWARE

Computer systems

Before deciding to use CAI material the teacher should have a good understanding of the available computer systems. Three conditions are necessary for CAI to be effective: firstly the computer system must be a proven one for reliability with minimal maintenance, secondly it must have the capacity to accept the student job during pre-arranged times, and thirdly the time between the student typing a response and receiving feedback should not exceed three seconds and should generally be less than one second.

The computer system to be used probably will fall into one of four categories:

1. Shared central computer

Such a system utilizes a medium to large computer belonging to the institution (e.g. IBM, DEC-10 CYBER) and implies sharing by a large number of people. The ease of obtaining a line, the response time and the scheduling of routine computer maintenance should be checked before embarking on a project. Good liaison with the computer centre is essential so that you can be informed of any changes in the usual routine. The main drawback with this type of system is that the teacher and students are 'users' of a complex system with no involvement in the computer's management. Communication with the central computing centre is generally by telephone or through messages received at the terminal. It is very disconcerting to be working through a program and to receive a message on the screen that the system is going down and to please log off!

2. Shared small computer

A small computer belonging to a department, used for both research and teaching (e.g. PDP11/34) allows the teacher to have more knowledge of the other activities taking place on the computer system, and therefore more freedom to plan group activities or tutorials at the terminals. The volume and complexity of research use are critically important in determining the suitability of such a computer for use in CAI.

3. Dedicated small computer

A small computer such as a PDP11/34 dedicated to CAI is probably optimal. It can provide several terminals for students running the same or different programs with almost instant response time as no other large programs are sharing the computer's storage. The computer's operating system can be modified to simplify logging in and logging out procedures, and running programs. This is important to retain student and staff enthusiasm, and particularly necessary when terminals are in use out of hours with no staff assistance. Routine maintenance and modification of the system can be scheduled for convenient times.

4. Microcomputer

This is a newcomer to the scene and it usually consists of a processor, memory, visual display unit (VDU) and cassette player or floppy disc drive(s) for online storage, with perhaps a printer. Programs prepared for one microcomputer and written onto a floppy disk may be run on similar models by making a copy of the disk. This is a very easy way of sharing programs between different institutions. On the larger systems all terminals are online to the central computer processor and when the system is 'down' all terminals are out of action; whereas each terminal on a micro-computer has its own processor so that if one terminal has a fault the others can still be used. It is entirely possible to develop a CAI program using two or more of these systems.

Terminals

Four popular brands are Teleray, Tektronix, Decwriter IV and Silent 700. The terminals most used for CAI are VDUs. These should display at least 80 columns and 24 rows to allow adequate spacing between questions and answers, with double spacing between lines of text wherever feasible for easier reading. There should be the option for lower case characters, as well as for 'cursor addressing' which allows a line to be deleted and another substituted without moving the text displayed above. The speed of the terminal should be set so that the rate at which characters appear on the screen does not retard the user. This usually means a speed of 1200 or 4800 baud which allows text to appear faster than one can read it. A speed of 300 baud becomes tedious, particularly when a program is rerun several times.

Printers

While VDUs are generally sufficient for students' use, teachers and programmers need hardcopy of programs, listing of text displayed on the screen, and records of students' progress. These can be obtained from a printer (e.g. Tally) or a hardcopy terminal (e.g. Decwriter) both of which can be connected to the computer system.

COMPUTER SOFTWARE

Languages

The link between textual material and its presentation at a terminal is the computer program. This program will be written in a high-level computer language such as Basic, Fortran or Pascal. Generally a person with programming expertise is needed to write CAI programs, but there is an alternative approach which incorporates the use of a CAI authoring language. These languages (e.g. Pilot, Decal) allow a teacher with little experience of computers to prepare material in a form which is directly converted to a CAI program. However, the teacher is forced to accept many constraints and the programs generally consume a large amount of computer memory.

Source

A number of categories of CAI programs have now been developed and are described in some detail below.

These include:
1. Computer patient management problems (CPMPs)
2. Simulation models
3. Multiple choice question (MCQ) sets
4. Tutorial exercises
5. Realtime problems

Some programs can be purchased from other sinstitutions. If this is done it may be necessary to modify textual content or pgoram structure. in either case programming assistance will be needed to make alterations and to test the program on the new computer system.

It is preferable for programs to be written to a teacher's specifications. In this way the material can be tailored to fit the requirements of the course and the level of experience of the students. The programmer might be a member of the institute's computer centre, be attached to the teachers' department or be a member of a unit responsible for the design and organization of CAI. A good understanding between programmer and teacher is essential for the material to be presented in optimal form. Both the material and the program can be modified *in situ* in the light of student feedback.

Computerized patient management problems

A computerized patient management problem is a computer simulation of a doctor-patient encounter in which a student or doctor tries to solve a clinical problem by seeking clinical information about the patient, ordering appropriate investigations and making management decisions, with immediate feedback from the computer. Responses are generally in the form of numbered options although provision can be made for a limited amount of free language. Additional information may come from slides and tape cassettes which can be interfaced with the computer, or from illustrated handbooks.

If a teacher or group of teachers wishes to develop their own CPMPs, a useful long term strategy, modelled on that which has evolved at Flinders University Medical School, might be as follows:

Step 1. The teacher and programmer work together to design a prototype CPMP, based on a real patient, with segments devoted to history, physical signs, investigation, diagnosis and differential diagnosis, treatment, prognosis and continuing care. A number of policy decisions must be taken at this stage, including:

1. Whether the CPMP will be used for instruction or assessment.

2. The proportion of information supplied and the proportion of information withheld, requiring active search by the student.

3. The extent to which a student is allowed to pursue incorrect decisions.

4. The wording of instructions on how to proceed through the problem.

5. The use of supplementary audio-visual material, such as X-ray, ECGs, and blood films (see Example 1).

Example 1 Use of visual material in a CPMP about a patient with rapid atrial fibrillation and bacterial endocarditis

---

What would you like to do now?
33. Chest X-ray
34. Blood cultures.
35. ECG
36. Echocardiogram.
37. Perfusion lung scan.
?33
33. You should start with an ECG before sending the patient away to have a chest X-ray. However, when the chest X-ray was done 1 hour later, the following film was obtained–
Look at slide 6, this shows:
38. Enlarged left atrium indicating mitral stenosis.
39. An enlarged heart with pulmonary plethora.
40. Slight cardiac enlargement with pulmonary venous congestion.
41. Left ventricular enlargement.
42. Large heart with pericardial effusion.
?38
38. The left atrium is enlarged, but the heart is generally enlarged too, and not typical of pure mitral stenosis. Look at this X-ray on slide 7, showing mitral stenosis with an enlarged left atrium.
?40
40. Correct. The heart is generally enlarged and the upper lobe vessels are particularly prominent.

In general terms it is wiser to start by developing CPMPs for instruction and self-assessment, without attempting to devise a scoring system for formal assessment until much later. It would also be easier to start with text alone, without using X-rays and other accessory audio-visual material until a later stage in development.

Step 2. As soon as the prototype CPMP is 'up' on the computer, a number of interested staff members work through the problem, preferably in the presence of the author and programmer, making criticisms and helping to modify the CPMP over a perido of 2–3 weeks, until it is regarded as satisfactory.

Step 3. Arrange a number of workshops (say 2 hours each) for groups of 6–8 staff members wishing to design CPMPs. At each workshop chaired by the author, or another teacher experienced in the use of CPMPs, the problem is attempted, discussed, analyzed and criticized. It is important to explain at this stage, that all problems need not follow the same format — some can end at 'diagnosis', others can start by giving the student the full diagnosis and posing questions on patient management, others can deal entirely with rehabilitation and continuing care.

Many suggestions will arise from the workshops and some can be incorporated into the design of new CPMPs. Some of the features that were added to the program at Flinders after a series of workshops were:

1. The cost of each diagnostic test and comparison of costs engendered by the student with the costs of investigations recommended by the author (see Example 2).

Example 2 Inclusion of cost factor in relation to laboratory investigations

---

It was necessary to carry out the investigations which are marked with an asterisk:
71. ★ 24 hour urinary protein ($4.70).
72. ★ Serum bilirubin ($4.70).
73. ★ Total serum proteins ($4.70).
74.   Uric Acid.
75.   3 day faecal fat study ($15.75).
76. ★ Prothrombin ratio ($5.95).
77. ★ Serum iron ($11.85).
78. ★ ESR-sedimentation rate ($1.95).
79. ★ Serum albumin ($4.70).
80. ★ Serum acid phosphatase ($7.90).
81. ★ Serum alkaline phosphatase ($4.70).
COST OF RELEVANT INVESTIGATIONS $29.45
YOU SELECTED THE FOLLOWING INVESTIGATIONS:
71, 72, 73, 75, 77, 79, 81
THE COST OF THESE INVESTIGATIONS
WOULD BE $51.30

---

2. The ability to return to earlier sections of the problem.

3. The ability to look at incorrect responses after the selection of correct ones.

4. The inclusion of references to alternate modes of management.

5. A comparison of author-student path through a problem.

6. The inclusion of normal ranges for all tests where appropriate.

7. The provision of more detailed feedback after incorrect responses in particular, but also after incorrect choices.

Step 4. The hardest task now is to cajole a number of staff members, all of whom are busy, to devote time to designing a CPMP. Depending on the individual's attitude and the complexity of the particular CPMP, a staff member may need to set aside between 5 and 10 hours to design a problem, spending some of these hours working together with the programmer. It might well take a year to accumulate a bank of 8–20 CPMPs.

Step 5. After a number of CPMPs have been in use for some months, and sufficient feedback has been obtained from students, new developments can be undertaken. These might include:

1. The development of scoring systems for use in formal assessment or self-assessment.

2. Interfacing the computer with random access projectors or tape cassettes so as to increase the range of material that can be presented within each problem.

3. The development of 'real-time' problems.

Tutorial exercises

An example of this type of program is the program package, TEACH, which has been developed at Flinders and provides computer management for whole courses or segments of courses. It has been extensively used for the respiratory system course in second year, incorporating eight tape slide programs and workbooks prepared by Dr John West, Professor of Medicine and Bioengineering at the University of California (San Diego). It is also used for tutorial exercises in renal physiology.

TEACH provides the medium for presentation of factual material, permits students to assess their own understanding and records their progress through a series of tutorial type exercises. Students can progress through these exercises at their own pace. A student who experiences particular difficulty with the material presented on the terminal can 'book' a personal tutorial with a staff member, and arrange the schedule for this tutorial there and then at the terminal.

In designing the program package the lecturer in charge of the course and the programmer decided that the main requirements were as follows:

1. The material presented in the eight tape slide programs should be systematically reviewed in corresponding computer based tutorial exercises, which would allow students to assess their own understanding.

2. Supplementary explanations and questions should be offered to students having difficulty with an exercise.

3. At set points in each exercise students who have made more than two errors should have the option of booking a tutorial.

4. As quantitative answers would be required, the initial values of parameters given to students should be randomly selected within a certain range, thus preventing the compilation of an answer sheet.

5. Students would be able to leave an exercise at the end of any question, and on reruning the program would be asked if they wanted to continue from where they left off or restart the exercise.

From this information and with the help of diagrams showing the various paths that could be taken through an exercise a suitable program was written. Several hours were needed by the lecturer and the programmer before the program was considered tested, modified and ready for student use. Here are two excerpts from TEACH:

1. WELCOME TO THE PROGRAM!
   THIS SECTION IS BASED ON CHAPTER 1
   LAST TIME YOU ENDED ON QUESTION 3
   TYPE 1 FOR BEGINNING OF EXERCISE
   TYPE 2 FOR QUESTION 4
   ?2
   4) The conducting airways are so called because they do not participate in gas exchange. They therefore include the

trachea, main bronchi, lobar bronchi etc. down to and including
1. Terminal bronchioles
2. Respiratory bronchioles
3. Alveolar ducts
?3

No. I know this is dry as dust, but do try to absorb the facts more efficiently next time. The conducting airways end at the terminal bronchioles, inclusive. Gas exchange takes place in respiratory bronchioles, alveolar ducts and alveoli.
PRESS RETURN KEY TO CONTINUE
****
2. No. That's two wrong answers in this exercise.
TYPE 1 FOR TUTORIAL You need human intervention
TYPE 2 IF TUTORIAL NOT REQUIRED You'll read up on your own
?1
AUGUST 13–17
1. TU:0800
2. TH:1100
3. FR:1120
?3
MICHAEL WILL SEE YOU FRIDAY AT 1120 IN THE LABORATORY — NOW LOG OFF PLEASE
****

Real time problems

In problems of this nature the student has the additional constraint that the patient is suffering from an acute disease and that the patient's condition begins to deteriorate as the student addresses the problem (Dugdale & Chandler, 1977). For example, the student might be faced with an accident victim whose airway is blocked, and as a result becomes hypoxic and cyanosed in a real time scale as the student ponders what to do. The patient's condition will continue to deteriorate either until he or she is dead, or until such time as the student chooses to clear the airway. The whole variety of intensive care situations are well dealt with using this approach which has been effectively developed at the McLaughlin Examinations and Research Centre in Canada.

Physiological simulation models

Physiological simulation models MACMAN, MACPUF and MACPEE, produced by McMaster University, Ontario, are especially useful in small group teaching. They allow students to apply physiological principles to important clinical problems such as organ failure, haemorrhage or hypoxia. One potential use for these models is to integrate a particular facet — say, responses to haemorrhage — into the fabric of a CPMP — say, a patient with haematemesis and melaena.

AUDIO-VISUAL EQUIPMENT

Supplementary audio-visual equipment adds immensely to the value of textual material, visual material and sound recording, and provides an optimal way of presenting a student with a wide range of data in a variety of media. A 'three-dimensional computerized system' of this nature has been devised at Flinders (Robbins et al, 1980) using a Kodak random access projector to show X-rays, ECGs or histological slides and a Phi-Deck cassette recorder for heart sounds, breath sounds and narrative. The combined cost of the terminal, projector and recorder is approximately $3000. Commercially marketed terminals incorporating all these functions are not yet widely available, and the best known one in the USA (PLATO, Control Data Company) costs approximately $12 000. However, accessory visual and auditory material can be provided without full automation, using separate projectors, handheld slide viewers, cassette recorders, or even booklets with illustrated material.

CONCLUSIONS

For effective development of CAI we would recommend a modest start with progressive expansion. The following ingredients are, in our view, essential:
1. A dedicated computer, however small.
2. A minimum of one full-time staff member on the computer side. This person should have skills in programming and systems design, and be responsible for operational management.

3. A staff member on the academic side responsible for coordinating the activities of the academic staff and liaising with the computer staff.

Establishing the first two units may be expensive. On the other hand a microcomputer system with dual floppy disk drives and printer can be purchased at very little cost. With careful selection of the microcomputer no difference need be detected in screen appearance, program structure or response time when material is adapted from a larger computer.

ACKNOWLEDGEMENTS

Contributions to the CAI program in the School of Medicine, Flinders University have come from the Ramaciotti Foundation, The Royal Australasian College of Physicians and the Faculty of Anaesthetists of The Royal Australasian College of Surgeons.

BIBLIOGRAPHY

Burzynski N J, Kupchella C E, Calhoon T B, Reid K H 1979 The CASE system for cancer education. Journal of Dental Education 43: 210–213
The computer-guided interaction of a student with a series of microfiche cards through a program in oncology

Dugdale A E, Chandler D 1977 Teaching diagnosis and treatment with an interactive computer terminal. Medical Journal of Australia 1: 145–149
Demonstrates the flexibility of an interactive computer terminal to present the student with exercises in clinical problem solving which may incorporate a time scale

Madsen B W, Bell R C 1977 The development of a computer assisted instruction and assessment system in pharmacology. Medical Education 11: 13–20.
A description of a computer based system for instruction and assessment in pharmacology which utilizes a large data bank of multiple choice questions

Murray T S, Barber J H, Dunn W R 1978 Attitudes of medical undergraduates in Glasgow to computer- assisted learning. Medical Education 12: 6–9
Attitudes of students to computer-assisted learning as part of the undergraduate course in general practice

Randall J E 1978 Teaching by simulation with personal computers. Physiologist 21: 37–40
The use of a microcomputer to simulate a classic peripheral nerve demonstration

Robbins G, Chalmers J, Higgs D 1980 A three-dimensional computerized patient management problem: and example of a computer system utilizing written text, sound track and visual projection. Medical Journal of Australia (in press)

Index